Women Writing
the Nation

The Bucknell Studies in Eighteenth-Century Literature and Culture

General Editor: Greg Clingham, *Bucknell University*

Advisory Board: Paul K. Alkon, *University of Southern California*
Chloe Chard, *Independent Scholar*
Clement Hawes, *The Pennsylvania State University*
Robert Markley, *University of Illinois at Urbana-Champaign*
Jessica Munns, *University of Denver*
Cedric D. Reverand II, *University of Wyoming*
Janet Todd, *University of Glasgow*

The Bucknell Studies in Eighteenth-Century Literature and Culture aims to publish challenging, new eighteenth-century scholarship. Of particular interest is critical, historical, and interdisciplinary work that is interestingly and intelligently theorized, and that broadens and refines the conception of the field. At the same time, the series remains open to all theoretical perspectives and different kinds of scholarship. While the focus of the series is the literature, history, arts, and culture (including art, architecture, music, travel, and history of science, medicine, and law) of the long eighteenth century in Britain and Europe, the series is also interested in scholarship that establishes relationships with other geographies, literature, and cultures for the period 1660–1830.

Titles in This Series

Juliette Cherbuliez, *The Place of Exile: Leisure Literature and the Limits of Absolutism*

Tita Chico, *Designing Women: The Dressing Room in Eighteenth-Century English Literature and Culture*

Dan Doll and Jessica Munns, ed., *Recording and Reordering: Essays on the Seventeenth- and Eighteenth-Century Diary and Journal*

Ziad Elmarsafy, *Freedom, Slavery, and Absolutism: Corneille, Pascale, Racine*

Regina Hewitt and Pat Rogers, eds., *Orthodoxy and Heresy in Eighteenth-Century Society*

Susan Paterson Glover, *Engendering Legitimacy: Law, Property, and Early Eighteenth-Century Fiction*

Catherine Jones, *Literary Memory: Scott's Waverley Novels and the Psychology of Narrative*

Sarah Jordan, *The Anxieties of Idleness: Idleness in Eighteenth-Century British Literature and Culture*

Deborah Kennedy, *Helen Maria Williams and the Age of Revolution*

Chris Mounsey, *Christopher Smart: Clown of God*

Chris Mounsey, ed., *Presenting Gender: Changing Sex in Early Modern Culture*

Frédéric Ogée, ed., *"Better in France?": The Circulation of Ideas across the Channel in the Eighteenth Century*

Roland Racevskis, *Time and Ways of Knowing Under Louis XIV: Molière, Sévigné, Lafayette*

Laura Rosenthal and Mita Choudhury, eds., *Monstrous Dreams of Reason*

Katherine West Scheil, *The Taste of the Town: Shakespearian Comedy and the Early Eighteenth-Century Theater*

Philip Smallwood, ed., *Johnson Re-Visioned: Looking Before and After*

Peter Walmsley, *Locke's Essay and the Rhetoric of Science*

Lisa Wood, *Modes of Discipline: Women, Conservatism, and the Novel after the French Revolution*

David Willinger, ed., *The Secret Life of Things: Animals, Objects, and It-Narratives in Eighteenth-Century England*

Chris Mounsey and Caroline Gonda, eds., *Queer People: Negotiations and Expressions of Homosexuality, 1700–1800*

Susan Manning and Peter France, *Enlightenment and Emancipation*

Judith Broome, *Fictive Domains: Body, Landscape, and Nostalgia, 1717–1770*

William Gibson, *Art and Money in the Writings of Tobias Smollett*

Leanne Maunu, *Women Writing the Nation: National Identity, Female Community, and the British–French Connection, 1770–1820*

http://www.bucknell.edu/universitypress/

Women Writing the Nation

National Identity, Female Community, and the British–French Connection, 1770–1820

Leanne Maunu

Lewisburg
Bucknell University Press

Associated University Press
2010 Eastpark Boulevard
Cranbury, NJ 08512

The paper used in this publication meets the requirements of the American National Standard for Permanence of Paper for Printed Library Materials Z39.48-1984.

Library of Congress Cataloging-in-Publication Data

Maunu, Leanne, 1971–
    Women writing the nation : national identity, female community, and the British-French connection, 1770–1820 / Leanne Maunu.
        p.   cm.
    Includes bibliographical references and index.
    ISBN-13: 978-0-8387-5670-6 (alk. paper)
    ISBN-10: 0-8387-5670-0 (alk. paper)
    1. English literature—Women authors—History and criticism.   2. English literature—18th century—History and criticism.   3. English literature—19th century—History and criticism.   4. Nationalism and literature—Great Britain—History.   5. Women and literature—Great Britain—History.   6. Nationalism in literature.   I. Title.
    PR116.M38   2007
    820.9′358—dc22   2006022356

In loving memory of my mother, Joanne La Carrubba Maunu
You are always in my heart

And for Mike Maunu
Always and forever

Contents

Acknowledgments

Portions of chapters 1 and 3 have previously been published as articles, and I would like to thank the publishers for granting me permission to reprint this work, as well as the anonymous reviewers who helped me refine my arguments, both for these journal articles and for Bucknell University Press. A modified version of the first chapter originally appeared as "Quelling the French Threat in Frances Burney's *Evelina*" (*Studies in Eighteenth-Century Culture* 31 [2002]: 99–125), under the imprint of The Johns Hopkins University Press. Chapter 3 originally appeared as "Home Is Where the Heart Is: National Identity and Expatriation in Charlotte Smith's *The Young Philosopher*" (*European Romantic Review* 15.1 [March 2004]: 51–71), and is reprinted with kind permission from Taylor & Francis (http://www.tandf.co.uk).

This work developed over the course of many years, and so I also wish to acknowledge and thank the many family members, friends, and colleagues who helped guide me along the path that ultimately led to this book. Back when I was an undergraduate at the University of California at San Diego, Fred Randel and Katheryn Shevelow made this period come alive for me, while serving as true mentors and teachers. They nurtured my desire to continue with my studies, and showed me that I could actually make a career out of literature.

This project grew directly out of the work I did as a graduate student while I was at Indiana University, where I benefited immensely from the guidance and critical acumen of Mary Favret, Kenneth Johnston, Janet Sorensen, and Nicholas Williams. To Mary and Nick I owe an especial debt of gratitude. Both Mary and Nick have always been so generous with their encouragement, time, and support, even when I was no longer officially their student. I feel fortunate to have had such wonderful mentors.

Since leaving Indiana, my friends and colleagues at Palomar College have provided me with an environment that has stimulated my thinking, and to them I owe many thanks for our lively discussions about teaching, research, and our profession. I especially want to thank Barbara Neault Kelber for her help in guiding me through the tenure process, and Deborah Paes de Barros, who offered so much advice and encouragement with this book.

All along this path, I have also benefited from the unflagging support and love of my family, especially my father, Howard Maunu, my brother and sister-in-law, Mark and Suzy Maunu, and my brother, Michael Maunu. Although she is no longer with us, my grandmother Lena Orcel La Carrubba also modeled for me what strength and love look like.

Most important of all, I would like to thank and dedicate this book to my two strongest supporters: my mother, Joanne La Carrubba Maunu, and my husband, Mike Maunu. When I was a young girl, my mother first introduced me to Austen and the Brontës, and thereby started my love affair with language and literature. She started me on the path that led me to where I am today and always gave me her fullest support in everything I ever did. I miss her greatly. My husband, Mike, has also been there every step of the way, and he has always believed in me, even when I did not believe in myself. I never could have done any of this without his love and faith. Thank you for everything.

Women Writing the Nation

Introduction—
British Women Writers and
the French Connection

I could frame in my own imagination a female community detached from the world, where every virtue might be nourished, every evil bias controled, all the comforts of society enjoyed, and all its cares mitigated. I can think of it sometimes till it is painful to me to give up the delusion; but alas! it is delusive; for whenever we attempt to establish general happiness, the frailty of our nature constantly introduces individual misery.
—Laeticia Matilda Hawkins, *Letters on the Female Mind, its Powers and Pursuits. Addressed to Miss H. M. Williams, with particular reference to Her Letters from France*

WRITING IN BRITAIN IN 1793, DURING THE REIGN OF TERROR, LAETICIA Matilda Hawkins sought escape from the political turmoil around her by imagining a female community—a community of women living and working together in safety and comfort. This society of women would become its own small nation, directing its own affairs and regulating its members' conduct. Living away from the rest of the world, this community would find peace and harmony in its members' shared commitment to ameliorating themselves and their environment, in creating a small paradise on earth. A group of women united by their gender, living "detached from the world," would provide the ideal soil for cultivating virtue and weeding out vice. And even though Hawkins must eventually dismiss her vision as too "delusive," its image and the regret it engenders lingers on in her mind.

Although Hawkins's vision of a female community detached from the larger British nation might strike the modern reader as utopic and unrealistic, it was, in fact, a vision shared by many British women writers of the late eighteenth and early nineteenth centuries. It was during this period, after all, that the people of Britain began to coalesce under the term "Britons," for most historians and political theorists agree that the eighteenth century was the defining moment in the creation of Britain's national identity.[1] Beginning in the mid-eighteenth century, an astounding number of tracts, pamphlets, articles, and novels—both hurriedly dashed off and painstakingly penned—detailed Britain's relationship with its neighbor France. Together, these texts serve as a revealing testament to the fears and anxieties of a nation that had been at war with France on and off since 1689; they are symptomatic of larger cultural concerns regarding the relative positions of France and Great Britain during this period, and attest to the growing fears and concerns of the British nation as it struggled to achieve a coherent national identity in the wake of political turmoil. Events like the Seven Years' War, which lasted from 1756 to 1763; the later French Revolution, which eventually led to the Napoleonic Wars; and the constant struggle to capture and keep colonial territories resulted in a strong sense of animosity between Britain and France. This animosity, in turn, led to the need to create and maintain a strong sense of British identity in the face of threats from without.

While men's involvement in the creation of national identity and the discourses of nationalism has been documented to a fairly large extent, the contributions of women writers have only recently begun to be explored. Past work on eighteenth-century and Romantic-era women writers has concentrated to such an extent on gender politics and the important contributions that women writers made to British literary history, that it has overlooked the nationalist context in which these women wrote their texts. Critics have looked closely at the French Revolution and the effects it had upon the political writings of the period, but even the connections that this momentous event has to nationalistic discourses have been part of the larger oversight of the connections between gender and the nation, an oversight that is only now being rectified.[2] Women—just as often as men—entered into debates about the British nation, and their discussions of gender politics took place, I will argue, within and through national politics, as they made use of nationalist rhetoric to promote their own claims about women's role within the nation. The discourses on national identity and nationalism circulating through the British body politic emerged as a rhetorical convenience for female writers, providing them with a framework through which they could express their own concerns. Yet by using the phrase "rhetorical convenience" I do not wish to suggest that these writers' conception of nationalism remained rooted in mere expediency. Nationalism as a concept was entrenched in their very beings—in their very notions of their identities as both women writers and political, national subjects. Analyzing their work demonstrates how gender identity and national identity interact with and complicate one another, ultimately leading to a new understanding of how discussions of gender politics took place within and through national politics in the work of many women writers of this period. Hawkins was not alone in her creation of a female community; other women writers availed themselves of these nationalist discourses to open up the possibility for another sort of imagined community—one that (they hoped) would rival that of the British nation.

THE CONFLICTING DEMANDS OF NATIONAL AND GENDER IDENTITY

Explorations of nationalism currently dominate late eighteenth-century and Romantic studies, and this book enters into these recent debates over the story of the British nation and the formation of British national identity. Yet the most significant of these recent studies, and the one upon which many of them are based, remains historian Linda Colley's groundbreaking text *Britons: Forging the Nation 1707–1837,* which laid the foundation for a new understanding of how the idea of Britain developed. Drawing upon Benedict Anderson's idea of nations as imagined communities,[3] Colley demonstrates how a unified Great Britain emerged out of a period of intense warfare with France. Britain and France had been traditional enemies for centuries, yet competition between the two nations intensified during the eighteenth century as each country struggled to expand its empire and establish new trade routes. Heightened competition led to war, and war led to the cohesion of Britons, who, for the first time, began to envision themselves as members of a larger collectivity. Since Britons had a "natural" enemy close at hand, this otherwise heterogeneous group therefore found commonality in a shared fear and hatred of their rival nation. Colley explains this model at greater length: "men and women decide who they are by reference to who and what they are not. Once confronted with an obviously alien 'Them,' an otherwise diverse community can become a reassuring or merely desperate 'Us.' This was how it was with the British after 1707. They came to define themselves as a single people not because of any political or cultural consensus at home, but rather in reaction to the Other beyond their shores."[4] As a nation traditionally despised by Britain, France conveniently became this "Other" against which Britons could define themselves. The constant warfare between the two countries made mass allegiance to the British nation and the invention of "Britishness" itself possible. In effect, Britons understood themselves relationally, as a group of people different from and superior to the French.

Once we recognize Colley's important claim, we start seeing these nationalist connections everywhere, in both the literature and politics of the time. In the literature of the eighteenth century, nationalist claims surface in Daniel Defoe's and Jonathan Swift's early separate attempts to reform the English language in an attempt to guard against French influence; in William Hogarth's and James Gillray's humorous and yet often grotesque depictions of French personalities and lifestyles; in the various attacks that began to be made after the 1760s on the Grand Tour and its emphasis on adopting a French *mode de vie;* and in the many (negative) frenchified characters who danced their way across the stage in both major and minor literary texts of the period by writers such as Tobias Smollett, Laurence Sterne, and Henry Fielding. Writers like Lord Chesterfield, who, earlier in the century, had encouraged their British readers to model themselves after the French, were increasingly attacked and reviled, for the British were no longer content to borrow the identity of a foreign and "insidious" nation. Literary characters like the French fop were now open to abuse, for the British began to see French "effeminacy" as a threat to both British manhood and British national identity.[5] Again and again, in text after text, the prose and poetry of the period reveals an anxiety about the influence that French culture was having on the British nation. Besides noticing such threats in fictional texts, we can also notice them in the realm of political life. Even the controversy surrounding the French Revolution was informed to a great extent by British paranoia and political jealousy over the French people's ascendancy, for if the French could obtain a liberty that rivaled the Britons', then Britons could no longer claim to be God's chosen people.[6] When Britain officially declared war on France in 1793, that hostility and fear increased, but when Napoleon crowned himself emperor in 1804, that hostility and fear reached a feverish pitch. In the wake of Napoleon's ascendancy, the British government responded with a reactionary backlash against civil liberties, essentially repressing many of the rights of Britain's subjects. Severe injunctions were placed on the holding of public meetings, and habeas corpus was suspended for the first time in over a hundred years. The British government became increasingly insular, ready to protect both its political and economic interests against the threat of France, regardless of the cost.

As much as Colley's model helps us better understand Britain's nascent sense of identity, it does not delve deeply enough into the often conflicting demands that exist between gender and national identity. Colley concedes that other identifications still exist for individuals, yet she downplays the connections between gender and nation. When it comes to the role of British women in the process of nation building, Colley believes that women pointed to their Britishness in order to be heard, and so she maps out the reasons why eighteenth-century British women used their national identity to make claims about their status as women. Linking Britain's nationalist concerns to the growth of the separate spheres ideology, Colley argues that eighteenth-century women participated in political life through the claim to being British: "Proclaiming their reputed vulnerability and moral superiority—and men's duty to respect both—provided them with a means to legitimise their intervention in public affairs and a means, as well, of protecting themselves. Posing as the pure-minded Women of Britain was, in practice, a way of insisting on the right to public spirit."[7] While Colley does point to the ways in which women used their gender identity to be heard, she contends that emphasizing their national identity—as "pure-minded Women of Britain"—was the primary way that women participated in political life.

If, however, we analyze texts written by late eighteenth-century women writers in more detail, we can see that it was often not their *national* identity that these women used to be heard, but rather their *gender* identity. Many women writers wanted to make it *seem* as if they were writing as members of a fairly stable community, even if such a community was composed of many different women with many different beliefs. In essence, because British–French relations dominated the national imagination, women had to think about their own gender concerns in national terms as well. The idea of France was thus not only a useful way for British men to discuss the welfare of the British nation, but it was also a useful way for British women to link their private concerns with public ones. British women took advantage, as it were, of the nationalist discourses dominating the political landscape to promote their own gender politics. To do so, they appropriated the model of collectivity posed by the nation, mimicking a national imagined community. As Benedict Anderson defines it, an imagined community only needs to exist in the minds of its members: "It is *imagined* because the members of even the smallest nation will never know most of their fellow-members, meet them, or even hear of them, yet in the minds of each lives the image of their communion."[8] This is the vision of the larger British nation that the general British populace held ever more strongly as the eighteenth century progressed, and it is also the vision an increasing number of British women writers began to hold as well. The political climate of the period demanded the cohesion of Britain's individual subjects into a unified group known as "Britons," and women writers responded to this same call by also imagining a distinct subgroup of women who were united as much by their gender as they were by their national affiliation.

This leads to the two main arguments of *Women Writing the Nation:* first, that gender concerns during the late eighteenth and early nineteenth centuries were repeatedly voiced against the backdrop of the nation and Britain's relations with France, and, second, that many British women writers during this same period created the idea of an imagined female community whose members were united not by national identity, but rather by gender identity and women's common concerns. What is crucial to note here is that what they imagined was not so much an alternative nation of women, but rather an alternative model of community that borrowed from standard nationalist rhetoric.[9] Again and again, the same themes and images occur in these women writers' texts: images of women without protection, of women being misrepresented and subject to gossip, of women meeting prejudice, of women forced to wander, of women gone mad. Yet the most significant of these images is that of female characters who inadvertently open themselves to doubt and blame because they possess an unstable national identity. In the face of such doubt, these women look to female community as an asylum, even though such community is often, to the chagrin of the authors who created them, denied by other women characters. What ultimately emerges from the more progressive of these novels, poems, and political treatises, then, is the belief that British women should adopt a more inclusive version of community, accepting into it other women whose national identities are fluctuating or open to question. *Women Writing the Nation* thus locates the various ways in which women writers borrowed from the discourses of nation to explore the role of the gendered individual within the larger nation through this concept of an imagined community that was defined by what it was *not.* Paradoxically, since fluctuating and mobile identities seem to resist community formation, late eighteenth-century women writers also opened up a rearrangement of the idea of community: by adhering to a model of community that accepted the unstable and the changing, they refused to abide by a model that defined them by categories that were not their own.

The very act of identifying and locating an imagined community of women during this period considerably revises existing theories of national identity, which largely hold that national identity dominates over any other kind of identity that individuals possess. Political theorist Anthony D. Smith argues in his important study *National Identity,* for instance, that the self is always composed of six categories and roles: gender, space/territory, socioeconomic class, religion, ethnicity, and national identity. Of all six identities that an individual possesses, Smith argues that only national identity leads to the formation of a stable community; national identity, according to Smith and other renowned political theorists such as Liah Greenfeld, is the strongest collective identity that people have.[10] When we ask the significant questions "[W]ho am I? Who are we?," Smith maintains, the answer is "the nationalist solution, which sinks or 'realizes' individual identity within the new collective cultural identity of the nation. The individual in this solution takes her or his identity from a cultural collectivity; she or he becomes a citizen, that is, a recognized and rightful member of a political community."[11] Smith's argument is that individual identity is lost within the larger collective identity of the nation, that national identity overrides all of the other identities that individuals also occupy. Even Colley's main argument implies that national identity remained the strongest hold over most Britons during this particular period in history. Although she concedes that Britishness as a category of identity did not actually "supplant" other loyalties during the late eighteenth and early nineteenth centuries, that "[i]dentities are not like hats. Human beings can and do put on several at one time," Colley still claims that "Britishness was superimposed over an array of internal differences in response to contact with the Other, and above all in response to conflict with the Other."[12] In Colley's assessment, national identity becomes the chief tie that binds together the various people of Britain.

The idea of an imagined female community resituates these theories. When women writers use their gender as a way to be heard, they demonstrate that gender identity is often stronger than, or at least as strong as, national identity. Choosing between one identity and another is not a position that most of these writers occupied, but they did explore the oftentimes complex relationships between the various identities that women could hold in ways that their male counterparts could not, since maleness was more unproblematically "British" than femaleness.[13] The notion that gender identity often supplanted national identity becomes particularly evident when we realize that the female community being created united both conservative and radical authors alike. When male writers—whether conservative, radical, or somewhere in between— indicated that there was a common bond among all men, that bond was more often than not the bond of being British, of holding a particular *national* identity. When female writers, on the other hand, indicated that a bond existed among all women, that bond was more often than not the bond of being a woman, of holding a particular *gender* identity.

In recognizing this bond, however, we need to be careful to recognize also the different ideologies upon which it is constructed. This idea of an imagined female community is not an innocent or static concept, and the women writers who used it as a way to assert their claims about the position of women in British society often overlooked fundamental differences between their readers.[14] Different writers imagined the existence of female community in different ways. For some, it could only exist within the larger realm of the British nation; for others, it was a transnational concept that existed outside of the nation and that could unite women who possessed different national identities. For a few, it could even be both, depending on the context. The various communities that these writers imagined were also often marked by exclusions that were race-, class-, sexuality-, and religion-based. By and large, the idea of a female community was constructed *by* middle-class white authors, *for* middle-class white readers. Many of the authors, for instance, drew upon the language of the abolitionist movement, not with the intent of supporting it, but rather to make their own claims, while others ignored or overlooked the situations of slaves who experienced the physical pain of oppression to a much greater and more damaging extent than they ever would.[15] A few writers, like Mary Wollstonecraft in her unfinished novel *Maria, or The Wrongs of Woman,* envisioned a protolesbian space for this community, while others, like Laeticia Matilda Hawkins, fretted over the dangers of women becoming too close to one another and thereby risking the loss of male protection. Other women writers reveal a strong anti-Catholic prejudice,[16] and still others a bias against the lower classes. There were thus limits to imagining this community, limits, we shall see, that were constructed as much by each author's individual prejudices as they were by society's demands. While the claims that were being made by the women writers differed according to the political inclinations and agendas of each individual author, each author still availed herself of the figure of the nation and its relation to France to further her own cause as it related to gender issues. An otherwise disparate group of writers was united in its members' interest in the role of women within the British nation as it defined itself in relation to France.[17]

"Exposing the Weakness of the Land":
Hannah More's Patriotic Cartography

Just as once we start looking for British–French relations in male writers' texts we see these connections everywhere, so, too, can we begin to recognize these relations in texts by women authors once we analyze them with these connections in mind. When these authors discuss women's issues, they are more fully able to do so by bringing the third term of France into their discussions—by making a triad of women, Britain, and France—and by locating themselves and their fellow women as members of a united entity, an imagined community in its own right. One of the century's most famous writers, for example, was the politically conservative Hannah More, who also contributed to the creation of a female community.[18] Asked to pen 1795–1797's *Cheap Repository Tracts* for the poor because of the reputation she had already established as a pious and moral writer, More soon followed this text up with 1799's *Strictures on the Modern System of Female Education, with a View of the Principles and Conduct Prevalent Among Women of Rank and Fortune,* one of her most popular works.[19] Written for women of "rank and fortune," the *Strictures* argue for reform in the manners of those women whom she feels are most able to influence society for the better. What at first appears to be a treatise on female education, however, soon reveals itself to be a diatribe against foreign influence. The two aims of education and nationalism might seem to be disjointed, but More soon makes it clear that they are more closely linked than we might otherwise have thought. One need read no further than More's own introduction to the *Strictures,* in fact, to locate her nationalist project. Her goal in addressing British women, she explains as early as the second paragraph, is to defend Britain's honor: "The Author is apprehensive that she shall be accused of betraying the interests of her sex by laying open their defects: but surely, an earnest wish to turn their attention to objects calculated to promote their true dignity, is not the office of an enemy: so to expose the weakness of the land is to suggest the necessity of internal improvement, and to point out the means of effectual defense, is not treachery, but patriotism."[20] Claiming to write for the good of the nation, More hopes to "lay open" the faults of her fellow British women. Such exposure, of course, revolves around the metaphor of British women as a "land" in need of protection from within. By equating women with the nation, the whole issue of reforming women's manners becomes a matter of defending the actual British nation against outside influence. More's self-described act of patriotism thus involves a critique of her fellow British women, with the implied purpose of uniting them against foreign invasion. Her focus on nationalist concerns functions as a thin disguise for her real interest in gender concerns.

The connection between More's desire to protect her fellow women and the connection to France becomes clearer as the introduction continues. In the very next paragraph, More extends her metaphor to elaborate on the similarities between the reformist writer and the geographer:

> In speaking on the qualities of one sex the moralist is somewhat in the situation of the Geographer, who is treating on the nature of one country:—the air, soil, and produce of the land which he is describing, cannot fail in many essential points to resemble those of other countries under the same parallel; yet it is his business to descant on the one without adverting to the other: and though in drawing his map he may happen to introduce some of the neighboring coast, yet his principal attention must be confined to that country he proposes to describe, without taking into account the resembling circumstances of the adjacent shores.[21]

The "adjacent shores" to which More refers belong, of course, to none other than France, the nation against which More has to "point out the means of effectual defense." More must make comparisons—however brief—between her own nation and that of the French since the British are so interested in the goings-on of their neighbors. More's choice of analogy in this passage is also significant, for in comparing the moralist to the geographer, More once again equates women with the terrain of the nation. Like the geographer, More "draws" the map of her own countrywomen so they can see the "true" state of affairs and subsequently effect change; in so doing, she metaphorically treats her imagined community of women as a nation itself. Her true interest lies not so much in protecting the British nation as it does in uniting her fellow countrywomen. Since plotting the perimeters of one's land is an important business, More's analogy also makes the study of women into an equally serious business, one that is just as necessary as other work carried on in the name of Britain. Understanding our British women, her words imply, helps us understand our own nation.

Although More claims in the Introduction that she will only occasionally make reference to France in her text—"to *introduce* some of the neighboring coast," as she phrases it—within the body of the *Strictures* More elaborates on the threat that France poses to a fairly large extent. Essentially, More blames the French (and, to a lesser extent, the Germans) for the current decay of British principles and values. "That cold compound of irony, irreligion, selfishness, and sneer, which make up what the French (from whom we borrow the thing as well as the word) so well express by the term *persiflage,*" More notes, "has of late made an incredible progress in blasting the opening buds of piety in young persons of fashion" (128). This *persiflage* has succeeded so well in chipping away at Britain's moral fiber that it has "unquestionably rent away some valuable parts of that strong, rich, native stuff which formed the antient (*sic*) texture of British manners" (132). The British nation may not literally be under attack in More's metaphor (although in 1799 Britain was still engaged in war with France), but that "strong, rich, native stuff" that Britishness comprises is. To defend themselves against the "French infidels" (138), women must collectively unite to defend their morality and honor: "At this period, when our country can only hope to stand by opposing a bold and noble *unanimity* to the most tremendous confederacies against religion and order, and governments, which the world ever saw; what an accession would it bring to the public strength, could we prevail on beauty, and rank, and talents, and virtue, confederating their several powers, to come forward with a patriotism at once firm and feminine for the general good!" (125–26).

More's encouragement to her fellow countrywomen to "come forward with a patriotism at once firm and feminine" essentially involves the joining together of these women—the formation of a female community. United as women against the French, female Britons can assert their "several powers," rendering both their homes and their homeland safe and comfortable once again. More's concern is therefore a national one, and she attempts to consolidate her readers not only because they are Britons, but also because they are *women.* By guarding against foreign influence, which infiltrates British society under the guise of seemingly innocuous pamphlets and works of literature, British women can protect themselves and their nation. Improving women's education and manners thus becomes a national concern of the utmost importance.

REGAINING LIBERTY IN MARY HAYS'S *APPEAL*

Swinging back to the other end of the political spectrum, we encounter Mary Hays, a professed radical and friend of Mary Wollstonecraft's, whose 1796 novel *Memoirs of Emma Courtney* caused a scandal when it first appeared since it quasi-autobiographically detailed the story of a woman who openly declares her (unrequited) love to the male object of her affection. Interested in women's issues throughout her writing career, Hays would expand on her views in greater length in 1798's *Appeal to the Men of Great Britain on Behalf of Women*. The *Appeal's* references to the French are not as explicit as those in More's *Strictures*, but they exist underneath the surface and, in fact, provide the basis for the entire text. Hay structures the *Appeal* around the basic argument that if British men really valued liberty to the extent they claim, then they would also value the rights of women. The premise for Hays's claim is thus the particularly eighteenth-century British belief that Britons possessed a superior degree of liberty as compared to other nations, particularly the French. As Linda Colley explains, during the eighteenth century Britons viewed themselves as "peculiarly free," with a "unique commitment to liberty."[22] United under a Protestant monarchy, most Britons believed that their nation was superior to that of the French, who, Britons firmly believed, were accustomed to being servile and passive. John Andrews, for instance, notes in 1783: "Subjection however of some kind or other seems necessary for a Frenchman."[23] Writing in 1789, Hester Lynch Piozzi makes the same point in her travel narrative *Observations and Reflections Made in the Course of a Journey Through France, Italy, and Germany*, where she remarks that "among the few comforts that result from a despotic government"[24] is the docility that the French display when in crowded venues.

Hays draws upon this rich tradition of depicting the French as impotent and weak when she appeals to her readers to effect change within Britain. Implicit comparisons between French servility and British liberty underlie all of her arguments. Opening her Introduction with an explanation as to why she chose to address a male audience instead of a female one, for example, Hays refers to this national interest: "But as the men of Great Britain, to whom in particular I chuse to appeal, have to their everlasting honor, always been remarkable for an ardent love of liberty, and high in their pretensions to justice with regard to themselves; it is not to be believed, if the subject of the present work were taken into their serious consideration, but that the same sentiments would be freely and generously extended to that class of beings, in whose cause I though unworthy appear."[25] By appealing to national vanity, Hays challenges her readers by piquing them in an area designed to rouse their interest. Throughout the *Appeal*, in fact, Hays continues to use this strategy, basing most of her injunctions on invocations to a British sense of liberty. To cite just one more example, in her chapter entitled "What Women Ought To Be," Hays writes:

The love of liberty, the desire of distinguishing ourselves by superior abilities of mind and body, the passions themselves are entailed upon us, and no doubt for the best of purposes, when kept within due bounds. But shall we presume to say that numberless ideas, or opinions, or principles, call them what we please, which we have taken up at random, and adopted upon trust, merely because they are ready made and handed down to us from our forefathers, who formed them to suit their own purposes, — or because men still find that they flatter their reigning vices, or prejudices, — shall we presume to say that such, are as obviously natural to the human character, as those I have named?[26]

Referring to the idea of Britain as a chosen land, Hays connects the idea of liberty to that of independent thinking: those who blindly accept the beliefs of their forefathers do not wisely use the "superior abilities" they have been given. Her fellow Britons owe it to their national heritage to cultivate these talents and to be defenders of their liberty. These abilities and freedoms are, after all, what separate the British from their less fortunate rival, who are, of course, the French.

Hays's discussion is, in many ways, also similar to those of Frances Burney, Mary Wollstonecraft, Charlotte Smith, and other popular women writers of the period, for an important link between Hays and these other women is their combined interest in unveiling prejudice for what it really is: a disfiguring form of hatred. In the Advertisement to the *Appeal,* Hays mentions her desire to demolish prejudice as one of the central aims of her book. She explains that when she first learned that other writers, both male and female, had already published books on the same topic as hers (women's issues), she was temporarily dissuaded from publishing her own text for fear of repetition. Upon further reflection, however, Hays decided to pursue publication since she knew that her project could help to further dispel prejudice: "Yet to manage with some degree of tenderness the prejudices of the generality of mankind; to respect even *these* till the multitude can be persuaded that ALL PREJUDICES are inimical to its happiness and interests; can neither justly be esteemed immoral, or deceitful."[27] *All* prejudice — whether relating to gender, nation, or personal situation — harms those against whom it is turned. To make this point in greater detail, Hays more plainly connects prejudice to British national pride: "I do suppose that all those high-sounding claims of the men, which they hold to be so natural, so reasonable, and so edifying for the other sex; must when impartially considered, be esteemed as but the fashion of this world, which passeth away. I do suppose that the subject is only to be examined by minds not prejudged to be convinced; that all opinions degrading to women, are grounded on the rude ideas of savage nations . . . . [and] all opinions degrading to women are founded in ignorance."[28] Hays's point is a sharp one, for she essentially informs British men that any degrading views of women that they hold make them ignorant fools. Even worse, if those views are shared by the British nation, as she implies they are, then Britain itself is nothing other than savage and barbaric. In addition to criticizing male Britons, Hays's words also convey a strong anti-Burkean stance, for any discussion of prejudice at this time would immediately bring Edmund Burke's *Reflections on the Revolution in France* to mind, a text in which Burke makes prejudice the key component in his configuration of the nation.[29] Burke centered his ideas about Britain around the idea of prejudice, which, he firmly believed, was the positive bond that united Britons. In critiquing prejudice, then, Hays is directly participating in conversations about nation formation and British national identity, and by portraying prejudice as harmful—not beneficial—Hays allies herself with those opposed to the Burkean camp. Her insistence on the outdated and "savage" nature of the British thus signals her nationalist, anticonservative agenda. By opening themselves up to new beliefs, the assumption is, British men would lose some of their nationalist prejudices, making their female compatriots' lives easier and more fulfilling.

Hays loses her subtlety at certain moments, when she more openly expresses her dislike of how British men treat British women. One particularly memorable passage seems designed to goad her male readers into action, a passage in which Hays compares British men to that most despised of all tormentors, William the Conqueror. Hays does not try to soften the analogy, which is anything but hidden: "Do not therefore endeavour to degrade women on the one hand, and in every material point in life, and then suppose you make it up to them, by a few idle ceremonies and unmeaning words; which as Sir Henry Wotton says of the new behaviour and habits introduced by William the Conqueror among the English; 'are under shew of civility, in effect but rudiments of subjection.'"[30] Hays's decision to compare British men with William the Conqueror takes on greater national significance when we realize that the image of William had strong political resonances during this period. As critic Matthew Bray explains, during the eighteenth century, a renewed interest in Anglo-Saxonism led Britons to look with disdain upon the vestiges of the Norman Conquest. Most eighteenth-century Britons viewed the conquest as an act that had forcefully imposed French influence upon an unwilling British people: "a central emphasis of patriotic Anglo-Saxonism . . . [was] the notion that the Norman Conquest imposed a short-lived, tyrannical 'yoke' upon nascent Anglo-Saxon liberties."[31] Hays's contemporary Thomas Paine, for instance, writes extensively about how "Conquest and tyranny transplanted themselves with William the Conqueror from Normandy into England" in 1791–1792's *Rights of Man*.[32] Historian Gerald Newman's analysis concurs with Bray's, for Newman notes that from the 1770s onward, Britons began to reemphasize their original sense of liberty.[33] William the Conqueror was to be particularly despised as the representative of such oppression, and, as Bray also points out, positive portrayals of either William or the Normans actually became dangerous in the late eighteenth and early nineteenth centuries, since "the Norman Conquest immediately brought to mind fears of a second French conquest by Napoleon. Thus, in the contemporary imagination, William the Conqueror equaled Napoleon, and the Normans represented the modern French, poised to invade England at any moment."[34] The figure of William the Conqueror thus inspired both fear and contempt in Hays's audience. By the time the *Appeal* was actually published in 1798, such feelings had been exacerbated to an extreme. That year—the same one that witnessed Napoleon's Battle of the Nile and the subsequent alliance of Britain, Austria, and Russia against the French general[35]—was one in which British men would have been particularly loathe to have themselves identified in any way with either of these two ravagers and destroyers.[36] With British liberty at stake, the treatment of British women thus becomes an issue of national importance. If British men continue to degrade women "in every material point in life" while simultaneously offering a "few idle ceremonies and unmeaning words"—gestures typically associated with the French—to attempt to soften such treatment, then those men are no better than the nefarious and pointedly French William the Conqueror or his present-day embodiment, Napoleon.

"So Small an Interest in Public Affairs": Helen Maria Williams's Reflections on France

Another woman writer of interest was that fervent supporter of the French Revolution, Helen Maria Williams, who was well known as one of Britain's finest sentimental poets before she began her foray into politics. In July of 1790, Williams made her first visit to France as the guest of the Du Fossé family. She arrived in Paris on July 13 (the Fête de Fédération, which commemorated the first anniversary of the Revolution) and stayed until September, when she returned to England. On this, her first acquaintance with France, she wrote *Letters Written from France in the Summer of 1790* as her version of the events she witnessed during those months. Subsequent volumes of letters began to be published serially in England as Williams continued her visits to France before permanently settling there in 1792 with her companion, John Hurford Stone. In all, Williams wrote eight volumes of *Letters from France* in the years from 1790 to 1796, letters that chronicled the Revolution firsthand for a primarily British audience.

Although Williams was enormously popular and influential during her lifetime (even inspiring the young William Wordsworth to compose his first published poem about her), she disappeared from literary criticism for a long while, and has only just recently returned.[37] Williams's contributions to the nationalist debate are significant, however, for Williams carefully positioned herself in relation to an audience whose views about the Revolution would fluctuate immensely in the years during which she wrote. In particular, Williams used her gender and subtle comparisons between France and Britain as ways to gain authority as a woman writer to talk about political events and the British nation. As historian Gregory Claeys has explained, the Revolution controversy was at its "most heated" state between 1791 and 1793,[38] at exactly that point when Williams sent out her first four volumes of letters. In looking at how Williams positioned herself in these volumes as a recorder of this great historic event, we can see that Williams ultimately tried to placate her more conservative readers by a seeming adherence to strict moral and behavioral codes, and often by using the language and tropes of romance, a genre associated with female readers. Doing so allowed her, through the intimacy of the letter form, to create an imagined community of women readers whose ability to take part in discussions concerning Britain was strengthened by Williams's own involvement in the actual political events of the day.

Understanding that her British audience would be opposed to a woman's involvement in political matters (especially French ones), Williams manipulated her readers' perceptions to purposely construct herself as an uninformed, emotional woman who, nevertheless, is able to write about the Revolution precisely because she possesses these same characteristics. Williams spends a great deal of time in Volume 1, for instance, justifying the writing of her *Letters*. Accused of betraying her sex by writing about such overtly political matters, Williams claims that such subject matter is only natural. She explains this to her correspondent (and hence her British audience):

> Yesterday I received your letter; in which you accuse me of describing with too much enthusiasm the public rejoicings in France, and prophecy that I shall return to my own country a fierce republican. In answer to these accusations, I shall observe, that it is very difficult, with common sensibility, to avoid sympathising in general happiness. My love of the French revolution is the natural result of this sympathy; and therefore my political creed is entirely an affair of the heart; for I have not been so absurd as to consult my head upon matters of which it is so uncapable of judging.[39]

De-emphasizing her own intelligence by claiming that it would be "absurd" for her to "consult" her head, Williams draws attention to her sensibility and extreme enthusiasm instead. Her claim that her "political creed is entirely an affair of the heart" significantly points to her role as a woman writer, for it is her "common sensibility," a sensibility shared among all women, that allows her to sympathize with the French.[40] Later on in this first series of letters, Williams will once again insist upon her own ignorance, remarking, "But, however dull the faculties of my head, I can assure you, that when a proposition is addressed to my heart, I have some quickness of perception."[41] Emotion supposedly allows Williams to respond perceptively to the Revolution's events.

In this earliest volume of letters, Williams also claims to be puzzled herself over her own interest in politics. At one point, she muses on this: "Did you expect that I should even dip my pen in politics, who used to take so small an interest in public affairs . . . ?"[42] Immediately after posing this question, however, Williams provides another answer for her "interest in public affairs," one that is also intimately connected with her sensibility. Her reason for becoming so involved has to do with her connection with the Du Fossés, who were victims of the *ancien régime*'s injustices. The Du Fossés' story, in fact, makes up a large portion of Volume 1 (over seventy pages in the original printing), and so receives great emphasis.[43] After relating how M. Du Fossé's father persecuted the couple for marrying against his wishes, Williams finishes their tale by once again emphasizing the emotional aspects of her interest in this French family. She concludes by pointing this out: "I am glad you think that a friend's having been persecuted, imprisoned, maimed, and almost murdered, under the ancient government of France, is a good excuse for loving the revolution. What, indeed, but friendship, could have led my attention from the annals of imagination to the records of politics; from the poetry to the prose of human life?"[44] Williams's literal turn from writing poetry to writing political prose was thus instigated by actual events, and her sympathy for the Du Fossés led her to "love" the Revolution. The "romantic" nature of the Du Fossés' history moves Williams, in fact, to a description of French society in general at the present moment. Linking the fantastic with the mundane, Williams opens her second volume of letters with a description of the extraordinary tenor of life in France:

> (Indeed living in France at present, appears to me somewhat like living in a region of romance. Events the most astonishing and marvellous are here the occurrences of the day, and every newspaper is filled with articles of intelligence that will form a new era in the history of mankind. The sentiments of the people also are elevated far above the pitch of common life. All the motives which most powerfully stimulate the mind in its ordinary state, seem repressed in consideration of the public good, and every interest is sacrificed with fond alacrity at the altar of the country.)[45]

Told as a parenthetical aside but receiving emphasis by placement in its own new paragraph, this comment calls attention to events which once would have been called "astonishing and marvellous," but which have since become common and ordinary because they are acted out daily. The French people are united in their concern for the "public good," which lends a heroic and romantic air to their actions. And if, of course, life is like a romance, then how could women not become involved, for are not romance and sensibility, as so many conduct book writers pointed out, the domain of women? By making this argument, Williams transforms romance into an *active* occupation for women.

After establishing her right in Volume 1 to comment upon the Revolution, Williams turns to a more active engagement in women's issues in Volumes 2 and following. Once she has constructed herself as interested in the Revolution because of her emotional attachment to it, Williams can now more openly make claims about women's status in society by comparing her fellow British women to the French. Her concerns thus lie not only with the larger political events unfolding in France, but also with the changes she witnesses in the lives of Frenchwomen. One of the letters in Volume 2 begins, for instance, with an account of how French girls who are destined to marry merchants are taught higher levels of mathematics. She explains the upbringing that such women receive:

> After she is married she acts as her husband's first clerk, and passes the whole day in his counting house. Some advantages arise from this practice; since a French woman, if her husband dies, is capable of carrying on his business till her children are of a proper age to succeed to it; and in the mean

time she knows exactly the state of his affairs. Whereas, the wife of an English merchant, sometimes from being entirely ignorant of his real situation, indulges herself in a mode of living which hastens on his ruin, and receives like a thunder-stroke the intelligence that her riches were a dream, and that her husband is a bankrupt.[46]

Williams's appraisal of this practice emphasizes its positive nature. Clearly approving of wives' involvement in their husbands' affairs, Williams points out how such involvement creates an economically stable family. When women occupy a significant role in their family's financial situation (for notice that the French merchant's wife is not just any clerk, but rather *first* clerk), they are able to manage effectively their home lives, even in the event of their husbands' deaths.[47] Williams attributes the differences between French and British women to the mentality of the French people as a whole, who, Williams notices, allow a much greater share of knowledge, activity, and mobility to their women than do the British. To make such points, which she does in many passages, Williams's rhetorical strategy is to slip these small observations in, without calling too much attention to them, but rather mentioning them in what she wants us to take as a nonchalant manner. A description of leisure time and the Paris cafés, for instance, suddenly turns into a commentary on how Frenchwomen meet with very different treatment than their British counterparts. Williams takes care to point out these differences: "There are coffee-houses on the Boulevards, where the people, while they drink their wine, lemonade, or orgeat, are entertained with a play gratis. Women, as well as men, are admitted to these coffee-houses; for the English idea of finding cafe, comfort, or festivity, in societies where women are excluded, never enters into the imagination of a Frenchman."[48] Something so widely accepted in England as not admitting women into the company of men is absolutely unthinkable in France, where women are allowed an equal share in the "cafe, comfort, or festivity" presently occurring. By mentioning this different mindset, Williams thus accentuates the arbitrary nature of how women are treated in her own native country. What one nation accepts as "natural" may, in fact, be contrived and absurd in another. Williams essentially adopts a cosmopolitan mindset, writing as a citizen of the world, rather than as a nationalist.

After her first volume of letters, Williams trades her timidity for temerity, becoming more daring in her comparisons of French and British women. Her comments now cover not only nationalist concerns, but gender ones as well. By emphasizing her own gender identity and its presumed claims to emotional superiority, Williams can engage in the Revolutionary debates and also make claims about the status of her fellow countrywomen. Her sensibility gives her license to comment upon political events—as she couches her arguments in terms designed to be palatable to an increasingly conservative British readership—and acts as a mode of unification. Williams essentially creates an imagined community of female readers, united by sensibility and a shared interest in the welfare of British women. Williams, like More and Hays, but in crucially different ways, thus draws upon the idea of France to talk about women's issues, and, in this case, their involvement in politics. France once again becomes the third term around which a woman writer could openly discuss women's current situation within Britain.

The Danger of the *Françaises:*
Laeticia Matilda Hawkins's Imagined Space

Try as she might to make her pro-Revolutionary views amenable to her British audience, Williams still met with criticism, and one of the more notable responses to her *Letters from France* came from the pen of reactionary Laeticia Matilda Hawkins, whose vision of female community opened up this chapter. Angered by Williams's overt treatment of political matters, Hawkins wrote her *Letters on the Female Mind, its Powers and Pursuits. Addressed to Miss H. M. Williams, with particular reference to Her Letters from France* in 1793 as a counter to Williams's earlier letters. Like her predecessor, Hawkins used the idea of France as a way to address her own concerns about the status of women in British society, as the title of her own text makes clear. Hawkins was, in fact, one of the few writers who recognized the subversive potential of Williams's text, especially Williams's cunning rhetorical strategy of discussing British women's concerns under the guise of offering supposedly "harmless" commentary on the status of Frenchwomen. The "inflammatory" nature of Williams's letters does not escape Hawkins's notice:

> Almost every page of your letters offers a subject of comment; but I pass over much, because I abhor hypercriticism, and because my only view in putting together these desultory remarks, is, I will candidly confess, to prevent, as far as I am able, your doing mischief, by inflaming the minds of my countrywomen with notions they had better be without. Society has already suffered abundantly by the ill-applied labors of republicans; and as women are most eager to see what women can effect, female republicans have had

it very much in their power to disturb domestic peace, by contending charitably, as we must believe, for those extensions of prerogative to wives and
daughters, which no wife or daughter has a claim to, or ought to be trusted
with.[49]

Although Hawkins claims not to be "hypercritical" of Williams, she
does, in actuality, offer an almost letter-by-letter assessment of Williams's text, with the palpable aim of preventing Williams from "doing
mischief" to British women. This particularly scathing account of the
effects of Williams's letters revolves around the idea that Williams incites women to "disturb domestic peace" by encouraging them to question their own positions in British society and to seek "extensions of
prerogative."

It is not until the Postscript to the *Letters on the Female Mind* that
Hawkins makes the dangers of these prerogatives explicit. In these final
pages of her text, Hawkins argues for the ongoing insulation of British
women, who, she firmly believes, should not be exposed to political
matters. Blessed because of where they live, English women occupy a
unique position in the world:

> from all the ten thousand miseries of power, we, happy women, and doubly
> happy as Englishwomen, are providentially exempt. Protected by the laws,
> by custom, and the general sentiment of our country; we may, if we chuse
> it, live undisturbed in the possession of every earthly good. Public calamity
> must become personal suffering, it must pervade the recesses of our dwell
> ings, before we, housed and sheltered as we are, in the hearts of our gener
> ous protectors, are exposed to it. The whole world might be at war, and yet
> not the rumor of it reach the ear of an Englishwoman—empires might be
> lost, and states overthrown, and still she might pursue the peaceful occupa
> tions of her home; and her natural lord might change his governor at plea
> sure, and she feel neither change nor hardship.
>
> And now, who would give up this peace, this security, this situation, so
> friendly to all the gentle virtues of the heart, and all the elegant powers of
> the mind, to make inroads into the hostile lands of public feud and political
> context?[50]

Hawkins's words, like those of Mary Hays, testify to her belief in the
idea that the British are a chosen people, a group enjoying the "possession of every earthly good." As Linda Colley notes, "An extraordinarily
large number of Britons seem to have believed that, under God, they
were particularly free and peculiarly prosperous. . . . large numbers of
Protestant Britons believed—believed precisely because they *were* Prot-

estant, and because it was comforting to believe it—that they were richer in every sense than other peoples, particularly Catholic peoples, and particularly the French."[51] In Hawkins's view, Englishwomen are particularly fortunate, "protected" as they are by the laws, customs, and "general sentiment" of their nation, which "allows" them to remain ignorant. They are "doubly happy," both because they are women and because they are English. Underlying Hawkins's claim, of course, is an implicit comparison to Frenchwomen, literal dwellers in the "hostile lands of public feud and political context." Unlike their French counterparts, British women remain willfully ignorant, "safe" in their domesticity. For Hawkins, ignorance is bliss.

Although they currently seem to possess more liberty than British women, however, French women will soon tire of their new-found freedom because, Hawkins asserts, it cannot provide them with the means of lasting happiness. She explains this at great length:

> It cannot be doubted that the privileges which this country allows the female sex, and the consequent comforts and enjoyments resulting from the consentaneous (*sic*) opinion of Englishmen in their favor, will excite as restless a spirit of envy and jealousy in the women of less-favored nations, as our public peace and prosperity has raised in the men. In France, notwithstanding all their boasted freedom and equality, women have suffered an irreparable, and a most barbarous degradation in the dissolution of the marriage union at pleasure. A few of the licentious may at first be pleased with this freak of liberty; but nine tenths of the Gallic ladies will soon be weary of it . . . . they will look with a malignant eye on the respectable English wife, repaid for all her sacrifices and absurdities, by that most gratifying of all returns, the esteem and affection of a worthy man.[52]

In an inversion of the jealousy model, Hawkins claims that Frenchwomen are actually jealous of the British, and not the other way around.[53] Drawing upon the stereotype of Frenchwomen as licentious and decadent, Hawkins paints an image of French marriages as disposable and insubstantial. The ability to dissolve their marriages might sound enticing to one-tenth of Frenchwomen, but it leaves these "Gallic ladies" without that most prized possession, the "esteem and affection of a worthy man."[54] English respectability (as opposed to French licentiousness)[55] provides the greatest comfort, and is guaranteed in Britain by the institution of marriage. Essentially, Hawkins positions marriage as the foundation of British society, the base upon which all relationships ultimately rest. Asserting that Frenchwomen themselves recognize this fact, Hawkins even goes so far as to claim that Frenchwomen are maliciously plotting to destroy the entire institution of marriage within Britain. She explicitly draws this connection for her readers: "One art which they [Frenchwomen] will certainly use, is that of exciting us, by their example, to take part in politics, in whatever can render us unamiable and ferocious. By this manœuvre, they will hope to lessen the mutual attachment subsisting between the sexes; they will set us at variance amongst ourselves, and then their next step needs no prediction."[56] Using a seduction metaphor, Hawkins describes the influence that Frenchwomen have on British women and the effects that involvement in politics has on women's lives in general. By "exciting" British women, French women destroy the affections that exist between British husband and wife. Through a cause and effect pattern, engaging in politics leads to women becoming "unamiable and ferocious," which in turn makes men despise them. Helen Maria Williams has herself been seduced by the arguments of the "Gallic ladies," and Hawkins wants to save other British women from this same fate.

It is this siren call of the *françaises* that also brings to the surface some of Hawkins's more hidden anxieties about the viability of a female community. In the passage that opens up this chapter, Hawkins, it is important to remember, envisioned "a female community detached from the world, where every virtue might be nourished, every evil bias controled."[57] Although Hawkins repeatedly imagines the existence of such a community, each time she does so she must eventually give up the illusion because of "the frailty of our own nature" (ibid.). Hawkins never specifies of what such a frailty actually consists, nor does she attempt to explain her vision of female community at any great length. It is not until we place her vision alongside that of the French sirens, in fact, that we can understand why female community cannot be sustained. In essence, the siren call of Frenchwomen compromises Hawkins's utopic vision of female community. Although she never directly names it, Hawkins's seduction metaphor essentially depends upon the veiled threat of lesbianism, of women turning to each other and completely excluding men. This veiled lesbianism acts as an incredible threat to Hawkins, for, as I have shown, heterosexual marriage is what makes English respectability possible for her; her version of nationalism depends upon an aggressive form of heterosexuality. The respect of men acts as a safeguard against the world, protecting women from those rumors of "empires lost" and "states overthrown" about which Hawkins wants to know nothing. Without male protection, woman would lose the "peaceful occupations of her home." The type of community that Frenchwomen represent is thus female community carried to an extreme—female community that exists without any reference to men. Hawkins is unable to sustain her own vision because of the fear that it, too, could reach this same extreme.

Also hidden beneath the surface lies another fear: that of economic insecurity. Marriage itself, Hawkins should well know, does not guarantee a man's affection or even decent treatment.[58] It does, however (or at least it does for upper- and middle-class women), usually guarantee financial well-being and security. Through their husbands' incomes, eighteenth-century middle-class women possessed peace and security, states of being that Hawkins seems to value above any others.[59] A female community carried to the extreme—carried out against men— would jeopardize all of the comforts that British women enjoy. For this reason, Hawkins immediately follows up her warning against French-women with a concrete plan of action. That plan is to have women unite in a collective effort to stave off French influence and to mitigate the weakening of English respectability. "[I]t behoves every woman, particularly at this crisis," Hawkins urges, "to be extremely tenacious of the real feminine character, and to improve to the utmost by every honest means, that favorable disposition, which Englishmen entertain towards us."[60] Like Hannah More's call for British women "to come forward with a patriotism at once firm and feminine for the general good,"[61] Hawkins's words act as a battle cry against any influences that destroy "the real feminine character." The irony of Hawkins's plan, however, is that Hawkins herself sets women "at variance" with one another, even though she denounces Frenchwomen for doing the same thing. That is, the call of the French is designed to lure British women away from their husbands and men, and toward other women. Yet the seduction metaphor that Hawkins uses to describe this call shows her own uneasiness with its lesbian tendencies. To deafen her readers' ears to the sound of the sirens' call, Hawkins then encourages them to do the best they can to please their men. Knowing as we do that the basis of British society depends for Hawkins upon the institution of marriage and a firm commitment to heterosexuality, we can read her remarks on keeping the men "favorabl[y] disposed" as a statement about Hawkins's commitment to the marriage market. After all, a group of women cannot usually be protected by the same man; each one needs her own protector (that is, husband). Her plan thus encourages women to unite in their efforts to rescue the "real feminine character," even though the goal of so doing is to compete with one another to win male protection. It is for these reasons that Hawkins cannot sustain her idea of female community. Remaining under the protection of their husbands and in the comfort of their domestic spaces would safeguard the attributes that separate British women not only from men, but also from French-women. At the same time, though, if women's attention is focused on marrying and keeping their husbands, then women will always be in competition with one another, looking at each other through veiled and suspicious eyes. Hawkins's vision of female community and her subsequent dismissal of it thus serve as a powerful case study; her text attests to the limits of female community, and to the fears and anxieties that often lie beneath what would otherwise seem to be a commonplace rhetoric.

THE BRITAIN–FRANCE–WOMAN TRIAD IN THE WRITINGS OF BURNEY, SMITH, AND WOLLSTONECRAFT

Although I have looked in detail at just four writers, this same interest in the relational role of France surfaces in texts by all of the more notable women writers of the period. It surfaces, for instance, in Anna Laeticia Barbauld's indictment of Britain because jealous of France in 1793's *Sins of Government, Sins of the Nation*;[62] in Mary Robinson's claim in her 1799 *A Letter to the Women of England, on the Injustice of Mental Subordination* that British women should become "citizens of the world";[63] in the Gothic novels of Ann Radcliffe and the threat of foreign influence;[64] and in Maria Edgeworth's association of the idleness of the upper classes with French *ennui*.[65] In the travel writing of the period, of course, the connections are even more obvious, especially in texts such as Hester Lynch Piozzi's 1789 *Observations and Reflections Made in the Course of a Journey Through France, Italy, and Germany*; Anna Eliza Bray's *Letters Written During a Tour through Normandy, Brittany, and other Parts of France in 1818*; and Lady Sydney Owenson Morgan's *France in 1829–1830*. Again, because the idea of France so completely dominated the political discourses of the period, even before the commencement of the Revolution, it became a useful way for women to discuss their own concerns and worries.

France therefore became the convenient third term around which female writers could make claims about their own status within Britain. It functioned as a vehicle: France was useful because relational, because of what it could (or, sometimes, could not) do in women's writing. While a reader can look, then, to many texts of the period to locate these claims about the merging of feminist or nonfeminist and nationalist or antinationalist agendas, *Women Writing the Nation* focuses on three of the better known women writers of the period: Frances Burney, Charlotte Smith, and Mary Wollstonecraft. Extended analyses of the intersections between gender and national identity in texts by these three particular writers enable me to pick up on the nuances of this formulation in ways that my shorter analyses of More, Hays, Williams, and Hawkins cannot. I also chose these three particular writers for several different reasons. First of all, these three writers were well known, widely read, and generally respected (though to varying degrees) during their lives and even after. They were major literary figures during this period: their contemporaries read them with interest, and ours have recently been doing so as well. Also, since *Women Writing the Nation* argues that women writers of the period deployed the figure of the nation and Britain's relations with France to further their own causes concerning gender, it is important to show that this deployment reached across political boundaries. Burney's political sympathies, for instance, were more "conservative," while Wollstonecraft's and Smith's were more "radical." A second reason, then, why I will be using these particular writers is to emphasize that the idea of imagined community exists in writings that ranged over the political spectrum, an idea that the analyses of More, Hays, Williams, and Hawkins has already shown. A third reason why this mix of writers works particularly well is because they used different genres to express their views. Smith used both poetry and the novel to further her political aims; Wollstonecraft used the political treatise, the letter, and the novel; and Burney used the novel and the political pamphlet. By alternating back and forth between different types of writing, *Women Writing the Nation* can better explore the possibilities gained by using various literary genres, while also showing that these ideas were not limited to one form of literature. Finally, the biographies of these particular women writers complicate even further the already intricate nature of the relationship between the private and the public. Their actual situations are reflected in their individual writings, opening up the question of how the personal inflects the political. All three women spent time in France at one point or another, and all three women had personal, familial, or professional relationships that brought them to their neighboring country. Choosing these particular three writers therefore illustrates how these claims hold true across political, literary, and biographical lines.

Mary Wollstonecraft's and Charlotte Smith's interest in France is probably better known than Frances Burney's, for the connections that both of these women had with the Revolution formed the basis for their texts and separate excursions into political matters. Charlotte Smith's

1792 novel *Desmond*, for instance, marks the beginning of Smith's explicit engagement in political affairs. Three years into the French Revolution, before the world was to encounter the Terror's frenzy of "judicial" murders or the sweeping victories of Napoleon, Charlotte Smith wrote *Desmond* in reaction to the changing world around her. Smith's novel, which was her fourth, tells the tale of the brave hero Desmond, a young man who is in love with the virtuous Geraldine, a woman who was married off by her parents to a cruel, profligate husband. Unlike her three previous novels, *Desmond* directly takes up political issues, weaving them in with the fictional tale of the characters whose lives we encounter against the backdrop of the Revolution. *Desmond*, which is one of Smith's best-known novels, makes strong the claim that the personal is political, that the national is gendered, and that the domestic is revolutionary. In particular, Smith uses the characters of Desmond and Geraldine to show why women should be allowed a voice in the political arena, how nationalistic prejudice encourages a narrow-minded view of the world, and that truth and reason are the best guarantors of both British liberty and understanding between nations.

Yet Smith's interest in gender and national identity became even more pronounced as the Revolution progressed. Instead of limiting her argument to the central idea that the concerns of British women should also be the concerns of the British nation, Smith extended her claims to insist upon the idea of choice in determining one's own national identity. The stories of Delmont and the Glenmorris family in 1798's *The Young Philosopher* exemplify Smith's new interest in exploring what it means to belong to a nation, particularly if that nation is spoiled and corrupt. Here imagined communities become a more real possibility for Smith than they had in any of her previous novels. Together, the two chapters on Smith highlight this movement toward imagined communities that Smith and other writers created.

Like Smith, Mary Wollstonecraft also shared an interest in the Revolution, and she is often remembered for her 1790 *A Vindication of the Rights of Men*, the first published response to Edmund Burke's famous *Reflections on the Revolution in France*. Yet Wollstonecraft's place in literary history has been guaranteed by her significant contributions to Western feminist thought, as mapped out in her 1792 text *A Vindication of the Rights of Woman*, a text dedicated to French diplomat Charles Maurice de Talleyrand-Périgord because of the educational reforms he had been encouraging in France. Both *Vindications* are daring treatises that expand on the rights of both men and women at a time when liberties were limited and political tensions in Britain were strong. Since Wollstonecraft's *Vindications* are her best-known works, most scholarship has focused on these two texts, especially the second *Vindication*. What has received very little critical attention, however, is the writing that Wollstonecraft did in the two years following the second *Vindication*. Her 1793 *Letter on the Present Character of the French Nation* and her 1794 *An Historical and Moral View of the Origin and Progress of the French Revolution* . . . deserve more critical attention because of the light they shed on Wollstonecraft's own views of nationalism and the role of women within the nation. I compare Wollstonecraft's ideas in her two *Vindications* to the ideas expressed in the *Letter* and *Historical View* in order to argue that Wollstonecraft merges her feminist agenda with a nationalistic one. More specifically, Wollstonecraft creates her version of feminism to unite her imagined community of women, and this feminism is a particularly British and nationalistic one. In a sense, it was as if Wollstonecraft helped invent Anglo-American feminism in contrast to what she saw as the perverted principles and misguided practices of French society. The chapter on this famous author thus reads the ways in which Wollstonecraft's feminist agenda emerges out of her nationalistic, anti-French sentiments.

While the chapters on Smith and Wollstonecraft lie at the core of *Women Writing the Nation,* it is Frances Burney's contributions that form the bookends to the project. Burney's nationalist connections have remained almost untouched in contemporary criticism, yet they are important indicators of the changing political climate in Britain during this period. Burney's work generally falls into the category of "novels of manners," as novels that represent genteel society and the mores, customs, and mannerisms of the "upper middle" (an anachronistic term) classes. No mention of Burney will you find in that section of Richard Polwhele's scathing 1798 poem "The Unsex'd Females" describing British women writers who have become "Gallic freaks, or [to] Gallic faith resigned."[66] Instead, Polwhele distinguishes Burney for her conservative politics, crediting Burney for "mix[ing] with sparkling humour chaste / Delicious feelings and the purest taste."[67] Burney's novels were all considered to be respectable and decorous, and they were admired by such eighteenth-century "conservative" illuminaries as Dr. Samuel Johnson and Edmund Burke. Burney herself was even given a position at Court as Keeper of the Robes for Queen Charlotte, whom she served for five extremely unpleasant (by Burney's own account) years. Together, the two chapters of *Women Writing the Nation* that focus on Burney will argue, however, that her views on the British nation are more revisionary than previously thought.

One of my main contentions is that Burney's last novel is a rewriting of her first in terms of its interest in nationalism and gender. Young and relatively inexperienced when she wrote 1778's *Evelina,* Burney chose stereotype and excess as devices to make the French and their nation into contemptible and even threatening characters. The characters who threaten Evelina also threaten England and English virtue, and no real space for a female community exists. By the time that she completed her last novel, however, Burney had been married to a Napoleonic general, and had experienced life within France first-hand. Although she repeatedly insists in her Introduction to 1814's *The Wanderer* that the novel is apolitical, Burney really does protest too much. In actuality, Burney pours her concerns about work, economics, gender roles, and identity into the forum of nationalist discourse in this later work, and provides a more complicated vision of the interrelationship between them. *The Wanderer*'s main character, a woman named Ellis/Juliet, almost starves to death because British society will not provide for her, but will also not let her provide for herself through work, and this is precisely what Burney criticizes. Burney's insistence on money, labor, and women's place in the nationalist project thus underscores her concern with Britain's role in the world arena. Revision of her earlier novel provides Burney with the chance to regain and reflect upon her past experimentation with French characters and with her own earlier misconceptions about national identity. In essence, Burney is kinder to the French nation and more critical of her own. Gender identity becomes a bond that unites several of the female characters, and Britain is criticized because its misplaced understanding of gender and national identity only contributes to "female difficulties," the subtitle of the novel.

Burney also explores two different kinds of nationalism, one in each novel. In *Evelina,* a nationalism based on violence, extremes, and aggression exists; in *The Wanderer,* however, a nationalism based on noblesse oblige is present. Such emphases are apparent because in *Evelina,* national identity is Burney's primary concern, whereas in *The Wanderer,* gender identity plays a more important role. While satire is also present in both novels, it works in the second novel to criticize not only France, as it did in *Evelina,* but also Burney's own nation. Burney offers a subtler version of the nation in her last work, and so the chapter on *The Wanderer* examines these subtleties and their significance in detail. In this chapter I also argue that by the time she wrote *The Wanderer,* Burney had modified her earlier views to express the idea that violence of any kind no longer has a place in the nation-state, and that female solicitude and danger are best mediated by a nation that allows women to provide for themselves, that allows for the creation of an inclusive, transnational female community. Dependence upon the state is undesirable, and, Burney argues, women should be allowed a space to contribute to a more acceptable, because accepting, vision of the British nation.

Just as France became the backdrop for a discussion of the rights of man for male writers, so, too, did it become the useful third term for a discussion of women's rights within Britain. The argument is a simple one really, but it has far-reaching effects on how we read and understand the literature produced during this period, for to read these women writers without understanding the national context is to not be fully aware of the cultural demands of their time. We have been reading these women writers with an eye toward their interest in gender concerns, but not with an eye toward their interest in the British nation. Once we recognize the role that France played in their exchanges, however, we can see how women writers linked gender issues with national ones to prove to their compatriots (both male and female alike) that the concerns of women should also be the concerns of Britain. Women writers of the late eighteenth and early nineteenth centuries demonstrated how gender identity and national identity interacted with and complicated one another, leading those of us writing in the twenty-first century to a new understanding of the great extent to which nationalism informs the work of so many women writers of this earlier period. And so, to see these interactions played out in more detail, we turn now to the texts of Burney, Smith, and Wollstonecraft—to the work of just a few of those women who helped write (and so shape) the modern British nation.

1

Quelling the French Threat in
Frances Burney's *Evelina*

A "LITTLE CHARACTER-MONGER," DR. JOHNSON ONCE CALLED Frances Burney as she was leaving an evening party at Lady Galway's London home shortly after the publication of her first novel, 1778's *Evelina*. Pleased herself with the description, Burney recorded the incident in both her journals and in her preface to *The Wanderer*, essentially registering the appellation in the annals of literary history.[1] The import of Johnson's epithet, of course, is that it draws attention to Burney's writing style, which Johnson meant to celebrate as one that used common character types in order to amuse and delight. Dr. Johnson was, however, not the only reader to point out Burney's facility with drawing interesting characters. In his 1843 review of Burney's published letters and diaries, Macaulay backs up Johnson's claim, stating, "It was in the exhibition of human passions and whims that her strength lay; and in this department of art she had, we think, very distinguished skill."[2] According to Macaulay, Burney's skill as an author lies in her ability to show "human passions and whims," emotions and behaviors that are shared by all humans, and so which can also be recognized as general personality types. Writing even earlier in the century than Macaulay, William Hazlitt also noticed this tendency in Burney's work, remarking that Burney's "*forte* is in describing the absurdities and affectations of external behaviour, or the *manners of people in company.*"[3] Hazlitt is quick to point out, however, that Burney's characters fall into general types and categories. While Burney is adept at recreating these "manners" of those in society, "Her characters, which are all caricatures, are no doubt distinctly marked, and perfectly kept up; but they are somewhat superficial, and exceedingly uniform."[4] Hazlitt recognized in Burney's early novels her tendency to make characters and actions appear simpler than they really are or could be, yet he failed to realize that this oversimplification resulted from Burney's own view of the world. The "superficial"

43

and "exceedingly uniform" characters she created in her early works were the direct result of her own belief that society is relatively superficial, relatively easy to interpret. The representation of Burney as a "character-monger" thus developed from the idea that Burney peopled her early novels with exaggerated personalities. The frenchified fop, the naive country girl, the handsome lord: all of these are characterizations that were easily recognized by Burney's readers.[5]

While Burney's skill in drawing these character types has long been recognized by many critics, what has gone relatively unexamined is the darker side of Burney's characterizations. *Evelina* in particular contains one of the most puzzling and disturbing pair of characters in an eighteenth-century British novel: Captain Mirvan and Madame Duval. *Evelina*'s other characters have received much critical attention over the past two hundred years, but few have stopped to question the function of these two in particular or the nature of their relationship. Having slipped through most of the cracks, the Captain and Madame Duval usually receive only cursory treatment, for most readers of the novel do not quite know what to make of these two odd characters. When discussed at all, the Captain and Madame Duval are rarely paired together, usually receiving separate treatment instead.[6] Despite their neglect, however, this fascinating couple is an important indicator of nationalist sentiment in Britain during the mid to late eighteenth century, for in creating these two ribald characters, Burney had to look no further than the nationalist rhetoric and anti-French propaganda of the day for inspiration. If, as Gerald Newman states, "To be truly English was to live up to a stereotype generated in anti-Frenchness,"[7] then Burney could draw upon the nationalist associations of her time period to draw characters that embodied the stereotypical traits of both the English and the French.

When examined through a nationalist lens, the roles that Captain Mirvan and Madame Duval play suddenly become clearer, and we can now see that the antagonisms that exist between this British sea captain and this Frenchwoman are a direct result of the antagonisms that had long existed between their respective nations. The threat of France is embodied in the figure of Madame Duval, and the most frightening force in *Evelina*, in fact, wears the guise not of a heartless seducer, as it did in many of the period's novels, but rather that of this old, bawdy woman. Evelina's grandmother represents the threat of a dual national identity, of being both French and English, which is a prospect that Evelina finds horrifying. To develop this idea, Burney draws upon nationalist stereotypes and prejudices to portray Madame Duval as a foul, almost monstrous woman. Despised by those around her, Madame Duval still possesses, however, the ability to force Evelina to return to France with her. Evelina is essentially powerless in her grandmother's grasp, and has no choice but to try to appease her. Yet Burney does not let Madame Duval get away with uncontrolled power. To contain Madame Duval, Burney brings in Captain Mirvan, a character who is even cruder and more savage than Evelina's grandmother. The Captain, who has an inveterate hatred of anything having to do with the French, absolutely abhors Madame Duval, so he does everything he can to torment and humiliate her. Their verbal and physical exchanges make up the bulk of the comedic scenes of the novel, yet, as will be emphasized towards the end of this chapter, these scenes also have a disturbing edge to them, one that reveals Burney's nascent sense of doubt about the nationalist rhetoric and imagery in which she engages. The young Burney thus draws upon some of the more nationalistic attitudes and stereotypes of her society, reinforcing a vision of France that adhered to the negative portrayals already put into place by her fellow Britons. Burney's novel serves as a useful case study to help us locate some of the most common nationalist stereotypes of the period, as well as some of the unsettling ambiguities that lie beneath them.

READING THE WORLD: THE LEGIBILITY OF CHARACTERS

Before Burney can introduce us to Madame Duval and overt investigations of nationalism, she must first establish Evelina's ability to fathom her world, so, throughout the novel and especially in the earlier scenes, Evelina encounters characters whom she can easily and accurately read. Within the various social situations in which she is placed, Evelina may not know what to say or how to act, but she immediately knows how to evaluate the people to whom she is introduced. This legibility that is inherent in Evelina's world is, of course, partly owing to the narrative constructs of the time period in which Burney wrote the novel. As Deidre Lynch has shown, in the earlier decades of the eighteenth century, character types "represented for their readers devices for thinking about typicality as such, for thinking about how, by expediting the diffusion and uniform legibility of information, printed characters supplied the social order with its impersonal mechanisms of coherence and comprehensibility."[8] Although *Evelina* was published after the period about which Lynch writes, the novel still retains these same elements of character type that made it possible not only for Evelina but also for Burney's readers to attach meaning to certain personalities.[9] From the moment she first meets him, for instance, Evelina knows that her eventual tormentor Mr. Lovel is a conceited fop. As he tiptoes, simpering and preening, toward Evelina and Maria Mirvan at their first dance in London, Lovel, Evelina notes in a letter, "had a set smile on his face, and his dress was so foppish, that I really believe he even wished to be stared at; and yet he was very ugly."[10] So very foolish are both his looks and behavior that Evelina has to conceal her laughter. This direct assessment of Mr. Lovel reveals Evelina's understanding of the place of this type of person in society; from the moment she first sees him, Evelina recognizes Mr. Lovel as a fool and a slave to society. His "set smile" is fixed, invariable, allowing for no adjustments to the circumstance or place. Recognizing this rigidity, Evelina cannot help but be amused. Her first meeting with her cousins the Branghtons also produces similar results. Based on this initial encounter, Evelina pronounces the father to be "very contracted and prejudiced"; the son to be a "foolish, over-grown school-boy"; Miss Branghton to be "proud, ill-tempered, and conceited"; and Miss Polly to be "rather pretty, very foolish, very ignorant, very giddy, and, I believe, very good-natured" (68). Before this first visit is over, the Branghtons prove themselves to be all that Evelina has imagined them to be. Although they have only just been introduced to her, for example, the family immediately begins to make pert inquiries into Evelina's personal history. Their rude questions will eventually drive Evelina from their presence: "I rose hastily, and ran out of the room: but I soon regretted that I had so little command of myself, for the two sisters both followed" (70). Evelina will learn just how correct her first candid remarks about the Branghtons were as she spends more time with them, learning more about their personalities. With time, too, Evelina will learn how to modify her own behavior more fully to accord with the dictates of society. She will learn that she cannot so boldly laugh at others, that she cannot run from a room if she is embarrassed and shocked by the behavior of others. Her initial evaluation of these characters, however, always remains intact. Another character, and this time a central one, that Evelina accurately reads is Lord Orville. When she meets him at the same ball where she meets Mr. Lovel, Evelina knows immediately what kind of person he is and the behavior that she can expect from him. Her understanding of Orville depends upon this same conception of the world and its members as relatively easy to fathom. When he first asks her to dance, for instance, Evelina describes Orville as a gentleman "gayly, but not foppishly dressed, and indeed extremely handsome, with an air of mixed politeness and gallantry" (29). As with Mr. Lovel, Evelina offers an initial assessment based upon superficial appearance. Whereas her other suitor wore a "dress . . . so foppish, that I really believe he even wished to be stared at," Lord Orville dresses with style and dignity. Even Orville's physical features attest to his superiority, for Evelina describes him as not just handsome, but rather as *extremely* handsome, using the adverb to emphasize his advantages.

Far from discrediting Evelina's tendency to judge others based upon an initial encounter, Burney gives Evelina's assessments value and credibility, which will become important later on in establishing Burney's nationalist agenda. Although Evelina immediately judges the characters she meets, her evaluations are always accurate, always precise. Even the external appearances of the people she meets reveal for Evelina their true inner natures. Granted, Lord Orville is handsome, but he would not be the perfect hero for our heroine unless he also possessed certain personality traits. Evelina acknowledges this superiority of manners shortly after she gets her first look at Orville. Having just finished dancing with Orville, Evelina rebukes herself for not possessing sufficient courage to speak with him openly and easily. Evelina is pleased, though, to see how much of an effort Orville makes to draw *her* into conversation. Recognizing his partner's timidity, Lord Orville draws upon his good breeding to make Evelina feel more at ease. She soon realizes that "the rank of Lord Orville was his least recommendation, his understanding and his manners being far more distinguished" (32). Orville's exterior thus reveals an interior that is equally excellent, equally meritorious. Evelina's initial assessment of Orville is an accurate one, and first appearances *are* what they seem. Orville is kind and protective, and, true to his nature, he will quite literally come to her rescue several times in the novel.

Even upon receipt of the false letter (actually written by Sir Clement Willoughby), Evelina's opinion of Orville is only temporarily clouded. The mix-up with the letter causes confusion, but is soon sorted out and even smoothed over by Evelina when Orville behaves so generously and kindly toward her afterward. The episode first begins when a small party composed of the Branghtons, Evelina, and Madame Duval find themselves without a coach on a rainy, stormy day. Noticing Orville's carriage and remembering that Evelina had once danced with the lord at a ball, the Branghtons, urged on by Madame Duval, use Evelina's name to secure Orville's coach for a ride home. Out of embarrassment and shame, Evelina writes a brief letter to Orville, begging his forgiveness for such an abuse of his kindness. Shock soon follows, however, when Evelina receives in response a letter that boldly proclaims that Orville loves her and would like to continue the correspondence. The letter contains a direct avowal of sentiments that Lord Orville should be loathe, as a proper gentleman, to communicate, causing Evelina to write to her close friend Maria Mirvan: "I could not find one sentence [in the letter] that I could look at without blushing: my astonishment was extreme, and it was succeeded by the utmost indignation. . . . how have I been deceived in this man!" (257). The "deception," in fact, incapacitates Evelina, eventually turning her into an "invalid" (268) and necessitating her trip to Bristol Hot Wells with Mrs. Selwyn so she can recover her health since her faith in humans is completely destroyed. Once there, Evelina learns that Orville will shortly arrive in Bristol, and she must once again force herself to think differently of him. She writes to Mr. Villars: "for how, my dearest Sir, how shall I be able totally to divest myself of the respect with which I have been used to think of him?" (277). Clearly, Orville's strong first impression has made a deep imprint on Evelina's mind. When she does meet him, however, Evelina is pleased to see that Orville makes no mention of the letter, instead assuming his habitual attitude of respect and polite interest. A panegyric opens her next letter to Mr. Villars: "Oh Sir, Lord Orville is still himself! still, what from the moment I beheld, I believed him to be, all that is amiable in man!" (278). Any doubts she had of his character are removed, and Evelina is once again secure in her assessments of the characters she meets. Misunderstandings can only be straightened out in this world, as characters' actions always coincide with their essential identities. Lord Orville's intentions are far from ambiguous, and he reveals himself to be the most suitable match for our heroine.

READING NATIONS: FRANCE AS THE SITE OF DECEPTION

This perspicuous understanding of the world carries over from the realm of characters to the realm of nations, for even our heroine's view of what Britain and France are like is straightforward. That is why it is important for Burney to emphasize to such a great extent Evelina's ability to read characters accurately: Burney needs to establish Evelina's character assessments early in the novel so that the judgments that Evelina makes about nations will also be read as valid. Burney thus uses Evelina to make her own nationalist claims. For Evelina, for instance, France is undeniably the land of deceptive women and of women who are deceived, the land where bad things happen to good people because of the villainous characters who dwell there. Although Evelina has never been there herself, France is where things first went wrong for her. Mr. Evelyn, Evelina's grandfather, was the first of the family to "abandon his native land" (13) upon his unhappy marriage to the Englishwoman who would later remarry and metamorphose into Madame Duval. Ashamed of this marriage to Madame Duval, "then a waiting-girl at the tavern," and "contrary to the advice and entreaties of all his friends," Evelyn relocated to France, where he died just two years later from extreme unhappiness (13). Although the initial mistake (the marriage to Madame Duval) took place at home in Britain, Mr. Evelyn's mismanagement of the affair is what ultimately led to his residence in France. His friends' "advice and entreaties" favor him staying in Britain and making the best of his chosen path; overwhelmed by "shame and repentance," however, Mr. Evelyn chooses France as the most appropriate place to hide from the world (14). France thus became a site of self-enforced exile for Mr. Evelyn, a place where he will try to lose his shame, although gaining misery in return.

Yet the Evelyn family's connection with France does not end here. Upon his death, Mr. Evelyn left his daughter Caroline Evelyn to Mr. Villars's guardianship back in Britain, knowing that his own wife would not care to raise their child. Mr. Villars provided for Evelina's mother until her own mother, recently married to Monsieur Duval, decided to send for her to come to France. Expecting to meet with maternal affection when she arrives in France, the young Caroline was instead faced with another episode of fraud. Madame Duval threatened her with a forced marriage, a marriage entirely abhorrent to Caroline. When Madame Duval "found her power inadequate to her attempt, enraged at [Caroline's] non-compliance, she treated her with the grossest unkindness, and threatened her with poverty and ruin" (15). In the face of such disaster, Evelina's mother chose to privately marry Sir John Belmont, since he "promised to conduct her to England" (15). Caroline's homeland thus becomes the site of potential freedom from persecution since a return home to Britain would safeguard her from her mother's cruelty.

France also serves as the site of deception regarding Evelina's true identity as Evelina Belmont. Mr. Villars and his friends have always believed that Sir Belmont has refused to acknowledge his marriage to Caroline Evelyn, but, by the end of the novel, they discover that Belmont *has*, in fact, acknowledged the girl whom he thinks is his daughter, although he has hid this daughter away in France for most of her life. Mr. Villars and his friends learn that within the year following Caroline's death, the nurse who had been with Caroline on her deathbed conceived the plan of substituting her own daughter for that of Caroline, bringing the false daughter to London to be raised by Belmont. This Dame Green's rationale was that Evelina's mother did not seem to care if her daughter received the fortune of Belmont, and "that, as *Miss* would never be the worse for it, she thought it pity *nobody* should be the better" (375). Belmont later validates the nurse's story: "unwilling . . . at that point in time to confirm the rumour of my being married, I sent the woman with the child to France; as soon as she was old enough, I put her in a convent, where she has been properly educated" (366). By sending the girl to France, Belmont assumed he was providing for her to the best of his ability. As Evelina explains in a letter to her guardian, "the child was instantly sent to France, where being brought up in as much retirement as myself, nothing but accident could discover the fraud" (375). Yet Belmont's hiding place for the girl is not merely coincidental, but rather symbolic. For not only is France the place where Belmont's initial deception took place, but it is also the place where he can perpetuate it, conveniently hiding the secret he wants to keep from the world. This decision to conceal the false daughter in France thus once more locates France as the novel's locus of deception.

The Evelyn lineage thus finds betrayal, cruelty, and regret, all while residing in France. Burney uses the image and idea of France in a nationalistic way, for she represents France, as so many other authors of this period also did, as a deceptive land. The family narrative has repeated itself from one generation to the next, as each member has invested the idea of France with feelings of peace and safety, only to find disappointment and disillusion. Just like her father, Caroline went to France to find refuge: while the father relocated to find peace from his own feelings of guilt and shame, the daughter relocated to find peace with her mother. Both father and daughter were deluded, however, in their choice of asylum. The father's unhappiness while in France led to his premature death, while the daughter's unhappiness while in France led to her marriage to "a very profligate young man" (15), and indirectly to her own premature death as well.

It is also significant that the arranged marriage that Madame Duval tries to force upon her daughter Caroline would take place in France since the British had traditionally maligned France for this practice. In this respect, the younger Burney again draws upon some of the more nationalistic attitudes and stereotypes of the day, reinforcing a vision of France that adhered to the negative portrayals already put into place by her fellow Britons. Writing in 1783, only five years after the publication of *Evelina,* for example, John Andrews set down some of these nationalist observations in his *Remarks on the French and English Ladies, in a series of letters; interspersed with various anecdotes, and additional matter, arising from the subject.* Whereas love, according to Andrews, is a "serious affair" in Britain, it is "too generally treated as a matter of little importance" in France.[11] Elaborating on this topic still further, Andrews points out that in France marriages are often arranged, and the young women are forced to choose between spending their days with the particular young man of their parents' choice or in the solitary realm of some convent.[12] Authority, however, is supposedly a concept that the French are used to, both in marriage and in other aspects of their lives, for the view that the French were a docile race because they were accustomed to adhering to the laws and rules of their tyrannical government was also a popular stereotype among the British. Burney's onetime dear friend Hester Lynch Thrale Piozzi would emphasize this in her 1789 travel narrative *Observations and Reflections Made in the Course of a Journey Through France, Italy and Germany.* In the section that records her observations on the Parisians, for example, Piozzi describes the effect that the sight of a hot air balloon up in the sky one afternoon has on its viewers. Noting that there is little confusion among the viewers, she remarks, "but I have really been witness to ten times as much bustle and confusion at a crowded theatre in London, than what these peaceable Parisians made when the whole city was gathered together. . . . Such are among the few comforts that result from a despotic government."[13] Although Piozzi begins by praising, she ends by damning, implying that the crowd control she has witnessed is only owing to the despotic French government, which keeps its people passive and docile.

British writers, on the other hand, presented marriages in their own nation as unions based on mutual esteem and the rational choice of the partners involved. Andrews, for instance, claims, "In England, even among persons of the highest order, nature and good sense are usually consulted in matrimonial connexions."[14] Unlike the French, the British use their "good sense" to rationally choose their life partners. In his extremely influential 1774 text *A Father's Legacy to his Daughters,* Dr. John Gregory makes a similar point. He explains "A man of taste and delicacy marries a woman because he loves her more than any other. A woman of equal taste and delicacy marries him because she esteems him, and because he gives her that preference." [15] Marriages in Britain are not forced, but are rather contracted for the mutual benefits they would bring to both husband and wife. Drawing upon portrayals of France and Britain such as these, Burney thus replicated in her own first novel the image of France as a land of tyranny and betrayal. France could never be the asylum that the Evelyn family desires it to be; instead, it becomes the place where mistakes are initiated and then perpetuated.

MADAME DUVAL'S SLIPPERY IDENTITY

The threat of France within Evelina's present world looms largest, of course, in the figure of Madame Duval. Returned to Britain to seek her granddaughter, Madame Duval represents Frances Burney's own early fears and anxieties about the French nation and her dislike of mixed, and so unstable, identities.[16] Within the pages of the novel, Madame Duval poses very real and serious threats to Evelina's personhood, threats that are both physical and emotional. Physically, Madame Duval represents the possibility of taking Evelina back to France with her; emotionally, she represents the possibility of unsettling Evelina's sense of personal identity. The first of these dangers, the physical one, is the more obvious of the two, and surfaces during Evelina and Madame Duval's first private conversation. After she has slandered Mr. Villars, to Evelina's great dismay, Madame Duval reveals her true reasons for being in England. Evelina describes her own emotions as the subject turns from her guardian to herself: "grief and anger mutually gave way to terror, upon her avowing the intention of her visiting England was to make me return with her to France" (53). The emphasis here is not on Madame Duval's *asking* Evelina to go with her, but rather on *making* Evelina go with her, and, based upon her past treatment of Evelina's mother, we know that Madame Duval typically relies upon force to get her way. Evelina's reaction to this threat is one of "terror," for she does not want to leave "that abode of tranquil happiness," Berry Hill (53). Her home is in Britain, and the idea of leaving it strikes terror into her.

Permanent removal from her homeland thus leaves Evelina in a state of panic, yet the more serious problem is the challenge to her sense of identity. From the moment of her first appearance in the novel, Madame Duval also represents the threat of a dual identity, an identity that challenges Evelina's way of seeing the world. If France is a dangerous land, then it is especially dangerous to encounter a woman from this country like Madame Duval, who is not quite French and yet not quite British, since this sort of woman is complex and difficult to decipher. Accustomed to easily assessing the people around her, Evelina is confounded when it comes to this strange amalgam of both the French and

British nations. Although in Great Britain and speaking English once again, the constant littering of her sentences with French exclamations and phrases marks Madame Duval as a Frenchwoman, although she is by birth British. This confusion as to Madame Duval's true national identity is present throughout the novel. Evelina's grandmother is first introduced to us in person, for instance, on what Evelina thinks will be her last night in London. Significantly, the Mirvan party has chosen to watch a fantoccini, a puppet show borrowing from both French and Italian traditions. On this night of dual nationalities, after the fantoccini has ended, the Mirvans are waiting outside for their carriage, when, as Evelina will write to Mr. Villars, "a tall elderly woman brushed quickly past us," exclaiming "'*Ma fois, Monsieur.* . . . I have lost my company, and in this place I don't know nobody'" (49). Describing the woman, whom Evelina does not yet know to be her grandmother, Evelina observes, "There was something foreign in her accent, though it was difficult to discover whether she was an English or a French woman" (49). This difficulty is exactly what upsets Evelina's worldview: confronted with an ambiguous national identity, Evelina can no longer trust her perceptions. This "supposed foreigner" (52), as Evelina will later refer to Madame Duval, throws Evelina's understanding of the world into question.

The fact that Madame Duval can pass as French although really English is a frightening prospect to Burney, and so to Evelina as well. Identities should be fixed, should be stable, and when a person has the ability to change an identity, whether national or other, the world is no longer as straightforward as it should be. Mutability thus represents a frightening prospect in this novel, one that undermines the basis of society and even the nation. One of the most telling passages in this respect is the one in which Madame Duval explains to her granddaughter how a French education would change Evelina for the better. A few days after she meets Madame Duval, Evelina calls upon her grandmother, who almost immediately begins a tirade against the British, concluding her harangue by once again threatening to take Evelina back to France with her. The physical threat of removal from Britain is severe, but even more severe is the national threat that this move would represent since it would mean that Evelina's identity would be disrupted. As Evelina explains in one of her letters to Mr. Villars:

> She talked very much of taking me to Paris, and said I greatly wanted the polish of a French education. She lamented that I had been brought up in the country, which, she observed, had given me a *very bumpkinish air*. How-

ever, she bid me not despair, for she had known many girls, much worse than me, who had become very fine ladies after a few years (*sic*) residence abroad; and she particularly instanced a Miss Polly Moore, daughter of a chandler's-shop woman, who, by an accident not worth relating, happened to be sent to Paris, where, from an awkward, ill-bred girl, she so much improved, that she has since been taken for a woman of quality. (67)

This passage is significant for two main reasons: first, because it undermines the value of "a French education," and, second, because it highlights Burney's ongoing critique of unstable identities. To address the first of these claims, it is useful to look at how Burney uses the tale of Miss Polly Moore to mock the Grand Tour. By the 1760s, as historian Michèle Cohen explains in *Fashioning Masculinity: National Identity and Language in the Eighteenth Century,* the Tour had already come under attack in Britain as the formative part of an Englishman's education.[17] Coming where it does in the novel, only a few pages after a heated discussion between Madame Duval and Captain Mirvan about the Grand Tour, this passage offers a strongly nationalist claim. During this previous discussion of the Grand Tour, Madame Duval insists that travel to France would make "quite another person" of the Captain. His reply, however, is a sarcastic commentary on what that other person would be like: "What, I suppose you'd have me learn to cut capers?—and dress like a monkey?—and palaver in French gibberish? . . . And, powder, and daub, and make myself up" (61). Taken to their extremes, the merits of a French education are seen to consist of nothing other than superficial and even ridiculous "accomplishments." The absurdities of what one learns abroad, the shine that comes from the "polish of a French education," are thus made obvious by the Captain's caricature, which is exaggerated, but held to be nonetheless true since the other characters laughingly seem to agree with the Captain's claims. When Madame Duval learns during this same conversation that her other nemesis, Sir Clement Willoughby, has spent three years abroad, she scoffingly criticizes the use of his time: "I dare say you only kept company with the English" (60).[18] If her remarks on his behavior are accurate, though, then Sir Clement *has* made good use of his time, for associating with the French would have contaminated his manners. At the very worst, Sir Clement could have become like Sir Lovel, whose French mannerisms and expressions are ridiculed throughout the novel, beginning with Evelina and Maria Mirvan's mockery of him at the ball.

Madame Duval's assessment of Evelina's education in this passage also remains subject to Burney's critique, as do Madame Duval's own manners. Far from viewing Evelina as possessing a *"very bumpkinish air,"* as Madame Duval claims she does, most of the characters in the novel see Evelina as charming. When Mr. Villars first agrees to send Evelina off to visit Lady Howard's daughter Mrs. Mirvan, for instance, he informs Lady Howard that she might find Evelina a little backward: "She is quite a little rustic, and knows nothing of the world; and tho' her education has been the best I could bestow in this retired place . . . yet I shall not be surprised if you should discover in her a thousand deficiencies of which I have never dreamt" (19). Lady Howard, however, responds to Mr. Villars quite differently, remarking, "She is a little angel! I cannot wonder that you sought to monopolize her. . . . Had I not known from whom she received her education, I should, at first sight of so perfect a face, have been in pain for her understanding" (21). At her first private ball, Evelina meets with a similar reaction from some of her gentleman admirers. Lord Merton will exclaim, "she is the most beautiful creature I ever saw in my life! . . . She looks all intelligence and expression" (35). Although Lord Orville is initially deceived in Evelina's personality, thinking her to be "a poor weak girl," he soon pronounces her to be "a pretty modest-looking girl," and will soon make every effort to seek her and her party out at sites of public amusement (35). Her air is far from rustic.

We know, then, that Evelina has had a solid education already. While it is true that she may be a little behind in her experience of the world, she has been sent to Mrs. Mirvan's to learn more, since, as Mr. Villars points out, "the time draws on for experience and observation to take place of instruction" (18). And, as a last piece of evidence against Madame Duval's claim of the superiorities of a French education, Burney takes care to emphasize that Madame Duval's own residence in France has done little to improve her own personality. In her role as temporary guardian of Evelina, she constantly places her ward in embarrassing and socially precarious positions, causing Evelina to ask at one point, "But is it not very extraordinary, that she can put me in situations so shocking, and then wonder to find me sensible of any concern?" (70). Evelina's grandmother obviously does not realize that British society places great importance on a young woman's actions. In France, chaperones might allow their young female wards to encounter "shocking" situations, but in Britain chaperones guard their young women's modesty and virtue. Britain's young women are more innocent and chaste than France's, as least in the prevailing stereotype. Madame Duval's control of the English language is also atrocious and her manners are abrasive, proving herself to be, as Lady Howard describes her, "as vulgar and illiterate as when her first husband, Mr. Evelyn, had the weakness to marry her" (12). She speaks her native tongue badly, and does not hesitate to use some of the choicest slang expressions of her adopted one. A "few years (*sic*) residence abroad" has thus done little to improve Madame Duval's manners, and Burney uses her readers' awareness of this fact to undermine Madame Duval's claims about the "polish" that time spent in France supposedly yields.

Besides offering commentary on education in this passage, Burney also shows the dangers of possessing an unstable identity. That is, in Madame Duval's words we can recognize not only Burney's doubts as to the value of a French education, but also once again her fears regarding individuals who are not really what they seem to be. This fear is best exemplified not in Madame Duval's comments on a French education, but rather in the tale that she relates of "a Miss Polly Moore, daughter of a chandler's-shop woman, who, by an accident not worth relating, happened to be sent to Paris, where, from an awkward, ill-bred girl, she so much improved, that she has since been taken for a woman of quality." Within the tale that Madame Duval weaves, Polly Moore comes to represent all individuals who smoothly glide their way across the strata of society, changing their identities in the process. In this respect, Madame Duval's, and hence Burney's, use of the indefinite article here is significant, for the fact that the young woman is not just "Miss Polly Moore," but rather "*a* Miss Polly Moore" emphasizes the commonness of her name and experience, as if there are more women who can tell the same story. Even the name "Polly" carries meaning with it, for it is a very general name, one shared by many women and one that also stands in for the actual full name of its possessor.[19] Polly Moore's transformation into "a woman of quality" is essentially a fraud, for society has been "taken" or fooled by this decoy, and, while Madame Duval approves of this deception, Evelina does not. If the "daughter of a chandler's-shop woman" can be "taken for a woman of quality," then there is no telling what frauds may be practiced upon society. Identities should be firm, should be stable, as we have already seen in Evelina's assessments of Lord Orville and Mr. Lovel, and in what critics have called her snobbery regarding the Branghtons' pretensions to gentility.[20]

Evelina's later "adventure" with the prostitutes also underscores Burney's desire to view the world as straightforward, and analyzing this episode alongside Polly Moore's story provides further insight into Burney's conception of the world. In this later incident, Evelina goes to Marybone-gardens with the Branghtons and Madame Duval, but be-

comes separated from her party during a fireworks display. In her quest
to find her friends, Evelina is repeatedly harassed by several young men
who prey upon her distress, until one finally tries to grab her hand. Exceedingly frightened, Evelina runs away from the man and right into
the arms of a pair of prostitutes, although she does not at first recognize
them as such. She describes the episode to Mr. Villars in a revealing
letter:

> I ran hastily up to two ladies, and cried, "For Heaven's sake, dear ladies,
> afford me some protection!"
>
> They heard me with a loud laugh, but very readily said, "Ay, let her walk
> between us;" and each of them took hold of an arm. . . .
>
> . . . But imagine, my dear Sir, how I must be confounded, when I ob-
> served, that every other word I spoke produced a loud laugh! However, I
> will not dwell upon a conversation, which soon, to my inexpressible horror,
> convinced me I had sought protection from insult, of those who were them-
> selves most likely to offer it! You, my dearest Sir, I well know, will both feel
> for, and pity my terror, which I have no words to describe.
>
> Had I been at liberty, I should have instantly run away from them, when
> I made the shocking discovery; but, as they held me fast, that was utterly
> impossible: and such was my dread of their resentment or abuse, that I did
> not dare make any open attempt to escape. (233)

Initially deceived in both who and what these two women are, Evelina
runs to them for protection, "taking" them to be "dear ladies." Her mistake soon becomes apparent, however, as the realization hits her that
these two women are, in fact, prostitutes. Evelina's ability to read the
world thus gives her the ability to figure out what kind of women they
really are, but not before the initial fraud is practiced upon her. She
is not, however, the only one deceived in the two women. Herself a
practitioner of artifice, Madame Duval is still also fooled by the two
new additions to their party: "As to Madame Duval, she was really for
some time so strangely imposed upon, that she thought they were two
real fine ladies" (236). This imposition, of course, has more disastrous
results for Evelina than it does for Madame Duval since it compromises
Evelina in front of Lord Orville, ultimately causing him also to question
the true appearance of things. Pinioned as she is between the two
women, Evelina must submit to being seen with them by Lord Orville.
In hindsight, the episode occasions her to remark: "Whatever may be
the construction that Lord Orville may put upon this affair, to me it
cannot fail of being unfavourable; to be seen—gracious Heaven!—to
be seen in company with two women of such character!" (237). Being

seen in the company of prostitutes discredits Evelina's reputation since, as Mr. Villars has earlier reminded her, "nothing is so delicate as the reputation of a woman: it is, at once, the most beautiful and most brittle of all human things" (164). Proper decorum forbids her from offering an explanation, so Evelina must submit to Lord Orville's own interpretation.

The encounter with the two prostitutes serves as a striking parallel for the story of Polly Moore. In both instances, Evelina is confronted with women who are something other than that which they appear to be. Just as Polly Moore "has been taken for a woman of quality," so, too, are the prostitutes taken for "two real fine ladies," first by Evelina and then by her grandmother. Like Polly Moore, then, the two prostitutes take on identities not truly their own, identities that, within the views expressed in the novel, they do not actually possess. Appearing to be something other than they really are, the prostitutes are dangerous to Evelina because her association with them threatens her precarious position as a proper young woman in British society. Although the reader is not privy to the rest of Polly Moore's story, one can easily imagine that she might pose a similar threat to some other unsuspecting young man or woman. And Madame Duval, as the possessor of a dual national identity, also claims membership in their group. All four women thus represent the threat of the world turned upside down as a result of deceptive appearances. Over thirty years later, when writing *The Wanderer*, the much older Frances Burney would embrace the complexity of the world, with all of its shadows and nuances; for now, however, she rejects false appearances, favoring a world that continues to uphold all of its first promises.

Evelina, however, is the only one of her circle to read Madame Duval as the possessor of a dual identity, since almost all of the other characters in the novel perceive Madame Duval as French. Madame Duval represents a threat to Evelina's own personal concerns, but also a more general nationalist threat to the rest of the Britons in the novel. For example, on the same night of the Fantocini, right after Evelina first notices the "something foreign in [Madame Duval's] accent" discussed earlier, Maria Mirvan, Evelina's young friend and confidante, pleads to help the woman based on this very fact, urging her father to admit the unknown woman into their coach: "She is quite alone, and a foreigner" (50). Maria's father, Captain Mirvan, also believes that Madame Duval is French. He refers to her at various points as "Mrs. Frog" (51), "*the old French hag*" (54), "old Madam French" (64), and "the old French-woman" (136). Because of her accent and liberal use of French expressions, the Captain assumes that she is French. Yet the Mirvan party is not alone in thinking of Madame Duval as a Frenchwoman. In fact, she herself aids in this deception by constantly associating herself with the French. When Captain Mirvan taunts her at this first meeting, for example, Madame Duval lividly retorts:

> "*Pardie, Monsieur* . . . I think the English a parcel of brutes; and I'll go back to France as fast as I can, for I would not live among none of you." . . .
>
> "Ay, do," cried [Captain Mirvan], "and then go to the devil together, for that's the fittest voyage for the French and the quality."
>
> "We'll take care, however," cried the stranger [Madame Duval], with great vehemence, "not to admit none of your vulgar, unmannered English among us." (50–51)

Her use of "you" and "your" signals her belief that she is not part of this "parcel of brutes," that she does not count herself among "your vulgar, unmannered English." Exchanges such as this one are common between Madame Duval and the Captain, and in each one Madame Duval references herself as French. Yet even when not with the Captain, Madame Duval still passes herself off as French. During one of Evelina's visits, Madame Duval will rail against "the horrible ill-breeding of the English in general, declaring that she should make her escape with all expedition from so *beastly a nation*" (67). Clearly, Madame Duval thinks of herself as anything but beastly, so here she is distancing herself from those of her native land.

While Madame Duval therefore specifically threatens Evelina because of her unstable identity, striking at one of Evelina's biggest fears—that of an opaque society—she poses more of a *national* threat to the other characters in the novel and, indeed, to Burney's contemporary readers. For them, Madame Duval represents France and its people, and, since France has already figured as the site of danger and deceit in the novel and was Britain's greatest enemy in 1778 (the year the novel was published), Burney's portrayal of Madame Duval as a French-woman would easily strike a chord with her more nationalistic and anti-French readers. Madame Duval thus serves two important purposes in the novel in the furthering of Burney's nationalist agenda. Her first purpose is to function as a threat for those (like both Burney and Evelina) who fear shifting, unstable identities and especially national identities that can be so easily and repeatedly adopted and discarded. The second purpose Madame Duval serves is to function as a more generalized threat of French invasion and influence. Madame Duval can simultaneously be read as an Anglo-French woman to Evelina and as a French-woman to the other characters, depending on the types of fears that each one of the novel's characters (and readers) possesses at any particular moment.

THE INFILTRATION OF FRENCH CULTURE

When she is read as a Frenchwoman, Madame Duval comes to embody the fears of a nation that had been at war with France on and off since 1689—for a period of almost 100 years. But Madame Duval represents less the threat of military invasion than of cultural invasion. One of the dangers that Madame Duval most represents by her "Frenchness," in fact, is the importation of foreign customs into Britain, customs that could eventually undermine the basis of British national culture. The French phrases, habits, and dress of Evelina's grandmother could pollute, as it were, the British characters she encounters. To provide a cultural context for these interactions, it is useful to return once again to John Andrews's *Remarks on the French and English Ladies* to see how these same fears surface in other texts from the period. In one of the letters from the *Remarks* on both the influence of Frenchwomen and the dangers of travel to France, Andrews makes this point clear:

> Now, as neither the deportment of the men, nor the corresponding manners of the women in France, are desirable objects of importation, the less we are tempted to fetch them over, the better it most certainly is for a people, who with, for a variety of substantial reasons, to retain the plainness of their own manners, and to keep at a distance from these pretended refinements in the exterior habits of intercourse, and in the system of living, which always degenerate into expensiveness and effeminacy.
>
> The danger of following the examples we see in France is the greater, as the people take so much pains to impress foreigners with the highest notions of their superior judgment and propriety.
>
> In other countries, the travelers are much less liable to be inveigled into an adoption of the ideas and customs prevailing among the natives.[21]

According to Andrews, French manners insidiously work their way into British culture when foolish British travelers make these manners into "objects of importation." The reason Andrews sees this one-way exchange as extremely dangerous is because these "pretended refinements" will ultimately "always degenerate into expensiveness and effeminacy." His fear, which was a common one of the period and which I will explain in more detail shortly, was that French influence would create a nation of effeminate and self-indulgent men. The trade metaphor that Andrews employs to discuss this process of gradual degeneration becomes literal only a few pages later when Andrews's fears about the French become even more pronounced. Within this same letter, Andrews's tone becomes more paranoid and hostile as he goes on to assert that French influence not only destroys English morals and manners, but also that "our trade, our manufactures, our whole commercial interest suffers through them" and that English gentlemen "cannot be too much forewarned of the necessity, of not suffering themselves to be imposed upon by the specious pretences of a rival nation" (263). This Scotsman's fear of French customs gradually reveals itself to be a fear of "a rival nation." If the British let French manners slowly seep their way into British culture, his argument runs, then the French will eventually overpower the British in political and economic matters as well. Enculturation not only destroys British national identity, but British commerce and power as well.

Examples of how Madame Duval's French habits risk infiltrating British culture exist throughout the novel. One morning, for instance, Evelina surprises her grandmother still in bed and with a male visitor. "I found Madame Duval at breakfast in bed," Evelina relates, "though Monsieur Du Bois was in the chamber; which so astonished me, that I was, involuntarily, retiring, without considering how odd an appearance of retreat would have, when Madame Duval called me back, and laughed very heartily at my ignorance of foreign customs" (66). Years later, the more cosmopolitan Mary Shelley would rather nonchalantly comment on this French practice in her 1817 *History of a Six Weeks' Tour through a part of France, Switzerland, Germany, and Holland,* casually remarking, "As usual in France, the principal apartment was a bedchamber."[22] The naive Evelina, however, is completely nonplussed by this French practice, so much so that she even forgets proper etiquette in her desire to rush from the room.[23] Knowing as we do Evelina's innocence and the value that both Burney and her other characters place on this quality of hers, we should agree with Evelina's negative assessment of this habit and so also be willing to make a hasty retreat when confronted with such "foreign customs." In essence, the influence of Madame Duval's Frenchness is a threat to Evelina's Britishness. Read alongside Andrews's passage, a habit like Madame Duval's takes on a stronger significance, one that reveals larger national, and nationalistic, concerns.

Besides importing French habits into Britain, Madame Duval also brings violence with her, another potential source of danger and disruption. Throughout the novel, Burney portrays Madame Duval as a frantic and garrulous Frenchwoman who wreaks emotional havoc on everyone she encounters. Unable to meet up with Evelina and her companion Mrs. Selwyn in Bristol Hotwells, for instance, Madame Duval is said to be detained not just by a cold, but rather by "a violent cold" (398). In her relations with subordinates, Madame Duval also reacts violently. During a journey with Evelina, in another example, the ride is so bumpy that Madame Duval declares, "I'd give a guinea to see them sots [the drivers] both horse-whipped!" (144). Blaming the drivers for the bad road, Madame Duval craves a violent punishment for them.[24] At another point, the Captain sends his servant after Madame Duval to give her a sarcastic message. After hearing it, "Madame Duval instantly darted forward, and gave him [the servant] a violent blow on the face" (88). Since she cannot retaliate against the much stronger Captain (and more will be said of their relationship later), she is forced to strike out at her social inferiors. Burney uses the word *violent* in its now-obsolete adverbial sense as well when she describes Madame Duval's feelings toward Captain Mirvan. On their way to Howard Grove from London, "Madame Duval was so very violent against the Captain, that she obliged Mrs. Mirvan to tell her, that, when in her presence, she must beg her to chuse some other subject of discourse" (120). In short, Madame Duval can do nothing without violence.

Madame Duval's violence is also repeatedly linked to her volubility. In the opening letter of the novel, for instance, we first learn of Madame Duval's existence through her own letter to Lady Howard. When Lady Howard writes to Mr. Villars to tell him about this initial contact, she points out that Madame Duval's "letter is violent, sometimes abusive" (11). Standing in for Madame Duval herself, the letter possesses the capacity to injure through its hostile nature. The letter, of course, is soon followed by the arrival of Madame Duval herself, who, as already mentioned, avails herself of threats and abuse, both forms of verbal behavior, to get her way.[25] The two characteristics that best describe Madame Duval are, then, her violence and her volubility, which are repeatedly linked together. By the time that *Evelina* was written, this particular pairing was also one that the British perceived as being decidedly French. As Michèle Cohen explains, in the early part of the eighteenth century, the French had been represented as vocal and lively speakers, whereas the British had already been typecast as naturally taciturn and reluctant to speak. To develop their conversation skills more, British men were urged by popular writers such as Addison and

Steele to engage in more conversation with women, who were also thought to be, like the French, natural talkers. *Spectator* 433, for example, makes this point clear. There, Addison remarks: "Man would not only be an unhappy, but a rude unfinished Creature, were he conversant with none but those of his own Make."[26] By the latter part of the century, however, conversation with women was no longer thought to help form and mold the British gentleman into a man of polite learning. Instead, increased hostility against France caused the British to devalue anything that was even remotely related to French culture. Conversing with women began to be viewed as dangerous because it led to effeminate British men and ultimately to the "enervation," to use Michèle Cohen's term, of the British nation itself.[27] John Andrews makes this nationalist stereotype clear in the first letter of the *Remarks on the French and English Ladies,* when he draws upon this, by 1783, already common stereotype of both French and British women. "As women have a much greater portion of native eloquence than men," he reasons, "the French ladies have consequently a larger share than the women of other nations, from their everlasting practice of it."[28] Drawing upon this tradition of representation allows Burney to create animosity in her audience against Madame Duval, who represents the largest threat to Evelina's sense of both self and national identity.

At one point in the novel, for instance, Madame Duval becomes more serious about taking Evelina with her to Paris to *"face to face,* demand justice" from Lord Belmont by forcing him to recognize Evelina as his daughter (159). Since Evelina and her grandmother are both staying as guests under Lady Howard's roof, however, Lady Howard refuses Madame Duval's request, referring Madame Duval to Mr. Villars to obtain permission to take Evelina to France. Enraged at Lady Howard's refusal, Madame Duval threatens to "make a journey to Berry Hill, and *teach [Mr. Villars] to know who she is.*" Worried that Madame Duval may actually follow through with this irrational plan, Evelina cautions, "Should she put this threat into execution, nothing could give me greater uneasiness, for her violence and her volubility would almost distract you" (160). Madame Duval's irascible temper is linked here to her ability to speak freely and without restraint. Such indeed is this power of Madame Duval's that she could easily "almost distract" Mr. Villars—could easily drive him mad and cause him to lose all restraint.[29] If her excessive talking, which is itself uncontrolled, ultimately causes Mr. Villars to also lose control, then Madame Duval will have essentially effeminated Evelina's guardian. Mr. Villars could lose control over his reason, possibly becoming as garrulous and unregulated as

Madame Duval. The danger of her unlicensed "violence and her volubility" makes Madame Duval a serious threat to British manhood.

Another example of Madame Duval's excessive temperament presents itself when the unexpected discovery of Monsieur Du Bois proposing to Evelina sends the Frenchwoman into an extremely vocalized and violent fit. Entering the dining room to seek Evelina, Madame Duval unintentionally surprises Evelina and Du Bois in the midst of a *tête-à-tête*, one that has surprised Evelina just as much as it has her grandmother. The sight of Evelina's hand in that of Du Bois sends Madame Duval into a rage, and although her entry causes the precipitate retreat of Du Bois, he cannot escape from the lash of her tongue. As Evelina observes:

> the rage of that lady quite amazed me! advancing to the retreating M. Du Bois, she began, in French, an attack which her extreme wrath and wonderful volubility almost rendered unintelligible; yet I understood but too much, since her reproaches convinced me she had herself proposed being the object of his affection. . . . and then, with yet greater violence, she upbraided me with having *seduced* his heart, called me an ungrateful, designing girl, and protested she would neither take me to Paris, nor any more interest herself in my concerns, unless I would instantly agree to marry young Branghton.
>
> Frightened as I had been at her vehemence, this proposal restored all my courage; and I frankly told her that in this point I never could obey her. More irritated than ever, she ordered me to quit the room. (252)

As she begins to "attack" Monsieur Du Bois for his infidelity, Madame Duval's "extreme wrath and wonderful volubility" become so excessive that her words are "almost rendered unintelligible." Despite this incoherence, Evelina can still manage to discern the cause to which her grandmother's rage is owing. The Frenchwoman's anger becomes even more severe, filled with "yet greater violence," however, when she turns to scold Evelina. Angered by the (false) belief that Evelina has purposely seduced the object of her own amorous intentions, Madame Duval repeats the injunction she made to her own daughter years before: the injunction of a forced marriage. Unlike her mother, however, who was trapped in France alone and without hope of outside help, Evelina opposes Madame Duval. Her previous fear at the "vehemence" of Madame Duval is transformed into courage at the idea of a forced marriage, and Evelina steadfastly refuses her grandmother's order. In France, Madame Duval had possessed enough power to try to force her daughter into a loveless marriage, and even though her plan ultimately miscarried (since Caroline secretly married the "very profligate" Lord

Belmont in order to escape), Madame Duval still maintained the upper hand in her ability to wreak chaos. In Britain, however, Madame Duval is rendered impotent, for in this episode the older Frenchwoman is put into her place by the younger British woman. Although the disagreement between the two women is eventually completely smoothed over by Evelina's assurances that Monsieur Du Bois does not interest her, the fact that Evelina stands up against her grandmother and wins on this important issue emphasizes Madame Duval's (at least temporarily) decreased authority and the dominance of British liberty. By presenting Madame Duval in such a stereotypical and negative fashion, Burney adheres to the nationalistic stereotypes of her day once again. This coupling of violence and volubility is therefore one more way that Burney draws upon the nationalist rhetoric of her time in order to portray Madame Duval as French and so an enemy to Burney's British audience.

Coupled with her volubility, Madame Duval's violence distracts and disarms, but its most serious danger is that it infects the world. Even though Evelina temporarily challenges her grandmother's commands, Madame Duval still has the potential power to disrupt the world through her violence.[30] Her violence contagiously spreads out, infecting the social world in which she moves. As critic William Ian Miller remarks, "Violence is understood to be disordering and hence disruptive of established boundaries and established orders."[31] Its potential for seeping past these boundaries makes violence particularly frightening, for it not only disrupts stable orders, but it also carries the risk of spreading out to an even greater extent. Within the pages of Burney's novel, the noun *violence* and the adjective *violent* are used more and more frequently, to the point where they become excessive, and, when they are used, these words are most often associated with Evelina's grandmother. Before meeting her grandmother, for instance, Evelina's letters to Mr. Villars are filled with excitement about the splendors of London life. Her world is threatened by nothing more serious than social embarrassments regarding proper behavior. The reader is hard-pressed, in fact, to find the word *violent* used at all. Even that first eventful ball of hers, the one where she first dances with Lord Orville, leaves only a slightly negative impression in her mind, nothing that could be characterized as violent. When Maria Mirvan's unintentional eavesdropping, for instance, uncovers Lord Orville's negative impression of her friend, Evelina is able to coax this information from Maria "between persuasion and laughter" (34). The laughter indicates Evelina's view that "the troubles of last night" (34), as she refers to them, have an effect on her that is more amusing than worrisome.

Once Madame Duval emerges on the scene, however, Evelina's letters become chronicles of pain and disorder. Violence soon dominates the novel, describing not only physical assaults, but also the emotions of many of the characters. Characters who possess dual national identities, Burney aims to show, introduce chaos into British society. A pleasure trip to Ranelagh turns disastrous for the Mirvan party (whose members are accompanied by Madame Duval), for instance, when the carriage breaks down, causing Evelina to observe: "I suppose we concluded of course, that we were all half killed, by the violent shrieks that seemed to come from every mouth" (63). In retrospect, Evelina can laugh at the group's excessive reaction to the accident; at the time, however, the event seemed serious enough to merit the "violent shrieks" that everyone emitted. Once introduced into her world, violence also disrupts Evelina's sense of tranquility. When Evelina travels to Bristol Hotwells with Mrs. Selwyn, she passes the first fortnight calmly enough, although she relates that "if I may now judge of the time to come, by the present state of my mind, the calm will be succeeded by a storm, of which I dread the violence!" (273). The habitual calm of Evelina's mind has long ago been replaced by violent emotions over which she has little control.

Even humor becomes violent when that humor is associated with Madame Duval.[32] For example, when Madame Duval first tells the Branghton family and Monsieur Du Bois the story of how she wound up in a ditch during the fake robbery, Monsieur Du Bois is rightfully shocked by what happened as he "listened to her with a look of the utmost horror, repeatedly lifting up his eyes and hands, and exclaiming, '*O ciel! quel barbare!*'" (169). The Branghtons, however, begin to laugh at Madame's retelling of the episode, so much so that she "was absolutely overpowered and stopped by the violence of their mirth" in the midst of speaking (169). The "violence of their mirth" gives them power over Madame Duval because they force her to suspend her story, making her unable to continue. The interruption also acts powerfully in the sense that it gives the Branghtons the space in which to imagine what happened to Madame Duval next; unable to continue speaking herself, she loses control over the telling of the event. The Branghtons' humor is described as violent because it is extreme, but it is also violent because it has the power to quell Madame Duval's volubility. The Branghtons demonstrate this same form of violence when Sir Clement Willoughby, Evelina's constant tormentor, pays a visit. In this latter scene, Sir Clement decides to call upon Evelina while she is a guest of her grandmother's. When Sir Clement first arrives, he knocks not lightly, but rather with a "violent rapping at the street-door" (208). His entrance also prefigures his comeuppance by Madame Duval, for she will soon chastise him in front of the Branghtons for his own rude and violent behavior toward her. Just as Madame Duval uses violence to control her inferiors, slapping the Captain's servant because she can, so, too, do the Branghtons use violence as a means to feel more assured in the presence of their social superior.[33] Although initially intimidated by Sir Clement's presence, the Branghtons lose their restraint when Madame Duval begins to verbally upbraid him for his insolent behavior, and they soon become overwhelmed by emotion: "The ha, ha, ha's, and he, he, he's, grew more and more uncontroulable, as if the restraint from which they had burst, had added to their violence. Sir Clement could no longer endure being the object who excited them, and, having no answer ready for Madame Duval, he hastily stalked towards Mr. Smith and young Branghton, and sternly demanded what they laughed at?" (211–12). No longer able to bear the insult of their laughter, Sir Clement shuts off "their violence" by drawing upon the credit of his social status. Violence thus marks not only Madame Duval's personality and actions, but it also punctuates the actions and emotions of many of the characters of the novel, most strikingly and most often when Madame Duval is involved in the events taking place.

CAPTAIN MIRVAN'S WAR AGAINST THE FRENCH

Although violence characterizes all of Madame Duval's relationships with the other characters in the novel, none of these relationships bears the same intensity as that between Madame Duval and Captain Mirvan. The relationship between these two aggressive individuals is one of the most underanalyzed aspects of the novel, and yet its role is central in understanding Burney's nationalist project. If Madame Duval represents a national threat to Burney's eighteenth-century audience, then that threat has to be controlled, and this is where the Captain comes in. Madame Duval is most marked as a Frenchwoman, and thus as a target of violence, through Captain Mirvan's interactions with her, and it is through the power of the Captain that Burney quells this French threat, rendering this obnoxious, vocal, and domineering old woman voiceless and so powerless. The primary way in which Burney achieves this representation of Madame Duval via Captain Mirvan is by using war metaphors. Throughout the novel, Burney figures the relationship between Captain Mirvan and Madame Duval as an ongoing battle, one that is waged against the French nation in the name of the British. In his capacity as Madame Duval's aggressor, the Captain becomes the representative of the British state, which is defined by political theorist Ernest Gellner as "that agency within society which possesses the monopoly of legitimate violence. . . . [and] the specialization and concentration of order maintenance."[34] When the state initiates or condones violence, that violence is usually not even thought to be violent since it comes from a "legitimate" power source. William Ian Miller provides additional insight on this point. He observes that violence that is condoned by the state is also sanctioned by society when it trickles its way down the social hierarchy: "Of course, the state does not monopolize legitimacy, for it is intimately involved in all social hierarchy and is an issue in most all social action. Violence that works its way down the hierarchy is viewed as legitimate, order-effecting, and is often thus not even recognized as violence, or when recognized as violence is seen as less violent than the same amount of force opposing it."[35] Miller's analysis applies especially well to our naval officer. A British seaman with a long history of aggressive behavior, Captain Mirvan's use of violence is most certainly "viewed as legitimate, [and] order-effecting" in Burney's novel. He comes to represent the force of Britain as it struggles to repel the French threat of enculturation and feminization as personified in Madame Duval. His battles with her take on an importance that has far-reaching effects for Burney's British readers.

Before going on to look at some examples of how the Captain uses military jargon to justify his assaults on Madame Duval, it is important to stop for a moment to consider the larger significance of these assaults. Many critics, both from Burney's period and our own, have laughed at Captain Mirvan's antics, pleased that he has the ability to put Madame Duval in her place in these battles.[36] By sympathizing with the Captain at the expense of Madame Duval, however, these critics only buy into Burney's nationalist agenda, without stopping to question it. They implicitly agree that Madame Duval is a specifically French threat that needs to be stopped at whatever cost. When we recognize Burney's nationalist project and her emphasis on Madame Duval's *Frenchness* and Captain Mirvan's *Britishness*, however, we recognize the cultural and political significations of the character portrayals and the roles that they played within eighteenth-century British society. Burney's specific choice of governing metaphor in these encounters brings with it a nationalist overtone that would greatly influence her readers' positive reaction to Captain Mirvan's treatment of Madame Duval. As the egregious fop Mr. Lovel will, in a rare moment of insight, point out, the Captain is "a fellow who has done nothing but fight all his life" (403). Although Mr. Lovel makes this statement in a condescending and rather offhand manner, the statement is a significant key to understanding the exchanges between the Captain and Madame Duval. As modern readers of the novel, we have to remember that the Captain has good reason for hating the French: he had been at war with this country for many years, and France represented Britain's greatest enemy, because greatest rival. Walter Dorn, in his now-classic study on the competition between the French and British empires, maps the development of this antagonistic relationship, explaining how these two countries finally emerged from the eighteenth century as the two great colonial and imperialist Western European powers, ahead of Spain, Portugal, and Holland. Pitted against one another, Britain and France became fierce rivals in their quests for expansion.[37] The situation finds its modern analogue in the mid-twentieth century, when the United States and the Soviet Union emerged as the two greatest superpowers of these years, and, subsequently, the two greatest rivals in what would eventually become the cold war. Burney's contemporary readers would have been greatly familiar with the hostilities between their own country and France, and would have recognized the Captain as the representative of Britain.[38] Battles won against Madame Duval thus symbolize battles won against France, even when those battles are read by a twenty-first-century audience. Not acknowledging this connection makes us complicit with Burney's nationalist agenda.

Returning to the novel, Captain Mirvan makes clear his antagonistic intentions toward Madame Duval by phrasing each of his plans in militaristic terms. Each time he confronts Madame Duval, he views the encounter as a battle. All of these attacks will ultimately cause Evelina to remark that Mrs. Mirvan's "principal study seems to be healing those wounds which her husband inflicts" (53). Leaving a series of wounds in his wake, the Captain engages in battle after battle with his sworn enemy. For example, when Sir Clement rejoins the Mirvan party as a guest at Howard Grove, Captain Mirvan declares that the Captain "was as glad to see him [Sir Clement] as if he had been a messenger who brought news that a French ship was sunk," before adding, "We shall have rare sport . . . for do you know the old French-woman is among us? 'Fore George, I have scarce made any use of her yet, by reason I have had nobody with me that could enjoy a joke" (136). The Captain's delight in seeing Sir Clement is only triggered by the fact that the two men can now "have rare sport" with the older Frenchwoman, sport that is anticipated through the use of a military metaphor. Like "a French ship," Madame Duval will soon be sunk both emotionally and physically as the Captain, encouraged by Sir Clement, begins his series of assaults against her. For his part, Sir Clement has already shrewdly noticed that the way to the Captain's heart is through his spleen, and that "he could take no method so effectual for making the master of the house his friend, as to make Madame Duval his enemy" (57). The two compatriots become "violent antagonists" whose "united forces so enraged and overpowered Madame Duval [at one point in the novel], that she really trembled with passion" (57).

Joined by this new accomplice, the Captain begins to plan the elaborate scheme of pretending that Monsieur Du Bois is imprisoned, a scheme that will culminate in the false robbery episode. Declaring that "he was going to read his commission to his ship's company," the Captain warns Evelina and the others present that they must go along with his mission: "I expect obedience and submission to orders; I am now upon a hazardous expedition, having undertaken to convoy a crazy vessel to the shore of Mortification; so, d'ye seem if any of you have any thing to propose, that will forward the enterprize, —why speak and welcome; but if any of you, that are of my chosen crew, capitulate, or enter into any treaty with the enemy, —I shall look upon you as mutinying, and turn you adrift" (139). The "crazy vessel" that the Captain has "undertaken to convoy . . . to the shore of Mortification" is, of course, none other than "the enemy" Madame Duval. Captain Mirvan's use of the word *mortification* also brings up a crucial aspect of his relations with Madame Duval. Any process of mortification involves the process of making a person aware of his or her flesh, of the very physicality of the body, since its roots lie in the word *death*. Also wrapped up with this meaning, though, is the possibility of humiliation. One definition that the *OED* gives for *to mortify* is: "To cause a person to feel humiliated; to cause (a person) mortification." The Captain's warlike relations with Madame Duval are thus founded upon his ability to humiliate his enemy, to bring her low. Yet humiliating Madame Duval also involves making her aware of her own pretentiousness. The work of William Ian Miller is once again useful to elucidate this point. In his explanation of the differences between shame and humiliation, Miller carefully discriminates between these two states of being: "It is humiliation that disciplines those who pretend to positions they are unworthy of filling. . . . One of the most salient distinctions between shame and humiliation is that, at root, humiliation depends upon the deflation of pretension. . . . Being cool or looking cool is asking for humiliation, as much as it is a defense against what it is asking for. . . . *humiliation is the consequence of trying to live up to what we have no right to.*"[39] Madame Duval's pretensions toward gentility and refinement, pretensions found in her self-representation as a Frenchwoman and hence superior to the British, is what particularly angers Captain Mirvan. He views her as an object in need of disciplining, an object in need of deflating, and he relies upon humiliation as his method of so doing.

A military strategist to the core, the Captain also carefully plans his battles and his line of attack. Each time he wages war against his enemy, the Captain sets his sights on Madame Duval's most prized possession: her voice. Since Madame Duval's two most dominant characteristics are her violence and her volubility, the Captain continually seeks to weaken her defenses, to humiliate her, by capturing her ability to communicate. Take away her speech, his strategy runs, and you take away her violence, and hence her power. The exchanges between Captain Mirvan and Madame Duval always begin as verbal quarrels, and slowly escalate to physical assaults that leave Madame Duval speechless. And, as the relationship between Captain Mirvan and Madame Duval progresses, so, too, does the intensity of the violence and the humiliation increase. Their initial encounters are violent ones, but the violence becomes more severe as the two characters interact more, each time forcing the loss of Madame Duval's voice to a greater and more damaging extent. On the night of the fantoccini, for instance, before the Captain even knows who Madame Duval is, he first exercises his talent for wounding. Separated from her own party, Madame Duval pleads for assistance from the Mirvans. When the Mirvans admit the foreigner into their coach, the two strangers immediately begin bickering. The argument's hostility increases until Madame Duval calls the Captain "a low, dirty fellow." At that point, the Captain's anger becomes too great, and he "seiz[es] both her wrists," yelling, "hark you, Mrs. Frog, you'd best hold your tongue, for I must make bold to tell you, if you don't, that I shall make no ceremony of tripping you out of the window; and there you may lie in the mud till some of your Monsieurs come to help you out of it" (51). This early episode culminates in a relatively minor act of violence: the Captain seizes her wrists and makes the threat of "tripping [her] out of the window" if Madame Duval refuses to "hold [her] tongue." The action makes the Captain's intention very clear, which is to render the foreigner voiceless. This intention becomes more obvious as the novel continues; severe as this first action may be, the assaults against Madame Duval only become worse.

Shortly after this first meeting, for example, on the night of the outing to Ranelagh, the Mirvan party finds itself separated from one another after their coach breaks down. Madame Duval remains missing, unable to be found, and only appears after Evelina is considerably worried. When she finally materializes with Monsieur Du Bois, both of them are filthy. Recalling the incident, Evelina relates, "She then entered,—in such a condition!—entirely covered with mud, and in so great a rage, it was with difficulty she could speak. We all expressed our concern, and offered our assistance,—except the Captain; who no sooner beheld her, than he burst into a loud laugh" (65). Madame Duval's rage, which makes it difficult for her to speak, is owing to a fall, a fall, the reader will later learn, initiated by the Captain. When she finally regains her ability to speak, Madame Duval explains that while Monsieur Du Bois was carrying her away from the fractured carriage, he accidentally fell, dropping both of them right into the middle of a large mud puddle. "This recital put the Captain into an extacy," Evelina will report, as, pleased at their misfortune, "he went from the lady to the gentleman, and from the gentleman to the lady, to enjoy alternately the sight of their distress. He really shouted with pleasure. . . . declaring repeatedly, that he had never been better pleased in his life" (65). The "extacy" that the Captain feels in their misfortune only sharpens Madame Duval's anger, which does not go unchecked for long, for she soon retaliates:

> The rage of poor Madame Duval was unspeakable; she dashed the candle out of his hand, stamped upon the floor, and, at last, spat in his face.
>
> The action seemed immediately to calm them both, as the joy of the Captain was converted into resentment, and the wrath of Madame Duval into fear; for he put his hands upon her shoulders, and gave her so violent a shake, that she screamed out for help; assuring her, at the same time, that if she had been one ounce less old, or less ugly, she should have had it all returned on her own face.
>
> Monsieur Du Bois, who had seated himself very quietly at the fire, approached them, and expostulated very warmly with the Captain; but he was neither understood nor regarded, and Madame Duval was not released, till she quite sobbed with passion. (66)

The pleasure that the Captain takes in Madame Duval and Monsieur Du Bois' fall, an act of physical violence that the Captain actually committed, leaves Madame Duval speechless, filled with a "rage" that is "unspeakable." Unable to give voice to her feelings, Madame Duval can only manifest her emotions through actions, by "dash[ing] the candle out of his hand, stamp[ing] upon the floor, and, at last, sp[itting] in his face." Madame Duval is relegated to a childlike state, forced to use forms of nonverbal communication to represent her anger because the

Captain has stripped her voice away from her. Her retaliation, however, only meets with a more severe punishment as Captain Mirvan continues to shake her until she once more loses the ability to speak. Although she can at first scream for help, she soon loses even that ability since the Captain assaults her until she can only sob, an extreme form of weeping that involves not only tears, but also the struggle even to breathe.[40]

THE CLIMAX OF VIOLENCE: CAPTAIN MIRVAN'S FAKE ROBBERY

The violence continues slowly to build after this encounter over Madame Duval's fall, until it finally crescendos in the fake robbery episode discussed earlier, an episode that also mirrors the movement of the novel, slowly building before it, too, reaches its final peak. In his desire "to convoy a crazy vessel to the shore of Mortification," the Captain stages an elaborate plan to put Madame Duval entirely at his mercy by pretending that her French companion Du Bois has been "taken up upon suspicion of treasonable practices against the government" (137). When she and Evelina set out to learn what has become of Du Bois, the carriage is attacked by two "thieves," who are really Captain Mirvan and Sir Clement in disguise. The thieves enter the carriage, and, while one holds Evelina, "the other tore poor Madame Duval out of the carriage, in spite of her cries, threats, and resistance," causing Evelina to admit, "I was really frightened, and trembled exceedingly" (145). The elderly woman is taken "out of sight of the chariot" by one of the men (whom *we* know to be Captain Mirvan), who then abuses her. Madame Duval will later fill in the particulars of the incident, telling Evelina that the robber had violently shaken her: "he takes me by both the shoulders, and he gives me such a shake! —*Mon Dieu!* I shall never forget it, if I live to be an hundred. . . . So when he had shooked me till he was tired, and I felt all over like a jelly, without saying never a word, he takes me and pops me into the ditch" (150). When Evelina goes to look for her grandmother after her own release from Sir Clement, she finds Madame Duval

seated upright in a ditch. I flew to her, with unfeigned concern at her situation. She was sobbing, nay, almost roaring, and in the utmost agony of rage and terror. As soon as she saw me she redoubled her cries, but her voice was so broken, I could not understand a word she said. I was so much shocked, that it was with difficulty I forbore exclaiming against the cruelty of the Captain, for thus wantonly ill-treating her; and I could not forgive myself for having passively suffered the deception. . . .

Almost bursting with passion, she pointed to her feet, and with frightful violence, she actually beat the ground with her hands.

I then saw, that her feet were tied together with a strong rope, which was fastened to the upper branch of a tree. . . . I assisted her to rise. But what was my astonishment, when, the moment she was up, she hit me a violent slap on the face! (147)

When Captain Mirvan earlier tripped Monsieur Du Bois, causing the Frenchman to land both himself and Madame Duval into the mud, the Captain laid his enemy low; this time, however, he lays her even lower, quite literally forcing her into a ditch. The Captain's penchant for fiercely shaking Madame Duval by the shoulders also reaches an extreme this time, for by the time he finishes maltreating her, Madame Duval is "sobbing, nay, almost roaring," capable only of producing the sounds of an animal. Her language abilities have once again been taken from her, for, as Evelina observes, Madame Duval's "voice was so broken, I could not understand a word she said." Unable to make herself understood through her broken cries and sobs, Madame Duval can only point to her source of discomfort, though in so doing, "with frightful violence, she actually beat the ground with her hands." Evelina's own sense of horror at her grandmother's condition is evident in this last remark in her use of the word *actually;* Evelina is extremely shocked to see Madame Duval act like an animal. Her extreme emotions also vent themselves in her treatment of Evelina, whom she viciously slaps. The Captain has succeeded once again in dehumanizing Madame Duval.

In this incident the Captain has not only taken away her voice, he has also taken away her pride by attacking her in her weakest and most pretentious area: her vanity. Besides physically assaulting Madame Duval, the Captain took care to leave her in an unsightly state, looking more monster than human. Describing her grandmother sitting in the ditch, Evelina observes: "so forlorn, so miserable a figure, I never before saw. Her head-dress had fallen off; her linen was torn; her negligee had not a pin left in it; her petticoats she was obliged to hold on; and her shoes were perpetually slipping off. She was covered with dirt, weeds, and filth, and her face was really horrible, for the pomatum and powder from her head, and the dust from the road, were quite *pasted* on her skin by her tears, which, from her *rouge,* made so frightful a mixture, that she hardly looked human" (148). In one of her earliest assessments of Madame Duval, Evelina had commented that "[s]he dresses very gaily, paints very high, and the traces of her former beauty are still very visible in her face" (53). At a later point in the novel, Evelina further elaborates upon this initial evaluation: "Indeed, had I not been present, I should have thought it impossible for a woman at her time of life to be so very difficult in regard to dress. . . . the labour of the toilette seems the chief business of her life" (155). Madame Duval is a woman who takes pride in her appearance, as, indeed, most women were thought to have. Dr. John Gregory, for instance, would comment on this supposed characteristic of British women just four years before *Evelina* was published in his influential conduct manual *A Father's Legacy to His Daughters*. Here Gregory remarks, "Dress is an important article in female life. The love of dress is natural to you, and therefore it is proper and reasonable."[41] Frenchwomen, however, were thought to love fashion even more than their British counterparts. John Andrews also wrote about this aspect of French culture in his chapter on female dress, condescendingly remarking: "The French are perhaps the only people we ever heard of, who pride themselves in the talent of inventing graceful modes of apparel," and, "The rage of being noticed in the world, is more prevalent in the females of this country than in those of any other."[42] In the description of her grandmother, Evelina even uses the French word *rouge*, linking Madame Duval's artificiality to her Frenchness. As a woman who makes the "labour of the toilette" the "chief business of her life," Madame Duval is excessively concerned with being noticed, with having pretensions to beauty and fashion. By leaving her in such a bedraggled condition, Captain Mirvan strikes at one of her most sensitive points. Mixed in with mud and dirt, the makeup and powder of Madame Duval make her face "really horrible," so much so, in fact, that she loses her human visage.

Evelina's sympathy for "so forlorn, so miserable a figure" does not last long, however, for Burney takes care to mock Madame Duval in her extreme pettiness and vanity, both of which are linked to her national identity. Once she and her granddaughter are both returned to the carriage, Madame Duval notices that her hairpiece is missing, and cries out, "the villain has stole all my curls," as if her curls were the booty that the thief was really after (149). Her anger now subsiding into grief, she begins most sorrowfully to lament her case. "I believe," she cried, "never nobody was so unlucky as I am! and so here, because I ha'n't had misfortunes enough already, that puppy has made me lose my curls!—Why, I can't see nobody without them:—only look at me, I was never so bad off in my life before. *Pardie*, if I'd known as much, I'd have brought two or three sets with me: but I'd never a thought of such a thing as this" (149). When Madame Duval claims that she "was never so bad off in [her] life before," she refers not to the physical stress she has suffered, but rather, ludicrously enough, to her physical appearance. After being dragged from a carriage, shaken by the shoulders, tossed around, tied up by the legs, and finally thrown into a ditch, all that this woman really seems to care about are her curls and that without them she cannot appear in public. The absurdity of these remarks work against her, taking away all of the sympathy the reader might have otherwise had for her. Vanity and national identity, not her unluckiness, have brought this vain French woman to such a state.

Although it is the Captain who has brought Madame Duval to such a low condition and who has humiliated her the most, however, it is the other characters in the novel who keep her in the position of victim. Characters such as Mrs. Mirvan discourage Madame Duval from seeking legal redress for her grievances, a discouragement that only works to condone the Captain's actions and keep him in a position of power. Immediately after the fake robbery, before she even suspects the Captain's involvement in the incident, Madame Duval decides to seek justice. Mrs. Mirvan, however, tries to convince her against taking such a step:

> Mrs. Mirvan, I found, had been endeavouring to dissuade her from the design she had formed, of having recourse to the law, in order to find out the supposed robbers; for she dreads a discovery of the Captain, during Madame Duval's stay at Howard Grove, as it could not fail being productive of infinite commotion. She has, therefore, taken great pains to shew the inutility of applying to justice, unless she were more able to describe the offenders against whom she would appear, and has assured her, that, as she neither heard their voices, nor saw their faces, she cannot possibly swear to their persons, or obtain any redress. (154)

Mrs. Mirvan has "taken great pains to shew the inutility of applying to justice" just to protect her husband. The pains she has taken will only, however, produce greater pains for others later on since the Captain will be left free to continue his violence. The "infinite commotion" that Mrs. Mirvan dreads is also never specified, but it certainly does not sound as serious as it should be. A complaint filed with the proper authorities would seem to merit a punishment for the Captain more serious than one that just produced "commotion," yet this is all that would seem to result.

Her first inklings of suspicion point Madame Duval toward the Captain, against whom she vows revenge. When Madame Duval does ultimately learn that the Captain is one of the thieves and the actual strategist of the entire affair, "her wrath was inconceivably violent. . . . Revenge was her first wish, and she vowed she would go the next morning to Justice Fielding, and enquire what punishment she might lawfully inflict upon the Captain for his assault" (167). A visit to the neighborhood Justice, however, reveals that her case will not hold; since she "has neither heard the voice, nor saw the face of the person suspected, she will find it difficult to cast him upon *conjecture,* and will have but little probability of gaining her cause, unless she can procure witnesses of the transaction" (171). Without such witnesses, Madame Duval has little chance of establishing a case, for the Captain had taken care to hide his own voice and face, even while doing such damage to Madame Duval's. *Her* voice was taken away from her by force, but *his* voice was taken away from him by choice. This important distinction once again points to the nature of their power relations, which always leave the Briton in the dominant position. Left with no form of retaliation, Madame Duval loses this final battle, leaving the Captain ultimately victorious.

The Disturbing Subtext of Violence

Although I have argued up until this point that the reader is cued to react to the Captain's violence in a sympathetic manner, seeing it as a humorous and even necessary way to deal with a national threat, a disturbing ambiguity still lies beneath the surface of this otherwise straightforward account of the Captain's treatment of Madame Duval. Violence against this Frenchwoman—violence committed by the very person who most closely represents the British state—is tolerated and even endorsed by the other characters, yet something fundamentally unsettling undergirds these acts of violence.[43] Our central narrator states this ambiguity concisely. Immediately after finding Madame Duval in the ditch and hearing her side of the tale, Evelina reflects on what has just occurred, remarking, "Though this narrative almost compelled me to laugh, yet I was really irritated with the Captain, for carrying his love of tormenting,—*sport,* he calls it,—to such barbarous and unjustifiable extremes. . . . Had I imagined he would have been so violent, I would have risked his anger in her [Madame Duval's] defence much sooner" (150–52). Torn between laughing at and grieving about Captain Mirvan's actions, Evelina raises two central questions regarding the Captain's violence: Is the violence even humorous? And, at what point does the violence become excessive? The Frenchness of Madame

Duval marks her as a prime target for nationalist prejudice and hence the Captain's forms of assault, but the violence still never quite sits right with the reader.

The ambiguity revealed through these two questions owes its birth to two narrative strategies that Burney uses throughout the novel. The first strategy has to do with the nature of humiliation itself, which always works through the medium of comedy. That is, part of the difficulty in choosing whether or not to laugh stems from the Captain's use of humiliation as his method of devoicing Madame Duval. Explaining the differences between humiliation, shame, and embarrassment, Miller notes:

> Although both shame and humiliation work by lowering, in contemplating shame the observer is more likely to be moved to pity than glee. In a rough, but very crucial sense, shame involves tragic justice, humiliation comic justice. . . . humiliation's [genre] is comedy. . . . Humiliation is dark . . . . Humiliation is rough justice . . . . if humiliation has anything to do with amusement, that amusement would be dark indeed. The observers would get to indulge their malice, while the victim would suffer his fury and chagrin. . . . There is always a tinge of brutality in [humiliation], the delight of kicking someone who is down, a delight we can indulge in because the justice and desert of the humiliation excuses us from having to make excuses for our failure of fellow-feeling. We can even congratulate ourselves on the labor we devote to the administration of such justice as a service to the community.[44]

Humiliation needs comedy to function successfully. Psychologically, humiliation works by cultivating our desire to see justice served; it encourages us as witnesses to take pleasure in the sight of the victim brought low because of his or her claims to superiority. Madame Duval, with her condescending airs and her strong belief in the supremacy of her adopted nation, would seem to merit "the justice and desert of the humiliation" that the Captain ultimately dishes out.

The second and most sustained strategy comes from an implied critique of the Captain, where Burney's representation of the Captain reinforces this strong ambiguity about his use of violence. Burney uses humiliation as a strategy to induce us to laugh, but she uses the representation of the Captain to force us to catch that laughter in our throats. Too xenophobic, too extreme in his beliefs, the Captain is capable of producing some of the most socially embarrassing moments for Evelina and her group, and Evelina can rarely mention him in anything but a tone of disgust. His abrasiveness and savagery ultimately end up undermining his own authority by causing us to question the righteousness of all of his actions. When first introduced to the Captain, for instance, Evelina describes him in purely negative terms:

> Captain Mirvan is arrived. I have not spirits to give an account of his introduction, for he has really shocked me. I do not like him. He seems to be surly, vulgar, and disagreeable.
>
> Almost the same moment that Maria was presented to him, he began some rude jests upon the bad shape of her nose, and called her a tall, ill-formed thing. She bore it with utmost good-humour; but that kind and sweet-tempered woman, Mrs. Mirvan, deserved a better lot. I am amazed she would marry him.
>
> For my own part, I have been so shy, that I have hardly spoken to him, or he to me. I cannot imagine why the family was so rejoiced at his return. If he had spent his whole life abroad, I should have supposed they might rather have been thankful than sorrowful. However, I hope they do not think so ill of him as I do. At least, I am sure they have too much prudence to make it known. (38)

Evelina's typically florid and spirited writing style has already been affected by her first meeting with the Captain. Direct and blunt, her first few sentences are simple ones, without any of her normal blandishments: "The Captain has arrived," "I do not like him," "He seems to be surly, vulgar, and disagreeable." Evelina's terse comments reflect her disapproval, and, knowing as we do her ability to accurately assess characters, we are trained to disapprove of the Captain also. Only a few pages later, Evelina makes her revelation even clearer: "I cannot bear that Captain; I can give you no idea how gross he is. . . . he seldom or never smiles but at some other person's expense" (48). These words appear before the group has even met Madame Duval or witnessed the Captain's acts of brutality against her, before the reader also realizes to how great an extent the Captain derives pleasure from imposing pain and humiliation on others. Once again, then, one of Evelina's initial assessments of another character, this time Maria's father, prevails for the remainder of the novel. Knowing as we do both Evelina's and Burney's penchants for seeing the world as stable and transparent, as well as Evelina's facility in reading the world around her, it is difficult to see the Captain as anything but boorish and aggressive. First introduced to us as "surly, vulgar, and disagreeable," the Captain retains these same traits throughout our relationship with him.

Most, if not all, of Captain Mirvan's remarks and antics, for instance, lead to embarrassment for his family and Evelina. His ill-timed and vulgar comments, as well as his tendency to pick fights with Madame Duval in public venues, make the Captain a reprehensible figure. Aggressive and confrontational, the Captain's manners embarrass his wife to such an extent that his behavior even becomes painful to her. Evelina notices this behavior soon after meeting the Captain, remarking of Mrs. Mirvan that "every dispute in which her undeserving husband engages, is productive of pain, and uneasiness to herself" (73).[45] Mrs. Mirvan's own "uneasiness" is owing to her "undeserving husband" and his constant warfare. The pain he brings to others is also indirectly brought to her through shame and her inability to put an end to the fighting. Besides embarrassing his wife, the Captain also hurts the other members of his party, including Evelina. One evening, while at Ranelagh, the Mirvan group is soon joined by Lord Orville. What would otherwise be a delightful outing for Evelina is turned sour by the fighting between the Captain and Madame Duval. "[T]he continual wrangling and ill-breeding of Captain Mirvan and Madame Duval," she shamefully admits, "made me blush that I belonged to them. And poor Mrs. Mirvan and her amiable daughter had still less reason to be satisfied" (58). On another occasion, Mrs. Mirvan suggests a visit to Cox's mechanical toy museum to try to put an end to yet another "disputation" between Madame Duval, her husband, and Sir Clement (76). Once there, however, the three again begin quarreling over French and British manners until the Captain assaults Madame Duval by forcing her to take up too large of a quantity of smelling salts. His behavior leads to another "violent quarrel," causing Evelina to remark, "Indeed, he laughs and talks so terribly loud in public, that he frequently makes us ashamed of belonging to him" (77).[46] Once again, the idea of embarrassment and shame dominate Evelina's commentary on Captain Mirvan.

The brutality that the Captain exercises against Madame Duval because she is French also reveals some of the underlying ambiguities surrounding Burney's views on nationalism in the novel. Madame Duval clearly represents the threat of French influence, and for that she "must" be punished, yet the Captain himself is often criticized for his nationalist beliefs, which are often represented as too narrow-minded. Striking examples of Evelina's reactions to the Captain's xenophobia appear throughout the novel. The fantoccini, conducted in both French and Italian, for instance, "both astonished and diverted us all," according to Evelina, "except the Captain, who has a fixed and most prejudiced hatred of whatever is not English" (49). Evelina's critical remarks emphasize her dislike of such an inveterate hate, a hate that is unreasonable in both its excessiveness and its cause. By closing himself off to whatever is of foreign origin, including an innocent puppet show, the Captain remains "fixed" and "prejudiced," unwilling to enjoy the arts and cultures of other nations. This hatred of his reveals itself again soon afterward, as the party leaves the fantoccini to return home. While waiting for their carriage, in a scene discussed earlier, they first meet Madame Duval. Before Evelina and the Mirvans even realize who Madame Duval is, the Captain begins to argue with her, and when they offer to give the stranger a ride home, the Captain "seemed absolutely bent upon quarreling with her: for which strange inhospitality," Evelina concludes, "I can assign no other reason, than that she appeared to be a foreigner" (50). This "strange inhospitality" of his is described as un-usual because it is grounded in nothing other than his dislike for "what-ever is not English." At this point, he has no other basis for arguing with the stranger. Evelina clearly thinks such reasoning is absurd, as should the reader. More chaos also ensues the first time Madame Duval comes to the Mirvan household in London for tea. Entering the house with Madame Duval is her friend Monsieur Du Bois, against whom the Captain also forms an immediate sense of dislike. The Captain greets his guest with extremely hostile words of welcome: "Do you know, Monsieur, that you're the first Frenchman I ever let come into my house?" (56). When the general conversation first starts up during tea, "Mrs. Mirvan endeavoured to divert the Captain's ill-humour, by start-ing new subjects; but he left to her all the trouble of supporting them, and leant back in his chair in gloomy silence, except when any opportu-nity offered of uttering some sarcasm upon the French" (56). Dis-pleased that he must welcome foreigners into his home, the Captain remains in a "gloomy silence," unable to take pleasure in the discussion unless he can register his dislike of the French. His behavior serves as yet another example of his "strange inhospitality," with which Evelina had earlier found fault.

Evelina's disapproval of the Captain's xenophobia becomes even more pronounced when we compare it with her reaction to the Bran-ghtons' behavior at the opera. Although Evelina has been chided by literary critics throughout the years for her "snobbishness" toward her cousins, her dislike of the Branghtons stems as much from their narrow-mindedness as it does from their low social standing. Like the author of her being, Evelina appreciates the art and music of other na-tions.[47] The Branghtons, however, like Captain Mirvan, can only mock all that is not British. Overdressed and feeling extremely out of place, Evelina is forced into accompanying them and her grandmother to hear Signor Millico sing. As soon as the opera commences, the Branghtons begin to belittle everything having to do with it. Commenting on the singing and lyrics, the elder Mr. Branghton declares, "What a jabbering they make! . . . there's no knowing a word they say. Pray what's the reason they can't as well sing in English?" His son soon takes on the role of dramaturge, exclaiming, "How unnatural their action is! . . . why now who ever saw an Englishman put himself in such out-of-the-way postures?" (92). The Branghtons, as Evelina points out, "made no allowance for the customs, or even for the language of another country, but formed all their remarks upon comparisons with the English theatre" (91). Their reaction to the opera is very similar to Captain Mirvan's reaction to Madame Duval, for he, too, makes no allowances for foreign customs or for foreigners. The Branghtons, like Captain Mirvan, do not attempt to understand national differences. And, just as the Captain's treatment of Madame Duval leaves Evelina feeling emotionally torn between the desire to laugh at the wrong being enacted and the desire to vindicate it, the Branghtons' comments also leave Evelina in a state of mixed emotions. "If I had not been too much chagrined to laugh," she admits, "I should have been extremely diverted at their ignorance of whatever belongs to an opera" (89). Amused by the Branghtons' ignorance, Evelina reveals her own appreciation for and knowledge of other cultures.

Throughout the novel, then, Captain Mirvan constantly displays his vulgar personality, his disagreeable temperament, and his extreme xenophobia and narrow-mindedness. Herself cultured, genteel, and open to new cultural experiences, Evelina finds the Captain to be distasteful and offensive. These characteristics on their own trouble Evelina, but the real seriousness of the Captain's behavior and personality lie not with the embarrassment that he often creates for Evelina and his own family, but rather with his disturbing use of violence against those he should protect. Essentially, Captain Mirvan uses some of the same violent tactics he uses with Madame Duval in his relationships with his own family and their young guest. He never actually physically assaults his wife or daughter, but he continually abuses them verbally, in addition to embarrassing them. At one point in the story, for instance, during a lively conversation with Lord Orville at the Pantheon, Evelina and Maria express their eagerness for the London sights they have seen, until the Captain breaks in by gruffly declaring, "What signifies asking them girls? Do you think they know their own minds yet? . . . they are a set of parrots, and speak by rote, for they all say the same thing. . . . and for you, [Maria] . . . I charge you, as you value my favour, that you'll never again be so impertinent as to have a taste of your own before my face" (109). The lively impressions of London society that Evelina has already recorded in her letters demonstrate that Evelina *does* know her own mind, that she does *not* just repeat the same fashionable ideas circulating among the young women of society. She has been presented to us as intelligent and capable of sharp discernment, not as one of "a set of parrots" that "speak by rote." Indeed, her observations make up most of the novel and contain some of the wittiest and most interesting passages in it. The misogynistic demand that the Captain makes—that his daughter cannot have an opinion of her own—is also subject to our critique, for if women should not be able to "have a taste of [their] own," Evelina's letters would not even exist for us to read. The Captain's remarks have the effect of highlighting his own foolishness and ignorance, ultimately causing us to question all that he says. Despite the harshness and inaccuracy of his comments, however, his words remain powerful ones, capable of intimidating the two young women into silence. As Evelina glumly states, "This reproof effectually silenced us both for the rest of the evening" (109). No longer able to enjoy Lord Orville's conversation, Evelina cannot help but resent the Captain's intrusion. When he asserts his power over Maria and Evelina to quell their voices, then, his action has the effect of opening up to interrogation his treatment of Madame Duval. Before this night at the Pantheon, the Captain has already repeatedly silenced Madame Duval; when he takes away the voices of Evelina and her friend, however, suddenly things are different because suddenly it is our British heroine who is being rebuked. If our reaction to the silencing of Evelina is one of shock, however, then should we not also be shocked by the silencing of Madame Duval? Is there really any difference in the Captain's treatment of both women? These are the kinds of questions that Captain Mirvan's behavior opens up.[48]

So why, then, does Burney undermine the Captain's power even while condoning it through his humiliating and yet "humorous" treatment of Madame Duval? The answer lies in two areas: in Burney's views on gender roles and in her own ambiguity about the nationalist project to which she tries to adhere. The Captain's treatment of the female members of his own family and of Madame Duval points, first of all, to Burney's adherence to a new sense of gender roles that were being codified in the late eighteenth century. As Claudia Johnson's important work on chivalry and sentimentality in *Equivocal Beings: Politics, Gender, and Sentimentality in the 1790s* has made clear, masculinity began to be re-characterized during the last decades of this period as a sensitivity toward the needs of women and as a desire to protect them.[49] The new "sensitive" masculinity that Johnson associates with Edmund Burke and his famous ardent defense of Marie Antoinette elucidates our understanding of the gender roles at work in Burney's novel. Although Johnson focuses her analysis on the age of chivalry that Burke ushered in during a period that occurred almost two decades after *Evelina* was published, we can see in Burney's novel the early roots of this idea taking shape. The gender-coding of Captain Mirvan's Britishness as being ungallant toward female characters seems to play a key role in Burney's qualification of his overall value. At work in this underlying critique of the Captain is a sense that his behavior toward his wife, daughter, and Evelina places the women in precarious situations. By denying them a voice, Captain Mirvan not only fails in his role as protector of female virtue, but also undermines their sense of selfhood.

The second answer to the question of why Burney undermines the Captain's power lies in Burney's ambivalence about the anti-French tone her characters adopt. Although the novel readily makes use of the nationalist stereotypes and rhetoric of Burney's day, including a character like Madame Duval, who is so easy for readers to hate, it also reveals an underlying difficulty about believing in such falsified and exaggerated representations. Burney might engage in the nationalist rhetoric of the period and her novel might be a product of the cultural climate of the times, but Burney does not seem to believe that such representations are always accurate or just. The reader's sense of uneasiness with the violent encounters in *Evelina* thus reflects Burney's own nascent sense of uneasiness with extreme nationalism and violence against women, stirrings of uncertainty that will surface as outright criticism in her last novel, 1814's *The Wanderer*. The ambiguity evident in *Evelina* slips away in *The Wanderer*, leaving in its stead a direct and sustained critique of nationalist rhetoric and of violence against women conducted on behalf of the nation. Female community and protection would also become paramount for Burney, as would the necessity for viewing the world and its inhabitants as ultimately much more complex and unknowable than the younger Frances Burney ever imagined they could be.

2

Change and Reform in
Charlotte Smith's *Desmond*

As the eighteenth century neared its close, the uneasiness about violence against women and national identity underpinning Frances Burney's 1778 *Evelina* would surface as outright critique in works by other female writers. As Harriet Guest explains, "by the early nineteenth century it had become possible or even necessary for some women to define their gendered identities through the nature and degree of their approximation to the public identities of political citizens. . . . By the early nineteenth century, the conditions (of consciousness or imagination at least) necessary to nineteenth-century feminist debate were emerging."[1] Reform, in particular, was a project shared by many women writers of the late eighteenth and early nineteenth centuries, and, in the works of some of the more radical thinkers, reform became a central theme of both their lives and texts. When they linked women's issues to national ones, the writers aimed to modify existing social structures so that they allowed more (or sometimes, as in the case of Hannah More, less) flexibility to women. In the works of some of the more radical writers, reform becomes the central concern, dominating the texts in which it appears. Charlotte Smith's novels and many of her poems, for instance, all prominently feature scenes of British injustice. Such injustice reaches down into the lives of Britain's subjects, but especially affects British women since they had so few rights with which to begin. Also like several of her fellow women writers, Smith made her concerns about women's issues heard by yoking them with issues of national prejudice and willful misrepresentation. Smith shows that gender concerns are wrapped up in concerns about the nation, and her plots move forward around the unstable roles of gender and national identity. Just as nations can be misunderstood, so, too, can women's characters. Misrepresenting other nations has negative consequences, but it has even more for women, Smith's novels show, because it takes away any form of protection they might otherwise have been granted. Women need a national identity, but they also need to connect across nations as *women* through the shelter of female protection.

Smith incorporates the link between national and gender identity into several of her novels, although 1793's novel *Desmond* makes the injustices of British society dominant and, for the first time in her career, is set during the actual period in which Smith wrote it.[2] Although the three novels that came before *Desmond* were also political, they were implicitly so, and all three were set in the distant past to create a rupture between Smith's own time and her political views. *Desmond* breaks that mold by chronicling the life of a young man who openly favors the French Revolution. As he narrates life in both England and France during the early years of the Revolution, Desmond encounters acts of prejudice and abuse in both nations. Such examples, however, fit into Smith's larger project of reformation: in *Desmond*, the possibility for change and reform exists, and the criticisms of Britain, while harsh, still leave open the possibility of improvement. By the time she wrote 1798's *The Young Philosopher*, as I argue in the next chapter, Smith's hope was gone, and so in that later novel she represents Britain as purely negative, the land where prejudice keeps fellow humans from helping one another, and actually makes Britons purposely harm one another; she explores the interconnections between gender and national identity within the British nation, as she struggles to understand the reasons why British women are unable to form any lasting connections with one another. National prejudice becomes more individualized and widespread, and women are increasingly the victims of the harm it brings. If *Desmond* depicts life during the Revolution, then *The Young Philosopher* depicts life after it.

Misrepresentation and Political Jealousy

Truth and misrepresentation emerge as central issues of *Desmond* before the novel even begins. In her preface, which was one of the longest and most detailed prefaces she wrote, Smith lays out the central arguments of the novel, explaining why she made the narrative choices she did. The entire preface, in fact, reads as a series of counterarguments — counterarguments made before the critics have had a chance to level their attacks. Smith's choice of genre (the epistolary novel), her choice of hero (a young man in love with a married woman), and her choice (as a woman) to intervene in political matters (the French Revolution) all fall under her notice, as she categorically defends each choice she makes. Each of her concerns, however, revolves around the unerring principle of truth, the standard to which the novel adheres. As she explains to her audience, "I have given to my imaginary characters the arguments I have heard on both sides [of the Revolutionary debate]; and if those in favour of one party have evidently the advantage, it is not owing to my partial representation but to the predominant power of truth and reason, which can neither be altered nor concealed."[3] Just as Mary Wollstonecraft argues in 1794's *Historical and Moral View of the Origin and Progress of the French Revolution* that a moral standard exists, so, too, does Smith argue that a "natural" standard of "truth and reason" exists, one that acts in a similar manner to Wollstonecraft's moral compass, as a standard against which political and social events can be measured. As soon as Smith's readers enter into her narrative, it quickly becomes clear which side of the debate truth and reason are on, for Smith's characters favor the Revolution and its principal tenets.[4]

Smith also clearly explains what she sees as the connections between misrepresentation and nationalism within these early pages. She continues her explanation of truth, for instance, by referring not only to national pride, but also to national prejudice: "I have not sacrificed truth to any party—Nothing appears to me more respectable than national pride; nothing so absurd as national prejudice" (7). Taking pride in the accomplishments of one's own country is honorable, but taking pleasure in animosity toward another people is disreputable. Smith even takes care to point out that such national prejudice is not truthful, because it is artificial. She comments upon the supposed differences between the French and the British:

> To those however who still cherish the idea of our having a *natural* enemy in the French nation; and that they are still more *naturally* our foes, because they have to be freemen, I can only say, that against the phalanx of prejudice kept in constant pay, and under strict discipline by interest, the slight skirmishing of a novel writer can have no effect; we see it remains hitherto unbroken against the powerful efforts of learning and genius—though united in that cause which *must* finally triumph—the cause of truth, reason, and humanity. (7–8)

Although Smith downplays her role as an author, she does so to placate an audience who might have a hostile reaction to a woman's involvement in the political arena. If, however, Smith really believed that women should be kept out of political matters, then she would never have attempted such involvement in the first place.

The emphasis of this passage, though, has more to do with Smith's claims about hatred between nations than it does about her role as a female novel writer. The main thrust of her argument is against the artificial basis of what most Britons see as a "natural" hostility against the French, for a large part of Smith's overarching project in *Desmond* involves a calling into question of the false basis of national prejudice. National prejudice, she points out, is an artificial construction, one that we tend to see as natural because the British nation, as an *interested* entity, wants us to believe so.[5] It is in the British nation's best interest to view the French as natural enemies, and so Britain's people do so, blindly believing their nation without stopping to question whether or not these representations of France are accurate. It is also important to emphasize here just how important Smith's arguments are. By pointing out that national prejudice is artificial, Smith ends up calling the very idea of Britain as a nation into question. Writing in 1882, Ernest Renan first explained how members of a nation must forget the birth of their nation in order to envision themselves as a united people. Renan defined the nation in his now-classic essay "What Is a Nation?" in terms that are still relevant. He notes that most nations are founded upon violent acts, but that nations must forget this violence, and that they were ever first *created*, in order to function. "Yet the essence of a nation," Renan writes, "is that all individuals have many things in common, and also that they have forgotten many things."[6] Members of a nation have to forget that their land is an artificial construct, an idea created long ago, in order to see their cohesive state as natural and right, present from the nation's inception.[7] By reminding her readers not only that distinctions in social class are artificial because they have not always been present, but also that differences between nations are artificial because propagated by the nations themselves, Smith destroys the fiction of the nation, the story upon which the nation depends.[8] If her readers see that national prejudice has not always been part of the British national character, then Smith can open their eyes to the true nature of political life, including the actual events of the French Revolution. Once exposed for what it really is, Smith believes, national prejudice will melt away in the face of truth, reason, and humanity.

Smith's emphasis on truth also leads her characters to a questioning of why events in France have been purposely misrepresented back home in Britain. Even Fanny Waverly, who is far removed from the events passing in France, notices that the Revolution has been falsely portrayed in Britain. She muses on this in one of her letters to her sister Geraldine, where she notes, "the people with whom I live are such inveterate and decided enemies to the revolution, that they exaggerate with malicious delight, all the mischief they hear of, and represent . . . [France] as a scene of anarchy, famine, and bloodshed" (306). Fanny recognizes that prejudice toward the Revolution leads many of her fellow Britons to misconstrue it. Instead of looking at what the Revolution hopes to accomplish, they look to what the Revolution has demolished. While Fanny's commentary is useful, however, it is Desmond's letters that contain the most detailed account of events not only in France, but also in England. As Desmond travels, for instance, he catalogues not only the abuses in his own country, but also the ways in which British public opinion has been turned against France. As Antje Blank and Janet Todd point out, "enemies to the Revolution in France are continually shown to ignore historical facts and distort events."[9] Through Desmond's letters, we see the "real state" (53) of France, a nation that is actually much better off than it was before the Revolution erupted; contrary to British popular opinion, French society is actually improving. Desmond notes that the "misrepresentations that have been so industriously propagated" (154) by the British government have made the majority of the British despise the primary tenets of the Revolution. He addresses these concerns at even greater length: "All the transient mischief has been exaggerated; and we have in the overcharged picture lost sight of the great and permanent evils that have been removed—All the good has been concealed or denied; and the former government, which we used to hold in abhorrence, has been spoken of with praise and regret" (154). As Desmond points out, the British used to condemn the *ancien régime;* now, however, they can only show scorn for the new government being put into place and regret the passing of the old one. The British essentially despised the French before, and they continue to despise the French now. The Revolution has made little difference in how the British understand the French, even though the French are fighting for a liberty not unlike that enjoyed by the British.

Misrepresentations of the principles and aims of the French Revolution therefore circulate throughout British society, but, the question then becomes, to what are these misrepresentations owing and why have they been put into circulation in the first place? One answer that Smith provides—and subsequently criticizes—is that the British government has been enforcing a policy of censorship. Since the British government believes that its subjects should be kept in the dark about certain matters, the characters in *Desmond* find that essential information regarding the Revolution and its progress is kept from them. At one point in the novel, for instance, Desmond meets Lord Fordingbridge, a

British noble who despises the Revolution's aims. During their conversation, the nobleman reveals his belief that the British government rightfully hides the truth to appease its people. The British peer argues that "it is not always proper to speak [truth]; nay, it is not always safe to the well-being of a nation" (186). Some information, Lord Fordingbridge believes, is best kept hidden from the general populace since it would cause them to question their own nation and its actions. Smith is quick to point out, however, that such actions violate the very foundations of British society. If prolonged, such willful misrepresentation would mean the end of British liberty. Through Desmond, Smith meditates upon the eventual destruction of British rights: "if facts, which cannot be denied, be repressed; and reason, which cannot be controverted, be stifled; the time is not far distant, when such a country may say, Adieu, liberty!" (186). In Smith's perception, the British nation depends upon truth and the free exchange of information among its people, ideals that align Smith with the Enlightenment thinkers that came before her. Without such freedom, the concept of liberty rings hollow.

Smith also provides a second answer to this question of why Britons have been purposely misrepresenting the Revolution, an answer more closely aligned with her larger project of attacking national prejudice. This answer has to do with political jealousy. As Desmond makes clear early in the novel, the French are "determined, in trifles, as well as in matters of more consequence, to change characters with us" (57). Basically, the French want to become more like the British. Montfleuri, the young French nobleman with whom Desmond bonds, best represents this interest in British principles. Great Britain, Montfleuri tells Desmond, is "a nation he loves and esteems" (63). In a symbolic act, Montfleuri has even demolished his ancestral house, "pull[ing] down every part of the original structure, but what was actually useful to himself; and brought the house, as nearly as he could, into the form of one of those houses, which men of a thousand or twelve hundred a year inhabit in England" (79). Even Montfleuri's house reflects his interest in middle-class British ideals. No longer content with extraneous details, Montfleuri has new-fashioned his house to accord more fully with British notions of simplicity and regulation.

The French people's interest in copying the British lies at the root of the problem as Smith constructs it. The French want to copy the British, but the British, Smith suggests, do not want to be copied for fear of being improved upon. The British are, essentially, jealous of any strides the French take in their struggle for greater freedom. Their dislike of the Revolution consists of nothing more than petty, misplaced jealousy. Smith, of course, was not alone in her critique of these misguided sentiments. Political jealousy was, in fact, such a major concern of the period that several other major women writers also leveled arguments against it. Helen Maria Williams, for instance, writes about France's desire to emulate Britain in the earliest volume of her *Letters from France.* She writes:

> And, therefore, when I hear my good countrymen, who guard their own rights with such unremitting vigilance, and who would rather part with life than liberty, speak with contempt of the French for having imbibed the noble lesson which England has taught, I cannot but suspect that some mean jealousy lurks beneath the ungenerous censure. . . . The French, on the contrary, seem to have imbibed, with the principles of liberty, the strongest sentiments of respect and friendship towards that people, whom they gratefully acknowledge to have been their masters in this science. They are, to use their own phrase, "devenus fous des Anglois (*sic*).'"[10]

Instead of being ashamed that they have so heavily borrowed from the English, the French acknowledge their debt to the "masters in this science," while the British, however, can only censure the French for having copied them, a censure that Williams attributes to "some mean jealousy."[11] Implicit in Williams's analysis is the concept that an equal exchange of ideas and the ability to learn from the other would afford each nation the means of self-improvement. A movement away from insularity would benefit the British, just as it has the French.

Another influential woman writer of the period who addresses political jealousy is Anna Laetitia Barbauld. In 1793, one year after *Desmond* appeared, the popular poet wrote her *Sins of Government, Sins of the Nation; or, A Discourse for the Fast, appointed on April 19, 1793.* The pamphlet encourages her fellow Britons to come forward and confess their sins to God, not as individuals, but rather as *British* subjects. Just as men and women should confess their sins, she reasons, "Nations have likewise their faults to repent of, their conduct to examine" (382). Those faults, she asserts, belong to England's people as a collectivity: "Those sins which, as a nation, we have to repent of, belong to national acts" (382), and each member of a nation needs to feel responsible for the sins of that nation. Those national acts consist of treating other nations not as fellow Christians, but rather as enemies. The same standards to which we adhere as individuals, we discard when it comes to other nations. Using the analogy of how we treat our neighbors, Barbauld comments upon the differences in our behavior, noting that "there are men who appear not insensible to the rules of morality as they respect individuals, and who unaccountably disclaim them with respect to nations" (386). Barbauld then provides several examples of how foolish such behavior really is:

> Most contrary to this [sense of justice] is a species of patriotism, which consists in inverting the natural course of our feelings, in being afraid of our neighbor's prosperity, and rejoicing at his misfortunes. We should be ashamed to say, My neighbor's house was burnt down last night, I am glad of it, I shall have more custom to my shop. My neighbor, thank God, has broken his arm, I shall be sent for to attend the families in which he was employed;—but we are not ashamed to say, Our neighbors are weakening themselves by a cruel war, we shall rise upon their ruins. . . . Our neighbors have bad laws and a weak government: Heaven forbid they should change them! for then they might be more flourishing than ourselves. . . . We are not ashamed to use that solecism in terms *natural enemies*; as if nature, and not our own bad passions, made us enemies. (397–98)

Just as we would be loathe to thank God for harm coming to our neighbor, we *should* be loathe to rejoice when a neighboring nation suffers a misfortune. The fact that we do rejoice nonetheless Barbauld attributes to jealousy: we do not want our neighboring countries (by which she means France) to "be more flourishing than ourselves."

Smith's voice was therefore one of several to warn the British against the evils of political jealousy, and yet she was also one of the first. Her dislike of national prejudice thus extends into the realm of political hostility and jealousy. Although many of *Desmond*'s characters insist that the Revolution is "dangerous to one's principles" (40), their rhetoric actually reveals their wish that the French do not prosper. Montfleuri once again exposes British pride for what it is:

> But, when I meet, as too often I have done, Englishmen of mature judgment and solid abilities, so lost to all right principles as to depreciate, misrepresent, and condemn those exertions by which *we* have obtained that liberty they affect so sedulously to defend for themselves; when they declaim in favour of an hierarchy so subversive of all true freedom, either of thought or action, and so inimical to the welfare of the people—and pretend to blame *us* for throwing off those yokes, which would be intolerable to themselves, and which they have been accustomed to ridicule us for enduring; I ever hear them with a mixture of contempt and indignation, and reflect with concern on the power of national prejudice and national jealousy, to darken and pervert the understanding.
>
> All, however, that I have ever heard from such men, has served only to prove to me, either that they fear for their own nation the too great political

consequence of ours, when our constitution shall be established; or know and dread that the light of reason thus rapidly advancing, which has shewn us how to overturn the massy and cumbrous edifice of despotism, will make too evident, the faults of their own system of government, which it is their particular interest to screen from research and reformation.—But how feeble are all the endeavours of this political jealousy on one hand, and the yet obstinate prejudices of papal superstition on the other, to obscure this light in its irresistible and certain progress.[12]

As Montfleuri's eloquent critique emphasizes, Englishmen hold a double standard: while they claim that the former French system of government was a good one, they would never submit to such political arrangements themselves and even condemn the French for adopting a system more like their own. With the commencement of the Revolution, the British have also begun to fear that the "faults of their own system of government" will be exposed for all of the world to see. This passage thereby testifies to the ways in which "national prejudice and national jealousy" cloud the truth. The British refuse to see imitation as the sincerest form of flattery. In addition, although Smith does not recognize it, behind the Britons' political jealousy lay another significant fear: that of losing their national identity. After all, the natural consequence of the French becoming more like the British is that of the British becoming more like the French. If this were to continue, then the distinct national identities of the British and the French people would be lost, and the very idea of the French and British nations would be exposed as fictions.[13]

Prejudice on the Individual Level

Jealousy and prejudice harm not only nations in *Desmond*, but also individuals. Just as a lack of connection among nations leads them to distrust and thus misrepresent one another, a lack of connection among humans leads them to also misrepresent the actions of others. The accusations against France are severe, but even more severe and harmful are the accusations made against individual characters. Desmond, for instance, is disliked by many of his acquaintances merely because he is different from them. His uncle, Major Danby, points this out to Bethel when he says that "he's not like any other young fellow of his age. Instead of sporting his money like a man of spirit on the turf, or with the bones, he goes piping about, and talks of unequal representation, and the weight of taxes, and the devil knows what; things, with which a young fellow of six-and-twenty has no concern at all. — And then, as for his amours; instead of keeping a brace or two of pretty wenches, he goes sneaking after a married woman" (335). Prejudice works by creating hostility against that which we do not understand. Because Desmond does not act as society thinks he should—because he does not game or keep "a brace or two of pretty wenches"—men like Major Danby retain a strong sense of prejudice against him. In a sense, individual difference becomes a figure for national difference here.

The most striking and damaging example of misrepresentation on the individual level is the rumor that circulates of Geraldine's having given birth to Desmond's child. Before Verney forces Geraldine to meet him in France, Geraldine moves her family to a place of retirement in the British countryside to avoid his creditors and to live more modestly than she could in a larger town. Unbeknownst to her, Desmond takes up residence close by. Although Geraldine later departs from the area, Desmond returns soon afterward with Josephine so that his French lover can have his child in a retired locale. Also living in retirement in the same part of the world, however, is the old gossip Miss Elford, who, having been deserted by her lover while on the verge of being married, is trying to lie low until the gossip surrounding her own story dies down. While staying with a relation, Miss Elford has little to do to pass the time, so she spends her days watching the comings and goings of the travelers at the inn across the way. As Geraldine's sister Fanny ex- plains to Bethel, this is where Miss Elford first noticed the party of French travelers with whom Desmond was journeying. Fanny explains how the rumors concerning her sister Geraldine first began: "A group much less marked by singularity of appearance, would have attracted the attention of an insulated being, eagerly attentive to every occur- rence that afforded any thing to gratify her natural love of malicious enquiry, now sharpened by internal wretchedness and discontent. — The foreigners no sooner appeared, then Miss Elford became stationary at her window" (340). A forerunner to the members of Jane Austen's network of neighborhood spies, Miss Elford spends her days vindic- tively meddling in the concerns of others. Already driven by a "natural love of malicious enquiry," Miss Elford's spiteful temperament is now further fueled by "internal wretchedness and discontent." Because she herself is so miserable, she wants everyone else to be miserable as well: jealousy fuels her discontent. When Miss Elford learns that one mem- ber of the party she notices from her window is with child, she also pronounces—with certainty—that the pregnant woman is none other than Geraldine. What is also interesting in this passage is how Smith's critique of Miss Elford mirrors Smith's critique of national concerns. For instance, Miss Elford's individual jealousy emulates the political jealousy that Smith ascribes much earlier in the novel to those Britons who are opposed to the political changes occurring in France. What is also curious here is that Miss Elford first notices the group because of their foreign appearance, yet, despite the fact that the pregnant woman is really the French Josephine, Miss Elford takes her for an English-woman. It appears to be a small oversight on Miss Elford's part, but it has significant consequences for what Smith asserts about national identities. If Miss Elford can mis-read the foreignness of this group, then perhaps national distinctions are not as clear-cut as most people assume them to be. After this juncture in the novel, Miss Elford spreads the rumor of Geraldine's supposed pregnancy with alacrity, and Fanny fears that there is little chance to salvage Geraldine's reputation: "There are, therefore, no hopes of stifling the report; and if I can judge by the manner of the ladies, there is not one of them who fails to hope it may be found true.—Geraldine is too lovely, and has been too much ad-mired, not to be disliked by women who are so remarkable for their wish to monopolize all admiration" (342). As Fanny's comments sug-gest, women will believe Miss Elford's vindictive comments because these women are spiteful enough to be jealous of someone like Geral-dine, who is both gracious and good-natured. Because she has been uni-versally admired, Geraldine has created enemies among her fellow women. Jealousy thereby impedes the establishment of female commu-nity, turning women against one another. Misrepresentation becomes personal once the local gossips think that Geraldine has had Desmond's child. Through this example, Smith demonstrates that jealousy and prejudice belong not only to the political realm, but also to the personal. Instead of reaching out to help a fellow woman in need, Miss Elford creates a divide.

At this point it is crucial to stop momentarily to point out the impor-tance of Smith's claims. Smith's decision to link national politics with individual morality was a daring analogy for her, as well as Barbauld, to make at this time because doing so meant that events that occurred in both the political and the personal realms should be judged according to the same standards. Instead of having two separate sets of standards, one for people and one for nations, Smith and Barbauld claim that na-tions should be accountable for their actions, just as people are. As women, Smith and writers like her would be more likely to make this claim than would male writers since women were believed to be the guardians of the individual morality that supposedly dominated the private sphere. Men interacted in two spheres—the public and the private—but women were entrusted with the guardianship of the private.[14] It would make sense, then, for them to adopt the same vision of morality that they were already familiar with in the private sphere to their discussions of national politics, discussions that occurred, of course, within the public sphere. This application of individual morality to national politics thus also accounts for the extensive use of domestic metaphors that female writers used to discuss the nation. Just as Barbauld uses the analogy of the French as neighbors, Smith repeatedly uses the analogy of the nation as a house or a household. Women writers employed analogies that they, along with their female readers, were familiar with to connect national politics with individual morality.

To return to an analysis of *Desmond*, besides showing that the French Revolution and its principal tenets have been misrepresented because of jealousy, Smith also analyzes Britain's claims of being the best nation in the world. Throughout the novel, Britain is seen to be a land of abuse, both of the poor and of the disenfranchised. Those aspects of British society that need to be reformed emerge through minor stories and through Desmond's conversations with the various men that he meets in his travels. During one such conversation (one mentioned earlier), for instance, Desmond enters into a debate with Lord Fordingbridge, who claims that "there is no cause of complaint in England: nobody is poor, unless it be by their own fault; and nobody is oppressed" (180). After hearing this, Desmond contradicts the noble, cataloguing the various instances of abuse that he has already witnessed firsthand in British society. Robbers and murderers being tried in the same manner, executions numbering higher than all of Europe's executions put together, property being protected more than human beings, lawyers abusing their vows to uphold the law: all of these are injustices that occur within Britain. Desmond concludes his argument by asking, "Why do we boast of the mildness and humanity of laws, which provide punishment instead of prevention? . . . we must, in spite of our national vanity, acknowledge, either, that the English are the worse and most unprincipled race of men in Europe, or, that their penal laws are the most sanguinary of those of any nation under heaven" (184). National vanity causes the British to wear blindfolds so as to avoid seeing their own faults. As Desmond notes, however, English laws are some of the most sanguinary laws in all of Europe.

The most sustained discussion of British liberty and British abuses occurs in an exchange of two letters between Desmond's mentor Mr.

Bethel and Desmond himself. Together, these two letters offer Smith's main critique of the British government and of the current state of its laws. In the first of the two letters, Desmond's mentor Mr. Bethel comments upon how honorably the French people acted when they discovered that their king was trying to flee the country. Bethel remarks:

> To unprejudiced minds, however, the conduct of the French, on the return of their ill-advised monarch, has certainly something great and noble in it.—I own I am one of those who wish that this magnanimity of character may be followed by a steady and well-directed pursuit of the present great object, the formation of a constitution, that, without its defects, may unite all the advantages peculiar to that of England, which, even with those flaws and imperfections, is undoubtedly the best in the world. . . . [the constitution] has not only been long our national boast, but admired and analized (*sic*) by foreigners of the most enlarged and enlightened understanding. . . . We have, indeed, a marvellous proof that our constitution has inherent excellence in no common degree . . . [when] it may, I believe, be truly asserted, that in no age or country, has there existed a people, to whom general happiness has been more fairly distributed, than it is among the English of the present day. (298–99)

Bethel's national pride finds its outlet in his choice of superlatives. Not only is the British constitution "undoubtedly the best in the world," but foreigners of "the most enlarged and enlightened understanding" have long studied it as a model. Also according to Bethel, no other civilization or nation—including both ancient and modern ones—has ever enjoyed such a distribution of "general happiness." Bethel's hopes for the future of France depend upon France's adopting a constitution similar to that already possessed by Bethel's own nation.

It speaks well, of course, to Bethel's overall character that he is willing to share Britain's successes with France, but his remarks about Britain being the best of all nations are countered in the very next letter that appears. In this letter, Desmond agrees with his mentor's claims, but only to a certain extent. What Bethel refers to as "the general good of the British constitution" (299), Desmond exposes to be exactly that: *general* good that does not apply to all of Britain's subjects. Desmond makes this clear: "much of your eulogium on the constitution of England is just; and that it is good, that it ought to be better" (327). From here, Desmond uses an extended analogy—one that links the individual to the nation—to illustrate that Britain still needs to make progress. Desmond explains how when we see a man with "a thousand good qualities" who yet also possesses several severe failings, we cannot help but wish that the man were perfect, "that any degree of perfection makes us regret that the object in which it exists is not perfect" (327). Even if kind, generous, and wise, the man does not live up to our expectations if he possesses faults that interfere with his overall temperament and personality. Extending his analogy to Britain and national concerns, Desmond further elaborates:

> Of this nature is the regret I feel in regard to my own country.—I would have us boast of her excellence just—I would not have it the mere cant which we have already learned by rote, and repeat by habit; though, when we venture to think about it, we know that it is vanity and prejudice, and not truth, when we speak of its wonderful perfection. . . . I cannot agree to unlimited praise—though most certainly willing to allow to you, that a greater portion of happiness is diffused among the subjects of the British government, than among any other people upon earth. But this rather proves that *their* condition is very wretched, than that ours is perfectly happy. . . .
>
> Thus, my dear Bethel, it seems to me, that instead of proving that we are extremely happy, you prove only that we are comparatively so. (327–30)

Desmond's rebuttal to Bethel challenges his fellow Britons to assess more accurately the current state of affairs in the nation. While Desmond concedes that most Britons benefit from living in prosperous conditions, his words call for a healthy and just analysis of British society. Through the words of Desmond, Smith encourages her readers to question their complacency with, to borrow William Godwin's phrase, things as they are. Smith encourages her readers to look through the lens of truth to see that Britain is not perfect, and that national vanity and prejudice can interfere with rational principles and the quest for self-improvement. And even if Britain's people are happier than the people of any other nation, a point that Desmond grants Bethel, that happiness only proves that other nations are less so. Britain, Desmond emphasizes, is only *comparatively* happy when other nations are brought into the equation. There is always room for improvement.

HOPE AND THE POSSIBILITY OF REFORM

Although large sections of *Desmond* catalogue the injustices and corruption present in British society, the novel ultimately remains optimistic about what Britons can do to ameliorate conditions within their society. This chapter, remember, opened with the idea of reform, and despite Britain's flaws, Smith still holds out the possibility of hope. Through Desmond, Smith encourages her readers to effect change. The need for reform becomes, in fact, one of the central arguments of the novel. In the letter from Desmond just discussed, Desmond concludes his reply to Bethel by making this point clear:

> Do not, however, misunderstand me: I think that our government is certainly the best—not that can be imagined—but that has ever been experienced; and, while we are sure that practice is in its favour, it would be most absurd to dream of destroying it on theory.—If I had a very good house that had some inconveniences about it, I should not desire to pull it down, but I certainly should send for an architect and say, alter this room—it is too dark—remove those passages—they are too intricate—make a door here, and a staircase there; make the kitchen more habitable for my servants, and then my house will be extremely good. (330)

Using a domestic analogy once again and in a passage that mimics Montfleuri's rebuilding of his ancestral home, Desmond compares the British government to a house in need of modernization. As Desmond points out, Britain retains the honor of being the most perfect nation *so far*, but that does not mean that there is no room for improvements to be made. Desmond's words, in fact, read as a challenge—as a call to Britain's citizens to make their government not just into the best government currently in existence, but into the best government imaginable. But Smith is careful to qualify her assessment, noting that Desmond's critique of Britain does not constitute a complete repudiation of its government, but rather a call for reform. That is, Smith does not advocate tearing down the British government as the French have done in their own country, but rather modifying some of its existing structures. Like a house in need of modern-day improvements, the British government needs to open itself up to modern, more enlightened principles. Making the British government into a place where the servant's needs are as important as the master's would mean making the British nation "extremely good." Although Smith wrote this novel as a direct response to Burke,[15] in some respects, interestingly enough, Smith's analogy is a Burkean one, for Burke's model of progress relied on a gradual reformation of the state. At this juncture in her political thinking, Smith promotes a model of change that is more conservative than one might otherwise think.

In order to educate British readers so that they can carry out these changes, part of Desmond's mission while in France is to invalidate both these false representations of France and also these false self-representations of Britain by explaining firsthand the events taking place around him. One of the most important letters for this purpose is the one in which Desmond records his French friend Montfleuri's account of the events leading up to the Revolution. As a French noble who supports the Revolution, Montfleuri is in an important position to comment upon France's situation. As Diana Bowstead remarks, "Montfleuri's function as a character in this fiction turns on the fact that reforms on his estate are an expression of his radical beliefs. . . . There is nothing naive about the political analysis that accompanies Montfleuri's history."[16] A common rhetorical device for English supporters of the Revolution was to include the thoughts of a prorevolutionary French aristocrat in their texts. Helen Maria Williams, William Wordsworth, and even William Blake in *The French Revolution,* for instance, use the same device, knowing, as did Smith, that an aristocrat's voice would lend validity to their claims. If even an aristocrat, as a member of the group most impacted by the Revolution, supports its aims, their argument runs, then those aims must be worthwhile. In *Desmond,* Montfleuri's tale serves as a history lesson for the novel's readers, a detailed chronology of all the episodes leading up to the storming of the Bastille and the subsequent changes it wrought. Montfleuri explains how France's former kings helped set the stage by forming the French national character, while also untangling the role that the Americans' own earlier revolution played. Once the French people saw the colonists rebel against the British government, they opened their eyes to the state of affairs in their own nation, realizing that revolution was also possible in the many nations that make up the vast continent of Europe (66–79). Not content with listening to the real causes of the Revolution, most Britons, Montfleuri points out, listen only to their political parties: "But thus it is, that, throughout the revolution, every circumstance has, on your side of the water, been exaggerated, falsified, distorted, and misrepresented, to serve the purposes of party" (405).[17]

Early in the novel, Smith offers an extended example of how these misrepresentations can do harm at the individual level. One of the most striking scenes that exemplify Smith's belief in humanitarian, truthful, and nonprejudiced principles is a scene that occurs before Desmond has even left for France. While waiting for Geraldine's brother Waverly to join up with him so they can set sail for France together, Desmond passes his time browsing amongst the shops of the small British town where he is staying. One afternoon, Desmond decides to enter a library, where he cannot help but overhear the conversation that passes between a reverend member of the Anglican Church and a certain Mr.

Sidebottom. Although Desmond does not interfere in their exchange, he relays their words to us through a letter written to his friend Mr. Bethel. The Doctor and Mr. Sidebottom's discussion of how Church lands have been confiscated in France gradually leads them into a discussion of French cuisine, which, both men agree, is decidedly lacking in merit. Essentially, their dislike of the French is fueled by their dislike of what the French eat. Yet Mr. Sidebottom's particularly vehement dislike of the French is also based upon his brief experience in France, where his physician advised him to pass some time in order to improve, or "find," his appetite (44).[18] After spending only one short day in France, however, Mr. Sidebottom was so much disgusted by the food that he returned home to Britain straightaway. All of which makes him conclude that if the French cannot even manage the making of their own food, then they certainly cannot manage the running of their new government. As Mr. Sidebottom tells the Doctor, "But for your French, I never desire to set eyes on any of them again—and indeed, for my part, I am free to say, that if the whole race was extirpated, and we were in possession of their country, as in justice it is certain we ought to be, why, it would be so much the better—We should make a better hand of it in such a country as that a great deal" (44). For some reason best known to himself, Mr. Sidebottom firmly believes that Britain should be in possession of France. Such notions, of course, are mocked by Smith and so, too, by Desmond, who overhears and engages in several conversations such as this one throughout his time in Britain. As we have already seen, most of the Britons that Desmond meets are remarkably ignorant about the actual events leading to the Revolution and about the true nature of the Revolution itself. Although men such as Mr. Sidebottom and the Doctor firmly believe they understand the roots of France's current problems, Smith shows such men to be ignorant and narrow-minded.

According to men like Mr. Sidebottom and the Doctor, the French, after all, little deserve liberty since they do not know what to do with it. Mr. Sidebottom argues this point with his usual loquacity: "it would be right and proper for our ministry to take this opportunity of falling upon them [the French], while they are weakening each other; and, if they will have liberty, give them a little taste of the liberty of us Englishmen; for, of themselves, they can have no right notion of what it is— and, take my word for it, its the meerest (*sic*) folly in the world for them to think about it.—No, no; none but Englishmen, free-born Britons, either understand or deserve it" (45). While it is true that both Mr. Sidebottom and the Doctor display national pride, the type of pride they exhibit finds its basis in its opposite: national prejudice. Instead of harboring a "natural," as Smith would have it, love of their country, they draw their emotions from a concomitant dislike of their neighbors: instead of being glad that other countries are following the lead of their own nation, these two men want to reserve liberty for Britain alone. They are, essentially, selfish. The irony of Mr. Sidebottom's statement, of course, is that his version of British liberty involves the "falling upon" of the French while they are at their weakest moment. British liberty, as these two representatives of the British nation conceive it, consists of nothing less than Britain bullying and brutalizing other nations weaker than itself. In this same passage Smith also exposes the circular reasoning inherent in common arguments concerning British liberty. As Mr. Sidebottom would have it, only the "free-born" are fit to be free. Desmond sums up the stupidity of Mr. Sidebottom and the Doctor's conversation by remarking that the two men "seemed unable or unwilling to distinguish declamation from argument, or prejudice from reason" (45). Their words are hollow, based on prejudices they do not stop to question.

Yet our association with these two Britons does not end here, for Desmond also gets the opportunity to witness the philosophy of Mr. Sidebottom and the Doctor in action. Immediately after hearing their conversation, Desmond follows "these two worthy champions of British faith and British liberty," as he mockingly refers to them, out to the street (46). As they exit the library, the minister and Mr. Sidebottom are "accosted" (47) by a French woman who pleads for their help. When she explains that she is a widow, Mr. Sidebottom cuts her short:

> "A widow," cried Mr Sidebottom, "why you are a Frenchwoman; what have you to do here? And why do you not go back to your own country? This is the time there for beggars—they have got the upper hand. Go, go, mistress; get back to your own country. . . . you had not business that I know of in England, but to take bread out of the mouths of our own people; and now I suppose you are going to join the fish-women, and such like, who are pulling down the king's palaces." (47)

As if widows and Frenchwomen are two mutually exclusive terms, Mr. Sidebottom refuses to give countenance to the poor woman's supplications. He does not ask her what her "business" in England actually is, supposing instead that any business she could have in England would only result in depriving England's own people of food. Assuming that she is a beggar, he dismisses her as one of the "fish-women, and such like," who, he mistakenly believes, led the march on Versailles.

The Doctor, however, reveals himself to be "more alive to the tender solicitations of pity" (48) than his companion, and makes somewhat of an effort to help the woman. Although up until this point we have heard little from the clergyman since Mr. Sidebottom has dominated the conversation, we now witness the Doctor's notion of Christian charity at work. Before he helps the Frenchwoman, though, he feels it necessary to reveal to her his true thoughts about her and her situation: "'Woman! though I have no doubt but that thou art a creature of an abandoned conduct, and that these children are base born; yet, being a stranger and a foreigner, I have so much universal charity, that, unworthy as I believe thee, I will not shut my heart against thy petition'" (47).[19] Refusing to acknowledge the dangerous situations that women of the period could easily find themselves in—alone and without male protection—the Doctor assumes that the woman must be a prostitute.[20] Despite his assurance of the woman's "abandoned conduct," however, the Doctor's "universal charity" moves him to give the Frenchwoman a sixpence, which he offers to her not alone, but along with a severe warning to leave town immediately, "'where, as people of fortune and consideration come for their health, they ought not to be disturbed and disgusted by the sights of objects of misery. I don't love to see beggars in these places; their importunity is injurious to the nerves. Let me hear of you no more—Our laws provide us to provide for no poor but our own'" (48). Echoing Mr. Sidebottom's views on charity, the clergyman admonishes the woman for being bold enough to beg British aid, when such aid would take away from British mouths. Even the mere presence of the Frenchwoman, as an "object of misery," disrupts the Doctor's sense of composure, as, he assumes, it does of everyone else who sees her. As a visual reminder of the poverty and deprivations resulting from the political changes currently going on in the European community, the widow serves as a token of events that some Britons would rather forget. The Doctor's unwillingness to help the Frenchwoman, other impoverished French émigrés, and even English beggars, signals his desire to remain outside of individual moral responsibility. He might repeatedly rail against the Revolution in public venues, but when it comes time for him to become personally involved with individuals affected by it, the Doctor stands to one side.

The scene does not end with the Doctor's callous dismissal of the widow, for Smith uses this scene to show of what true "universal charity" actually consists. For Mr. Sidebottom and the Doctor, national identity works to divide instead of to unite. Because the widow is French, they believe that their selfish refusal to help the poor woman is justified. Desmond, however, thinks (and acts) differently. After the Doctor and Mr. Sidebottom stroll off in quest of some "good dishes" (48), Desmond approaches the Frenchwoman and asks if he can help her. Interested in the widow's well-being and knowing that her command of the English language is weak, Desmond talks to her in French, a language he does not mind speaking, even if it is supposed to be the language of a rival nation. Unused to being treated with compassion, the widow, as Desmond relates, is momentarily stunned: "The voice of kindness, in her own language, was so soothing, and I fear so new, that she was for some moments unable to answer me" (49). When she does finally speak, the woman explains her situation to Desmond, and, because he listens attentively, he hears the truth of her story. Unlike the Doctor, who assumed that the widow was a prostitute, Desmond sets aside his national prejudices in order to interact with the woman as a fellow human being. By doing so, Desmond soon learns that the woman was the wife of a gentleman's companion, who died of an illness shortly after honorably attending to the sickbed of his British master. Because the master's new wife disliked the French and showed little concern for the sufferings of the poor, the French widow was forced to leave the residence of her husband's late master and make her way, as best she could and with two young children to care for, back to France. After hearing her tale, which Desmond does not doubt because it was told with the "simplicity" that always signals truth (49), Desmond gives the widow enough money to pay for her return voyage to France. Desmond, unlike Mr. Sidebottom and the minister, recognizes his fellow humans when they are in need of charity and aid. His humanitarian principles reach across national borders, and he is able to recognize truth when he sees it.[21] Desmond's act of kindness toward the French widow reveals Smith's belief in individual accountability toward other human beings, regardless of the nation from which they might hail.

Women's Vulnerability and the Development of a Female Perspective

The pathos present in the French widow's story remains with the reader even after Desmond moves forward with his own tale. Placed as this story is at the crossroads when Desmond is about to leave for France, it opens up the issue of women's special vulnerability in a society that casts them aside. Up until this point, I have looked at the ways Smith exposes the truth about the French Revolution so that her British readers would have a more accurate and less prejudiced understanding of its principal goals. Yet another of Smith's central concerns in *Desmond* is illustrating how women are especially subject to the injustices that beset them in British society. Anne K. Mellor directs our attention to this issue, observing that Smith devotes much of the last part of the novel "to an exploration of the gender politics that sustain both conservative and republican political ideologies. In order to uncover the most extensive and most profound oppression experienced by British subjects, namely, by women, she must turn away from abstract political theory and debate towards a fictionalized account of the probable experiences of particular women."[22] While Mellor grounds her discussion in an analysis of the ways in which Smith personalizes political events through the use of her female characters, I want to look more closely at how Smith uses the figure of Geraldine to expose the dangers inherent in being a female political subject. The British nation, as it is currently constructed, leaves its women vulnerable and open to abuse.

Exposure of the truth—whether that truth relates to national prejudice or social and political abuse—becomes most pronounced when recorded by the pen of Desmond's primary love interest, Geraldine. Completely silent throughout the first book of the novel, Geraldine finds her voice when she leaves her native country to join her degenerate husband, at his command, in France. This event, of course, finds its parallel in Smith's own life, for she followed her own profligate husband to France during the winter of 1784–85, when her husband was fleeing from creditors back home in Britain. As most readers of Smith know, Smith used autobiographical elements in all of her fictional texts, often referring to the personal, lengthy lawsuit she was involved with for forty years in an attempt to recapture the inheritance that her father-in-law left her children after Smith left her husband in 1787. Antje Blank and Janet Todd, among other critics, have remarked on this autobiographical tendency, commenting: "Many of Smith's marginal plots are thinly veiled accounts of her own life."[23] Once Geraldine arrives upon French soil, many false accounts of the Revolution are set right. Up to this point, we have encountered Desmond's correctives, but they are correctives that Smith's readers could easily dismiss since Desmond is, after all, a somewhat obsessed young man. When Geraldine begins to discuss the Revolution, however, we, as readers, have already been prepared to accept her comments as an objective account of the Revolution. This is especially true considering that Smith has spent the last two books of the novel—which comprise almost 300 pages in modern-day reprints of *Desmond*—building up the strength of Geraldine's character based upon the remarks of other characters (including the austere Mr. Bethel), as well as upon her own virtuous conduct. In her analysis of the novel, Angela Keane explains how "[i]n both the pro- and counter-revolutionary imaginary, women were valued primarily as bearers and moral guardians of the nation."[24] As a mother who is constantly looking out for the welfare of her children and who rebuffs Desmond's untoward advances, Geraldine proves herself to be a woman of virtue. As several critics, including Chris Jones and Eleanor Ty, have argued, Geraldine stands as the paragon of conservative womanhood during the late eighteenth century.[25] Forced by her parents to marry against her will, Geraldine remains obedient and passive, an ideal wife and mother. She is a woman with whom few could find fault.

Geraldine's most extensive comments about the Revolution appear in the tenth letter of Book 3, which is one of the novel's longest and most important letters, and the first letter that Geraldine actually sends from France. Just as Desmond's letter to Bethel about the British constitution provides Smith with the opportunity to reflect upon the necessity of reform, Geraldine's letter to her sister Fanny provides Smith with another forum in which to correct the false assertions made about the Revolution. To prepare her readers for Geraldine's chronicle and also to explain why the new government might not yet be running as smoothly as one might expect, Smith makes it clear that the Revolution is still in its earliest stages. Geraldine likens the changes in France to changes within a smaller unit, one more familiar to the novel's middle-class female readers: the family. Using an analogy that her female readers would understand,[26] Smith connects the political changes in France to changes within a household. Geraldine links the two units for her readers: "We know, from daily experience, that even in a private family, a change in its œconomy or its domestics, disturbs the tranquillity of its members for some time. — It must surely then happen, to a much greater degree, in a great nation, whose government is suddenly dissolved by the resolution of the people; and which, in taking a new form, has so many jarring interests to conciliate" (308). Like Wollstonecraft and even Burke, who both view the family as a microcosm of the state, Smith has Geraldine compare the smaller household to the larger nation by using yet another domestic image of the nation.[27] Just as a slight change in economy or in the number of domestics upsets the delicate balance of the domestic sphere, so, too, does a change in government have far-reaching effects. This passage also differs from Desmond's earlier comparison of the British government to a house in need of remodeling in that this time it is a *woman* who is in control. In Desmond's analogy, he—a man—was the person who oversaw the changes being made in the "house"; in Geraldine's analogy, on the other hand, women supervise the "household economy." Women once again become the guardians of public morality.

Despite such forebodings, however, Geraldine's depictions of France are positive, more full of surprise at how grossly distorted the true state of affairs has been than full of despair, as she had anticipated they would be. Overall, the people of France are in a period of great possibility, with the potential to affect profound changes in their nation. This particular letter offers a firsthand account of the events in France, beginning with Geraldine's first few hours abroad. Although she had been told in Brighthelmstone, for instance, that she would find the entire nation *"en feu & en sang"* (314),[28] the French are actually orderly and well behaved. Recording her first impressions of the neighboring country in this same letter to her sister Fanny, Geraldine writes: "I expected . . . to have seen some symptoms, in the town, of the misery, which I was assured, the revolution had occasioned; but every thing is the same as it was when we passed this way to England, six years since" (308). The only difference she notices, in fact, is that the French soldiers are actually in better condition than they were before; this time they are well-fed and nicely dressed, whereas before they were in such a miserable condition that Geraldine would not have been surprised if the soldiers had ransacked their own towns, so desperate were they for food (308). While passing through Rouen on her way to the capital, Geraldine also encounters an evening *fête* under the stars. Charmed by what she sees, Geraldine muses on the inaccuracy of what she had been told in Britain: "this is a specimen of universal national misery—of the fierce and sanguinary democracy so pathetically lamented by Mr Burke!" (314). Even religion, which Geraldine had believed to be eradicated, still exists: "All religion, however, . . . is not abolished in France—they told me it was despised and trampled on; and I never enquired, as every body ought to do, when such assertions are made—*Is all this true?*" (310, emphasis added).

This last question of Geraldine's—*"Is this all true?"*—emerges as particularly significant, for in it we see Geraldine first beginning to question the lies that she has always been told. Before coming to France, Geraldine had submissively accepted everything that she had been told or taught. Once she arrives in France, however, she begins to question what she had before taken for granted; once she realizes that the events in France have been misrepresented to her, Geraldine realizes that other circumstances in her own life have been misrepresented to her as well. "[E]very body," she makes clear, whether man *or* woman, should question the truthfulness of accounts they have heard. Although she has been taught that politics are not part of woman's sphere, Geraldine now understands that such teachings are as false as the blood that she had been told was spilling throughout France.[29] She remarks upon this change in the same letter to Fanny, noting that the revelation of truth has led her to take an active part in her own destiny, even as a woman:

> This excursion into the field of politics, where, for the most part, only thistles can be gathered, and where we, you know, have always been taught that women should never advance a step, may, perhaps, excite your surprize. . . . The truth is, that whenever I am not suffering under any immediate alarm, my mind, possessing more elasticity than I once thought possible, recovers itself enough to look at the objects around me, and even to contemplate with some degree of composure, my own present circumstances, and the prospect before me, which would a few, a very few months since, have appeared insupportable. . . . .
>
> . . . my inconsequential opinion would not be put in the other scale, were I not convinced, that every principle, all that we owe to God, our fellow creatures and ourselves, is clearly on the other side the question. (311–12)

Situations that only a few months ago would have overwhelmed her have actually made Geraldine stronger and more assured. Not only does she now venture into the muddled realm of politics, but she also dares to assert her "inconsequential opinion" that the Revolution is right and just. In her own Preface to the novel, Smith had made a similar claim as to why she decided to write overtly about political events in this, her third novel. "But women," Smith writes, "it is said have no business with politics.—Why not?—Have they no interest in the scenes that are acting around them, in which they have fathers, brothers, husbands, sons, or friends engaged!" (6). Because women have connections to the political world, they have a right to be interested in what passes within it. Religion even enters into Geraldine's argument here, for her words issue a challenge to those, like Mr. Sidebottom and the Doctor, who call themselves Christian: if we truly wish to serve God, she notes, we should support the French cause.

Geraldine's agency in denouncing those who have misrepresented the Revolution also leads this formerly silent character to denounce those individuals who have been cruelest to her, including her own parents and husband, Verney. The same woman who had repeatedly reprimanded her sister Fanny for speaking badly of their parents or of Verney,[30] and who purposely stifled her own complaints,[31] now finds a voice with which to complain against maltreatment. In previous letters, Geraldine had meekly accepted her dead father's wishes, refusing to demur. In this letter from France, however, the father meets with severe censure. Geraldine now recognizes him as "a very Turk in principle," a man who "hardly allowed women any pretensions to souls, or thought them worth more care than he bestowed on his horses, which were to look sleek, and do their paces well" (312). While living, his interest in his two daughters only extended to how well they were set off to advantage so that they could attract suitable husbands. Yet even worse than their father is their mother, a woman who cares for nothing other than "riches and high birth" both in her own choice of personal acquaintances and in that of suitors for her two daughters (312). As the first of the sisters to be married—or rather, sold—off, Geraldine is "most unhappily the victim of this mercenary spirit" (313). Her sacrifice was offered, of course, to Verney, whom Geraldine also indicts in this same letter. In the past, Geraldine did not like to complain against him out of duty and respect. He is, after all, the father of her three children, as she so frequently points out, and, as such, should be the entire family's "natural protector" (318). Now that she recognizes general abuse of power, however, Geraldine complains about her husband, "a man, whose conduct is a continual disgrace to himself, his family, and his country" (316). Not only does Verney disgrace himself and his family, but he also disgraces Britain. Smith's inclusion of country in this trio once more shows how strongly she believes in the interconnections between political and personal duty, as well as how closely they are tied to morality. The same standards that determine how well Verney succeeds as an individual and a father also determine how well he succeeds as a Briton.

Ashamed of how Verney treats both herself and their children, Geraldine now openly regrets her union with him. Even worse, she now admits that she also fears him. She reveals these feelings to Fanny: "other circumstances that have accidentally come to my knowledge, have raised in me such a dread of him, that there is no humiliation to which I had not rather submit, than that of considering myself as his slave" (316). Essentially, though, Geraldine has been just that: a slave to her husband and his every whim. Each time Verney makes (or rather, demands) a request of her, she is forced to comply.[32] Now that her eyes have been opened, however, Geraldine recognizes her situation for what it truly is. She realizes that she has been sold in slavery (marriage) to a man who treats her even more terribly than he would a horse. As several critics have pointed out, Geraldine's distresses are not romanticized, melodramatic concerns, but rather everyday concerns that still have a profound impact on her life. Diana Bowstead perceives that "Geraldine's predicament is not at all the kind that sentimental heroines suffer. Melodramatic resolution at the end of the novel notwithstanding, Geraldine's story is about the dismal facts of wretched marriages, and especially those (like Smith's) that have been arranged by self-absorbed parents. Geraldine's difficulties are never, until the end of the novel, dramatic or extravagant enough to be captivating." Mary Anne Schofield concurs, noting that Smith blends her own life with those of her female characters to express the "life and movements of a prototypical eighteenth-century woman."[33] The radicalness of such an approach—of showing that the concerns of the ordinary woman are of the upmost importance—is that it makes Everywoman's contemporary problems into problems severe enough to be treated in a novel. By focusing her attention on the average woman, Smith can better argue for reform.

Other characters also point out this ill-treatment of Geraldine on Verney's part. Earlier in the novel, Desmond had railed against the abuses that Verney could legally bestow upon his wife, exclaiming, "for England is not my country, when I can hear only, in whatever company I go into, of Geraldine's unhappiness, and the folly, extravagancies, and utter ruin of her husband" (231). Desmond cannot believe that his own nation would allow Verney to treat Geraldine so cruelly, and so Desmond refuses to claim allegiance to England. Later on, Fanny makes a similar point when Geraldine departs for France. Before her sister's letters assure her that events in France have been greatly exaggerated, Fanny fears for Geraldine's safety. Yet Fanny also recognizes that Geraldine's worst enemies are not the French Revolutionaries, but rather her *British* husband: "how decidedly convinced I am, that the greatest evil that can befall you would be meeting with your husband" (307). Mayhem and murder little compare to the evils that Verney brings with him. At the time, of course, Geraldine brushed off such comments as nonsense; now that she recognizes Britain's faults, however, Geraldine agrees. She questions her world and develops a newfound ability to judge and think for herself.

In many ways, Geraldine's awakening is the most important development in the novel. While Smith's critique of the Revolution and her plea for British reform are still significant, it is Geraldine's new understanding of the world that offers the greatest possibility for change. As previously discussed, many critics have focused on how Geraldine (as a passive, subservient woman) is used to convey support for the Revolutionary cause. Gradually, slowly, Geraldine begins to speak her mind, and, since we trust the values of this "ideal" wife and mother, we listen to her claims. She helps determine our understanding of the Revolution before we are even aware that we are being influenced. Yet while this is certainly a valid assessment of how Smith uses Geraldine to comment upon the Revolution, an assessment with which I also agree, most of these critics read Geraldine as static and unchanging, a woman who remains docile and tractable throughout the entire novel. Such assessments of Geraldine, however, overlook the fact that Geraldine—she who was formerly so silent and submissive—finds her own voice *through and because of* the French Revolution.[34] Once her eyes have been opened up to the predominance of misrepresentation and the subsequent importance of truth, she can see how her own situation as a woman in modern British society has also been misrepresented to her. Significantly, by the end of the novel, Geraldine is no longer jealous of Josephine. She has been able to set aside her personal jealousy to such an extent that she even raises Josephine and Desmond's illegitimate child as her own.

Since the key to renouncing misrepresentation lies in one's ability to think and judge for oneself, Geraldine is able to change both her and our understanding of the Revolution. Geraldine's growing understanding of herself and her ability to express her own thoughts finds its best representation, in fact, in two passages that incorporate her thoughts on natural scenery. Read side by side, these two passages reveal Geraldine's own changed nature. Once Geraldine begins writing letters to her sister Fanny, for instance, we first learn of Geraldine's interest in nature and of her own "poetic" nature. Her letters written from the British countryside contain descriptions of the natural scenery, and her melancholy tone carries over into the landscape.[35] When she arrives in France, Geraldine continues to describe the natural vistas she encounters. Her earliest description, for instance, encompasses the area around Rouen, a location "infinitely more beautiful than any I ever saw.—The Seine winding through a lovely vale of great extent, and the port of Rouen crouded (*sic*) with vessels—the town and suburbs—the old and magnificent cathedral—all embossed in trees, with the finest meadows beyond them, and an infinite number of *châteaux* scattered throughout the whole landscape, render it altogether such a view as I never saw equalled in England; but, indeed, I have not, in my own country, been a great traveller" (309). Geraldine's description uses superlatives to note the scenery around her: the area in general is "infinitely more beautiful" than any she has ever seen, and the entire view is something she has never seen "equalled" in her own country. France, her sketch makes clear, is more beautiful than Britain. Still afraid at this point to trust her own words, however, Geraldine immediately qualifies her statement by remarking that she has not actually traveled much at all. "Of what importance is an opinion such as hers?" her words imply. As Geraldine becomes more aware of her own voice, though, she begins to assert her views more strongly, with less hesitation. Once she begins to recognize the lies around her, she trusts her own opinion more forcibly. In her next letter to Fanny, after she has inveighed against her parents' and husband's cruel treatment, Geraldine once more comments upon the scenery around her. Her description of a French sunset is particularly striking: "The first yellow tints of Autumn are hardly stealing on the trees, encreasing, however, where they have touched them, the beauty of the foliage.—The sky is delightfully serene; and a sunset in the gardens here exceeds what I ever saw in England for warmth and brilliancy of colouring" (323). Whereas as recently as in her last letter Geraldine qualified her own assessment of natural beauty, afraid to grant France any superiority over Britain, here Geraldine recognizes that one nation can have superiorities over another. This time, France surpasses Britain in natural beauty, with sunsets that "exceed" in beauty all that she has seen back home. Just as Desmond disavowed national prejudice in helping the French widow and her children, so, too, does Geraldine disavow national prejudice in allowing for the merits of a French sunset. In essence, judgment of taste parallels political judgment in these two passages. Nature has become the determining point around which Geraldine can now freely express her opinions.

By the novel's close, Geraldine and Desmond are able to overcome the obstacles that have kept them apart from one another, and their ultimate "reward" is their ability to be united in marriage. The novel's increasing focus on Geraldine as an independent voice and as an active woman, I would also like to suggest, mirrors Smith's growing exploration of what female agency looks like. At this point in her writing career, Smith was not yet able to articulate clearly the idea of an alternative concept of female community and of alternative ways of thinking about national identity, but she was able to show the dangers inherent in Britain's legal and social systems and of misguided national prejudice. Geraldine models the process of awakening that Smith's female readers should then mimic themselves, undergoing a revolution in how they understand their own position as British women. In this respect, Geraldine's awakening is both political and national in nature, although expressed in individualistic terms. Like so many other women writers of the period, Smith uses the idea of France to help her character find a voice. The Revolutionary cause provides Geraldine with the opportunity to observe impartially her own position within British society and to recognize her own lack of rights.[36] The idea of France allows her to recognize her own subservient position as a British woman, as little more than a slave to her supposedly enlightened British husband.

3

National Identity and Expatriation in Charlotte Smith's *The Young Philosopher*

IN 1792, WHEN *DESMOND* FIRST APPEARED IN PRINT, SMITH STILL BELIEVED that Britain could be reformed. By 1798, when *The Young Philosopher* appeared in print, Smith would lose that hope altogether. In many ways, the two novels contain similarities in both content and theme. In one, the hero Desmond seeks vindication for the French Revolution and throws doubt on the myriad ways in which the Revolution has been falsely portrayed; in the other, the hero Delmont seeks vindication for his American lover, Medora, and her parents as they return to Britain to seek retribution in a lawsuit that would grant Medora a significant inheritance. Yet in many ways the two novels are also very dissimilar. In both novels, misrepresentation is also a central issue, but it is a more pressing one in *The Young Philosopher* because it has more serious personal consequences, particularly for women.[1] Smith's later novel also concerns itself more explicitly with national identity—with how individuals view themselves as possessing the traits associated with a particular nation, whereas *Desmond* concerns itself more with national-ism—with how individuals align themselves with one particular nation instead of another. *The Young Philosopher* is, above all, an exploration of what it means to be a member of a nation and to hold a particular na-tional identity; her primary interest lies in understanding the formation of community and interactions between humans. In this, her tenth novel, Smith is less concerned with nationalism and its acts of political jealousy, and more concerned with national identity, with what makes us identify ourselves as members of a particular nation. National iden-tity is a theme that lay beneath the surface in *Desmond*, but that would fully emerge in *The Young Philosopher.*

REFLECTIONS ON NATIONAL IDENTITY

As in *Desmond*, the French Revolution is still present in *The Young Philosopher,* but it is not Smith's main concern. Instead, Smith focuses

114

on national identity and on nations in general. Her interest in the Revolution primarily lies in her interest in aligning her characters either with or against humanitarian values, where each character's level of support for the Revolution determines that character's level of interest in doing general good.[2] The French Revolution makes its appearance in the novel in the earliest pages, for instance, in a conversation that passes between George Delmont and his unexpected guest Dr. Winslow.[3] When the minister blames philosophers for all the "bloodshed and misery" that has occurred in France,[4] Delmont feels himself compelled to respond with a defense of all that has been accomplished by means of the Revolution. He retorts: "The truth is, that the gloomy and absurd structures, raised on the basis of prejudice and superstition have toppled down headlong; many are crushed in their fall . . . the bastilles of falsehood, in which men's minds were imprisoned, are levelled with the earth, never, never to rise again!" (45). Delmont's support for the Revolution establishes him as a character we can trust. Because he supports the end of prejudice and superstition, we know that his principles are just.[5] The next time that the Revolution appears to any great extent is when Delmont's mentor Armitage defends his own character to the evil Mrs. Crewkherne. Because Armitage had supported the Revolution since its inception, Mrs. Crewkherne particularly despises him, even though she does not completely understand the principles by which she actually does so. Armitage finally decides to confront Mrs. Crewkherne so that she will stop spreading rumors about the Glenmorris family and himself.[6] When he braves her wrath, he makes sure to clarify how he understands the term *Jacobin,* the principal crime of which Mrs. Crewkherne accuses him. He corrects her assertion of his being a Jacobin by explaining what a Jacobin actually is:

> if you mean, among other heavy misdemeanors included under [the term Jacobin], that I either approve, or ever did approve of the violence, cruelty, and perfidy, with which the French have polluted the cause of freedom, you are greatly mistaken; far from thinking that such measures are likely to establish liberty, and the general rights of mankind, I hold them to be exactly the means that will delay the period when rational freedom, and all that its enjoyment can give to humanity, shall be established in the world. I deny many of their maxims, and I abhor almost the whole of their conduct. I never do believe that axiom of politicians, which says, that evil may be done to produce good. (247)

Like Delmont's conversation with Dr. Winslow, Armitage's discussion with Mrs. Crewkherne establishes Armitage's character for us. This passage defines Armitage as a man to be trusted. He has a right sense of honor, and can recognize that the ends do not always justify the means. Liberty, for him, can only be based upon a "rational freedom" that does not involve violence of any kind. This scene thus clarifies Armitage's beliefs for us, while also justifying Smith's own involvement with the Revolution, for Armitage's battle with Mrs. Crewkherne is Smith's own opportunity to defend herself against charges of supporting the more recent violence of the Revolution. When she wrote *Desmond*, Smith supported the French people's cause before their cause had turned them against one another. Like so many of those who initially supported the Revolution, Smith became disenchanted with it after the Reign of Terror. Once the Revolution deviated from its original path, Smith no longer supported its new principles of violence and chaos. Armitage's praise for the Revolution lets Smith's readers know that Smith herself has not forsaken her values, even if she does not support the turn the Revolution has taken. This scene is Smith's way of dealing with the changes of the Revolution.

While the Revolution makes its appearance in small scenes, then, it never does steal the show. The star of Smith's production is, instead, her own nation. Smith's emphasis in *The Young Philosopher* is not on the potential that the Revolution promises, as it was in *Desmond*, but rather on the injustices that seem as if they will always exist within British society. In her earlier novel, Britain's weaknesses were exposed so that its subjects could eliminate them through personal and national reform. In her later novel, Britain's weaknesses are exposed because Smith herself feels that they will always endure, and she wants to offer an alternative. The novel reads, in fact, as a catalogue of various injustices that can (and do) occur within Britain. From the beginning, a critique of Britain and its laws becomes a central theme of the novel, even before we realize it as such. In an early passage describing Delmont's education, for example, the narrator describes how Delmont's eyes are first opened, while still an adolescent, to the injustices he sees in the society around him:

> his heart swelled with indignation against those whom these real or apparent sufferers described as having been the cause of their wretchedness, and against the systems through which only they could be inflicted. From detestation against individuals, such as justices and overseers, he began to reflect on the laws that put it in their power thus to drive forth to nakedness and famine the wretched beings they were empowered to protect; and he was led to enquire if the complicated misery he every day saw (a very very small part of so wide an evil) could be the fruits of the very best laws that could

be framed in a state of society said to be the most perfect among what are called the civilized nations of the world. (21)

Delmont's reaction to these abuses emphasizes their source. Although first inclined to attribute this suffering to individuals, Delmont soon realizes that the actual source of the problems lies in the system itself. Britain's laws protect tyrants at the expense of the innocent, and make it possible for the strong to abuse the weak. The customs, institutions, and prejudices inherent in British society further perpetuate these injustices, protecting the same justices and overseers who dispense the misery in the first place. The central irony, of course, is that Britons pride themselves on possessing "the very best laws" and "the most perfect" society of any modern nation. Such thinking, however, only testifies to their smugness and self-complacency.

At an early age, then, Delmont began questioning Britain's laws, and so the seed of doubt had already been planted and well-tended long before he meets the Glenmorris family. When he does meet them, Delmont encounters even more examples of the degeneracy of British laws, for all of the negative things that have happened to the Glenmorrises have happened while residing in Britain. When Laura Glenmorris narrates how she and her husband first met, for instance, her tale revolves around prejudice and injury. Because she loves a man considered to be socially beneath her (and a Scotsman on top of that), Laura is cast off from her family without any form of monetary aid. Glenmorris's subsequent kidnapping and their separation are all owing to the fact that Laura's parents have tried to separate her from her rightful inheritance. Their return to Britain from America is due, in fact, to their attempt to claim this inheritance for their daughter Medora. When Glenmorris himself finally arrives in Britain towards the end of the novel, his welcome is symbolic, for he is almost immediately thrown into jail for not paying the interest on an old debt for £4,000 that he had long ago contracted to help a friend marry. We soon learn that the accusation is false, contrived only to get Glenmorris out of the way so that he would not try to claim his daughter's inheritance (344–45). The fact that Glenmorris can be thrown into prison under such circumstances, however, testifies to the fact that what the narrator mockingly refers to as "the boasted widely spreading English oak of jurisprudence" (341) actually provides limited shade for those who try to repose beneath it. Although the oak symbolizes the liberties of the British nation and was already an image associated with Burke, Britons do not share in equal measure the comfort of its protection.

NASCENT STIRRINGS OF FEMALE COMMUNITY

Britain is therefore portrayed throughout the novel as a land of injustice, but Smith takes care to emphasize that these injustices are much worse for women than they are for men. After Smith develops a strong case against the injustices of British society and its institutions, she therefore turns to an exploration of the impact of these injustices upon women, who feel the effects of abuse much more deeply than do men. At one point in the novel, for example, Medora accepts a ride with a man who is returning a sick woman and her small children to their home parish. When he notes that Medora is shocked to see such an ill woman undergoing the difficulties of travel, the cart driver explains to her that even though the family was starving, British poor laws did not require their current parish (that of the woman's dead husband) to provide for them. Here Medora sees the maxims of *Desmond*'s Mr. Sidebottom and the clergyman at work, for just as they believed that the French widow was no concern of theirs—that "Our laws provide us to provide for no poor but our own" (*Desmond*, 48)—so does British society as a whole feel the same, especially in regard to women. Instead of helping the woman, who, because she is a woman, has no means of earning money on her own, her parish sends her and her young children away. Amazed by what she both hears and sees, Medora remarks: "I never had seen poverty and misery till this moment; I never had an idea of the degree of wretchedness which the laws of England permit a set of men called parish officers to inflict upon the poor" (321). Like Desmond with the French widow, Medora aids the woman, comforting her and her children and alleviating their sufferings to the best of her ability throughout the ride.

The two Glenmorris women also remain particularly vulnerable to the British legal system: because lawyers manipulate their case, Laura and Medora must struggle to be heard, and, with no recourse to the law, they are left open to attack.[7] When they travel to London alone to meet once again with lawyers, Medora ends up being kidnapped, and Laura, as a result of her daughter's disappearance, ends up mad. Yet the primary reason that such catastrophic events come about is because the Glenmorris women are misrepresented to the very people best suited to act as their allies and advocates: other women. Smith's novel reads, in fact, as an extended exploration of the means of protection available to British women when the patriarchal nature of the British legal system refuses to countenance their claims. One solution Smith wants to believe in is that of a female community whose members would offer support to each other in times of need. Like other women writers of the period who also explored the possibilities of such a community, Smith would like to believe that British women would help each other out when they encounter a fellow woman in a distressing situation; unlike some of these other authors, however, Smith is more pessimistic in her assessment of such aid. Smith wants such community to exist, but must ultimately conclude that female community is just not feasible given the current nature of British institutions and customs. More particularly, one of Smith's central critiques of British society in the novel is that British women do not protect or help their fellow women, largely due to the powerful influence of gossip, which Smith portrays as a symptom of larger societal evils.

Before looking at the impact gossip has on Laura and Medora, I would like to pause momentarily to emphasize to a greater extent than I did in my discussion of *Desmond* the powerful role gossip could play in a woman's life during this period. In *Desmond*, Geraldine was subject to whatever notions the tattling tongue of Miss Elford contrived. While the rumors tarnished Geraldine's reputation to a certain degree, they never do her (or Frenchwoman Josephine, whom the rumors are really about) any lasting harm. In *The Young Philosopher*, however, gossip has much more serious ramifications for the female characters. The work of Patricia Meyer Spacks is useful here to illuminate the dangers that these pernicious rumors represent. In her insightful and now classic study on the nature of gossip, Spacks explains that the various modes of gossip spread along a continuum, with vicious intent at one end, "idle talk" in the middle, and "serious" intimate gossip at the other end.[8] At its most harmful point, "gossip manifests itself as distilled malice. It plays with reputations, circulating truths and half-truths and falsehoods about the activities, sometimes about the motives and feelings, of others."[9] Especially significant is that gossip works to distance women from any forms of protection that might otherwise be available to them. "[T]he dynamics of gossip," Spacks notes, "regardless of class, create a we–them dichotomy: *we* who talk, *them* whom we discuss."[10] This imposed dichotomy creates an inside group and an outside group, and when women are members of the outside group, their reputations are especially vulnerable. Misrepresentation opens women to abuse because it makes them unable to protect themselves or their honor. Gossip, as the primary determinant of whether or not a woman's character will be praised or blasted, thus acts as a powerful form of social interaction and control.

Throughout *The Young Philosopher*, gossip is the means whereby false impressions circulate, ruining the credibility of those who become entangled in its web.[11] Laura and Medora, for instance, repeatedly attempt to seek protection from other women when they find themselves alone and without help, but most of the time they are turned away because other women have maligned their reputations. In Smith's earlier novel *Desmond*, as just mentioned, the main female character Geraldine suffers because of the rumors circulating about her, but the worst that happens to Geraldine as a result of the false allegations against her is that society thinks poorly of her. Laura and Medora, however, are left in the much more serious position of finding themselves unprotected and without means of financial support, literally running the risk of starving to death since they cannot find the means to support themselves or pay their outstanding debts.[12] When Armitage confronts Mrs. Crewkherne about her spreading of rumors, he emphasizes the effects of such viciousness: "I came to you to represent to you the injustice and cruelty of the attacks you have made on the reputation, and, for ought you know, on the peace of two persons" (248). As Armitage makes clear, when a woman's reputation is attacked, her peace is interrupted as well. Men can continue to move about in society with tarnished reputations, but women are all but lost.[13] As Spacks explains, "Women have no way to wipe out stains to their good names. . . . women depended vitally on their reputations. As late as 1800, moralists observed that a wound to a person's name, however frivolously originated, lasts forever."[14] Armitage, for instance, may possess a bad (although falsely so) reputation, but it is Laura who suffers as a result of her association with him. Because she is afraid to be further linked with Armitage via gossip, knowing as she does that rumors about them having an adulterous affair are currently circulating, Laura refuses to seek his aid when she needs it most—when she and Medora start running out of money while pursuing their lawsuit in London. Laura "has been deterred from applying to [Armitage] by this infernal crew" (233), afraid of the stigma that applying to this old family friend would have on her reputation and of being made into an outcast. Gossip can easily ruin a woman's credibility, and, without credibility, women are refused protection. Thus it is that an intelligent and virtuous woman like Laura can find herself alone and "so destitute of protection" (215), even with a loving husband and friends like Delmont and Armitage.

Since Laura is afraid to be indecently associated with her male friends, she must find alternate sources of protection. Other women, however, refuse to help, choosing instead to believe the worst about her.[15] Even Laura's own mother, Lady Mary, is swayed against Laura because of the rumors she has heard. Never interested in Laura (as a younger daughter) to begin with, Lady Mary first decided to have nothing to do with her when Laura eloped with Glenmorris years ago, convinced as she was that Glenmorris was beneath her daughter's notice. When Laura returns to England so many years later to salvage a portion of her fortune, Lady Mary lets herself be swayed by false opinion. Mrs. Crewkherne, in particular, as well as her "agents and deputy gossips" (342), represent Laura's connection with Armitage as a disgraceful one, which "contributed as much as any thing to harden the heart of Lady Mary, and to confirm her, instead of the protectrice, the persecutor and oppressor of her daughter and grand-daughter" (343). This last comment is significant, for it makes explicit the role that Lady Mary *should* occupy, but does not. As a mother, Lady Mary should assume the role of "protectrice," but since she has allowed herself to believe all that she has been told about Laura, Lady Mary assumes instead the role of "persecutor and oppressor." Smith's decision to use the feminine form of "protector" also provides an important clue as to the nature of her interests. Lady Mary should be a specifically *female* protector, one whose gender should provide her with the natural desire to help other women. Because Lady Mary has been influenced by the false information she has heard, however, her sentiments have masculinized her, making her into one of her own daughter's worst enemies.

GOSSIP AND THE MARRIAGE MARKET

Lady Mary's treatment of Laura signals not only Smith's disbelief in the ability of one British woman to help another, but also her disenchantment with the system that causes women to behave in such a way in the first place. That is, Smith's analysis of the powerful effects of gossip does not end with just a critique of women who refuse to overlook false claims and help their fellow women; instead, she takes her critique one step further by showing how gossip is linked to the very institutions of the British nation itself. Gossip is a gendered offshoot of the systemic abuses that characterize the British system of governance and human interaction; it is one of the few avenues open to women in which they can exhibit some degree of power and control over others in a nation that gives them precious few means of asserting influence. The gossips in the novel are not simply women who refuse to help, but are instead symptoms of a system whose institutions continually exacerbate division amongst its women.[16] Gossip therefore occupies two important positions within the vision of British society that Smith portrays in her novel: first of all, gossip grants power to women, and, second, it creates envy and jealousy among women because of the strong competition inherent in the marriage market. The most malicious women in the novel—Lady Mary, Mrs. Crewkherne, and Mrs. Grinsted—all refuse to help Laura and Medora either because spreading gossip gives them control or because they have been swayed by a marriage market that relies upon competition among women along class and national lines.

The first role that gossip plays—that of granting power over others—is inherent in the very nature of gossip itself. If we think about how gossip works, we realize that it depends upon the possession (or dispossession) of information. Those in the "we" group that Spacks mentions are in positions of power because they hold information they can use against others.[17] Gossip essentially gives its proponents power over the reputations of others and therefore, indirectly, over those persons they choose to discuss. This power, of course, was particularly important to women during this period since they lacked other means of influence. Gossip was one of the few avenues whereby women could exert control; it gave them power because it made them arbiters over the destinies of other human beings, who happened to be, most often, other women. To look at a very basic example from the novel, even Lady Mary, a woman who occupies a relatively powerful position in society, uses gossip's influence to assert control over her daughter, Laura. When Laura fell in love with Glenmorris against Lady Mary's injunctions years ago, Lady Mary had no way to stop Laura from going through with the marriage. Now that her daughter is believed to be a disgraced woman, however, Lady Mary takes Laura securely in hand, certain that Laura's new state puts her under Lady Mary's jurisdiction. And, although she had earlier refused to acknowledge Laura's ties to her when the issue of the inheritance was ever mentioned, Lady Mary acknowledges her daughter when it reinforces her own power; she asserts her authority over her daughter to give Laura a false identity and to confine her to a madhouse.

More extended discussions of the power of gossip and its connections to social standing also occur throughout the novel. When Delmont's aunt, Mrs. Crewkherne, first learns of her nephew's interest in Medora, for example, she purposely tries to manipulate Delmont's two sisters into thinking that Delmont has made a dishonorable attachment. While explaining Medora's background to the Miss Delmonts, Mrs. Crewkherne "related it with several additions, which her own *candid* imagination failed not to invent; and then putting in the very worst light the future prospects of the family, she lamented the probability there was, that this occasion of securing to it so handsome a fortune as Miss Goldthorp's should be so senselessly lost" (63). Mrs. Crewkherne has long ago given up the hope of marriage for herself, but she recognizes that a marriage between her nephew and Miss Goldthorp would have considerable advantages not just for Delmont, but also for herself. Since money confers a higher social status on its possessors, Delmont's social standing would be raised by allying himself with the heiress, as would her own. Because Mrs. Crewkherne wants Delmont to marry Miss Goldthorp and her £50,000, she maliciously misconstrues Medora's true character, and continues to do so throughout the novel.[18] Gossip is the means whereby Mrs. Crewkherne can achieve her materialistic goals. Yet Mrs. Crewkherne not only uses gossip to attempt to raise her own social position, she also uses it to gain power over others.[19] Later on in the novel, when Armitage decides to confront her about the lies she is spreading, he explains to Delmont that the reason for choosing to become involved through such a confrontation is because of the powerful effects gossip has. Such slander, Armitage emphasizes, is not harmless, but actually destructive: "in this instance, where the character of a blameless, an amiable woman, is traduced—where my affection for my friend, and my consequent protection of his family, is converted by the diabolical malice of an old woman, impotent in every mischief but this, into the means of blasting the fair fame of the wife and child of my friend, and has perhaps been the cause to them of irreparable evils, I must endeavour to stop it" (236). Gossip grants power here by giving those who possess its secrets control. As a woman in late eighteenth-century British society, Mrs. Crewkherne, despite her £18,000, has little power or control over others. Gossip, however, gives Mrs. Crewkherne, a woman "impotent in every mischief but this," power that she otherwise lacks. Through the confabulations of gossip, Mrs. Crewkherne gains power over other women, for through it she possesses the ability to annihilate the "fair fame" of Laura and Medora. Their own claims to respectability and hence protection are jeopardized by Mrs. Crewkherne's attacks on their characters. Gossip therefore empowers its advocates not just indirectly by giving them an increased social standing, but also directly by putting the reputations—and so lives—of others in their hands.

Besides granting women power over other women, the second role gossip plays in the novel has to do with its relevance to the marriage market. As many historians and literary critics have noted, "middle-class" women in the eighteenth century had relatively few options available to them in terms of what roles they could fill within society. Elaborating on these roles, Judith Newton explains just how limited women really were: "Aware that dependency on the family was a burden, subject to ridicule as spinsters, and given almost no options for self support which would not sink them below the rank of gentlewoman, they were constrained to marry."[20] Yet entering into the institution of marriage, we well know, was not as (relatively) simple or as pleasant as it is today. Besides the various economic factors that came into play through entitlements and dowries, women were also subject to intense competition: since women greatly outnumbered men in this period,[21] women were in direct competition with one another in their attempts to "attract" husbands. It is precisely this aspect of the marriage market that comes under Smith's scrutiny in *The Young Philosopher*. Not only does gossip impede the formation of female community through the desire for power that it creates in women, but it also impedes community by giving voice to the competition among them. The marriage market, as well as the financial arrangements that go along with it, forces women to vie for suitable husbands. Gossip thus becomes a powerful weapon in getting rid of the enemy, in blasting the fame—and so future fortune—of a fellow woman. The connection between gossip and the marriage market becomes clear in the novel in Smith's several discussions of Mrs. Grinsted's role in the rumors being passed around about the Glenmorris women. Mrs. Grinsted, we must remember, is the other main gossip in the novel who abets Mrs. Crewkherne in propagating false information. Motivated by some of the same impulses as Mrs. Crewkherne, Mrs. Grinsted derives pleasure in spreading spurious accounts of Laura and Medora. Although Mrs. Grinsted is "naturally malignant," with a "temper selfish and arrogant" (211), much of her anger has an earlier cause, derived from a period in her life when she was a frequent visitor to Lady Mary's residence. On one such visit, Mrs. Grinsted first met Glenmorris, for whom she felt an instant attraction. Glenmorris, however, soon became the object not of her passion, but rather of her hatred, for he rejected Mrs. Grinsted's advances in favor of Laura's charms. Admiration turned to detestation as her emotions overpowered Mrs. Grinsted: "To this masculine, or rather universal propensity to govern, she added one purely feminine—a latent hatred toward Glenmorris because he had not made love to her when he might, but preferred the little baby-faced Laura to her mature and ripened beauties" (343). The situation is further explained:

> she had never forgotten that when Glenmorris was a young man, frequenting the house of Lady Mary, where she was occasionally an inmate, she had

vainly endeavoured to attract his notice, and that he had never shewed . . .
attention to her person, though she was then thought young. . . . She still
bore in mind, that he and Laura were once overheard to turn into ridicule
her supposed attempts to engage the heart of Mr. Vanhugheynbourg . . .
and these recollections were sufficient to add personal hatred to the other
motives, which engaged her to assist in delivering from the importunity of
her daughter, or claims of her grand-daughter, her dear, venerable friend
Lady Mary, from whom she also expected for her services, a very considerable addition to a legacy. . . . [and] like Mrs. Crewkherne, she held it to
be perfectly justifiable to alter, change, or falsify any thing, if the *existing
circumstances* required it. (211–12)

Mrs. Grinsted thus first began to despise Glenmorris when he ignored
her and chose Laura instead, leaving her unmarried and alone. Her rancor is further exacerbated by the mockery she must endure when she
later decides to pursue Mr. Vanhugheynbourg, who also ultimately rejects her in favor of another woman. In both instances, Mrs. Grinsted
loses out in the marriage market, retaining her single status after repeated attempts to gain a husband and thereby a higher social standing.
Spinsterhood is not a sisterhood that Mrs. Grinsted aspires to, but is
instead one that she is forced to belong to.[22]

Gender Reversals and Women in Need

Competition among women in the marriage market and their desire
to gain power over other women thus led British women to abandon
each other in times of need. British patriarchal institutions perpetuate
division, pitting woman against woman in a battle to "win" husbands
and assert authority over those who are less fortunate. Yet Smith does
not stop here with her critique of the British system; she pushes her
analysis even one step further to show her readers how the system
causes both women and men to act in ways that run counter to what
Smith sees as our "true" gendered natures. When individuals adhere to
the belief systems of Britain's institutions, they let those beliefs infiltrate
their gender identity, ultimately influencing behavior patterns for the
worse. Humanitarian principles, which Smith clearly believes are gendered, are left aside in the desire to dominate others. Each time Medora
or Laura encounters another woman in her own attempt to get help,
Smith takes pains to emphasize either that woman's masculine or that
woman's feminine characteristics. The characteristics that woman displays then determines her level of desire to protect her fellow women in

need. This point becomes clearer by looking at a few examples from the novel. Years earlier, shortly after Laura and Glenmorris's marriage, Glenmorris was captured by pirates, and Laura was left completely by herself. Finally forced to live with the Kilbrodie clan, Laura describes the cruel Lady Kilbrodie as "this *unfeminine*, this inhuman woman" (116, emphasis added). Later on, afraid that Lady Kilbrodie might try to poison her, Laura temporarily refuses to eat or drink, until Lady Kilbrodie "with the most *unwomanly* menaces of force" (141, emphasis added) makes her. The reason Lady Kilbrodie is so violent toward Laura, of course, is because the death of Laura and her unborn child would mean the succession of the Glenmorris estate to Lady Kilbrodie's own two sons and the subsequent increase in her own stature (109). Such desires have so dominated her nature that Lady Kilbrodie no longer resembles a woman. When Laura finally escapes from the Kilbrodies, she puts herself under the protection of Lord Macarden and his family. Yet the lord's sister, Mrs. Mackirk, jealous of Laura, does everything she can to make Laura feel unwelcome in their house. She is another unfeminine woman. While the brother demonstrates proper "*manly* politeness" (135, emphasis added) in his behavior toward Laura, the sister demonstrates "*unfeminine* and malicious conduct" (151, emphasis added) because she does not want Laura to marry her brother and usurp her place in his household. When the action is finally brought back to the present day and Laura becomes mad after she discovers that Medora has been kidnapped, it is the kindness of a servant that determines Laura's fate. Laura ends up right outside Lady Mary's doorstep, deliriously ranting about her stolen daughter. Although Lady Mary does not want to take the woman in (whom she does not yet know to be her own daughter), her maid Mrs. Battin shows more compassion and "had probably more *feminine* feelings than her lady," for "she had not the heart to shut the door against a poor lady in distress" (213, emphasis added). Unlike her servant, Lady Mary is devoid of "feminine feelings." When she is finally taken into Lady Mary's house, Laura meets with the worst treatment she has yet received at the hands of Mrs. Grinsted, a woman, we have already seen, who has abhorred Laura ever since Glenmorris chose Laura over herself. During Laura's stay at Lady Mary's, Mrs. Grinsted, she who possesses a "*masculine*, or rather universal propensity to govern" (343, emphasis added), takes pleasure in exacerbating Laura's pain. By insisting that Medora has run off with a lover, Mrs. Grinsted torments her hostess's daughter (209). Laura, of course, has a difficult time believing that anyone, but especially a fellow *woman*, would do such a thing: "Mrs. Glenmorris, however, did not expect—it was not in her nature to suppose it possible, that there could exist in a human form—in the form of a woman—a being, who would feel an horrible and malignant pleasure in aggravating the misery of a mother for the loss of an only child" (208). When Mrs. Grinsted continues to assault Laura's feelings, Laura is again surprised to see such behavior, refusing to believe that a *woman* could be so cruel: "it would be almost incredible that any creature, in the form of a woman, could delight to irritate the anguish of a mother weeping over misfortunes that might be even worse than death" (211). Unused to such treatment by a woman, Laura cannot fathom the idea that a fellow woman could behave in such a way when such behavior seems so much against what she views as woman's very nature.

Medora also meets with similar treatment from similar women. When the law clerk Mr. Darnell kidnaps her and takes her to his mother's house to hide her, Medora pleads with Mr. Darnell's mother to help her escape. Medora's supplication is from one woman to another, for the sake of a third woman: "I call upon you, *as you are a woman,* and I am willing to suppose a gentlewoman, to influence him that I may be restored to my mother" (313, emphasis added). When Mrs. Darnell refuses to help her, however, Medora insults Mrs. Darnell, and meets with the threat of violence: "for a moment she even lifted up a fist, the apparent prowess of which a butcher might have envied" (313). Although Mrs. Darnell is not explicitly called masculine, Medora's comparison leaves little doubt as to Mrs. Darnell's true "nature." A few days later, after she manages to escape from the Darnells, Medora is taken in by a certain Mrs. Crowling, who claims to want to help her. Medora, however, does not trust Mrs. Crowling, for she was "tall and confident, and had a something of a daring and *masculine* air both in her walk and manner, which there is no describing" (327, emphasis added). Unaccountably, Mrs. Crowling troubles Medora, and for good reason, for we soon learn that Mrs. Crowling is an evil woman, one who is paid by a wealthy man to lure young, innocent women to their ruin. Because Medora trusted her instincts, which warned her against this "masculine" woman, she is able to save herself from total devastation.

Each woman who refuses to help Laura or Medora thus exhibits traits that Smith purposely describes as not being in line with the "feminine" traits that Smith assumes are part of woman's nature. Yet these "unnatural" gender traits are exhibited not only by the female characters, but also by the male characters. That is, while Smith's primary concern is an investigation of the causes that impede the creation of community among women, she is also interested in investigating how these gender concerns play out in the interactions not only between women, but also between women and men. I will soon look at how Smith's interest in male gender identity also directly connects with her interest in national identity, but at this point I want to emphasize how Smith also explores the construction of masculinity. When Medora is taken away from her mother by the law clerk who hopes to force her into marriage and thereby become possessor of her fortune, for example, she must seek out protection from those around her. More often than not, however, she meets with insult instead of respect, and abuse instead of assistance from the men she meets. The best example of this occurs when Medora, escaping from her kidnapper, mistakes Delmont's brother, Adolphus, for Delmont himself while she is hiding at an inn. Before approaching the stranger, however, Medora has enough forethought to verify her belief with a servant. When she asks the servant for the name of the man she has seen, Medora hears the name she longs to hear. Forgetting, however, that her George has a brother with whom he shares the name of Delmont, Medora rushes over to the man, knowing that Delmont would, she explains, "afford me that protection which would end my perils and fears" (322). Her mistake, however, soon becomes apparent when Adolphus treats her disgracefully. A re-union with Delmont would have provided Medora with protection, but she instead meets with mortification, insolence, and verbal abuse from his brother. Because he has heard such damaging rumors about her, Adolphus treats Medora as a member of the class to which he believes she belongs: as a prostitute. When Medora tells this story to Delmont, he becomes enraged, but Medora reasons with him, pointing out that Adolphus was only judging by appearances, by the face that the local gossips had put upon their relationship. Medora interprets Adolphus's treatment of her for Delmont:

> You should recollect . . . that your brother knew nothing of me, or that if he had ever heard me mentioned, it was probably in a way very much to my disadvantage. . . . I own I did hope when I explained, or attempted to ex-plain who I was, that I should have found protection from your brother; but I know not why, unless because he had received some false impressions from Mrs. Crewkherne as to my mother and myself, he seemed to disbe-lieve, and to turn into ridicule all I said. (323)

The "false impressions" Adolphus has received have colored his view of Medora, illustrating yet once again the damaging effects that gossip has upon women. Since Adolphus has heard Medora being compared to a prostitute, he treats her as he thinks she should be treated, putting her in a precarious and threatening situation. As Delmont's betrothed, of course, Medora should have found protection from his brother; instead, she finds the worst treatment she has met with so far, treatment that scares her from attempting to journey to London (and hence her mother) by herself. Even the landlady who has thus far aided Medora in her escape now views Medora differently, seeing Adolphus's attitude as a reflection on Medora's character.[23] Forced to leave her temporary asylum, Medora must flee from Adolphus before she meets with further insult from him. His behavior literally threatens her safety.

Although Medora attempts to justify Adolphus's conduct toward her in her conversation with Delmont afterward, Delmont remains upset. Medora might forgive Adolphus, but Delmont cannot, as his reaction to her story makes clear. "Do not attempt to palliate his conduct, Medora," Delmont tells her, "there is no palliation, no excuse; it was cruel, it was unmanly" (323). Delmont's last comment is especially significant, for it brings up an important behavioral distinction: Adolphus's behavior is particularly reprehensible because he does not act as he should—as a man. By tormenting her instead of offering her protection, Adolphus acts not only cruelly, but also "unmanly." This distinction is the key to understanding Smith's own understanding of how women should be treated within British society. By refusing to help a British woman in need of protection, Adolphus defies the gendered role he should play: by molesting instead of aiding a woman, Adolphus himself becomes less than a man. His behavior lies in sharp contrast to that of his brother, Delmont, for while Adolphus reveals himself to be "unmanly," Delmont consistently demonstrates "manly compassion" (74) throughout the novel. Dr. Winslow's son also possesses these same attributes. The primary reason Miss Goldthorp prefers Delmont over young Winslow, in fact, is because Winslow is so "unmanly." Miss Goldthorp had even "sometimes rallied her cousin on his effeminacy, and asserted that he was designed for a woman" (11), whereas she "romantically" envisions Delmont as "an hero sent in her rescue, such as fables feign when they tell of demigods and knights endowed with supernatural powers" (35).

Protection, Gendered Behavior, and Community Formation

All of these scenes, taken together, point to Smith's belief that men and women have certain gendered roles to fill within British society.

Men should be "manly" and women should be "feminine," and when they violate these roles, women end up suffering the most. Protection, for Smith, thus initially seems to depend upon a clear-cut understanding of how men and women should behave within British society.[24] When men (like Delmont's brother, Adolphus) act "unmanly," they hurt innocent women like Medora and leave those women open to further abuse. When women (like Lady Kilbrodie, Mrs. Mackirk, Lady Mary, Mrs. Grinsted, Mrs. Darnell, and Mrs. Crowling) act "unfeminine," they refuse to establish female community with other women. When both men and women believe the false rumors they hear and continue to propagate gossip, they further undercut any sense of connection with their fellow human beings. In contrast, humanitarian principles exist in the "manly compassion" of Delmont, the "manly politeness" of Lord Macarden, the "feminine feelings" of Mrs. Battin, and—in the ultimate act of self-sacrifice in the novel—Miss Cardonnel's decision to give half of the inheritance money to her cousin Medora.[25] These are the instances of human connection that Smith advocates, and her insistence on the gendered nature of such connections reinforces her belief—one shared by so many other women writers of the period— that gender identity unites individuals.[26]

At first glance, then, Smith's characters seem to either adhere or not adhere to her notions of what constitutes "proper" behavior for both men and women, and Smith chastises her characters, and thereby her readers, when they deviate from the path of moral virtue. A closer look at the characters' actions, however, reveals a central paradox that lies underneath the surface of Smith's character portrayals: the paradox that both "feminine" and "manly" behavior really amount to the same thing. In each instance, morally virtuous behavior depends upon compassion, politeness, and sympathy, and yet these are the defining traits not just of "manly" behavior, but of "feminine" behavior as well. If we, as individuals, whether male *or* female, discover a woman in distress, Smith seems to be saying, then we should make every effort to help her as much as we can. Honorable characters of *both* sexes thus share the same moral attributes in their willingness to help the less fortunate, while dishonorable characters (the "unmanly" and "unfeminine") share a love of slanderous talk, comments that demean, and the callous treatment of others. This paradox is a significant one, and it raises an important question that profoundly affects our understanding of the outcome of the novel: if "feminine" and "manly" behavior share the same qualities, then why does Smith choose to locate her definition of what constitutes moral behavior in gendered terms? To answer this question we must look more closely at Smith's belief in the humanitarian principles mentioned above, as well as at her interest in national politics. Smith insists to such a great extent upon the gendered nature of her characters' actions, even though the traits exhibited through those actions are the same in both men and women, because she believes that such positive moral traits are both cross-gender and cross-national. That is, Smith's belief that both the men and women of Britain share the same moral attributes also extends to her belief that people from different nations share the same moral attributes. Just as concerned British men and women display the same traits, so, too, do individuals possess the same natural sympathies, even when they hail from different nations. By emphasizing that British men and women behave the same way, Smith underscores her belief in the transnational nature of human emotions. Her beliefs about gender identity are ultimately closely wrapped up with her beliefs on national identity.

Smith's emphasis on national identity and transnationalism is worth noting, for both concepts underlie the action of the last half of the novel and become, in fact, Smith's hope for the future. As I have argued, Smith spends a great deal of time in the early and middle parts of the novel exploring the possibility of female community before finally dismissing the idea as unfeasible given the current state of British society and the unjust nature of its institutions. Female community would seem to be a woman's best hope in a nation that otherwise leaves her without much protection, but such community is thwarted by the envy, jealousy, and spite that Britain's institutions spawn amongst its women. Since female community does not seem possible, Smith turns in the latter half of the novel to an exploration of an alternative form of community, not just one that would unite women amongst themselves, but rather one that would unite both men and women together. That alternative form of community is none other than national identity, which Smith looks to, with utopic vision, as the best way to forge connections between humans. National identity is, after all, a way of connecting with others. It is, according to Gerald Newman's definition, "the distinctive pattern of traits more or less commonly shared by all members of a culture, hence a pattern of enculturation, hence a common history."[27] It is this sense of commonality that underscores Smith's nationalist project in the concluding pages of *The Young Philosopher*. Since British society reeks of corruption and antipathy, Smith must look outside her own nation to find a solution to her grievances.

AMERICA AS DOMESTIC UTOPIA

Before she can establish her claims about the commonality of national identity, however, Smith must first demonstrate to her readers that British society is corrupt when compared to nations like America, and this is why she spends a great deal of time developing the differences between the British and American nations. Again, like other women writers of the period, Smith linked gender concerns with national concerns to advocate reform not only for women, but also for men. In her previous novels, British society was corrupt, but not so corrupt that the potential for change did not exist. Smith still possessed hope. In *The Young Philosopher*, however, Britain is a land so full of abuse that little chance for reform exists.[28] Even the French Revolution, which held the promise of regeneration for Britain, has turned into an event of violence and chaos. Yet Smith does not completely give up. Although her own country and that of the French have disappointed her, America still holds possibility. America, in fact, substitutes for the role that France played in *Desmond*, as the land with the most promising outlook for the future. Smith essentially fashions America into a political and social utopia, which she had never done with France in any of her previous texts.[29] As Angela Keane points out, "America provides the setting, or at least the projected setting, for the most Utopian ending of any of Smith's novels."[30] Smith had, of course, discussed life in America in 1793's novel *The Old Manor House*, but only in regard to the Revolutionary War. In this earlier novel, her hero Orlando fights on the side of the Americans, but returns afterward to Britain. In *The Young Philosopher*, glimpses of America show us vistas of uncompromising majesty and force. In her many conversations with Delmont and her mother, for instance, Medora returns again and again to comparisons of what life was like before coming to Britain, almost making it her motif. Her complaints center around the idea that her family was always completely happy until they left their home. In America, she tells her mother, "we had always enough for our wishes. . . . We may be very happy again, if we determine to hasten back to America, and think no more about [the lawsuit]" (192). When Laura determines to pursue the lawsuit, Medora can only note the toll that this pursuit is taking upon her mother. Each day, Laura returns home tired and worn out from her meetings with the lawyers. As Medora later tells Delmont, "for almost the first time in my life I heard her complain, and repent that in coming to England she had sacrificed substantial happiness to the pursuit of a chimera, which, even if it could be attained, was not worth one year, nay, not one month, of the tranquil happiness and domestic comfort we had known in America" (301). Life in America is full of "tranquil happiness and domestic comfort," of the joys that accompany a stable and fruitful home life. Medora's representation of America essentially fashions it into a domestic utopia. Since coming to Britain, however, this stable existence has been shattered. Medora bemoans her situation to Delmont at greater length:

> Why did my father ever suffer himself to be persuaded to send us to England to engage in it [the lawsuit]?—We never had these hateful perplexities in America.—My mother never lost her spirits there, and sunk into dejection as she does here!—Of what use will this money be to me if I should get it, if my mother loses her health and cheerfulness to obtain it? Oh! that we had never left America! . . .
>
> . . . were it not for you [Delmont] England would be utterly intolerable to me,—I never recollect a moment's uneasiness till I came to England, and since I have been here I am sure I have felt a great deal . . . but I know not how it is, the pleasure of our country rambles here, or the more agreeable hours of study, which would have charms as great as I used to find in the same occupations in America, are now always dashed by something which embitters our delight—Politics, and lawsuits, and old ladies finding out that we are people of bad character, and gossips repeating the malignant nonsense of other gossips—Oh! my dear Delmont, if ever I should belong to you, take me, take me, to America! (154)

Passages such as this one create the image of America as a utopia in the novel, a place where life is idyllic and where nothing can go wrong. In Britain, in contrast, something is always going wrong. Even when trying to forget her worries through the pursuit of her favorite pastimes, Medora finds her pleasure interrupted through politics, lawsuits, old ladies, and the self-perpetuating chain of gossip.

Glenmorris shares his daughter's enthusiasm for America. One of our earliest views of life in America, in fact, comes to us through Glenmorris, who relates to Laura what happened when the pirates who kidnapped him first took him to this new continent. America's inhabitants, he explains, were unlike those of any other nation he had ever been to:

> I was now among a new race of people—a people who with manners, customs, and general habits of thinking quite unlike my own, had one great and predominant feature in their character which I loved and honoured—they were determined to be *free*, and were now making the noblest exertions to resist what they deemed oppression. I found that with a few of them the inveterate hatred generated by the unnatural war they had been driven into,

> extended to me, merely because I was an Englishman, or, what was the
> same thing to them, a Scotsman; but in others the noble flame of liberty
> seemed to have purified their minds from very narrow and unmanly preju-
> dice, and when they found that my heart beat in unison with theirs, when
> they heard me declare that, Englishman as I was, I would never have drawn
> my sword against men struggling in that glorious cause . . . they forgot that
> I was born a Briton, a North Briton too, . . . and embraced me as a brother.
> (148)

Although the American sensibility is quite different from his own,
Glenmorris finds commonality in their shared desire to live their lives
free from oppression and prejudice. Although he is a Briton, the Americans welcome him "as a brother," as one united with them in their fight
against tyranny. Significantly, national identity is lost in the mutual dislike of injustice, just as gender difference was earlier lost in a desire to
help Laura and Medora. Glenmorris and his new friends—strangers to
"unmanly prejudice"—embrace as *men* and as *brothers,* rather than as
members of different nations, or, significantly, different families.
America is a place where national difference, and hence national prejudice, is lost, and this is a sign of its people's freedom.

Throughout the novel, these scenes of idyllic life in America are contrasted with scenes of British superficiality and prejudice. The injustices
present in Britain do not exist in America. When Glenmorris looks
around him in London,

> he envied no one, but rather beheld with wonder the toil and fatigue which
> were incurred to make a splendid appearance at such immense expence as
> would have supported in America fifty families in more real comfort and
> plenty. . . .
>
> To cultivate the earth of another continent . . . had in it a degree of sub-
> limity, which . . . sunk the petty politics and false views so eagerly pursued
> in Europe, into something more despicable than childish imbecility. . . .
> When he reflected on the degradation to which those must submit, who
> would make what is called a figure in this country; that they must sacrifice
> their independence, their time, their taste, their liberty, to etiquette, to forms
> and falsehoods, which would to him be insupportable, he rejoiced that he
> had made his election where human life was in progressive improvement.
> (299)

Glenmorris's critique of Britain centers around a dichotomy between
that which is trivial and petty and that which is meaningful and substantial. In his analysis, British men and women of fashion waste an
extravagant amount of money and energy on making a fine figure. Yet

such expenditure forces Britons to give up their independence and liberty as they become enslaved to empty and meaningless forms. The sense of sufficiency that most fashionable Britons think they enjoy finds its basis in nothing other than superficial customs, without lasting value. In contrast, Americans lead a more substantial life, one with "*real* comfort and plenty,*"* and Glenmorris's own decision to farm the earth of a "new" continent carries with it "a degree of sublimity." Glenmorris made the decision to live a rural life closely in touch with the land and, as a result, also closely in touch with his family. Through his own manual work, Glenmorris, we can assume, was able to provide for his family, essentially retaining the independence that the Britons have given up. Life in Europe—banal, shallow, and petty—fails in comparison.

Besides offering another comparison of life in America and life in Britain, this passage also brings up one of Smith's most important claims about nations and national identity in the novel, and that is the idea of *choice*. Because he cannot be happy with the way things are in Britain, Glenmorris "made his election where human life was in progressive improvement." Essentially, Glenmorris has chosen to leave his homeland to seek a new life in America. The radicalism of such an act becomes apparent when we realize that Glenmorris has not just become an American, but has renounced his own nation in so doing.

ACTS AND INSTANCES OF NATIONAL IDENTITY

Before delving further into the significance of Smith's proposition, however, now is a good time to step back momentarily and consider the extent to which issues of national identity inform the novel. One of the most striking aspects of *The Young Philosopher* is, in fact, how much it resonates with acts and instances of national identity. In *Desmond*, a few of the characters are non-British (in particular, French), but none possess a dual or conflicted national identity; all of the characters claim either a completely French or a completely British nationality.[31] Nationalism and (its concomitant emotion) prejudice are Smith's focus, and national identity is just not an issue. In *The Young Philosopher*, on the other hand, national identity becomes a concern with most of the main characters; the novel is, above all, as I said in the opening of this chapter, an exploration of what it means to be a member of a nation and to hold a particular national identity. Since, as we have seen, Smith must dismiss the idea of female community as a way to unite women, she must look elsewhere for unity, and she finds that common bond through national identity. As the various subnarratives unfold, glimpses of national identity emerge, never overtly, but still always there. National identity is not an issue that Smith's narrator dwells upon, but it nevertheless surfaces as an essential component of each individual's unique character. Slyly and subtly, Smith sneaks descriptions of her characters' national affiliations into the novel as a way, we shall soon see, to justify her larger project of choice.[32]

Each time an issue of national identity appears, however, it startles us since it at first seems so unrelated to the action of the novel. When we first learn about Delmont's education, for instance, we find out that Delmont's mother was his primary teacher, and that she was a woman who took care to instill in him just and rational principles.[33] Her method for so doing was to teach him about other nations and other philosophies through what Mrs. Crewkherne derogatorily calls "the nonsensical schemes of some wicked aetheistical French or German writer" (63). Mrs. Crewkherne's comment, of course, reveals only her own ignorance and narrow-mindedness, for she does not even know the name of the particular writer to which she refers. Later on in the novel, we hear an account of Delmont's education that has much more of good sense in it. When Glenmorris gives his approval to the marriage of Medora and Delmont in a letter to Laura, he recognizes Delmont's noble character and intelligent mind, noting that he would not have granted his consent if Delmont had possessed anything less. In his letter, Glenmorris makes it clear that he never would have consented to letting his daughter marry anyone who did not possess a transnational, nonlocalized identity, as Delmont does:

> Of an ordinary character . . . of one of those men who cannot exist without the accommodations, the luxuries, the frivolous amusements of London or Paris, I know this would be asking a great sacrifice: but it is not to the fastidious fine man of the day I give my child; it is to a citizen of the world; to one divested not only of local prejudice, but I hope of all prejudices; to him, who can live wherever his fellow men can live; to him who can enjoy the spectacle of a new continent rising into a great state by its cultivators. . . . Such a man, I know from his letters, and from your account of him, Delmont is. (169)

What Glenmorris most admires about his future son-in-law is that Delmont's upbringing has made him not into a presumptuous bigot (a "fastidious fine man of the day"), but rather into a thinking, rational being—a "citizen of the world," and so of all nations and times. Because he is "divested" of all prejudices, Delmont is not bound to any one nation or place; his national identity is nonfixed and flexible, and this attribute adds to his personal integrity. Glenmorris clearly sets a high value on the transnational mind frame of Delmont.

Laura's story is also one where national identity plays a significant role. When she first begins to tell her story to Delmont, she never mentions her national affiliation, and so the reader, like Delmont, has no reason to question it or to assume that Laura is anything other than English. In fact, her mother, Lady Mary, dislikes Glenmorris not just because he is poor and without social standing, but also because he is Scottish, and, we would presume, because Laura is English. As Laura progresses in her narrative, however, we unexpectedly discover that she lays claim to a much broader national heritage herself. After Glenmorris had been abducted by the pirates, we must remember, the Kilbrodies lock the pregnant Laura away, refusing her multiple requests to contact her family back home in England. When she realizes that Lady Kilbrodie and her son are purposely trying to make her miscarry her child, Laura is able to resist their depraved attempts because she holds on to the secret of her national identity. She details Lady Kilbrodie's actions in her narration to Delmont:

> As the time of my lying-in approached, she caused the superstitions of the country to be brought forward, to alarm me with ideas of danger and dread of death.
>
> Sometimes portentous sounds were heard in the air; and at others the corpse candle was seen to go from my chamber to the burial ground of the abbey. The cry of an English bogie or sprite was heard, intimating the death of a person of that nation—but that was rather a miscalculation on the part of those who directed this machinery, for I was not only *not* a native of England, having been born at Florence, but I had never been naturalized. This, however, the *graunie* did not know; though it helped me to repress such fears as might have arisen from the "cry of an English ghaist!" (112)

Lady Kilbrodie's plan to frighten Laura into miscarrying her baby inadvertently backfires on her because she is unaware of Laura's true national identity. Assuming that Laura is English because she comes from England, Lady Kilbrodie causes the sounds of "an English bogie or sprite" to echo near the house. Since she is by birth Florentine, however, Laura is able to draw strength from these hoaxes, knowing that the cries are artificial. No further explanation, though, is ever offered as to why Laura was born in Italy or as to why Lady Mary—a stickler for the rules and customs of English society—never had her younger daughter naturalized. Smith introduces the topic only to let it fall again, but it occurs early enough to stay with us throughout most of the novel, letting us know that Laura is not really English and that she retains no strong ties to any one nation—until, that is, she goes to America. Her national identity is essentially in flux. Laura's place of birth is thus revealed to us in an insignificant manner, but one that has important consequences since her birthplace ends up saving her life and prolonging the life of her unborn child.

Like her mother, Medora also possesses an ambiguous national identity. Although we assume that Medora is American, having been born and raised there, her identity is open to question. Many characters do not trust her, in fact, because she possesses what they see as an unstable national identity.[34] When we first meet Medora through the gossiping tongue of Mrs. Crewkherne, for instance, Medora seems to be French. She and her mother, after all, live "after a sort of French way" (40) and their French-speaking servant teaches their new English servant to make "strange [French] dishes" (41) for them. Yet as Mrs. Crewkherne learns more about Medora, she discovers that Medora comes from America. This is precisely why Mrs. Crewkherne does not like Delmont's young lover, for the older woman, like many of the other foolish characters in the novel, is prejudiced against all things American, even though she does not know what life is really like in this new nation. When her friend Mrs. Nixon first informs Mrs. Crewkherne of Medora's existence and of Delmont's attachment to her, Mrs. Crewkherne gasps her surprise: "Marry an American girl, who may be a stroller for aught he can tell!—Here in the very face of his family, and next door almost to *me* and to his sisters! Here, on the very spot where his family, inferior to none in England, have been the very first people since the conquest?" (41). The irony of Mrs. Crewkherne's comment, of course, is that Delmont's family, which she praises as being so very "English" in nature, is actually French in origin, planted in Britain only since the Norman Conquest.[35] Her inability to notice this foreign genesis of the Delmont family attests to the very sort of narrow-mindedness that Smith ridicules in many of her novels. Yet Mrs. Crewkherne's myopic vision of national identity is, unfortunately, also shared by other characters in the novel. The gossip Mrs. Nixon, for instance, also fears individuals with a non-British identity. When she first discovers that Delmont has feelings for Medora, Mrs. Nixon's worst fear is not that Delmont might marry beneath him, but rather that Delmont might marry someone with a different national identity, a viewpoint that Smith once again takes care to satirize. The possible marriage, Mrs. Nixon warns, is a "national concern for nothing can be worse than for great families to

demean themselves by low alliances, and especially with folks not properly born according to the laws of England—and then an American
too!—a race that for my part seem to me not to belong to Christian
society somehow. . . . I am assured that they are excessive bad people,
and that it is a dangerous thing to have any communication with them"
(41). Although Mrs. Nixon spreads such gossip to purposely exacerbate and frustrate her "friend" Mrs. Crewkherne, she still believes such
things herself. Marriage with an American thus becomes a "national
concern" of the utmost importance, a threat against Delmont's "British"
heritage.

Throughout the novel, however, Medora is never just referred to—
plain and simply—as an "American." At various points, Medora becomes this "Caledonian-American" (72) who hails from "the wilds of
America" (73), a "fair American" (73), a "little American" (163), a "fascinating yankey" (163), a "little Yanky" (264), a "pretty" or "fair" Co-
lumbian (156, 265), a "Columbina" (167), "a sad little vagabond girl
from the rebel Americans" (165), "that American" (255), a "young
squaw from the wilds of America" (265), and "George's American girl"
(256).[36] While it is true that Delmont's brother Adolphus concocts most
of these epithets, the point is that Medora is never just simply an American: there is something else about her that Adolphus cannot quite put
his finger on. The issue reaches a pinnacle when Adolphus asks their
sister Louisa about the whereabouts of Medora, making a significant
query: "has nothing happened lately in regard to that girl, that American, that, *what is she?*" (255, emphasis added).

The final element of Adolphus's question— *"what is she?"*—resonates
throughout the novel since those who do not know Medora well are
unsure of who or what she is.[37] Medora possesses an unstable national
identity, which makes characters like Adolphus and Mrs. Crewkherne
mistrust her. As readers, though, we are privy to more information than
the gossips who spread allegations without even knowing the people to
whom they attribute such scandals. We soon learn—in passing, and,
again, without much emphasis—the answer to Adolphus's question, or
at least part of it. Medora, we find out, is actually Swiss by birth, and
so is not really a native American at all.[38] Years ago, when Laura and
Glenmorris first decided to leave for America, they made Switzerland,
which is itself the ultimate locale for split identities, a stopping-off place.
"At Lausanne, where we resided near two years," Laura reveals to Delmont, "Medora was born, and is thus, like her mother, a foreigner in
this country" (152). Laura emphasizes that mother and daughter are
connected by their shared lack of connection to England: their differ-

ence further unites them. As Delmont learns more about his betrothed and the many talents she now possesses as a result of her expansive education, we also discover that Medora speaks several languages: "Having learned to lisp her first accents in Switzerland, the French was in some degree her native tongue; and the servant who had brought her up, and had attended Glenmorris and his wife to America, being of that country, and still remaining with them; the French language as being most familiar to the whole house, was that in which their domestic conversations were always carried on.—There were few Englishmen so well acquainted with the Italian as Glenmorris, and he had taken great pains to teach it to Medora" (170). We learn here of Medora's language capacities in detail, yet never hear anything else about them afterward. As with Laura's Florentine birth, Medora's multinational background is an issue that Smith de-emphasizes, but one that she still chooses to include. Such information could just as easily have been left out of the novel, since it so far seems to add little to our understanding of the narrative—or, the question then becomes, does it?

HOME IS WHERE THE HEART IS: NATIONAL IDENTITY AS CHOICE

It is, in fact, at the end of the novel that all of these earlier instances of fluctuating national identity, including some not mentioned here,[39] as well as their connection to the idea of female community, become clear. It is at this point that we return, then, to the idea of election that Glenmorris had earlier mentioned and to Smith's larger project of choice. These moments of unstable national identity emerge in the novel in what at first appears to be a haphazard manner. Once we recognize Smith's belief that individuals are free to choose their own nation and hence their own national identity, however, these moments suddenly coalesce into a unified picture of how Smith envisions national identity. When Armitage confronts the gossip Mrs. Crewkherne about her meddling in the Glenmorris family's affairs, for example, one of the more interesting points he brings up in his argument is that being a democrat does not mean opposing his own nation. "I respect the established government of my country," Armitage declares, "and never disturb it. If I could not live contented under it, I would go to another" (247). The significant part of his statement is the last half: if he were truly unhappy in England, then he would not hesitate to leave. Glenmorris shares his friend's view. When Glenmorris first convinces Laura to elope with him, for instance, he urges her to imagine a life outside of England.

"The great fortune your father has amassed makes him look on mine as a contemptible nothing; and it is true that in this country it would not enable me to live as well as his maitre d'hotel," he tells her, "—But, Laura, we are not confined to this country!" (89). Life in Scotland would enable the couple to live happily and well. The two Glenmorris women, we have already seen, have also left their countries of origin in order to live their lives as Americans. Although their respective birth-places—Florence and Switzerland—were strongholds of democracy, republicanism, and political freedom during the eighteenth century, Smith still chooses to have them become American citizens to demon-strate the importance of choice in national identity. Nationality, the place of one's birth, Smith maintains, is merely an accident of time and place; national identity, the national group with which one chooses to identify him or herself, on the other hand, is a choice that each individ-ual must make after weighing the advantages and disadvantages of be-longing to a particular nation. Being a Florentine or Swiss citizen might have its merits, but being an American has more. For Laura and Med-ora, choosing a national identity also has the built-in advantage of allowing for connection; British women might refuse them aid, but they will always be welcome in America. National identity thus substitutes for the lack of female community in British society, allowing for individ-uals to connect with one another.

Hints of this claim therefore appear throughout the novel, but it is not until the novel's close that the claim materializes in its full form. The strongest argument in favor of having the option to leave one's native land, in fact, occurs at the very end of the novel, once the Glenmorris family is finally reunited. In a conversation between himself and Armi-tage, Glenmorris explains once again that he chose life in America be-cause he was tired of Britain's abuses. Yet the new and most striking part of his argument—one that we have not heard developed so far, besides the small hints mentioned above—is that a person's country is the place where that person is surrounded by his or her loved ones. Glenmorris's decision to permanently leave his native land was spurred on by Britain's treatment of him:

> "If I have those I love with me," said he, "is not every part of the globe equally my country? And has not this, which you are pleased to call my native land, thrown me from her bosom when I *might* have served her? Did she leave me any choice between imprisonment and flight? Now, averse from the means by which political power and influence can be obtained, and without a fortune to live but in continual pecuniary difficulties, why should I ask an asylum of this haughty mother country for my declining days? . . .

> . . . I do not love to be in a country where I am made to pay very dear for advantages which exist not but in idea. I do not love to live where I see a frightful contrast between luxury and wretchedness; where I must daily witness injustice I cannot repress, and misery I cannot relieve." (351)

In a decision that parallels Laura's choice to permanently remove herself from the house of her own "haughty mother," Glenmorris chose to leave Britain since Britain had already chosen to cast him off: "Did she leave me any choice . . . ?" he asks. Ironically, he chose to make America his new home only because Britain had already made that choice for him; if he had stayed in England, he would have been jailed for crimes he did not commit. Glenmorris continues his argument by painting a picture of an England dominated by figures of the poor and miserable, of those who have been persecuted for not being part of a higher social standing and for not possessing wealth. Glenmorris expands upon his critique of England, saying, "can I love to live in such a country only because I drew my first breath in a remote corner of it? No. . . . wherever a thinking man enjoys the most uninterrupted domestic felicity, and sees his species the most content, *that* is his country" (352). Just because Glenmorris was born on the island of Britain does not mean that he should be content with living there. Domestic happiness, being with "those I love," ranks as the most significant reason for choosing to belong to a nation. His decision to become an American, a process Laura describes as "his metamorphose from a Scottish chieftain to an American farmer" (152), is a natural one. Glenmorris chooses life in his "adopted country" (352) since life in Britain is intolerable to him.

The fact that Armitage, Glenmorris, Laura, and Medora, and even Delmont,[40] choose their nation and thus their national identity marks them as informed and knowledgeable individuals. We are meant to read their decision as an honorable one, since such a decision is presented as rational and just within the pages of the novel. In direct contrast to the Glenmorris group's decision to choose, however, is the decision of a marginal group that makes a brief, but significant, appearance. That other group is the band of pirates who kidnap Glenmorris just after he and Laura marry. Although their appearance is brief, the pirates have a considerable role in developing Smith's claims about national identity. When Glenmorris tells Laura about his life with the pirates, for instance, he focuses on the pirates' motley makeup: "The men who plundered our house . . . were a crew of an American privateer, or rather of a large vessel fitted out at Morlaix, under the American colours, but commanded by an English outlaw, and manned by English, American, Scotch, Irish, Portuguese, and even three or four Genoese sailors; they were literally a party of buccaniers, holding themselves accountable to no government, and ready to use their arms against all" (146). Pirates, we must remember, occupied a marginal role in the British imagination during this period. Although most of Europe's pirates hailed from Britain, historian Hugh F. Rankin notes, most of them "prey[ed] not only on foreign commerce, but on the shipping of the nation that had used them in a time of crisis and had then tossed them aside with so little concern for their future."[41] As former British seamen who were no longer valuable outside of a military context, the pirates felt they had been badly treated by their own nation, a sentiment not unlike that felt by Glenmorris. That these originally British pirates constituted a group outside of the nation made them particularly discomforting to Britons. Referring to a number of eighteenth-century piracy trials, for instance, Anna Neill concludes that in each case, "it is the rootlessness of pirates, their willful renunciation of all national ties, that constitutes the primary offense against the law of nature."[42] The American buccaneers, a group like that which took Glenmorris away to this new nation, were especially charged with "nationless barbarism," since "according to sailors' law, having passed the tropic, they had left behind all their former obligations to the state, as well as to their families."[43] The pirates who kidnap Glenmorris have also left aside these national and familial obligations. Although an American man commissions the pirates and the ship sails "under the American colours," Glenmorris emphasizes that things are not what they seem. The ship is not really American or even French, just "fitted out at Morlaix," since the men on board refuse to choose a national affiliation. Being composed of sailors from many nations and regions, however, does not in itself signify the wrong; after all, America itself claims a similar makeup. What does signify the wrong is that the men refuse to hold themselves "accountable" to a particular government, and so remain enemies to all. The pirates' choice is to choose no national identity at all, and Smith clearly sees this as wrong. Without a national identity, the pirates can only be isolated aggressors, literally living on the outskirts of society because they refuse to be affiliated with a nation. When individuals do not identify with a nation, they become marauders and murderers, willing to abandon all laws to plunder and steal, never fitting in anywhere.

Throughout the novel, then, we encounter these instances where national identity becomes an issue, albeit seemingly a minor one. Yet the full significance of all these moments of fluctuating national identity only becomes clear when we see that they function to prepare us for the radical claim that Glenmorris makes at the end of the novel. Although earlier in *The Young Philosopher* Glenmorris had hinted at the idea of *election* in national identity, that hint takes a dominant place in the close of the novel in Glenmorris's and Armitage's extensive discussion of life in Britain and America. In her earlier novels, Smith believed that Britons could reform their nation by noticing the abuses that their system allowed. In *The Young Philosopher,* Smith no longer held out hope. Whereas the conclusion of Desmond's story leaves our hero happy within England (although living with his small, utopic group in the isolated countryside), the conclusion of Delmont's story leaves our hero and his coterie secure in the knowledge that happiness can only be found when one chooses one's own nation. For the women in the novel, this realization is especially significant, for it allows them to establish connections in the wake of rejection from other (British) women. Hoping to find that women could connect as part of a female community, Smith must ultimately dismiss this idea as impossible, accepting national identity instead as the most common bond among individuals. Delmont, Laura, Medora, Glenmorris, and even Armitage may thus all have been born within the geographical confines of a particular nation (whether that nation be England, the Italian provinces, Switzerland, or Scotland), but their national identity is a part of their identity that they are free to determine for themselves. The flexibility they all earlier displayed is what allows them to make this choice: if they had imagined they were rigidly tied to one nation, they would never have realized they could adopt the national identity of their preference. For Smith's characters, therefore, the place of one's birth does not create one's national identity; national identity is determined not by where one was born, but rather by where one *chooses* to live.

In the early 1790s, Smith's primary concern was to argue for reform within her own nation, but by the late 1790s she no longer possessed such hope for change. By that point, the Britain that Smith portrayed in her novels was a land of corrupt politicians and lawyers, and also of gossiping women who refused to help their fellow women in need. Britain was a dangerous land in 1798, one that, for Smith, had become even more prejudiced during the backlash against the French Revolution. America was where the future lay, and Smith advocated expatriation and the choosing of one's national identity as the only remedy for life in an intolerant and abusive nation. What is ultimately important for Smith is not what nation one comes from, but rather how and where one forges community with other human beings. An individual—whether man *or* woman—is at home when and where he or she finds loved ones near. For Smith, home is where the heart is.

4

Mary Wollstonecraft's Nation-Building Project

MARY WOLLSTONECRAFT'S TWO MOST FAMOUS TEXTS WERE WRITTEN within two years of one another, during a period of intense political and social turmoil in Wollstonecraft's own country as well as abroad. The first of these two treatises—1790's *A Vindication of the Rights of Men*—was written to counter Edmund Burke's version of the French Revolution, while the second treatise—1792's *A Vindication of the Rights of Woman*—was written to counter the various claims made about women's "proper" position within society by the most prominent male educational writers of the day.[1] These facts, of course, are common knowledge to any reader of Wollstonecraft, and both texts have received much critical attention during the past 200 years. Shortly after writing the *Vindications*, however, Wollstonecraft began work on two texts more closely related to the French Revolution, younger siblings that have, over the years, remained in the shadow of their elders since Wollstonecraft's two greatest works have garnered most of the critical attention. Although relatively ignored, however, her two French texts provide important insights into Wollstonecraft's political doctrines, shedding new light on her theories of both gender and national identity. Begun in 1793, *Letter on the Present Character of the French Nation* lays out Wollstonecraft's larger project of "sketching"[2] the French character for her British readers. The following year, in 1794, she completed the much longer *Historical and Moral View of the Origin and Progress of the French Revolution; and the Effect it has produced in Europe,* which chronicles the early years of this momentous event.[3]

Within a short five-year time span, then, Wollstonecraft concentrated her energy on exploring the implications of men's rights, potential changes in women's education and social status, and the development of the French Revolution, all in response to the French issuance of the *Droits de l'Homme*. We know that Wollstonecraft's writing about gender and political rights grew out of a period of intense intellectual fermentation, but the connection to her nationalist beliefs has not yet been fully

145

explored.[4] Since gender and the nation shared space in her thoughts, however, it was only a matter of time before these topics would begin to influence each other. Her ideas about gender and nationalism would particularly intertwine, mutually forming and feeding off one another in what could be described as an almost symbiotic relationship. Gender and the nation were both foremost concerns of hers, and Wollstonecraft, like so many of her female contemporaries, borrowed the language and beliefs of nationalism to make explicit her views about women's role within British society. Wollstonecraft's work in these texts can, in fact, be read as a cycle of influence: the commencement of the French Revolution inspired her to write about women's issues, and then women's issues inspired her to write more about nations. That is, the fact that she wrote the two *Vindications* in reaction to the French Revolution shows that the idea of nations influenced her writing and beliefs about gender politics, for the political changes going on in France encouraged her to reflect upon the situation of women within her own nation. Merging her feminist agenda with her nationalist one, Wollstonecraft also attacked those aspects of identity that weakened what she conceived of as a particularly pro-British and masculine morality. United in Wollstonecraft's mind by vanity, an extreme love of pleasure, and excessive emotion, British women and the French people are particularly weak exemplars of the moral standard that she advocates. In her representations of both groups, Wollstonecraft also dwells on the "effeminating" identity traits they share. Her arguments about why women should be more rationally educated and more compassionately treated are thus remarkably similar to her ideas about why the French should also be treated the same way. They share her concern, and she approaches their situations from a similar perspective. Gender and national identity resemble one another in surprising ways in Wollstonecraft's texts, and yet her ultimate goal is to move both groups toward a masculine, British morality—one firmly grounded in nationalist beliefs and best personified in the form of an ideal male British subject.

Vanity, Pleasure, and Emotion:
Linking British Women and the French

Before looking more carefully at the ways in which Wollstonecraft links gender identity and national identity, it is important to look first at the connections Wollstonecraft created between her fellow countrywomen and all French people. By comparing Wollstonecraft's discussion of British women's characters as she presents them in *A Vindication of the Rights of Woman* with her discussion of the French national character as she presents it in her French texts, it becomes clear that Wollstonecraft thought of the two groups in a similar fashion. That is, Wollstonecraft's portrayal of the current state of British women and their morals is almost identical to her portrayal of the current state of the French and their morals (or lack thereof), for the French, I would like to argue, have replaced women as Wollstonecraft's primary interest by 1792. In particular, those aspects of the French national identity that irritate her the most are the same that irritate her the most about her own countrywomen: both groups share vain natures, an excessive love of pleasure, and extreme emotions.[5] These three traits have led to the weakened condition of both groups, but Wollstonecraft has a plan to make lasting changes for both.

Vanity is the first of the ties that bind British women to their Gallic neighbors, and Wollstonecraft spends a great deal of time pointing out how both groups share this particular character flaw. Members of both groups are united in their desire to beautify their persons and set themselves off to their best possible advantage. Looking and behaving in a particular way is what motivates British women in particular to neglect their duties as mothers and wives. A typical woman, Wollstonecraft despairs, "has enough to think of to adorn her body and nurse a weak constitution" than to look after her children or to attend to their needs.[6] Women are essentially vain coquettes, interested only in how prettily they are dressed or how they can best set off their beauty. "Taught from their infancy that beauty is woman's sceptre," Wollstonecraft explains, "the mind shapes itself to the body, and, roaming around a gilt cage, only seeks to adorn its prison" (*VRW* 44). The education in beauty that women receive teaches them not only to devalue their own educations, but also to spend an inordinate amount of time and energy on making themselves as attractive as possible. Adorning their "prisons" thus leads them to an extreme interest in keeping abreast of the latest fashions: "Ignorance and the mistaken cunning that nature sharpens in weak heads as a principle of self-preservation, render women very fond of dress, and produce all the vanity which such a fondness may naturally be expected to generate, to the exclusion of emulation and magnanimity" (*VRW* 186). Superficiality replaces any depth or magnitude of feeling, as women become more concerned with living beautiful, rather than meaningful, lives.

The French people share these vain tendencies. In her *Letter*, Wollstonecraft briefly touches on this issue when she claims, "Their chief enjoyment, it is true, rises from vanity" (*Letter* 443). In the *Historical and Moral View*, Wollstonecraft elaborates on this character trait even further, claiming that vanity is "the national foible" of the French, and that it must be "insisted upon . . . [that] frenchmen are the vainest men living."[7] Yet this character trait has led to more serious consequences in the French nation than it has among her own women, for Wollstonecraft traces the current political situation to their vanity, arguing that "the disasters of the nation have arisen from the same miserable source of vanity, and the wretched struggles of selfishness" (*Historical* 144). Even the Revolutionaries, she claims, are motivated by a much greater share of vanity than we would otherwise think, for many of their actions are performed to make names for themselves, rather than to do good for the French nation.[8] To offer proof of this, Wollstonecraft refers to the night when the National Assembly first decided to draft a Declaration of Rights. Instead of rejoicing in the decision they had made, the Assembly members also decided to permanently mark the occasion: "And then, not forgetting their national character, it was proposed, that a medal should be struck in commemoration of this night" (*Historical* 139). Wollstonecraft is obviously irritated with such an action, which she attributes to the French people's desire to regale their own actions, and believes that such vanity is closely connected to the French people's love of the theatrical. As Wollstonecraft notes, "Nothing can equal the fondness which the french suck in with their milk for public places, particularly the theatre. . . . Their national character is, perhaps, more formed by their theatrical amusements, than is generally imagined: they are in reality the schools of vanity" (*Historical* 25).[9] The breast-feeding imagery that Wollstonecraft uses here calls attention to the "naturalness" of this national characteristic, a characteristic that is, however, only further nourished by constant exposure to the theater.[10] This love for the theater even carries over into the French people's approach toward political events; "Such in fact was the inconstancy of a people, always running after theatrical scenes" that at one point they even denounced financial minister Necker in one part of Paris while they celebrated him in another (*Historical* 133). The royal family particularly engages in this love of performance, and to prove this Wollstonecraft spends a great deal of time describing the night of October 1, 1789, when Louis XVI held a banquet for the palace guards. Although the feast was presumably given to welcome the new soldiers, Wollstonecraft notes that it was really a propaganda event, a "preconcerted business" designed to secure the guards' loyalty (*Historical* 194). Marie

Antoinette, whom Wollstonecraft considers to be an actress herself, led the assembled men in regaling their king, and, according to Wollstonecraft's account, there was then a "theatrical display of sensibility, carried to the highest pitch, [that] produced emotions almost convulsive in the whole circle, of which an english reader can scarcely form an idea" (*Historical* 195). "Convulsive" is the word Wollstonecraft chooses to describe the guards' emotions, emotions that their queen was able so carefully to draw out of them through her own "theatrical display of sensibility."

Such extreme emotion, of course, is a completely foreign idea to the British, who, Wollstonecraft's tone implies, should rightfully disdain such empty gestures. Extreme sensibility is, and should remain, incomprehensible to the British, a part of the French national identity that the British are unable to identify with themselves. This love of theater also carries over into the conversational skills of the French, for the language of the theater has made the French into smooth and "oily" talkers (*Historical* 228). The melodramatic flourishes of plays, in which "a sentimental jargon extinguishes all the simplicity and fire of passion," has caused the French to adopt the language of the stage even in their everyday conversations with one another (*Historical* 228). Although most other nations usually celebrate the French for their exquisite conversational skills, Wollstonecraft links these skills to artificial rhetoric and false emotion. She thus concurs with the assessment of the French as experts in the art of conversation, but adds her own modification as she searches for the foundation of this art: "As a nation, the french are certainly the most eloquent people in the world; their lively feelings giving the warmth of passion to every argument they attempt to support. And speaking fluently, vanity leads them continually to endeavour to utter their sentiments, without considering whether they have any thing to recommend them to notice, besides a happy choice of expression" (*Historical* 156). Even their famous conversational skills find their origin in vanity: for vanity leads to eloquence, but that eloquence, in turn, lacks substance. "The french therefore are all rhetoricians," Wollstonecraft asserts, "and they have a singular fund of superficial knowledge, caught in the tumult of pleasure from the shallow stream of conversation" (*Historical* 228). Compared to the British, who had an established reputation as being phlegmatic and taciturn,[11] the French are "too light" and "too giddy," too prone to regarding themselves as fluent speakers of their native tongue (*Historical* 166). Toward the end of the *Historical and Moral View* she even goes so far as to term this national characteristic not just mere vanity, but rather a "disgusting conceit and wretched egotism" (*Historical* 231). These are strong words against the French, one that sets them up as a counterpoint to the British.

Besides sharing a strong sense of vanity, the second connection that Wollstonecraft makes between British women and the French is the love of pleasure that motivates their actions. Both British women and the French in general are, in Wollstonecraft's estimation, driven by their desire for pleasure, for both pleasing and being pleased. Throughout the second *Vindication,* for instance, Wollstonecraft insists upon this shared facet of British women's lives, repeatedly emphasizing that the collective end of all of their individual actions is to find bliss in the passing moment. "Pleasure," Wollstonecraft claims, "is the business of woman's life, according to the present modification of society, and while it continues to be so, little can be expected from such weak beings" (*VRW* 55). While British men leave the home each day to work as active and productive members of society, "women seek for pleasure as the main purpose of existence. In fact, from the education, which they receive from society, the love of pleasure may be said to govern them all" (*VRW* 60). Lack of an enlightened education causes women to become weak and vapid, insipid creatures whose energies are all directed toward living lives of bliss. Their entire education, in fact, contributes to this demand for continual delight. "The same love of pleasure, fostered by the whole tendency of their education," Wollstonecraft insists, "gives a trifling turn to the conduct of women in most circumstances" (*VRW* 60). British women differ from their husbands, brothers, and fathers, all of whom can engage in useful and meaningful activities within society, because their educations constrict both their minds and their bodies.

Like British women, the French also share this passion for enjoyment, and, also like most middle-class British women, the French as a people have been educated to give free reign to their quests for pleasure. While analyzing the French educational system in the second *Vindication,* for instance, Wollstonecraft takes care to point out, "In France, boys and girls, particularly, are only educated to please, to manage their persons, and regulate their behaviour" (*VRW* 81). Of the three aspects of education that Wollstonecraft chooses to describe—pleasing, managing, and regulating—pleasure comes first because it is the basis of all of the other arts that French schoolchildren learn: the only reason they take such care with their appearance and conduct is because such care will eventually repay them in their abilities to please others. In her *Letter on the Present Character of the French Nation,* Wollstonecraft expands upon this point even more. The text's purpose, according to its author, was to "attempt to trace to their source the causes which have combined to render this nation the most polished, in a physical sense, and probably the most superficial in the world" (*Letter* 444). At the heart of her text is the desire to root out the reasons why the French have become not only extremely cultured, but also extremely superficial. One of the more striking passages in the *Letter* lays out this superficiality even more clearly. In one of the opening paragraphs, Wollstonecraft sketches a portrait of the French that leaves little doubt for her British audience of how inundated with pleasure the French really are. Describing life in France, Wollstonecraft draws upon the French language (through her anglicized use of the word *aimable*) to record her observations on what she sees passing around her:

> The whole mode of life here tends indeed to render the people frivolous, and, to borrow their favourite epithet, amiable. Ever on the wing, they always sipping the sparkling joy on the brim of the cup, leaving satiety in the bottom for those who venture to drink deep. . . . they alone understand the full import of the term leisure; and they trifle away their time with such an air of contentment. . . . They play before me like motes in a sunbeam, enjoying the passing ray; whilst an English head, searching for more solid happiness, loses, in the analysis of pleasure, the volatile sweets of the moment. (*Letter* 443)

Wollstonecraft's portrait of the French is obviously an exaggerated and prejudiced one, but it is one that nevertheless marks her displeasure with this particular lifestyle. The French are too prone to spending their lives chasing after superficial pleasures; instead of spending their time in meaningful activities, they can only "sip" from the grand cup of life. The British, on the other hand, "venture to drink deep," for they are the ones who seek not fleeting fancies, but rather more lasting, more "solid," forms of happiness. Like bits of dust caught in the morning rays of light, the French are blown about by the whims of the moment, unable to ground themselves in a careful analysis of the motives or causes behind their pleasure. Their inability (or perhaps lack of desire) to analyze their lives leads to the general feeling of frivolity that pervades their nation. Life across the Channel, as Wollstonecraft portrays it, is too light to ever offer any lasting joy. In their endless pursuit of the amiable, the French have rendered themselves superficial and petty.[12]

Wollstonecraft clearly links her own countrywomen with the French in her analysis of pleasure and its role in the lives of these two groups. Yet the reason pleasure receives such a strong emphasis in her texts is because of its connection to an even more dangerous character trait:

excessive sensibility. Critics have long recognized Wollstonecraft's deep concern for the effects that this trait has upon women, but what has gone relatively unnoticed is how strongly she associates it with both pleasure and the French. As Wollstonecraft sees it, the education that British women receive makes them particularly vulnerable to extreme behavior. As she makes clear in her second *Vindication,* "Most of the evils of life arise from a desire of present enjoyment that outruns itself" (*VRW* 72). What Wollstonecraft sees as particularly dangerous, however, is not just that British women are too prone to "present enjoyment," but that this strong desire for immediate gratification and an impulse to find pleasure solely in "sensual feelings" also causes women to become foolish mothers and wives. "Women subjected by ignorance to their sensations, and only taught to look for happiness in love," Wollstonecraft explains, "refine on sensual feelings, and adopt metaphysical notions respecting that passion, which lead them shamefully to neglect the duties of life, and frequently in the midst of these sublime refinements they plump into actual vice . . . . The mighty business of female life is to please, and restrained from entering into more important concerns by political and civil oppression, sentiments become events" (*VRW* 183). Without a proper outlet for their energies, emotions become exaggerated, magnified into large events when they should really only be feelings experienced during the normal course of the day.[13]

Wollstonecraft also takes this opportunity to expound on one particular way in which these emotions are heightened. The regression towards "actual vice" is further perpetuated by the reading material that most women choose: the novel. Because of its overly sentimental language and exaggerated demands for passion, the novel as a genre only exacerbates women's condition. The hyperbolic nature of both the language and the style of novels carries over into the language and style of the women who read them: "Besides, the reading of novels makes women, and particularly ladies of fashion, very fond of using strong expressions and superlatives in conversation; and, though the dissipated artificial life which they lead prevents their cherishing any strong legitimate passion, the language of passion in affected tones slips for ever from their glib tongues, and every trifle produces those phosphoric bursts which only mimick in the dark the flame of passion" (*VRW* 186). The main complaint that Wollstonecraft has with novels is that they create artificial passions in their readers, and, while many critics over the years have discussed Wollstonecraft's dislike of the novel, what has gone unanalyzed is the connection between this dislike and Wollstonecraft's views on the French.[14] Just as the theater has made the French people as a whole into superficial conversationalists, the novel has made British women into weak and vapid creatures. Although novel readers might use "strong expressions and superlatives" when they speak, underlying this excessive emotion is an empty core; they remain unable to maintain "any strong legitimate passion." Endurance of any kind is therefore out of the question, for women's emotions lack a firm basis in reality, and the legitimacy of what women feel is ultimately called into question by the superficial quality of their feelings. Without a foundation upon which to create a meaningful relationship—a foundation of education and intellect—women can only play at the grand passions of life.

Women are not the only ones who share this excessive quality of emotion, for, according to Wollstonecraft, the French are an emotionally overwrought group as well. Just like British women, the French are subject to their passions, which tend to dominate the individual. The introduction of the second *Vindication* outlines this national characteristic briefly, but with great emphasis. Although she concurs that the people of France are perhaps the most knowledgeable of any of those in Europe, Wollstonecraft still charges them with an excessive interest in indulgence. She remarks that "in France the very essence of sensuality has been extracted to regale the voluptuary, and a kind of sentimental lust has prevailed, which, together with the system of duplicity that the whole tenour of their political and civil government taught, have given a sinister sort of sagacity to the French character, properly termed finesse" (*VRW* 3–4). The "sentimental lust" that she describes has created a nation controlled by artificial desires, for the sagacity that the French demonstrate is not true wisdom, but rather the sense of knowing about worldly affairs and desires. It is also worth noting that Wollstonecraft mentions the French in the introduction to a text that focuses on her own countrywomen; in her mind, the two groups are linked, for many of her thoughts about British women grew out of her thoughts about the discussion of human rights during the French Revolution. In her *Letter on the Present Character of the French Nation*, however, Wollstonecraft particularly details the influence that sensuality has had among the French people. She explains to her British readers that "every thing has conspired to make the French the most sensual people in the world" (*Letter* 444). Once again, Wollstonecraft's biggest worry lies in the artificial and superficial aspects of emotion. Like British women, whose novel reading makes them particularly vulnerable to falsified and exaggerated emotions, the French people's desire to be polished and refined leads them into lives of artificial emotion without any solid foundation. A lack of emotional depth has made the French a nation of sensualists, a nation ready to enjoy the passions of the present moment.[15]

THE DIFFICULTIES OF LINKING GENDER AND THE NATION

Up until now, I have looked at the three primary ways in which Wollstonecraft connects her own countrywomen with the general French population. Yet at this point it is important to consider momentarily the implications of what Wollstonecraft is doing and, especially important, why her focus would move from British women to the French people as the 1790s progressed. The events of the Revolution, we must remember, inspired Wollstonecraft, just as they did for Charlotte Smith, to write about her own country and its faults; comparisons with Britain's rival nation led Wollstonecraft to envision changes in her own nation. Wollstonecraft's vision of a female imagined community essentially grew out of comparisons with France and the subsequent desire to provide more solid educations for women. However, I would like to suggest, the influence that nationalism had upon Wollstonecraft's gender beliefs did not just flow in one direction. While political changes going on in France caused her to rethink the positions of British women, the positions of British women also caused her to rethink the events in France. That is, in the *Vindications* Wollstonecraft had portrayed the French Revolution in a more positive light. But as the Revolution progressed and Robespierre's Reign of Terror swept the nation, Wollstonecraft, like so many other Britons who had supported the Revolution's early aims, became disenchanted and even disgusted with it.

Wollstonecraft, of course, experienced the Terror firsthand, for she lived in revolutionary France from 1792 to 1795, as, first pregnant and alone and then as a new mother and alone, she waited the return of her American lover Gilbert Imlay. Many critics have argued that the depressed state of Wollstonecraft's mind may have colored her depiction of events in France, but, true as this might be, it was also equally true that her residence coincided with some of the darkest moments of the Revolution. Wollstonecraft's personal letters from these months actually rarely mention the progress of the Revolution, but this was most likely because she was worried about censorship by the French government. One of the most striking exceptions to this is the letter Wollstonecraft wrote on December 26, 1792, to her friend and publisher Joseph

Johnson. In it, Wollstonecraft recounts her thoughts when she sees Louis XVI pass before her window on his way to the treason trials:

> I can scarcely tell you why, but an association of ideas made the tears flow insensibly from my eyes, when I saw Louis sitting, with more dignity than I expected from his character, in a hackney coach going to meet death, where so many of his race have triumphed. . . . I have been alone ever since; and, though my mind is calm, I cannot dismiss the lively images that have filled my imagination all the day.—Nay, do not smile, but pity me; for, once or twice, lifting my eyes from the paper, I have seen eyes glare through a glass-door opposite my chair, and bloody hands shook at me. . . . I want to see something alive; death in so many frightful shapes has taken hold of my fancy.—I am going to bed—and for the first time in my life, I cannot put out the candle.[16]

The letter is spellbinding in its vivid imagery, and also because of the absolute shock that Wollstonecraft experiences afterward. Analyzing the same passage, Anne Mellor remarks that Wollstonecraft continued to be "horrified by the execution of the king and the numerous deaths that followed at the hands of the Jacobin Convention. . . . She feared that the golden age of which she had dreamt for France . . . was forever lost."[17] Wollstonecraft's increasing revulsion to the events taking place in France certainly colored the texts that she was writing.

Although she was limited in her ability to write about the events of the Terror while she was in France and while the Terror was taking place, in the text that she wrote immediately after the *Historical and Moral View*, Wollstonecraft revealed how terrible things really had been.[18] In her 1796 *Letters Written During a Short Residence in Sweden, Norway, and Denmark*, she compares her feelings while viewing a picturesque landscape in Norway with those she experienced while living in France during those months from 1792 to 1793: "How silent and peaceful was the scene. I gazed around with rapture, and felt more of that spontaneous pleasure which gives credibility to our expectations of happiness, than I had for a long, long time before. I forgot the horrors I had witnessed in France, which had cast a gloom over all nature, and suffering the enthusiasm of my character, too often, gracious God! damped by the tears of disappointed affection, to be lighted up afresh, care took wing while simple fellow feeling expanded to my heart."[19] The "horrors" that she had observed remained in her mind, even when surrounded by fresh scenes.

Although Wollstonecraft never did reject the original aims of the Revolution, what she had earlier seen as promise she now saw as pollution, and so she took it upon herself to rectify her earlier portrayal of France by tracing the Revolution (and its failures) to what she saw as its source: the national identity of the French people.[20] This is why, I believe, France replaces women in her political thinking as the 1790s progressed: because Wollstonecraft was trying to understand what had gone wrong. Her *Historical and Moral View* recounts the primary events of the Revolution in order to understand it more fully. Wollstonecraft's initial plan, after all, was to continue writing the *View* right up to the present day, but her personal circumstances got in the way, and she was never able to write about the Terror itself.[21] What is especially significant is that as Wollstonecraft moves away from the universalist rhetoric of revolutionary reason she had used in her earlier *Vindications*, she also moves away from the large category of woman, looking instead to national character and national identity as the focus of her critique. The connections she draws (whether inadvertently or not) between British women and the French are not, therefore, equivalent in her thinking; women and the French are not equated in her mind, but, instead, she replaces the former with the latter in her political thinking.

Although Wollstonecraft does draw comparisons between women and the French, however, there are several problems that arise in her formulations—problems that, again, are worth considering, if only briefly, since they shed light on the difficulties that women writers often ran up against when they tried to reconcile their thinking about gender politics with their thinking about national politics. As I argued in the previous section, those female characteristics and attributes that Wollstonecraft describes in *A Vindication of the Rights of Woman* find their mirror image in the French. In Wollstonecraft's formulation, however, British women possess these superficial traits of vanity, a desire for pleasure, and excessive emotion largely because British society perpetually inculcates these traits through its educational systems and treatment of women, while the French possess these traits because of their national identity. Trying to connect British women to an entire nation of individuals of both genders is, of course, an almost impossible task since, we well know, gender and national identity were then—and are now—open to flux. Additionally, Wollstonecraft viewed gender (at least in part) as a constructed, rather than essential, category. An even larger difficulty this equation poses, though, is that of trying to reconcile the universal with the local, for Wollstonecraft writes herself into a logical quandary when she dissects the shared traits mentioned above. The language that Wollstonecraft uses is often equivocal, and nowhere is this more apparent than when she discusses women. In the examples we have looked at so far, we know from the context that Wollstonecraft is specifically referring to British women. At times, however, she slips into ambiguous language, referring to "woman" as a universal category. The title of her second *Vindication* reveals this slippage, for instance, for *A Vindication of the Rights of Woman* implies a universal understanding of "woman," one that reaches across nations and across history. Throughout the second *Vindication*, Wollstonecraft also refers to "the history of woman" (*VRW* 54), as if women share a unique sense of time and being. These references are part of her attempt to establish a female community, but she cannot seem to make up her mind as to whether this community is transnational and transhistorical or, instead, firmly located in the here and now of the British nation. At times, Wollstonecraft seems to favor the first version, but at other times she favors the second; at times, all women belong to a universal category that unites them, but at other times British women possess an identity that sharply distinguishes them from the French. Wollstonecraft seems to alternate between these two versions depending on her aim at the particular moment. To make things even more complicated, when Wollstonecraft does employ "woman" as a universal term, her doing so raises an asymmetry in the equation she tries to formulate. If "woman" is a universal category, then that category would have to transcend time and place—it would have to transcend national identity. But, at the same time, her depiction of the French people places them into a category of a localized identity; their national character is what distinguishes them, say, from the British. So when Wollstonecraft discusses British women, her discussion involves an odd disjunction between the universal and the local: for how can British women have all of the faults both of women and of the French? Perhaps Wollstonecraft's answer to this question lies in the idea that gender identity and national identity are categories she believes are constructed rather than essential, and that are caused by political oppression in both cases. Nevertheless, this slippage consequently illustrates the problems that often come up when we try to think of gender and the nation together.[22]

The Importance of Morality

Imagining women and the nation is not as simple as it otherwise might appear to be, but Wollstonecraft does not let this stop her from following through with the implications of her equation. Three character traits—vanity, pleasure, and excessive emotion—link British women with their French neighbors in Wollstonecraft's analysis, and it is precisely in these three areas that Wollstonecraft most severely reproaches the groups under attack. Yet her criticism of both the French and British women lies in her heavy emphasis on morality, which she strongly believes should form the basis of society. Wollstonecraft's understanding of morality involves a differentiation between morality and manners. The primary difference between the two, according to Wollstonecraft, is that manners are local, changing, and variable, whereas morals have an unchanging foundation that extends across cultures and even genders. Her distinction between the two extends at least as far back as her *Elements of Morality for the Use of Children,* a German text originally written by Christian Gotthilf Salzmann, but later translated (from 1790 to 1791) into English by Wollstonecraft while she was working for publisher Joseph Johnson. Yet even though the text, a collection of stories designed to teach correct morals to children, purports to be a translation, Wollstonecraft herself is the first to admit that she heavily modified parts of it: "I term it a translation, though I do not pretend to assert that it is a literal one; on the contrary, beside making it an English story, I have made some additions, and altered many parts of it, not only to give it the spirit of an original, but to avoid introducing any German customs or local opinions. My reason for naturalizing it must be obvious—I did not wish to puzzle children by pointing out modifications of manners, when the grand principles of morality were to be fixed on a broad basis."[23] The "German customs and local opinions" that she is so worried about importing into Britain are variations on manners, on the behavioral differences between groups of individuals. Morals, however, have a fixed, consistent foundation that does not vary amongst nations and people. "Naturalizing" these German tales involves removing the local mores and substituting "grand principles" in their stead. The British and the Germans share the same principles, and so, by extension, should the French as well. Morality crosses national borders, remaining consistent no matter what the nation.

A few years later, in the second *Vindication,* Wollstonecraft makes this same point, this time in her discussion of women's rights. "Moralists have unanimously agreed," she explains, "that unless virtue be nursed by liberty, it will never attain due strength—and what they say of man I extend to mankind, insisting that in all cases morals must be fixed on immutable principles; and, that the being cannot be termed rational or virtuous, who obeys any authority, but that of reason" (*VRW* 191). When it comes to judging good from bad, right from wrong, actions should also be subject to one standard: "Surely there can be but one rule of right, if morality has an eternal foundation" (*VRW* 36). The "immutable" and "eternal" nature of morality means that its standards apply equally to both men and women, without any sort of difference in how those standards are applied. These ideas on morality culminate in an image that appears in her *Historical and Moral View*. Here she asserts that there exists in the world a "compass of moral principles, which alone render the character dignified or consistent" (*Historical* 215). Although standards of morality were greatly contested throughout the eighteenth century by writers as diverse as Ralph Cudworth, Lord Shaftesbury, Francis Hutcheson, and David Hume, Wollstonecraft adheres to the belief that all decisions can be measured against one consistent, unchanging "compass." When confronted with a difficult moral dilemma, an individual has only to consult his—or her—internal compass to choose the proper direction. The same yardstick should thus measure both the actions of man, and those, too, of mankind (that is, women).

Wollstonecraft therefore believes in the existence of a moral standard, but the question then becomes, "Of what does that moral standard consist?" Far from leaving her readers in a state of ignorance on this point, Wollstonecraft has a definition of morality clearly in mind. Order, reason, and understanding are, in fact, its defining traits. Morality, for instance, is predicated on order. Unregulated behavior leads to unconcerned citizens, both male and female, and consequently to unconcerned participants in the political state, for, "Whoever rationally means to be useful must have a plan of conduct" (*VRW* 68). Without a carefully detailed scheme for conducting one's life, chaos abounds. After all, "order [is] the soul of virtue" (*VRW* 68), whereas, "Disorder is, in fact, the very essence of vice" (*Letter* 445). Plans provide structure in life, and structure is necessary, in Wollstonecraft's estimation, for the regulation and control of the events of the world. Lack of a moral compass means lack of a moral guide, and such a lack leaves individuals free to act and do as they please, even if those actions bring harm to others. Society becomes unregulated and uncontrolled without order, and so, too, do morals. Believing in the existence of a moral compass, however, provides discipline and structure, a standard by which a person can regulate his or her own behavior and against which he or she can judge the behavior of others. Far from being arbitrary, morality is consistent and concordant with set principles.[24] A second component of morality is reason, which figures greatly in all of Wollstonecraft's texts because it binds human beings together.[25] She makes this belief clear in the *Vindication of the Rights of Men*, where she attacks Burke for his failure to recognize this point. "I know not of any common nature or common relation amongst men but what results from reason," she contends. "The common affections and passions equally bind brutes together; and it is only the continuity of those relations that entitles us to the denomination of rational creatures; and this continuity arises from reflection—from the operations of that reason which you contemn with flippant disrespect."[26] As Angela Keane notes, "In much of Wollstonecraft's analysis of the effects of social inequality, women, the most abused, are, consequently, first to reach the level of the brute, the first to lose their powers of reflection, the most alienated from their labours and from their bodies."[27] According to Wollstonecraft, humans are superior to animals because humans possess the ability to think. Reflection leads them to ponder their many relationships, which in turn leads them to forge an even closer emotional bond with others in a continual cycle of evaluation and recommitment. Developing our reason also allows us to control our emotions and passions, which further separates us from animals. In essence, "reflection must be the natural foundation—of *rational* affections" (*VRM* 64). The third element in the triad of morality is understanding. In her *Letter,* Wollstonecraft poses a significant question: "what can render the heart so hard, or so effectually stifle every moral emotion, as the refinements of sensuality?" (*Letter* 444). The answer, of course, is nothing since sensuality, in Wollstonecraft's opinion, lies at the root of most of society's problems. Because sensuality and its close relation sensibility both depend upon corporeal and fleeting pleasures, they work against the true principles of morality, which are ever fixed and unchanging. Wollstonecraft makes this clear in her *Historical and Moral View* when she explains that "the highest degree of sensual refinement violates all the genuine feelings of the soul, making the understanding the abject slave of the imagination. But, when the advances of knowledge shall make morality the real basis of social union, . . . men cannot lose the ground so surely taken, or forget principles" (*Historical* 111). Until that day, however, the understanding risks being infiltrated by false passions. Mere emotions can be contrasted, in fact, with understanding, which is based upon a more solid foundation of reason, and Wollstonecraft greatly laments the fact that emotions and reason are so often confused: "So weak is the tenderness produced merely by sympathy, or polished manners, compared with the humanity of a cultivated understanding. Alas! It is morals, not feelings, which distinguish men from the beasts of prey!" (*Historical* 126). The "genuine feelings of the soul" are thus held up against the feelings associated with sensual enjoyment, and the latter come out looking the worse for wear.[28]

Wollstonecraft therefore clearly lays out what she feels are the primary attributes of morality, and yet she also wants us to believe that she herself believes that morality has no basis in gender. She insists that morality is sexless, an option available to both men and women. David F. Venturo also notes this aspect of Wollstonecraft's thought, remarking that she believed that "women should be educated in the same fashion as men and held to the same, sexless standards of virtue."[29] As she explains in her first *Vindication*, most men writing about female education limit virtue to the masculine domain:

> Thus confining truth, fortitude, and humanity, within the rigid pale of manly morals, they [the writers] might justly argue, that to be loved, [is] women's high end and great distinction! . . . The affection they [women] excite, to be uniform and perfect, should not be tinctured with the respect which moral virtues inspire, lest pain should be blended with pleasure, and admiration disturb the soft intimacy of love. This laxity of morals in the female world is certainly more captivating to a libertine imagination than the cold arguments of reason, that give no sex to virtue. (*VRM* 72–73)

Truth, fortitude, and humanity, some of the main offshoots of virtue, are "confined" by men to themselves—to the "rigid pale of manly morals." Women, however, do possess the same virtues, since they, too, possess the ability to act rationally. Reason gives, after all, "no sex to virtue." Wollstonecraft makes this same point in her second *Vindication* as well, although this time she does so more forcefully: "I here throw down my gauntlet, and deny the existence of sexual virtues, not excepting modesty. For man and woman, truth, if I understand the meaning of the word, must be the same" (*VRW* 51). Her metaphor emphasizes her willingness to argue over this important belief, for the moral compass functions equally well in both men and women. When the day finally arrives "when morality shall be settled on a more solid basis, then, without being gifted with a prophetic spirit, I will venture to predict that woman will be either the friend or slave of man" (*VRW* 35).

THE CREATION OF A MASCULINE MORALITY AND THE COMMONWEALTH TRADITION

At first glance, then, Wollstonecraft's understanding of morality appears to be a morality that is tied to neither nation nor gender; a closer look, however, reveals it to be thoroughly grounded in a masculine, pro-

British sensibility. Although she claims otherwise, I suggest that the standard of morality Wollstonecraft believes in is essentially a "masculine" and British one. Even though Wollstonecraft insists that a standard set of moral principles exists between the sexes and even between nations—a standard to which all of a person's actions might be compared and to which each individual might aspire—she purposely constructs that morality in gendered and nationalist terms. Order, reason, and understanding characterize Wollstonecraft's version of morality, and so this morality is based upon traits that British women and the French decidedly do *not* share, even though they share the *potential* for these traits. This latter group—as vain, pleasure-driven, and sensual—possess none of the traits that distinguish male Britons from themselves.

Throughout several of her texts, for instance, Wollstonecraft comes back to the idea that reason and morality are masculine traits.[30] In the Preface to the *Historical and Moral View* she purposely genders rational thought, referring to "the enlightened sentiments of masculine and improved philosophy" (*Historical* 6). Morality, in her formulation, is grounded upon reason, which is itself based upon what she views as the "manly" dictates of a Christian God.[31] While Wollstonecraft retains hope for future progress, that hope lies in a specifically masculine sense of reason: "But should experience prove that there is a beauty in virtue, a charm in order, which necessarily implies exertion, a depraved sensual taste may give way to a more *manly* one—and *melting* feelings to rational satisfactions" (*VRM* 74–75; first emphasis added). When that day finally arrives, the world will see that the more "manly" taste that Wollstonecraft refers to is one that will encourage its possessors to do all that they can to help others.[32] Both "manly ardour" and the "manly exertions inspired by the voice of reason," as she elsewhere calls them, will ultimately lead individuals to adopt changes (*Historical* 108, 113). Conforming to "the law of God" therefore means trying to make the world a better place: "to labor to increase human happiness by extirpating error, is a *masculine godlike* affection" (*VRM* 85; emphasis added). Working to rid society of false beliefs makes individuals more masculine and godlike, more perfect in their abilities to reason and feel. In each of these texts, then, Wollstonecraft exhorts her readers to develop and exercise a specifically masculine mode of reason.

Wollstonecraft's insistence on the masculine was not unique, however, given her surrounding context. Before looking at Wollstonecraft's own writing in more depth to see how she constructs this British masculinity, it is important first to situate Wollstonecraft's thoughts within the larger political context in which she was writing. As G. J. Barker-

Benfield has shown in a now-classic essay, Wollstonecraft's political views grew out of the Commonwealth tradition with which she was so closely allied.[33] When Wollstonecraft first established her small school at Newington Green in 1784 with her two sisters Elizabeth and Everina and her close friend Fanny Blood, she entered into the midst of a Dissenting tradition led by the Reverend Richard Price. Wollstonecraft's mentor and ally Hannah Burgh, who assisted Wollstonecraft financially and emotionally and who thought of Wollstonecraft as a surrogate daughter, also shared with Wollstonecraft the work of her now-deceased husband, the famous Dissenting writer James Burgh. Positioned as she was within this community, Wollstonecraft learned more about the Commonwealth values in which these thinkers believed. Barker-Benfield explains their views in detail: "The Dissenting edge of this tradition emphasized that to be virtuous one must be free. Time and again Dissenters insisted that independence of mind was the individual's essential right. . . . Like other Commonwealthmen, they were deeply critical of the luxury and dissipation of the 'ins,' the ruling class. Conversely, they presented 'the middling people' as the repository of morality and civic virtue" (97). While the community of thinkers Wollstonecraft found herself in did treat her as an ally, the republican beliefs to which the Dissenters subscribed excluded women: they believed in what was a specifically "male civic consciousness" (110). Although she focuses on Revolutionary America, historian Ruth H. Bloch's work on the nature of virtue during this period also sheds light on the same principles and concepts of morality that the Americans and the Dissenters shared. Like Barker-Benfield, Bloch points to "the intrinsic maleness of the term virtue" associated with the republican tradition, where "the term refers not to female private morality but to male public spirit, that is, to the willingness of citizens to engage actively in civic life and to sacrifice interests for the common good."[34]

Barker-Benfield therefore locates the particular tradition from which Wollstonecraft developed her ideas, while also touching upon the many ways Wollstonecraft tried to extend the Commonwealthmen's views—views that up until then had focused only on men—to women as well. Wollstonecraft essentially drew upon the same principles, arguments, and rhetoric that her mentors and predecessors had used, and, throughout the first *Vindication*, Barker-Benfield notes, Wollstonecraft's "use of 'manly' . . . is the same as the Commonwealthman's usage, manifest, say, in Burgh's *Political Disquisitions*; but it also represents Wollstonecraft's extension to women of the principles of true Whiggery and political radicalism. . . . Her standards of healthy citizenship, the receipt of a good education, and the exertion of mind and body under the bracing condition of liberty in order to produce virtue, look back to the 'manly' political, moral tradition emphasized by Price, Burgh, and Priestly. . . . The significance for the manhood on which civic virtue depends, is clear."[35]

Although she tried to extend the Commonwealth's views to women, Wollstonecraft still fell back upon the gendered construction of the morality and virtue that surrounded her. As Claudia Johnson's recent revisionary work on Barker-Benfield so usefully explains, one of Wollstonecraft's main concerns about British society was that its own men were becoming too feminized and sentimental for the good of their nation, and that sentimental masculinity was basically destroying republican notions of virtue.[36] During the new Age of Chivalry in which Wollstonecraft lived and wrote, illustrious figures, such as Wollstonecraft's nemesis Edmund Burke, perpetuated the figure of the hypersensitive male, a figure that threatened the already precarious foundation upon which women's own sensibility rested. Wollstonecraft's "early career," Johnson points out, "is marked by hope that republican masculinity—as distinct from chivalric masculinity—can save men and women alike from such degradation."[37] Johnson also suggests that Wollstonecraft's main focus in *A Vindication of the Rights of Woman* is on the ways in which society has "systematically vitiated men's character and deformed women's along with it. . . . [and that the text] is preoccupied with championing a kind of masculinity into which women can be invited rather than with enlarging or inventing a positive discourse of femininity."[38] Wollstonecraft, in other words, urges women to become more masculine, rather than urging them to reformulate the feminine. What I particularly want to emphasize here is how Wollstonecraft's own repeated emphasis on the masculine nature of morality in several texts and her encouragement to the (mostly male) readers of the second *Vindication* in particular to reinstitute this morality, both demonstrate her belief in the gendered nature of virtuous principles. Part of Wollstonecraft's project was to reestablish a masculine mode of morality that she saw as largely missing among British men.

This belief in the gendered nature of morality carries over into Wollstonecraft's discussion of the current state of British women and of the French nation that I have been discussing thus far. A main complaint against both groups is, in fact, that they are made effeminate by their current modes of behavior.[39] In the case of British women, this argument for a masculine morality is best exemplified through Wollstonecraft's own personal references in her nonfiction texts. For example, she sets up her own rhetorical model in the first *Vindication*—for the move is deliberately pointed out to her readers several times—as one based upon the very principle of reason that Burke lacks. Her own ability to argue precisely and clearly sets her apart from her rival and makes her writing a prime example of the "manly" sentiment she so strongly advocates. While Burke, for instance, indulges in emotional cant, Wollstonecraft engages in the higher realm of rational conversation. In one of the opening passages of the first *Vindication*, she enjoins Burke to engage with her in reasonable dialogue.[40] Her now-famous injunction rings forth from the page: "Quitting now the flowers of rhetoric, let us, sir, reason together" (*VRM* 16). Further on, Wollstonecraft takes up the issues of government representatives: "And, sir, let me ask you, with manly plainness," she forthrightly declares, about the nature of those representatives (*VRM* 58). As she views it, Burke's use of fanciful rhetoric allies him with women, whereas her own more succinct style allies her with men. Her ability to lose her gender, to take up the voice of masculine reason, signals her belief that women can be rational individuals, and that that very rationality she condones is a gendered one. If women can be rational, it is only because they cast off their feminine traits in favor of masculine ones.

Wollstonecraft's belief that women could be "manly" also carried over into the ways in which she lived her own life, for even in her personal life Wollstonecraft attempted to cast off what she saw as feminine weaknesses. Personal letters detailing the birth and early years of Wollstonecraft's first daughter, Fanny, for instance, demonstrate this desire to create more masculine women. Writing on May 20, 1794, just a few days after the birth of Fanny, Wollstonecraft proudly mentions in the closing lines of a letter to friend Ruth Barlow, "My little Girl begins to suck so *manfully* that her father reckons saucily on her writing the second part of the R—ts of Woman." A few months later, on September 20, Wollstonecraft tells her sister Everina how greatly she longs for Everina to meet her little niece Fanny, who was only four months old at the time: "I want you to see my little girl, who is more like a boy—She is ready to fly away with spirits."[41] Clearly pleased with the energy of her little daughter, Wollstonecraft compares Fanny to a young male. Two days afterward, in a letter to Fanny's father, Gilbert Imlay, Wollstonecraft reassures Imlay that their daughter has gotten over her recent illness: "and you will want to be told, over and over again, that our little Hercules is quite recovered."[42] A Demeter or Hera little Fanny is not; instead, her mother describes her as that most powerful of the heroes—one who was also of paramount importance in revolutionary iconography—Hercules. Joan B. Landes traces, for instance, the ways in which the female figures of Liberty and Marianne at first served the Revolutionaries by "excising the excessively feminized and feminizing dimension of the old body politic" associated with King Louis XVI and his predecessors, before eventually becoming displaced by Hercules, "the masculine representation of popular strength."[43] This was an iconography with which Wollstonecraft would have been familiar since she was still living in France when Fanny was born, and her decision to describe her newborn daughter as this male mythic figure highlights not only her conflicted feelings toward the Revolution, but also her underlying belief that women can take on masculine characteristics.[44] What is worth underscoring in each of these several examples, above all, is that Wollstonecraft chooses to describe her daughter by listing attributes that call attention to her masculine nature, demonstrating how Wollstonecraft enacted the views she espoused in her writing.[45]

Wollstonecraft's dislike of the effeminate becomes even stronger and more vocalized in her writings about the French, where she portrays this rival nation as a weakened, effeminate land. The portrait she paints of the French national character also owes its genesis to the tradition out of which Wollstonecraft wrote. Steven Blakemore points out the connections between France's effeminacy and Wollstonecraft's Commonwealth concerns: "Using the conventional language of the seventeenth-century Commonwealthman's concern over the effeminacy of men degraded by antirepublican institutions," Blakemore suggests, gave Wollstonecraft a ready explanation for the reasons why the French could not maintain their "enlightened ideas."[46] Before, in earlier times, at least according to Wollstonecraft, these effeminate traits were at least dampened to some extent. The foresight of Louis XIV, for instance, led him to encourage his people to read some of the most renowned British authors: "for introducing the fashion of admiring the english, he led men to read and translate some of their masculine writers, which greatly contributed to rouse the sleeping manhood of the french" (*Historical* 28). Reading British male writers should have led the French to adopt some of the Britons' more masculine traits. Only now, in recent times, however, have the feminine traits of the French been renewed and reactivated. Because of their sensual natures, the entire nation, she asserts, has been "emasculated by pleasure" to such an extent that they have become "an effeminate race of heroes" (*Letter* 445; *Historical* 213). Even individuals active within the Revolution and praised for their heroic exploits, like the famous Duc d'Orléans, in actuality lack the "courage of a man" (*Historical* 207). Her contempt for this trait of the French national identity is further exacerbated by her belief that French men are becoming more and more like women; instead of progressing, they are regressing. In Paris particularly, "a variety of causes have so effeminated reason, that the french may be considered as a nation of women . . . . Every thing, in short, shows the dexterity of the people, and their attention to present enjoyment" (*Historical* 121). Wollstonecraft's dislike of the "feminine" is evident in her scorn for this "nation of women," whose "dexterity" gives them a lassitude detrimental to morality. Even the social polish associated with the French character really only amounts to false refinement. Social graces enervate the masculinity of Frenchmen, making them capable only of pleasing themselves and others. "Thus a frenchman, like most women," she remarks, "may be said to have no character distinguishable from that of the nation; unless little shades, and casual lights, be allowed to constitute an essential characteristic. What then could have been expected, when their ambition was mostly confined to dancing gracefully, entering a room with easy assurance, and smiling on and complimenting the very persons whom they meant to ridicule at the next fashionable assembly?" (*Historical* 230).[47] These tendencies have been especially magnified amongst the nobility: "the encouragement given to enervating pleasures, and the vebality [*sic*] [venality] of titles, purchased either with money, or ignoble services, soon rendered the nobility as notorious for effeminacy as they had been for heroism in the days of the gallant Henry" (*Historical* 225).[48]

While reading each of these examples, it becomes clearer and clearer that Wollstonecraft's sense of morality remains firmly rooted in the Commonwealth tradition that so strongly informed her views beginning in the early 1780s. In these examples and in many other places in her writing, not only does she take pride in the masculine characteristics of her daughter, Fanny, and criticize the French for having turned into a "nation of women," but she also encourages her readers and Burke to exhibit more "manly" behavior.

A Pro-British, Masculine Morality: Wollstonecraft's Ideal Citizen

Besides being decidedly masculine, I would like to suggest that Wollstonecraft's version of morality is also emphatically pro-British, and this, too, becomes more evident when we compare her writings about women and the French. Although, as discussed earlier, Wollstonecraft insists that morality is transnational, she actually tempers her vision of morality by infusing into it a nationalist blend of pro-British rhetoric and anti-French sentiment. Her portrait of the ideal British male sets up the paradigm for her model, as she explains how this man's character is formed: "The character of a master of a family, a husband, and a father, forms the citizen imperceptibly, by producing a sober manliness of thought, and orderly behavior" (*VRM* 38). What is most noteworthy about this description is that "the citizen" she has in mind is not gender-less, but clearly a man. This master, husband, and father is the litmus test against which other versions of citizenship can be compared.[49] This paradigm of the British nation is clearly British in Wollstonecraft's mind, and we can see this if we compare her ideal citizen to her representations of the French. Wollstonecraft's outline of the typical Frenchman as vain, pleasure-driven, and overly sensual, forms a sharp contrast to this vision of British manhood—a vision that is decidedly *not* French. Sober, orderly, and reasonable, the rational father adheres to the primary principles of morality, as Wollstonecraft defines them.

Once again, we can extrapolate from other passages in the Wollstonecraft canon to fill in the details of Wollstonecraft's model of British statehood. For Wollstonecraft, the family is the locus of public good. At one point in the first *Vindication,* for instance, she discusses "that first source of civilization, natural parental affection" (*VRM* 37). From this virtue, other virtues come forth, and this is a point worth emphasizing. What it signifies is Wollstonecraft's belief that family affections provide the soil into which other affections can be planted. In her second *Vindication,* she also points out: "A man has been termed a microcosm; and every family might also be called a state" (*VRW* 177). If each individual is his or her own little society unto him or herself, then each family is composed of these smaller societies, just as nation–states are composed of smaller subunits as well. Family affection thus forms the basis of society, and yet it is also from private virtues that the flowers of public virtues can shoot forth. As Wollstonecraft makes clear, "The happiness of the whole must arise from the happiness of the constituent parts, or the essence of justice is sacrificed to a supposed grand arrangement" (*VRM* 84). Those "constituent parts" are the people who not only possess but also act upon their private virtues. "Public spirit," Wollstonecraft insists, "must be nurtured by private virtue" so that "private virtue [can] becom[e] the cement of public happiness" (*VRW* 140, 144). Toward the close of her second *Vindication,* she makes this even clearer, declaring it to be one of the central arguments of her treatise: "I have endeavoured to shew that private duties are never properly fulfilled unless the understanding enlarges the heart; and that public virtue is only an aggregate of private" (*VRW* 192).[50]

If domestic affection, which is based upon strong morals, is therefore to be seen as the basis of the social order, then, following through with Wollstonecraft's logic—a logic that is, admittedly, circular—it also stands to reason that a lack of morals creates bad citizens. This, in fact, is what Wollstonecraft considers to be the primary result of depraved morals. The ostentation and love of the sensual that British women and the French share makes them unfit candidates for inclusion in the moral and principled nation. Sensuality and a lack of principles lead to bad parents, bad patriots, and ultimately bad public servants, all of whom eventually weaken the moral fiber of the state. To be better citizens, they need to become more like the ideal Briton—that "master of a family, a husband, and a father." In the case of British women, we can trace this argument back to Wollstonecraft's intolerance of their French counterparts. The very reason Wollstonecraft chose to write the second *Vindication*, as she herself explains, was because she wanted to write a British version of womanhood. The introduction clarifies her goals for the project. Addressing herself to Charles Maurice de Talleyrand–Périgord, upon whose influential report the French government was to base its system of public education, Wollstonecraft explains that she would like the French diplomat to extend his claims to women: "I dedicate this volume to you; to induce you to reconsider the subject, and maturely weigh what I have advanced respecting the rights of woman and national education" (*VRW* 3). Yet, as her introduction continues, Wollstonecraft makes it clear that her true concern is not so much women in general, as it is British women. Her model might be borrowed from the French (an important issue that I will shortly address), but her audience is purely her own countrymen and women. In the third paragraph of the opening, for instance, Wollstonecraft makes the connections between the French project and her own clear:

> In France there is undoubtedly a more general diffusion of knowledge than in any part of the European world, and I attribute it, in a great measure, to the social intercourse which has long subsisted between the sexes. It is true, I utter my sentiments with freedom, that in France the very essence of sensuality has been extracted to regale the voluptuary, and a kind of sentimental lust has prevailed, which, together with the system of duplicity that the whole tenour of their political and civil government taught, have given a sinister sort of sagacity to the French character, properly termed finesse; from which naturally flow a polish of manners that injures the substance, by hunting sincerity out of society.—And, modesty, the fairest garb of vir-

tue! has been more grossly insulted in France than even in England, till their women have treated as *prudish* that attention to decency, which brutes instinctively observe. (*VRW* 3–4)

This entire passage is based upon an implied comparison between British and French women. In Wollstonecraft's portrayal of French society, woman and men communicate freely, which has led their nation to become the most knowledgeable one in Europe. Yet that knowledge has also been bought at the cost of the morality of France's women. Sincerity, modesty, and decency are lacking, and their missing status has ultimately led to the degenerate status of the French people. Polished and refined they might be, but their morality has been sacrificed to sensuality. The implication is that British women, in contrast, are not subject to the same lack of morality—or at least not to such a great extent. Wollstonecraft hardly approves of her own countrywomen, but even though their modesty may have been insulted, it has not been replaced, as it has in France, by "a kind of sentimental lust."

Even though Wollstonecraft favorably compares British women to French women, one of her primary claims is that British women are not British enough—that they are too close in nature to their French neighbors. If the ideal citizen is the orderly, rational, and, above all, manly father who participates in the workings of the nation, then women, too, should be subject to this ideal. Wollstonecraft's main project is, of course, to make British women into "better citizens" (*VRW* 150), citizens who are neither French nor effeminate, and whose formulation owes its genesis to the close ties that Wollstonecraft retained to the Commonwealth tradition. Cora Kaplan speaks for many critics over the years who have noticed that "Wollstonecraft thought gender difference socially constructed but she found practically nothing to like in socially constructed femininity."[51] She urges women to model themselves after an ideal British manhood, and the way to achieve such an ideal is by making women useful. She carefully lays out this argument: "To fulfil domestic duties much resolution is necessary, and a serious kind of perseverance that requires a more firm support than emotions, however lively and true to nature. To give an example of order, the soul of virtue, some austerity of behaviour must be adopted, scarcely to be expected from a being who, from its infancy, has been made the weathercock of its own sensations. Whoever rationally means to be useful must have a plan of conduct" (*VRW* 68). This last line of the passage is one worth dwelling on. Knowing as we do Wollstonecraft's predilection for "order, the soul of virtue," we know that she favors rational thought and logical arguments. A plan, as a methodical formulation of action, best represents a strategy designed with clear guidelines in mind. To be useful therefore means having a clear set of principles in mind. Later on in the *Vindication,* she makes this same point: "I cannot help lamenting that women of a superiour cast have not a road open by which they can pursue more extensive plans of usefulness and independence" (*VRW* 147).[52] Once again, the word "plan" signifies Wollstonecraft's emphasis on the regulated and controlled aspects of her desire to make British women closer to her masculine ideal.

So how exactly are women supposed to be useful, and of what do these duties she so emphatically insists upon actually consist? The answer is most clearly spelled out in *A Vindication of the Rights of Woman.* Throughout this text, Wollstonecraft asserts that British women need to become better mothers, and so better citizens. "Would men but generously snap our chains," she reasons, "and be content with rational fellowship instead of slavish obedience, they would find us more observant daughters, more affectionate sisters, more faithful wives, more reasonable mothers — in a word, better citizens" (*VRW* 150). The argument, of course, is not a new one, for critics have long since pointed out Wollstonecraft's interest in making women into good members of society by making them into good mothers and wives first.[53] Yet the argument merits deeper analysis here because of its close tie to Wollstonecraft's own connections between nationalism, women's issues, and French national identity. Her construction of British womanhood depends upon a concomitant construction of British manhood. Wollstonecraft continues to argue not only for the increased need for strong moral principles, but also for the increased need for strong patriots. She explains the relationship between the two in detail:

> Manners and morals are so nearly allied that they have often been confounded; but, though the former should only be the natural reflection of the latter, yet, when various causes have produced factitious and corrupt manners, which are very early caught, morality becomes an empty name. The personal reserve, and sacred respect for cleanliness and delicacy in domestic life, which French women almost despise, are the graceful pillars of modesty; but, far from despising them, if the pure flame of patriotism have reached their bosoms, they should labour to improve the morals of their fellow-citizens, by teaching men, not only to respect modesty in women, but to acquire it themselves, as the only way to merit their esteem.
>
> Contending for the rights of woman, my main argument is built upon this simple principle, that if she be not prepared by education to become the companion of man, she will stop the progress of knowledge and virtue; for

truth must be common to all, or it will be inefficacious with respect to its influence on general practice. And how can woman be expected to co-operate unless she know why she ought to be virtuous? unless freedom strengthen her reason till she comprehend her duty, and see in what manner it is connected with her real good? If children are to be educated to understand the true principle of patriotism, their mother must be a patriot. (*VRW* 4)

The "factitious and corrupt manners" of Frenchwomen in particular has led them to despise what Wollstonecraft considers to be the best aspects of domestic life: a reserved nature and an adherence to delicacy. Without such attributes, Frenchwomen cannot be modest themselves or teach their husbands and brothers to be modest, either. Only when "the pure flame of patriotism" reaches them can they hope to effect such changes in the morality of their nation. After making this argument, Wollstonecraft then turns to a discussion of the current state of women within her own society. Since the focus of the second *Vindication* is on Britain's women, her "main argument," as she outlines it, focuses on the value of educating women: education will lead to stronger morals in women, which will in turn lead them to be better mothers, which will in turn lead them to educating their own children in a more patriotic fashion. The causality of her argument underscores the close connections between women, the nation, and the family: since public good depends upon moral and content individuals—moral and content *family* members—then British mothers have a serious duty imposed upon them. The family members determine what the nation will be like, but the mothers determine what the family members will be like. Wollstonecraft insists upon this role for women throughout the rest of the second *Vindication*. At one point, for instance, she states: "The being who discharges the duties of its station is independent; and, speaking of women at large, their first duty is to themselves as rational creatures, and the next, in point of importance, as citizens, is that, which includes so many, of a mother" (*VRW* 145). Women's role in the nation is thus, in many ways, similar to the role played by men, for "man must fulfil the duties of a citizen, or be despised, and that while he was employed in any of the departments of civil life, his wife, also an active citizen, should be equally intent to manage her family, educate her children, and assist her neighbors" (*VRW* 146). Activity is the key word here, for women must energetically take on the demands required of them. Instead of being passive beings, interested only in superficially pleasing or being superficially pleased, they should manage, educate, and assist those in need of their help.[54] Her argument for reform is therefore based upon use value, on how women can more effectively contribute to the goals of their own mother Britain.

CREATING BRITISH *CITOYENNES*

The irony of Wollstonecraft's vision, of course, is that she actually borrows her ideas from the French—from French Revolutionary discourse. When she wrote her second *Vindication*, Wollstonecraft was inspired by the political changes going on in France regarding women's rights, and her decision to write about women in her own nation was the direct result of the Revolutionaries' interest in addressing women's concerns. In these early days of the Revolution (before the Terror), women's rights were given a consideration that they had never been given before, and the work of writers like Marie-Jean-Antoine de Caritat Condorcet and Olympe de Gouges was particularly influential in changing the position of women in French society, who, Carol Blum points out, now "enjoyed the beginnings of some direct influence in political affairs."[55] Yet, as Lynn Hunt notes, although the early legislators granted women some political power, "They were not willing, however, to grant women equal status as citizens. Women were by definition citizens since they were not slaves, but they could not vote or hold public office."[56] There were limits to what French women could and could not do, and, as Hunt also notes, "It was only after they had fulfilled their private functions that women would be permitted to enter the public sphere. Similarly, legislators were most likely to proclaim the virtues of republican motherhood at those moments when they were concerned to deny women more public roles" (152). Wollstonecraft, familiar with these discourses and the political changes occurring in France, sought similar changes in Britain, and her positive portrayal of republican motherhood was essentially based upon a French model. In effect, Wollstonecraft was borrowing from the revolutionaries in order to improve upon their claims, expanding their claims so that British women could have more of a say in the goings-on of their nation, too. Wollstonecraft was basically advocating the creation of French *citoyennes* within Britain,[57] although she modified and expanded upon the Revolutionaries' claims to grant more rights to the women of her own nation. Despite her claim to be creating British patriots, she was actually creating French ones instead.

Women's "duty," then, is to be useful, to fulfill the function of moral caretaker, for her family, and yet this purpose, too, connects to Wollstonecraft's vision of morality. As already explained, Wollstonecraft's formulation of morality includes a heavy emphasis on order, on a strict adherence to uniform and regulated principles of conduct. Her ideal Briton, is regulated, too; he possesses "a sober manliness of thought" and demonstrates "orderly behavior." Consistency and responsibility are the trademarks of his actions. Because sensibility, however, involves a chaotic flood of emotions—the letting-in of arbitrary emotions that are not properly screened—sensibility undermines the patriotic responsibilities of both men and women. Right now, in the current state of society, women are neither useful nor orderly; their actions reflect the changing whims of their emotional states. Wollstonecraft thus makes a clear connection between women's sensibility and their inability to function as proper citizens. As sensual and pleasure-driven creatures, for instance, women resist action in favor of obscure emotion: "This word [humanity] discriminates the *active* exertions of virtue from the vague declamation of sensibility" (*VRM* 86; emphasis added).

Although Wollstonecraft's initial claim implies that she wants to erase national differences in order to make everyone subject to the same model of virtuous behavior, her model of ideal citizenry is actually based upon a masculine, pro-British rhetoric. Since the private family creates public citizens, who then influence the larger public for either better or worse, the welfare of the nation depends upon what goes on within the family. In Britain, the mother should take primary responsibility for raising principled, orderly Britons, and Wollstonecraft's goal is to convince her fellow countrymen and women to allow women greater freedom and more rational educations for them to do so. In France, however, or at least in Wollstonecraft's estimation, the argument is the same, but the situation is less optimistic. She criticizes the French even more than she does women for not adhering to standards she views as essentially British. Her portrayal of the French conveys the image of a people unable to harbor either domestic sympathy or private virtues. In the *Historical and Moral View*, for example, she makes this assessment several times. Since the French have been so concerned with living lives of pleasure, she explains to her British audience, "some few really learned the true art of living; giving that degree of elegance to domestic intercourse, which, prohibiting gross familiarity, alone can render permanent the family affections, whence all the social virtues spring" (*Historical* 147). This quotation is an important one, for it concisely expresses Wollstonecraft's belief in the connectedness of the family and the nation. The French people's quest for the sensual implies that they have failed to establish permanent bonds with their families, for the "true art of living" that she refers to is essentially a domestic happiness based upon probity and a regulated moral code. The failure to create such lasting bonds has serious consequences, though, for it means that their social affections have also been thwarted. Social virtues cannot exist without a strong degree of affection between husband and wife, brother and sister. Even the choice of amusements in France reinforces this lack of connection between family members: "the lascivious provocations to vice, exhibited at the opera, which, by destroying the social affections that attach men to each other, stifle all public spirit; *for what is patriotism but the expansion of domestic sympathy, rendered permanent by principle?*" (*Historical* 54; emphasis added). Love of one's country is rooted in love of one's family; without that first basis of order, little connection to one's own nation can be expected. Domestic affections are therefore moral because "true" and "natural." As she cries out at the end of one chapter, "When will a change of opinion, producing a real change of morals, render thee truly free? . . . When will thy sons trust, because they deserve to be trusted; and private virtue become the guarantee of patriotism? Ah!—when will thy government become the most perfect, because thy citizens are the most virtuous!" (*Historical* 85).[58] As she portrays them, the French are essentially moral vacuums.

This lack of domestic affection has ultimately led the French to becoming false patriots, just as it has caused British women to become bad mothers. In the preface to her history of the Revolution, Wollstonecraft explains that France is "often tottering on the brink of annihilation; in spite of the folly, selfishness, madness, treachery, and more fatal mock patriotism, the common result of depraved manners, the concomitant of that servility and voluptuousness which for so long a space of time has embruted the higher orders of this celebrated nation" (*Historical* 6). The depravity that characterizes the French has created a form of "mock" patriotism that is as artificial as the people themselves. Even those members of French society in a high enough position to make lasting changes in the French government have been "embruted" by their sensual natures. The difference between being a true patriot and being a mock one lies in the difference between morality and vanity. Using the ancient Greeks and Romans as an example, she argues that, actually, although they are praised for their heroic exploits,

> these heroes loved their country, because it was their country, ever showing by their conduct, that it was only a part of the narrow love of themselves.
> It is time that a more enlightened moral love of mankind should supplant,

or rather support physical affections. It is time, that the youth approaching
manhood should be led by principles, and not hurried along by sensations.
(*Historical* 21)

In Wollstonecraft's assessment, egoism and a narrow jingoism, not patriotism, lay at the core of the Ancients' actions. Physical affections—
affections based upon sensations—cannot function as a lasting mainstay
for the nation. Without "a more enlightened moral love of mankind,"
the nation has a hard time acting as a true nation. Its members are not
united by a bond that would bring together its members underneath the
rubric of "France." They cannot recognize each other as members of an
imagined community. "For a vain glorious ambition, mixing with the
abortions of giddy patriotism," Wollstonecraft further explains, "acts as
the most fatal poison to political disquisitions, during seasons of public
ferment" (*Historical* 143). As opposed to this "giddy" patriotism, true
patriotism "is of slow growth; requiring both a luxuriant public soil,
and to be fostered by virtuous emulation. Yet this emulation will never
flourish in a country where intriguing finesse, supplying the place of
exalted merit, is the surest ladder to distinction" (*Historical* 143). If
France's people remain vain and devious, they will never develop an
"honest" and "true" love of their country.[59]

A Revolution in National Character

Although Wollstonecraft deliberately points out the failings of both
groups under her observation, she still holds out the possibility for
change, unlike her compatriot Charlotte Smith who ultimately gave up
on the idea that Britain could be reformed. Because Wollstonecraft believes in the constructed nature of both people and nations and because
she posits that environment forms the individual, she can argue for the
possibility of directed growth toward her ideal. Identities—both gender
and national ones—have, she explains, been formed by society, but they
can also be changed with proper application and exertion. As mentioned earlier, Wollstonecraft's plan for the two groups she focuses on
is to make them into better citizens. How she actually advises them to
do so involves making them into more useful members of society. Yet
those more "extensive plans of usefulness and independence" (*VRW*
147) first involve making individuals aware that they can change. She
makes this claim, for instance, upon a more general level when she discusses individuals at large. "It is of great importance to observe," she

notes, "that the character of every man is, in some degree, formed by his profession. . . . Society, therefore, as it becomes more enlightened, should be very careful not to establish bodies of men who must necessarily be made foolish or vicious by the very constitution of their profession" (*VRW* 18). Performing the same duties on a daily basis forms a cycle of repetition that augments both positive and negative personality traits. As nations become more enlightened, she hopes, they will rid themselves of those professions most detrimental to their citizens. In addition, she emphasizes that not just a person's profession, but also a person's environment contributes to creating that person's nature: "it is the multitude, with moderate abilities, who call for instruction, and catch the colour of the atmosphere they breathe" (*VRW* 68–69).

Individuals' natures are thus constructed by their surroundings, and yet so, too, are genders. One of Wollstonecraft's main contributions to feminism, in fact, is her emphasis on the socially constructed nature of femininity.[60] Throughout the second *Vindication*, for instance, she insists that women have been formed by how others have treated them. Rousseau and other educational writers have always believed that women are naturally dependent and weak. Yet Wollstonecraft takes care to demonstrate how society has constructed and then reinforced this image of woman through its mores and codes. Repetition has made women take on the identities that these male writers have assumed they have always possessed. In essence, "the effect of habit is insisted upon as an undoubted indication of nature," even when that habit is imposed (*VRW* 81). A habit, as an arbitrarily assumed mode of behavior, makes random actions take on larger significance because of the repetition involved. Like prejudice, habit reinforces arbitrary actions while making those actions seem both reasonable and natural.[61] Just because women have been assigned roles to fill does not mean that those roles are natural, consistent, or even right; in fact, those roles do more harm than good, making women, as we have already seen, into pleasure-driven, vain, and overly sensual creatures. Yet Wollstonecraft's criticism does not just fall upon educational writers, for they are not the only ones who reinforce this constructed version of womanhood. Governments assert control over the actions of women to a much greater extent than we might think. Wollstonecraft traces this connection for her readers, noting that "the very constitution of civil governments has put almost insuperable obstacles in the way to prevent the cultivation of the female understanding:—yet virtue can be built upon no other foundation!" (*VRW* 54). Since most governments refuse women a rational education, they impede the progress that women could make. She also compares women to wealthy aristocrats: "Such are the blessings of civil governments, as they are at present organized, that wealth and female softness equally tend to debase mankind, and are produced by the same cause; but allowing women to be rational creatures, they should be incited to acquire virtues which they may call their own, for how can a rational being be ennobled by any thing that is not obtained by its *own* exertions?" (*VRW* 52). The ability to act and think for oneself gives each individual a sense of dignity, of accomplishment. Without virtue, women can claim no share in the principles of freedom. "Debased" by their gentle and mild "natures," their positions remain low and their morality remains even lower.

Women's current position, then, can be traced back to the ways in which society and governments have treated them. Haphazardly and thus poorly educated, women have become foolish and narrow-minded, unable to understand the larger world that lies outside of their windows. Gender identity–at least as it applies to women and their femininity since she otherwise outlines an essentialist British masculinity and sense of manhood–is therefore a constructed concept for Wollstonecraft, and so, too, is national identity. In Wollstonecraft's schema, not only do men and women—as gendered beings—become the creatures their societies' standards force them to become, but men and women also become national subjects who adhere to imposed standards of *national* behavior. She makes this clear in the opening lines of the *Letter on the Present Character of the French Nation* when she explains her reasons for choosing to write the letter in the first place: "it is not the morals of a particular people that I would decry; for are we not all of the same stock? But I wish calmly to consider the stage of civilization in which I find the French, and, giving a sketch of their character, and unfolding the circumstances which have produced its identity, I shall endeavour to throw some light on the history of man, and on the present important subjects of discussion" (*Letter* 444). Emphasizing once again that morality is consistent across nations—"for are we not all of the same stock?"—Wollstonecraft explains that she will focus on understanding the "character" and "identity" of the French. Particular circumstances have created the French national identity, and her goal is to draw the connections between this identity and the causes of the French Revolution.[62]

She makes these connections even more explicit in the *Historical and Moral View*. There, she shows how France's geographical position and even choice of food have contributed to the French national identity. Wollstonecraft attributes the differences in temperament between the

British and the French to a difference in climate; France's location has made it literally a brighter and cheerier land than Great Britain, a "great" nation nonetheless plagued by perpetual fog and rain. "Besides," she writes, "the climate of France is so genial, and the blood mounted so cheerily in the veins, even of the oppressed common people, that, living for the day, they continually basked in the sunshine, which broke from behind the heavy clouds that hung over them" (*Historical* 122). Basking in the sunshine may at first sound well and good, but for Wollstonecraft it signals an inability to engage in the more serious issues of the present situation, a refusal to acknowledge the presence of foreboding signs of approaching storms. When discussing the bread shortages of the summer of 1789, which occurred immediately before the storming of the Bastille, she also remarks on how gullible and ignorant the French had been. Commenting on their credulity, she remarks:

> The supplying of Paris with provision always depended on a nice arrangement of circumstances, capable of being controlled by the government of the state. It is not like London, and other great cities, the local position of which was previously pointed out by nature, and of which the welfare depends on the great and perpetual movements of commerce, which they themselves regulate. . . . Paris, on the contrary, might be famished in a few days by a secret order of the court. All the people of the place would feel the effect, and no person be able to ascertain the cause. (*Historical,* ftns 92, 93)

In contrast to Britain, France possesses a capital that reflects the duplicity that its people practice upon one another everyday. Insinuating that the French government started the recent famines, Wollstonecraft notes that the people are naive enough to be played upon by the hoax. Even their geographical location thus works against them, for it allows the French to be manipulated by their government. Indirectly, Paris's location renders its inhabitants even more artificial and foolish than they already are.

Similarly, Wollstonecraft points out how even the French cuisine and government have contributed to shaping the French. She begins her discussion by first noting how lifestyle contributes to the national character. "Besides," she remarks, "the very manner of living in France gives a lively turn to the character of the people" (*Historical* 226). Using an argument that dates at least as far back as Montaigne and that was also used by writers as diverse as Voltaire and Thomas More, Wollstonecraft explains that even the French people's food makes them too vivacious and sensual. She investigates the French mode of eating even further: "for by the destruction of the animal juices, in dressing their food, they are subject to none of that dulness, the effect of more nutritive diet in other countries; and this gaiety is increased by the moderate quantity of weak wine, which they drink at their meals, bidding defiance to phlegm" (*Historical* 226–27). Although she does not say as much, clearly her ideal, the citizens whose food renders them as a whole the most phlegmatic of nations, are those consummate eaters of roast beef, the British. While the French have been formed, then, by both their location and their alimentary affiliations, they have also been formed, just as British women have, by their government. Just as the British government has been an active contributor to the formation of British womanhood, so, too, has the French government played an active role in creating its own subjects. Throughout her history of the Revolution, for example, Wollstonecraft attributes the recent events in France to the actions of the rulers. "The late arrangement of things seems to have been the common effect of an absolute government, a domineering priesthood, and a great inequality of fortune," she notes (*Historical* 231). Yet most of all, she blames the government: "Let us investigate the causes which have produced this degeneracy, and we shall discover, that they are those unjust plans of government, which have been formed by peculiar circumstances in every part of the globe" (*Historical* 235).

How have the actions of the government affected France's people? Basically, the same government that produced the Revolution also created corrupt morals. Tracing the cause of the current state of depravity, she writes, "The morals of the whole nation were destroyed by the manners formed by the government.—Pleasure had been pursued, to fill up the void of rational employment; and fraud combined with servility to debase the character" (*Historical* 123). By encouraging its subjects to seek pleasure, the French government has exacerbated the superficial, disingenuous, and servile nature of its people. Wollstonecraft even goes as far back as the Crusades to establish this pattern of immorality. The Crusades, she explains, first gave rise to chivalry, and marked the period when "the character of a *gentleman*, held ever since so dear in France, was gradually formed; and this kind of bastard morality, frequently the only substitute for all the ties that nature has rendered sacred, kept those men within bounds, who obeyed no other law" (*Historical* 23–24). The "bastard morality" to which she refers is chivalry, a concept that is usually associated with regulated rules of behavior. But Wollstonecraft takes care to point out that gentlemen who possess the semblance of being refined and regulated may actually lack morality. Appearance and the desire to be thought by others to be a gentlemen have held these men in check. Besides being slaves of plea-sure, as the nature of being a gentleman implies, the French have also become cunning. Fearful of their government, they have resorted to fraud and deception: "Arbitrary decrees have too often assumed the sa-cred majesty of law; and when men live in continual fear, and know not what they have to apprehend, they always become cunning and pusil-lanimous. . . . This leads, likewise, to an observation, that partly ac-counts for the want of industry and cleanliness in France" (*Historical* 75). Dirty and lazy, the French lack strength of character. This "despo-tism in the government" ultimately "account[s] for the contradictions in the french character" (*Historical* 232).

Even though Wollstonecraft's portrayals of her fellow countrywomen and the French are, to put it mildly, negative, she nevertheless presents an optimistic portrait of the future. That the natures of both women and the French are constructed makes the possibilities for change that much greater. Wollstonecraft's belief in the environmentally and socially con-structed nature of identity is, in fact, what lies behind her idea of revo-lution. By the time that Wollstonecraft wrote her French texts, however, her understanding of revolution was more aligned with the Burkean model of gradual change than it had been in her earlier *Vindi-cations*.[63] In her formulation, the British government serves as a model of the process of gradual improvement. "With respect to the improve-ment of society," she notes, "England seems to have led the way, ren-dering certain obstinate prejudices almost null, by a gradual change of opinion" (*Historical* 70). The British constitution developed as a result of "slow improvement," and has thereby become "the sublimest theory" of government ever created (*Historical* 167). This regulated and contin-uous vision is central to Wollstonecraft's analysis: "The revolutions of states ought to be gradual," she insists; "All sudden revolutions have been as suddenly overturned, and things thrown back below their for-mer state" (*Historical* 183, 166). And why exactly should revolutions be gradual? Because if they are not, those affected will be unable to com-prehend the new state of affairs. There is a "necessity of gradual reform; lest the light, suddenly breaking-in on a benighted people, should over-power the understanding it ought to direct" (*Historical* 183).[64]

This vision of revolution closely aligns with Wollstonecraft's vision of gender since revolution opens the possibility of change. Just as women have learned certain behaviors, they can, though not quite as easily, un-learn them, aligning themselves more closely with Wollstonecraft's "masculine" ideal in the process. This belief underlies her desire for what she refers to as a "revolution in female manners." Early in the second *Vindication,* she mentions her goal: "It is time to effect a revolution in female manners—time to restore to them their lost dignity—and make them, as a part of the human species, labour by reforming themselves to reform the world. It is time to separate unchangeable morals from local manners" (*VRW* 45). Wollstonecraft's terminology is important, for she advocates not a revolution of morals, but rather a revolution in *manners.*[65] Once again, she insists that morality has an unchanging nature, a fixed core, whereas manners are variable and mutable. Since we have already looked at Wollstonecraft's theory of manners in a national context through her translation of the German text *Elements of Morality for the Use of Children,* we know that the term "manners" also carries a nationalist connotation for her. Just as national identity—national *manners*—can be altered, so, too, can gender identity. In the last chapter of *A Vindication of the Rights of Woman,* she dwells on the idea of revolution at greater length, making the concept of a female revolution part of her chapter title: "Concluding Reflections on the Moral Improvement That a Revolution in Female Manners Might Naturally Be Expected to Produce" (*VRW* 178). Within the pages of this chapter, she expands upon various examples of the "follies" that women commit, ending with the changes she would like to see accomplished.[66] The changes, she hopes, will take effect as a result of this revolution: "That women at present are by ignorance rendered foolish or vicious, is, I think, not to be disputed; and, that the most salutary effects tending to improve mankind might be expected from a REVOLUTION in female manners" (*VRW* 192). Wollstonecraft's use of the passive voice in this passage once again signals her understanding of how women are not born a particular way, but rather created. Ignorance and viciousness are the culprits, for they have made women into weak beings.

A MODEL OF GRADUAL CHANGE

It should be clear by now that Wollstonecraft's idea of female revolution depends upon the constructed nature of gender. Each error a woman commits, whether that error is one of vanity, pleasure, or excess emotion, directly results from that woman's improper education. If taught to think rationally and morally—and this is what constitutes Wollstonecraft's revolution—women will become more productive citizens. The key to making women into useful beings thus lies in educating them about their nation and their own role within it as mothers and wives. As Wollstonecraft repeatedly emphasizes, women cannot fulfill their duties unless they understand of what those duties consist. They must use their reason to understand their place within British society. By exercising their faculty of reason, women can learn to become independent thinkers and more able contributors to the welfare of the British nation. As slaves of opinion, the role that women currently *do* occupy, they are vain and shallow, overly concerned with what others think. As rationally educated creatures, the role they *could* occupy, they are respectable and informed, concerned with helping others. Later on, she sums up the point rather succinctly: "In short, in whatever light I view the subject, reason and experience convince me that the only method of leading women to fulfil [*sic*] their peculiar duties, it to free them from all restraint by allowing them to participate in the inherent rights of mankind. Make them free, and they will quickly become wise and virtuous" (*VRW* 175). Women can change through education, by becoming more rational creatures. In essence, "To render women truly useful members of society, I argue that they should be led, by having their understandings cultivated on a large scale, to acquire a rational affection for their country, founded on knowledge, because it is obvious that we are little interested about what we do not understand" (*VRW* 191–92).[67] Wollstonecraft states her main point even more directly: "The conclusion which I wish to draw, is obvious; make women rational creatures, and free citizens, and they will quickly become good wives, and mothers; that is—if men do not neglect the duties of husbands and fathers" (*VRW* 178).[68]

Effecting a female revolution signifies change—or at least the potential for it. Yet Wollstonecraft does not limit her hope to only one of her two focus groups, for she also believes that the French Revolution represents France's best hope for transformation. A *gender* revolution (for that is, essentially, what a female revolution is) can be brought about in Britain because manners possess the ability to be altered; in the same way, France's *national* revolution—a revolution, of course, already in progress—can be brought to a successful close because its people can alter their manners so that those manners are more closely allied with the eternal moral compass that should guide us all. After all, part of the reason the Revolution has met with so many difficulties thus far, she explains, is because the French are not ready to change their manners. Their national identity is still tied to their ideals of pleasure and emotion, creating a soil too superficial and light for any lasting changes to take root. Because of their national identity, the French are prone to extremes, and this is a point she repeatedly emphasizes. "But, from the commencement of the revolution," she argues, "the misery of France has originated from the folly or art of men, who have spurred the people on too fast; tearing up prejudices by the root, which they should have permitted to die gradually away" (*Historical* 159). If the French had possessed a "consistent government," that government "would have prevented those clamours, which were sure to draw together an host of enemies, to impede the settlement of rational laws; flowing from a constitution, that would peaceably have undermined despotism, had it been allowed gradually to change the manners of the people" (*Historical* 160). Because the French were "constitutionally attached to novelty and ingenious speculations," however, they "gave themselves little trouble to examine the gradual steps by which other countries have attained their degree of political improvement" (*Historical* 226). Acting on their own, they decided (out of vanity, of course) not to refer to the actions and ideas of those nations that had gone before them; they decided to conduct their revolution in their own way. Even the National Assembly perpetuated these initial mistakes. When this able group of men first began meeting, they avoided gradual reform, favoring abrupt action instead: "instead of looking for gradual improvement, letting one reform calmly produce another, they seemed determined to strike at the root of all their misery at once" (*Historical* 45). This tendency pervades the entire nation, for so many of them refuse to listen to reason: "And so apt are men, in the moment of action, to fly from one extreme to the other, without considering, that the strongest conviction of reason cannot quickly change a habit of body; much less the manners that have been gradually produced by certain modes of thinking and acting" (*Historical* 53). Accustomed to "thinking and acting" a particular way, a nation's people will change slowly, even when reason acts as a catalyst to that change.

Despite the tendency to fly from one whim to the next, however, the French can still attempt change because their national character can be modified, even if slowly. Change, however, she makes clear, "ought not to have been expected, before an alteration in the national character seconded the new system of government" (*Historical* 196). The fact that such an "alteration" can take place, however, is where her hope lies. As she earlier explained, "It was a revolution in the minds of men; and only demanded a new system of government to be adapted to that change. This was not generally perceived; and the politicians of the day ran wildly from one extreme to the other" (*Historical* 183). She develops this point to a greater extent toward the end of the next chapter:

> To consult the public mind in a perfect state of civilization, will not only be necessary, but it will be productive of the happiest consequences, generating

a government emanating from the sense of the nation, for which alone it can legally exist. The progress of reason being gradual, it is the wisdom of the legislature to advance the simplification of it's [*sic*] political system, in a manner best adapted to the state of improvement of the understanding of the nation. The sudden change which had happened in france, from the most fettering tyranny to an unbridled liberty, made it scarcely to be expected, that any thing should be managed with the wisdom of experience: it was morally impossible. (*Historical* 212–13)

Wollstonecraft's emphasis on the morality of France's sudden change calls attention once again to her pro-British stance. Sudden change is least likely to produce lasting effects, and yet it is also least in tune with the gradual process of reform that Britain itself underwent during the Glorious Revolution, a revolution that Wollstonecraft and her Commonwealth associates supported. Aligning itself with Britain's model of change would also mean that France ally itself not just with the abstract concept of a nation, but also with the unrelaxing moral standards that distinguish Britons from themselves.

So although the negative aspects of their national identity have thus far caused the French to live degenerate, extreme lives, they still have time to change their national identity in order to fulfill the promise of their revolution. One way they can accomplish this goal, as just suggested, is by following Britain's model of gradual reform, and yet a second method also exists. By first perceiving and then analyzing their areas of weakness, the French can also adapt to Wollstonecraft's British ideal. She explains this belief for her readers: "Every nation, deprived by the progress of it's [*sic*] civilization of strength of character, in changing it's [*sic*] government from absolute despotism to enlightened freedom, will, most probably, be plunged into anarchy, and have to struggle with various species of tyranny before it is able to consolidate it's [*sic*] liberty; and that, perhaps, cannot be done, until the manners and amusements of the people are completely changed" (*Historical* 213). British women, she had argued in *A Vindication of the Rights of Woman*, need their method of education changed so that they can, in turn, change their manners and adhere more strongly to a correct set of moral principles. The French, she argues in the *Historical and Moral View*, can also be changed. If their manners are changed so that they adhere more closely to the one standard of morality—the moral compass that guides the actions of the moral individual—then they can become free. Their revolution will succeed if they conform to Wollstonecraft's ideal—if, that is, they become more like the British. After all, their manners should not just be changed, but should rather be "completely," if gradually, changed. The "improvement of manners" she envisions for the French will serve as the "harbinger of reason," as the forerunner of the subsequent "progress of political science" (*Historical* 225).

"A New Order of Things": Wollstonecraft's Hope for New National Citizens

Most readers believe that Mary Wollstonecraft held an uncompromisingly positive view of the Revolution, that she was an unfailing supporter of it—and of the French people—no matter what the cost. Critics have long recognized Wollstonecraft's admiration of the French Revolution and her love–hate relationship with "French" *philosophe* Rousseau,[69] but what has not been explored up until this point is her complicated view of the Revolution and the connections between her nationalist and feminist beliefs. Her feminism is therefore more closely related to her views on the French and her own nationalist impulses than has been previously recognized. Although she believed in the progressive nature of the Revolution, Wollstonecraft also maintained a pessimistic view of the French people. She preserved the view that their national identity made it uncertain as to whether or not their Revolution could be successfully accomplished. In much the same way, Wollstonecraft was also uncertain in her hopes for her own fellow countrywomen. While she advocated a "female revolution," she also knew that little could be accomplished until women's gender identity was to also change. British and French society would have to be modified in order for progress to take place.

The merging of Wollstonecraft's nationalist and feminist projects was not unique; the rhetorical strategies she used were also adopted by writers as diverse as Hannah More, Helen Maria Williams, Charlotte Smith, and Frances Burney. Like these other female writers, Wollstonecraft had to treat her gender concerns against the backdrop of French–British relations since nationalist concerns so completely dominated the public discourses of the late eighteenth century. Her interest in comparing her fellow countrywomen to the French makes her project unique, however, for ultimately Wollstonecraft differs from her peers because she figures a masculine, pro-British morality at the core of her program for change.

Drawing heavily upon the nationalist rhetoric that she herself was so familiar with, Wollstonecraft advocated a vision of morality that, she believed, was both cross-gender and cross-national. However, making British women into better mothers and the French into better citizens actually involves making them adhere more strongly to a program of productivity that is closely allied to a morality best exemplified in the figure of the British male. Despite possessing vain, impetuous, and pleasure-driven natures, and despite being subject to their emotionally overwrought sensibilities, British women and the French can, she argues, still become serviceable members of society. Usefulness is, in fact, the best way to render both women and the French productive members of their respective nations. Writing at the dawn of the nineteenth century, Wollstonecraft was thus able to foresee what she would refer to several times in the *Historical and Moral View* as a "new order of things" that was just beginning to take place in the world (*Historical* 129, 142, 208). Rational, regulated, and principled, this new order would, Wollstonecraft believes, bring with it new national citizens, able to participate more fully in the goings-on of their countries. The revolutions she hopes to see accomplished would issue forth moral and concerned citizens, ready to change the world and its inhabitants for the better.

5

Reconciliation and Revision in Frances Burney's *The Wanderer*

Writers constantly practice the craft of revision as they pore over their pages, making changes in their work that will ultimately affect their readers' understanding and appreciation of the text. Yet when a writer sends a final manuscript off to press, to be printed and made available for mass distribution, rarely will he or she have the opportunity to change the book to any great degree before it reaches its final audiences. Scenes may be expanded and words may be modified when the writer corrects the book for a second or possibly third edition, but usually the changes are insignificant ones. If ideas alter or a new vision of the world emerges to replace an older one, the author usually has no choice but to live with the creation that has been sent out to the public. Frances Burney, however, was not ready to live with the choices she had previously made.

Between the writing of her first and her last novel, Burney's worldview underwent a change, a change that would make the ideas and characters in her first novel obsolete to her. This first novel, *Evelina, or, a Young Woman's Entrance into the World*, which appeared in 1778, was an instant success. Burney's diaries and letters record, in fact, her delight at the immense popularity of her book. She took great pleasure in listening to people, not knowing that she was the author, discuss it in her presence, and meticulously copied down both their words and those of the published reviews.[1] Praise for the novel centered around the lively characters, whom most of the critics appreciated for their amusing antics and vigorous dialogues.[2] The ribald exchanges between the characters and the flagrant comedy appealed to her readers, who could literally not get enough of the novel. Although the next two novels that Burney wrote, 1782's *Cecilia, or Memoirs of an Heiress* and 1796's *Camilla; or, a Picture of Youth*, were relatively well received, audiences then, as even now, preferred her first attempt. The serious tone of these later

188

novels was no match for the comedic one of *Evelina,* which has always remained the favorite. Her fourth and last novel, 1814's *The Wanderer; or, Female Difficulties,* met with the worst fate of all, however. Although the first edition of it sold quickly, the reviewers came down hard, criticizing Burney for her choice of content, tone, and character.[3] Despite these harsh appraisals, though, many modern-day critics agree that *The Wanderer* is the richest and most complex of any text in the Burney canon.[4] By the time she wrote it, Burney had experienced life in France firsthand, and had developed an appreciation for its people and culture. Her worldview had been enlarged, and Burney was ready to think of national identity in new ways. Whether consciously or not, Burney rewrote her first narrative, the story of Evelina, to reflect these changes. The similarities between the two tales, which both detail the life of a young woman, make Burney's project of reconciliation and revision clear. Although the two narratives are not identical, their areas of overlap make the connections between them, as well as Burney's modifications, prominent.

While *Evelina* consistently delights its readers, its premise, that of a young woman making her entrance into fashionable British society, is light. Evelina must learn to regulate her behavior and to negotiate her place in the world, but she learns her lessons quickly and well. Her metaphorical journey to maturity, as I argued in chapter 1, is made easier by the fact that her world is a straightforward one, uncomplicated by characters that exhibit unusual or incomprehensible behavior. Although she does manage to get herself into a few dangerous situations (most notably at Vauxhall, in the Marybone-gardens, and with Sir Clement Willoughby), most of the time her mistakes are nothing more than faux pas, social embarrassments that she must live down afterward. The most threatening force in the novel, in fact, wears the guise not of a heartless seducer, as it did in many of the period's novels, but rather that of an old, bawdy woman by the name of Madame Duval. Evelina's grandmother represents the threat of a dual national identity, of being both French and English, which is a prospect that Evelina finds horrifying. To develop this idea, Burney draws upon nationalist stereotypes and prejudices to portray Madame Duval as a foul, almost monstrous woman. Despised by those around her, Madame Duval still possesses, though, the ability to force Evelina to return to France with her. Evelina is essentially powerless in her grandmother's grasp, and has no choice but to try to appease her. Yet Burney does not let Madame Duval get away with uncontrolled power. To contain Madame Duval, as I argued, Burney brings in Captain Mirvan, a character who is even cruder and more savage than Evelina's grandmother. The Captain, who has an inveterate hatred of anything having to do with the French, absolutely abhors Madame Duval, so he does everything he can to torment and humiliate her. Their verbal and physical exchanges make up the bulk of the comedic scenes of the novel, yet these scenes also have a disturbing edge to them, one that reveals Burney's nascent sense of doubt about the nationalist rhetoric and imagery in which she engages.

The Wanderer, in contrast to its predecessor, is a dark novel. British society is more complex and unfathomable than it was in Burney's earlier novel, and many of the characters remain as shrouded in mystery as the heroine Juliet. Even the premise of the novel has undergone revision. This story, like Burney's previous one, is also about the entrance of a young woman into British society; the difference, however, lies in the seriousness of the adventures that our heroine encounters. Whereas Evelina's most constant fear was the risk of social embarrassment, Juliet's is that of sustaining herself physically and emotionally. If she does not find work, she will literally starve to death because she has no other way to live. Another aspect of *Evelina* that Burney revised is the characters. In this novel, *Evelina*'s cast of characters appear once again, ready to make their final performance, but they both look and act differently. Replacing Evelina is Juliet, an older and more mature heroine who must still negotiate the world and find asylum. Unlike Evelina, however, Juliet has no friends and family members to guide her or offer her financial help; she must rely upon her own abilities to support herself and must constantly seek out protection to do so. In place of Captain Mirvan is Admiral Powel, a man full of prepossessions against the French, but who is benevolent nevertheless. And Lord Orville, that most perfect of all Burney's heroes, appears as that most disliked of all Burney's heroes, the rather bland Harleigh.[5] Yet Burney's most significant revision appears in the changes made to Madame Duval, who at first glance seems to have been left out of the cast. Far from excluding Madame Duval, however, Burney has allowed her to metamorphose into none other than our heroine, Juliet. This time, though, Burney presents a much more favorable portrait of a character who possesses a dual national identity, and the principal villains of the novel are not French, but rather *British* women. Whereas in *Evelina* we are trained to be amused when Madame Duval is "rightfully" punished for her claims to a dual identity, in *The Wanderer* we are trained to sympathize with Juliet and to condemn those who mistreat her for the very same reason we earlier disliked Madame Duval—for possessing a French–English heritage.

Burney's most substantial revision is also her most liberatory, for by reading about Juliet's trials we reach a better understanding of the difficulties of life for women in modern British society, a society that, as Burney depicts it, is based upon prejudice and distrust. Each of the major themes of the novel—friendship, protection, work, and prejudice—is thus wrapped up with larger concerns about gender and the role of women within the British nation. These concerns, which are all inextricable from one another, also reinforce Burney's emphasis on the necessity of female community. Like other women writers of the period, Burney argues that bonds between women should traverse national barriers, and that women should set aside their nationalist prejudices to help and protect those in need. The revisions she made to her first novel thus reflect Burney's own changed conceptions of British society and nationalist discourses between the mid to late eighteenth century, as well as those of other women writers. These alterations gradually take shape as we watch the ways in which Burney reweaves her original tale.

Prefacing the Reconciliation of Differences

Burney begins her last novel by laying out her project of reconciliation, of aligning opposites, even while she embraces contradictions. Her Preface to the novel is worth examining in detail since it establishes some of the major themes in the novel and because in it Burney presents herself as an arbiter and reconciler of differences. Before the Preface even begins, Burney establishes this role. Charles Burney, her father and one of the most prominent musical historians of the eighteenth century, is the addressee, for the novel is dedicated to "Doctor Burney, F.R.S. and Correspondent to the Institute of France," and, to make things even clearer for her readers, Burney adds a footnote explaining the latter designation: "To which honour Dr. Burney was elected, by the wholly unsolicited votes of the members *des beaux arts*. His daughter brought over his diploma from Paris."[6] Although Burney takes care to emphasize that her father had not sought the votes of the French council members, that the French made the first gesture of unification and the great musical historian had merely accepted a place in their Institute, she herself takes on a more active role. Her emphasis upon the dual titles her father has received and that she herself has acted as liaison between France and her father places Burney in the role of ambassador between nations. French music is united with British music through the figure of her father, yet she has had a central role in bringing about that unification by conveying the diploma from Paris to Britain. She continues to assume this role of reconciler throughout the rest of her Preface. At one point, for instance, she mentions her friendship with "those two celebrated, immortal authours (*sic*), Dr. Johnson, and the Right Honourable Edmund Burke; whose sentiments upon public affairs divided, almost separated them, at that epoch; yet who, then, and to their last hours, I had the pride, the delight, and the astonishment to find the warmest, as well as the most eminent supporters of my honoured essays" (5). These two otherwise hostile men were still able to achieve unity through their appreciation for Burney's work and, although they may have disagreed in their views on political matters, Johnson and Burke could remain friends through their shared affection for their young friend. Burney credits herself with bringing about peace not only between nations, but also within them.

As she continues with her Preface, Burney further discusses her aim of adopting a neutral stance in her relations with both France and Britain within her novel. Her marriage to Frenchman Alexandre D'Arblay, she explains, has made her particularly desirous of avoiding any topics that would give rise to hostile relations. She clearly explains her rationale: "If, therefore, then, . . . I held political topics to be without my sphere, or beyond my skill; who shall wonder that now,—united, alike by choice and by duty, to a member of a foreign nation, yet adhering, with primæval enthusiasm, to the country of my birth, I should leave all discussions of national rights, and modes, or acts of government, to those whose wishes have no opposing calls; whose duties are undivided; and whose opinions are unbiased by individual bosom feelings" (5). In this passage, Burney carefully situates herself as a woman who can easily maintain more than one national identity, something fearsome and undesirable in *Evelina*. She is "united" to her French husband not just through "duty," but also through "choice": she loves him and wants to be with him. So that her British readers do not mistake her allegiance to Britain, however, Burney is careful to state that she still adheres, "with primæval enthusiasm, to the country of [her] birth." Her wishes *do* have opposing calls, her duties *are* divided, and her opinions *are* biased by her feelings; she is truly split by loyalty to both nations. In *Evelina*, the possibility of holding a dual national identity was one of the central problems for the protagonist. Thirty-six years later, however, the same author welcomes a dual identity, for she herself now possesses one. By representing herself as a woman who can occupy several spaces at once,

Burney prefigures the role that *The Wanderer*'s protagonist, Juliet, will have, for we will soon learn that the novel's heroine will also have these same dual allegiances to both Britain and France. Burney sets up our understanding of Juliet, prepares us to read and appreciate her, by referencing her own situation. The two women have much in common. A return to the idea of dual identities occurs when Burney explains how she carefully chose the subject matter and time period of *The Wanderer* to further avoid any hostile relations between France and Britain. She explains her decision in cautious language, emphasizing that the Reign of Terror is looked upon by both countries—what she refers to as "my adoptive country" and "the country of my birth"—as a time of "horrour" (6). Essentially, France and Britain are united through their feelings about the Terror and its effects on the modern world. The French and the British, despite their other differences, both look back to the Terror as one of the darkest moments of history, and even future generations of French and British will be linked by this historical tie.

Even Burney's choice of setting thereby lends itself to her larger project of reconciliation, and yet there are some significant resonances in this choice as well as some others. While it is true that her novel takes place during the Terror, the true subject matter of her novel lies outside the sphere of overtly political events. The Terror serves as more of a backdrop to the lives and themes that Burney wants to take up, and the novel is not so much about the Revolution and the Terror as it is about some of Burney's own concerns regarding gender and the nation. "Female difficulties," the subtitle of the novel, is where Burney's interests really lie, and so by claiming that her novel is about the Revolution, Burney tosses her audience a red herring. Reconciliation thus involves telling lies, lies that Burney herself might not be aware of telling, but which still color her explanation of the choices she made when writing her novel. Putting together the pieces of the puzzle makes it clear that unification between France and Britain occurs at the expense of truth.

The desire to forge these connections leads Burney to slightly alter her explanation of how she brought her manuscript through customs. The French custom officers' behavior was actually marked by suspicion and hesitancy when Burney left France to return to Britain in 1812. Burney brushes over this, however, in her rush to come to the rescue, as it were, of both nations. Like its author, "The early part of this immediate tribute ha[d] already twice traversed the ocean in manuscript" form (4). This second crossing was upon her final return to Britain, and Burney describes the event in detail:

And, to the honour and liberality of both nations, let me mention, that, at the Custom-house of either—alas!—hostile shore, upon my given word that the papers contained neither letters, nor political writings; but simply a work of invention and observation; the voluminous manuscript was suffered to pass, without demur, comment, or the smallest examination.

A conduct so generous on one side, so trusting on the other, in time of war, even though its object be so unimportant, cannot but be read with satisfaction by every friend of humanity, of either rival nation. (4)

Although Burney claims that the "voluminous manuscript was suffered to pass, without demur, comment, or the smallest examination," her personal journal actually gives a completely different account of the border crossing. When the small case that the manuscript was packed in was opened up, the officer, according to Burney, "began a rant of indignation & amazement at a sight so unexpected & prohibited. . . . He sputtered at the Mouth, & stamped with his feet."[7] Although the officer's reaction appears humorous in its absurdity, it held serious consequences. Accusing Burney of "traitorous designs," the customs official could have arrested Burney and had her novel destroyed. Burney herself acknowledges this when she writes that "this Fourth Child of my Brain had undoubtedly been destroyed ere it was Born, had I not had recourse to an English merchant" who helped establish her identity.[8] Using the metaphor of an aborted birth, Burney records her true feelings toward her work and the impact that the manuscript's destruction would have had on her. Even though she does not openly avow her emotions, by linking her novel to a living human being, to a child, she makes those emotions apparent. These personal feelings, however, are subsumed within the Preface so that Burney can seek her "greater," because more public, goal. Deviating from the truth of the episode allows Burney to assert the generosity and trust of both "rival nation[s]."[9] Her purposeful misconstruction of the actual circumstances is done to achieve harmony. Only a few pages later, Burney continues this deception. While separated from her "native friends and country," she asserts that "during the ten eventful years, from 1802 to 1812, that I resided in the capital of France, I was neither startled by any species of investigation, nor distressed through any difficulties of conduct" (6). Margaret Doody points out the falsity of this claim by referring to Burney's letters and journals. As Doody explains, Burney was "always conscious of oppression in living under Napoleon's dictatorship."[10] Her life was fraught with emotional and economic difficulties, and Burney greatly missed her family and friends at home in Britain.[11] Once again,

Burney consciously misrepresents her personal life in order to serve as a "neutral" arbiter.

Burney's claim in the passage cited above that "the papers contained neither letters, nor political writings; but simply a work of invention and observation" brings up another type of falsification that Burney practices in her Preface. Claiming that her novel is not political, she asserts that she is only continuing what she has already tried to accomplish in her three previous works:

> Such, therefore,—if any such there be,—who expect to find here materials for political controversy; or fresh food for national animosity; must turn elsewhere their disappointed eyes: for here, they will simply meet, what the Author has thrice sought to present to them already, a composition upon general life, manners, and characters; without any species of personality, either in the form of foreign influence, or of national partiality. I have felt, indeed, no disposition,—I ought rather, perhaps, to say talent,—for venturing upon the stormy sea of politics. (4)

Yet Burney *had* already been swayed by "national partiality" and *had* given her audience "fresh food for national animosity," despite her claims that she lacks "talent" for so doing. She seems to have forgotten that much of *Evelina* involves nationalist stereotype and a comic relief that is achieved through the humiliation of a pretentious Frenchwoman. If we cannot believe Burney in her claims about her previous novels, the question becomes, then why should we believe her now? In fact, her last novel, just like her first, *is* a political novel; the nature of Juliet's story *is* one of "political controversy." That controversy may not have to do with the events of the French Revolution, but, we shall soon see, it does have to do with the status of British women within society and with the nationalist discourses with which Burney was already so familiar.

"A VOICE OF KEEN DISTRESS"

As the novel opens, the voice of the author slowly fades away, to be replaced instead by "a voice of keen distress resound[ing] from the shore, imploring, in the French language, pity and admission" (11). The figure of Juliet emerges from the darkness as the possessor of this voice, as a woman who brings with her a more experienced understanding of the world than did her predecessor, Evelina. Complexity and shadows define the world for Juliet, and she herself is shrouded in mystery and darkness. If Burney's project of reconciliation, of uniting France and Britain, reveals itself through her overarching project of revision, then some of the most substantial revisions she made from her first novel to her last were in the form of her heroine. Juliet is both Burney's rewriting of Evelina and her rewriting of Evelina's grandmother, Madame Duval, for the two figures are combined into the lone figure of Juliet. Multiple identities are no longer problems to be resolved, but instead act as indicators of the larger instability of the world and the favoring of a transnational approach to understanding others. Juliet's interactions in British society also reflect Burney's changed views on nationalism and the idea of community.

Juliet's story, like Evelina's, involves betrayal and deception on the part of her parents, although this time France figures not as the nation of treachery, but rather as the nation of redemption. When her personal history is finally revealed to us late in the novel, we learn that her history is also closely connected to the neighboring country of France. Like Evelina's mother, Juliet's mother, Juliet Powel, "came not, indeed, from an ancient race; but she was a pattern of virtue, as well as a model of beauty" (641). When the Earl of Melbury's only son, Lord Granville, married her, however, he decided to keep his marriage a secret, just as Evelina's father, Sir John Belmont, did, because the lovely Juliet was the daughter of a mere businessman. When Lord Granville's wife died soon after the daughter, Juliet, was born, Lord Granville decided "to guard the secret, till his child should be grown up; or till he should become his own master" (642). A second marriage reinforced his desire to keep his daughter a secret, so he sent her to France with her grandmother to be brought up and educated, under the care of his French friend the Bishop, in a convent where the Bishop's own niece Gabriella was also being educated. Gabriella's mother, the Marchioness, also acted as guardian to Juliet, offering advice and acting as Juliet's substitute mother. Here again the stories of Evelina and Juliet overlap, for the false daughter of Lord Granville, the actual child of Evelina's nurse, Dame Green, was also sent to France to be educated and kept hidden from the world. Whereas the Evelyn family found deception and guilt in France, the Powel family finds redemption and friendship. When Juliet's grandmother died, the French Bishop "constituted himself guardian and protector of the young orphan" (644), taking her under his care. He proves to be an excellent guardian for Juliet, and his niece Gabriella, who has long been Juliet's closest companion, becomes more of a sister than a friend. Juliet's French advocate the Bishop proves to be more principled and scrupulous than her own countrymen and relations, in fact, and Juliet repays this virtue with a fondness and loyalty of her own by letting herself be married to the corrupt commissary so as to save the Bishop from the guillotine.[12] "My life, indeed, at that horrible period," Juliet later rationalizes, "had lost all value but what was attached to the Bishop, the Marchioness, and my beloved Gabriella" (746). Juliet's French friends give her life value and meaning, and she is willing to make whatever sacrifices she can to help them. In her associations with them, Juliet crosses national barriers. With her French friends, her oldest and truest friends, she is known for who she is: a virtuous and honorable woman. France is thus the home of "her cherished and cherishing friends" (646) and no longer represents, as it did in *Evelina,* a nation of guilt and betrayal. The representation of France is one of the several issues and themes that Burney revises.

This is where we meet Juliet in the opening pages of the novel, for Burney's text opens in medias res. All of the events in France happened before the novel opens, and we learn them slowly as the novel unfolds. Having just escaped from her false marriage, Juliet now seeks asylum in Britain, where she hopes to find the Bishop and Gabriella. Juliet's personal story, like Evelina's, is thus intertwined with life in both France and Britain. In this novel, however, *Britain* is the land of deceptive relations and *France* is the land of trustworthy and faithful friends. France is home to characters who aid the heroine and who themselves are kind and virtuous. Juliet's closest ties are to those who possess a national identity different from her own, an identity that is no longer hostile or threatening to her own. Besides possessing a much more positive relationship with France and its people, Juliet also possesses a more solid understanding of the world and its dangers. In revising her heroine, Burney chose to present a more experienced and mature individual. Naive and gullible, Evelina is prey to her own ignorance of the mores and customs of British society. Indeed, much of the humor of the earlier novel, as we have seen, comes from Evelina's social blunders and the knowledge she gains from making those mistakes. Juliet, in contrast, is more experienced and more knowledgeable to begin with. In this world of complex characters and darkness, Juliet is more equipped to handle herself independently, and much of her novel is devoted to the struggle to attain independence and monetary freedom.

This major difference is most striking in a story that Burney tells twice, once in each novel, where an abduction sets the stage for the presentation of our heroines' different levels of experience. The story begins in *Evelina* on the night of the Opera that Evelina attends with her cousins the Branghtons. Anxious to separate herself from her relatives as soon as the performance concludes, Evelina allows Sir Clement Willoughby to conduct her home. Shortly after commencing their journey, however, Evelina discovers that Sir Clement's coachman is heading in the wrong direction. Combined with Sir Clement's amorous talk, the misdirection causes Evelina extreme panic: "Never, in my whole life, have I been so terrified. I broke forcibly from him, and, putting my head out of the window, called aloud to the man to stop" (99). Once Sir Clement learns that she is serious, he conducts her home, with Evelina keeping watch the entire time: "[I] kept my head at the window, watching which way he drove, but without any comfort to myself, as I was quite unacquainted with either the right or the wrong" (99). When they finally reach the Mirvan house, Evelina still does not seem to recognize the seriousness of the attempted kidnapping, which Sir Clement cajoles her into keeping a secret. Reflecting on the incident, she later writes in a letter to Mr. Villars, "The adventures of the evening so much disconcerted me, that I could not sleep all night. I am under the most cruel apprehensions, lest Lord Orville should suppose my being on the gallery-stairs with Sir Clement a concerted scheme, and even that our continuing so long together in his chariot, was with my approbation" (100). Oblivious to the fact that she could have been raped, Evelina is more concerned with how Lord Orville might perceive her behavior. Knowing that she should not be seen alone with a man causes her more pain than any awareness of her own vulnerability to Sir Clement. Further reflection on her part only leads to a slightly more heightened sense of the danger she was actually in: "the more I reflect upon it, the more angry I am. I was entirely in his power, and it was cruel in him to cause me so much terror" (104).[13] Evelina's reaction to her abduction reveals a naïveté that is unsettling, and the deflated nature of her retrospective anger emphasizes her inability to comprehend just how perilous her situation was. Admitting that she was terrified is not the same, in this case, as realizing to what that terror owed. Reacting with anger only lessens the severity of what Sir Clement has done, providing him with a slap on his wrist when his crime calls for a much greater punishment. Evelina also even continues to countenance his presence throughout the rest of the novel. While it is true that she always makes her dislike for him clear, she still remains in his company. Evelina's naïveté thus signals Burney's own possession of this same trait: as Burney portrays it, virtuous women may find themselves in distracting situations, but they will always manage to find a way out.

In her last novel, Burney rewrote this same incident, this time, how-

ever, empowering her heroine and making her aware of the severity of
her danger. In Juliet's world, as we shall soon see in more detail, people
are not always what they seem to be, and naïveté in women serves as a
liability instead of an asset. Women must be strong and intelligent in
this society, Burney has come to realize, aware of the perils that sur-
round them. When Juliet finds herself in a similar situation as Evelina,
she also panics, not because of an unknown and unvoiced danger, but
rather because she knows what danger lies in this event. This second
abduction, unlike the first, involves a pre-planned scheme to convey
Burney's heroine to the kidnapper. Unlike Evelina, Juliet has not accepted a ride from a man with whom she will travel alone. A letter,
supposedly from the mother of her friend Flora Pierson, arrives one
afternoon, urging Juliet to come visit her young friend, who is presumably suffering from a high fever. Without hesitation, Juliet enters the
post chaise that she assumes will carry her to Flora, realizing her mistake when a horseman stops the carriage and forces his way in. Immediately recognizing Sir Lyell Sycamore as her persecutor, "A change, but
not a diminuation of alarm, now took place, yet [Juliet] assum[ed] a
firmness that sought to conceal her fears" (458). Showing weakness
and fear, Juliet knows, would give Sir Lyell even more power over her,
so she assumes a firmness that she perhaps does not even possess. Without even listening to what Sir Lyell has to say on his behalf, Juliet loses
no time in seeking an escape from the carriage. Noticing that the cart
in the middle of the road belongs to two men within view, "Juliet, lean-
ing out, as far as was in her power, from the chaise-window, called with
energy for help" (458). Evelina had earlier contented herself with looking out the carriage window during her journey home to ensure her
safety, but Juliet will seek help more actively, refusing to remain in the
carriage any longer with her aggressor. Fortunately, the two men that
Juliet calls out to turn out to be her friends Mr. Tedman and the young
farmer Gooch, the former of whom agrees to follow the carriage she is
in until it reaches the safety of Lewes. Unlike Evelina, Juliet knows the
danger she is in with a more seasoned fear, since she has already saved
this same Flora Pierson from the sexual prowess of Sir Lyell. Although
Juliet at first assumes that the abduction was spontaneous, upon further thought she realizes that the event had been carefully conceived of
and planned out by Sir Lyell. This realization makes her danger even
more apparent: "a plan thus concerted to get her into his power,
changed apprehension into certainty, and indignation into abhorrence"
(463). Juliet's abhorrence of Sir Lyell carries a greater weight than
Evelina's anger, for abhorrence, unlike anger, according to the *OED*,

involves feelings of "detestation, repugnance, or utter dislike." Juliet, an outsider with little power in the community, cannot denounce Sir Lyell for his actions, but she knows to abhor and avoid him in the future. Juliet, unlike Evelina, recognizes the severity of her danger.

Another difference between Burney's two heroines is in their relative levels of complexity. Evelina could easily decipher her world and the people in it, judging good from bad and right from wrong, as she interacted in London society. In the same way, as readers, we could easily decipher Evelina. Naive and innocent,[14] Evelina and her motivations, as revealed in her letters, readily lend themselves to analysis. We know that Evelina loves Lord Orville, for instance, before she herself even seems cognizant of the fact. We even learn her family history in one of the first few letters of the novel, and even though her history is not common knowledge for the other characters, as readers we are privy to this classified information early on. Burney's last novel, in contrast, reveals not only a world but also a heroine that is more complex. One of the central themes of *The Wanderer*, in contrast to its predecessor, is that nothing is straightforward. The world is no longer as simple as it once was for the twenty-five-year-old woman who wrote *Evelina*, and the older Burney leaves us with doubt and uncertainty about the society in which she lives. In this last novel, the world is infinitely more complex, infinitely more dangerous, and no longer full of characters that can easily be deciphered by even the most inexperienced of heroines. We can no longer neatly and safely place a Merton and a Lovel, two of the fops from *Evelina*, into one category and an Orville into another. Juliet's world, as opposed to Evelina's, is peopled with characters and personalities that neither she nor the reader can easily fathom. Human beings manifest personalities of nuanced and complex natures.

As part of the third-person narration, for instance, we do not learn Juliet's story, or even her actual name, until late in the novel. She remains an enigma, a woman who takes on multiple roles and multiple identities. When Juliet first emerges from the fog in the opening scene of the novel, she appears in the guise of a black woman covered in patches and rags.[15] Yet this is not the last shape she will take, for as her patches and coverings drop off, she will become in turn an actress, a harp instructor, a performer, a private seamstress, a milliner, a paid companion, a haberdasher, and a runaway wife. Riley, a passenger on the boat that first takes her to Britain and the future bounty hunter for her French husband, comments upon this shape-shifting tendency of Juliet's when he remarks, "But you metamorphose yourself about so, one does not know which way to look for you. Ovid was a mere fool to you" (771). Even though Juliet assumes many of these various roles herself, her ability to "metamorphose" opens her character up to interpretation. Because Juliet lacks a name, the other characters in the novel see her as lacking a fixed identity as well. They assign her roles that *they* think she fills.[16] They refer to her as an "adventuress"(570), an "adventurer" (642, 820), a "pauper" (101), a "professional parasite" (543), "the frenchified stroller" (75), "that bold young stroller" (74), simply a "stroller" (101), "a mere female fortune-hunter" (75), "a needy traveling adventurer" (75), a "vagabond" (75, 101), "the stranger" (71), "the creature" (642), "this wretch" (106), and an "impostor" (571). The terms "Wanderer" and "Incognita" also get used almost too many times to keep track of. Yet when these roles fail to apply to Juliet's behavior, when they are not sure what to make of her, the inhabitants of Brighthelmstone also annihilate her identity altogether. They often perceive her as a blank, as a nobody. She becomes "a mere nothing" (258), "such a body" (61, 75), "a nobody . . . if not worse" (147), "anybody" (296), simply "nobody" (147, 226, 437, 557), a "no one" (74, 214), and merely "a body" (61, 75, 88, 550).[17] When the blank that is Juliet does need to be filled, the community members also take the initiative of naming her. Knowing that Juliet is expecting a letter addressed to "L.S.," the characters assume that these are her initials. A miscommunication shortly afterward leads Juliet to first be called "Elless," although this is soon modified into "Ellis," the name that ultimately stays with her (81–82).[18] Not present herself at the moment that this transformation in her "name" takes place, Juliet learns from Selina Joddrel that "they have all settled, below, that your real name is Ellis" (82). When mockery or cruelty come into play, however, and even the name of Ellis will not do, then Juliet becomes "The Rose" (314), "The Doll" (314), "The Ellis" (230–31), "Mrs. Betty" (759), and "Citoyenne Julie" (740), all before she can finally claim her real name and title of "the Honorable Miss Granville" (646), and assume the role of sister to Lady Aurora and Lord Melbury.

QUESTIONING IDENTITIES

Juliet thus holds many identities, both those that she chooses to take and those that are thrust upon her. Yet perhaps one of the strongest identities she holds, one that is itself multiple, is that of being both French and British. In this respect, Juliet is not only a revision of Evelina, but also a revision of Evelina's grandmother, Madame Duval. In her first novel, Burney had already experimented with a character who possesses a dual national identity. Madame Duval's Frenchness/Britishness had marked her as the "sport" of the Captain and made her fair game, if you will, for the exercise of that sport. Burney, we have seen, was adhering to the nationalist rhetoric and imagery of her day. Yet Juliet also bears the mark of a dual national identity, as retaining characteristics of both the French and the British, although, we shall soon see, she receives a much different treatment than her predecessor did. Although raised in France and loyal to what could be called, taking our cue from Burney's own appellation in the Preface, her "adopted country," Juliet still retains a strong connection to her native land of Britain. Although only seven years old when first sent to live in France, she preserves essential components of her British heritage. This was no doubt aided by conversation with her British maternal grandmother, herself a pensioner at the convent where Juliet was educated, and with whom Juliet conversed in English: "By this means, and by books, Juliet had perfectly retained her native tongue, though she had acquired something of a foreign accent" (643). Yet Juliet's connection to her homeland lies in something stronger than just being able to speak English. When Sir Jasper Herrington finally learns her complete story late in the novel, and when we, too, hear it for the first time, we learn that Juliet has always guarded a love of her native country. Describing her narrow escape from her wicked French "husband," the commissary in Robespierre's regime, Juliet relates her joy at returning to Britain. "I set sail," she reveals, "for my loved, long lost, and fearfully recovered native land" (751), even though Lord Denmeath had a plan "for making me an alien to my country" (752). Afraid that Juliet will return to England to gain her rightful inheritance, Lord Denmeath has tried to keep her in France. Yet his plan to alienate her has only made her homesickness, what the French call, significantly enough, *le mal du pays*, stronger. His plan has succeeded in alienating her from her homeland, but this sense of alienation has only increased her desire to return to her native shores.[19]

Besides bearing these marks of a British heritage, Juliet also bears the marks of her French education. When Juliet first cries out for help, in a quotation previously cited, for example, she "implor[es], in the French language, pity and admission [into the boat]" (11). We first hear her as a Frenchwoman, even though her native tongue is English. The first words she actually speaks in English also bear the mark of her French upbringing. Escaping from France in the small boat that holds the Brighthelmstone residents she will soon come to know much better,

Juliet thanks her rescuer Admiral Powel for his kindness in persuading the other passengers to let her on board the vessel. When she does finally speak, she "replied in English, but with a foreign accent" (17). She carries this accent with her, we can safely assume, for the remainder of the novel. It will mark her as a foreigner, a Frenchwoman, in the eyes of others. Once she finally settles down in Brighthelmstone, however, Juliet's credibility increases once her cultural merits become known: her French connection gives her cultural cachet in the eyes of the town's residents. Her harp lesson business prospers, for instance, when word spreads that she has just recently "come over from France" (260), supposedly armed with the latest music and playing techniques. When she later works as a seamstress for Miss Matson, what is actually her "native taste" in fashion is instead attributed to her residence in France (429). After having arranged some ornaments with "an elegance so striking," for instance, Miss Matson displays them "as a specimen of the very last new fashion, just brought her over by one of her young ladies from Paris. . . . The phrase, therefore, that went forth from Miss Matson, that one of her young ladies was just come from France, was soon spread through the neighborhood; with the addition that the same person had brought over specimens of all the French *costume*" (429). Exquisite taste and an eye for the beautiful eventually lead to Juliet's becoming known as the "famous French milliner" (430).[20]

Yet Juliet's accomplishments can only get her so far in British society. Although the general populace of Brighthelmstone appreciates Juliet's French tastes, the members of the smaller circle in which she moves distrust her for possessing them. Simultaneously sought and shunned, Juliet must negotiate a space from which to be heard.[21] Essentially, she occupies the same position as Madame Duval—both are "foreign" women who are mistrusted because of their dual identity. Madame Duval's dual nationality, however, opens her up to threats and mistreatment by British subjects, behavior that is condoned by the novel although uncertainty about this use of violence still exists underneath the surface. Madame Duval's younger counterpart does not meet with actual physical assault from any Britons, but she is still subject to the threats and abuse of those who refuse to grant her personal credit. The shadows surrounding Juliet and her identity lead the other characters to doubt her and her intentions. In scene after scene, Juliet is verbally abused and threatened to be driven out of whatever house she happens to be staying in at the time. When Mrs. Howel learns, for instance, that Juliet has come across the Channel under mysterious circumstances, she refuses to acknowledge that Juliet may be innocent:

"Inncocent? . . . without a name, without a home, without a friend?—Innocent? presenting yourself under false appearances to one family, and under false pretenses to another? No, I am not such a dupe" (133). Mrs. Howel's questions are the questions that most of the characters also ask of Juliet. Refusing to see Juliet as innocent, they assume that because she is without a name and a single fixed identity, she is also duplicitous. False appearances and false pretenses are strikes against her, and lead to the questioning of her fundamental nature, even though she is in reality a paragon of feminine virtue and honor as defined at the time.

Juliet herself recognizes that "her credit and consequence" (327) rest on a precarious foundation, and although her refusal to acknowledge her true identity leads the other characters to mistrust her, she understands their doubts. Faced with ill treatment, she must continually remind herself that her situation merits such behavior from others. Supplicating Elinor for mercy upon her arrival in London, for instance, Juliet sympathizes with Elinor's confusion at the mysterious state she is in. "I am truly shocked at the strange appearance which I must make," Juliet admits. "I am in so forlorn a situation, that I must not wonder if you conclude me to be some outcast of society, abandoned by my friends from meriting their desertion,—a poor destitute Wanderer, in search of any species of subsistence!" (49). Her own "strange appearance" and condition are so shocking to even herself that she cannot blame others for supposing her to be an outcast. At another point, after meeting yet again with verbal insults and mockery from Elinor, Juliet once more reflects on her situation and the doubts that she must necessarily excite in others:

> upon more mature reflexion, she enquired by what right she expected kinder treatment. Unknown, unnamed, without any sort of recommendation, she applied for succour, and it was granted her; if she met with the humanity of being listened to, and the charity of being assisted, must she quarrel with her benefactors, because they gave not implicit credit to the word of a lonely Wanderer for her own character? . . . .
>
> This sober style of reasoning soon chased away resentment, and, with quieter nerves, she awaited some termination to her suspence and solitude. (72–73)

"Unknown, unnamed," Juliet lacks the credentials that would grant her a higher standing within the social hierarchy. Her own word, "the word of a lonely Wanderer," does not carry the weight that a recognized name, a recognized identity, would. Unable to vouch for her character, she must submit to the evaluations that others make of her. Without the proper credentials, she lacks credit within British society. "And how can I expect to be judged but by what is seen," Juliet later questions, "[by] what is known?" (297). Aware of how mysterious a figure she must be, without a name or story to provide a context for her life, Juliet acknowledges the judgments that society passes.

THE POSSIBILITY OF KNOWING OTHERS

Yet Juliet's query also opens up an ultimately more troubling and significant question, one that resonates throughout the novel: In the modern world, is it ever possible to actually know and understand another human being? Juliet's question comes up repeatedly, as she interacts with characters who are themselves complex and unknowable. Burney takes care, though, to answer the question that her heroine poses, and her answer reveals a fundamental critique of the same mistreatment of Juliet that was once condoned for Madame Duval. In answer to this question, then, Burney offers a yes—but a qualified one: yes, it is possible to understand other human beings, but only if prejudice is discarded, replaced instead by an actual desire to listen to and thus learn about other people's "true" natures. Juliet's world, unlike Evelina's, is much more complex and enigmatic, and not easily readable. Despite this difficulty, however, it *is* still possible to understand others if we realize that such understanding depends upon a more nuanced understanding of both human nature and British society.

If the residents of Brighthelmstone actually took the time to really see and know Juliet, Burney makes clear, they would learn that she has a very good reason for her silence. Juliet must assume these false identities to protect her French friends, and she constantly tries to make this clear to those she meets. She repeatedly insists she is innocent and has good motives for refusing to reveal her name and history. To yet another of Mrs. Maple's incessant demands that she reveal her identity and situation, for example, Juliet can only once again plead with her benefactress: "I am truly ashamed, Madam, so often to press for your forbearance, but my silence is impelled by necessity! I am but too well aware how incomprehensible this must seem, but my situation is perilous—I cannot reveal it! I can only implore your compassion!" (75). Pleas such as this frequently escape Juliet, and yet they fall on deaf ears again and again. If the other characters would only listen to her rationale more carefully and trust what she had to say, they would realize that her silence is literally a matter of life and death. The mystery that surrounds Juliet is necessary for her safety as well as for the safety of her French friends caught in the turmoil of the French Revolution. Although she cannot reveal the specificity of her problems and her own connection to the Revolution, she tries to make this danger felt and known on a general level. By securing her identity from those around her, Juliet protects her friends. She herself is even loathe to appear out of character, for "all disguise was disgusting to her, if not induced by the most imperious necessity" (773). This "imperious necessity" is, however, exactly what the other characters refuse to acknowledge. They refuse to believe that Juliet could be innocent, even though she repeatedly points out the faultlessness of her actions. When Mrs. Howel taunts Juliet yet once again, for instance, Juliet declares, "I may bear with cruelty and injustice, for I am helpless! but not with insult, for I am innocent!" (564). Her innocence should protect her from insult, not make her subject to it, yet the only character who actually listens to this repeated emphasis on her innocence is Harleigh. In one encounter with him, Juliet comments on her use of concealment, remarking, "Disguise, I acknowledge, Sir, you may charge me with; but not deceit! I give no false colouring. I am only not open" (340). Confronting the charges against her, Juliet can only plead guilty to not remaining open to inquiry. She has not purposely misled anyone, and has not presented any "false colouring" to society.

Harleigh's response to Juliet's claim that she is "only not open" meets with what we, as readers, are meant to see as the appropriate reaction to our heroine. Despite her mystery, despite her refusal to reveal her name and story, we are meant to see the underlying virtues of her character. Addressing Juliet's avowal of her innocence, Harleigh enthusiastically exclaims, "That, that is what first struck me as a mark of a distinguished character! That noble superiority to all petty artifice, even for your immediate safety; that undoubting innocence, that framed no precautions against evil constructions; that innate dignity, which supported without a murmur such difficulties, such trials" (340). Indeed, illustration after illustration is given in the first volume of the novel, before any part of her story is revealed, to show Juliet's innate modesty, her strong sense of honor, and her high morals. Different, special, Juliet bears the marks of a distinguished upbringing, if only someone besides Harleigh would set aside his or her prejudice long enough not just to notice her accomplishments, but also to reflect upon what they must ultimately reveal about the nature of her character. When Mrs. Maple's household returns early from an excursion one day, for instance, they surprise Juliet playing elegantly upon the harp. Their discovery causes them to momentarily reassess their opinion of Juliet: "All, except Harleigh, remained nearly stupefied by what had passed, for no one else had ever considered her but as a needy traveling adventurer" (75). In this scene, which occurs early in the novel, Juliet's accomplished performance announces her to be a gentlewoman. Her playing has changed the perceptions that her housemates have of her, causing them to be shocked with how wrong their initial assessments of Juliet seem to have been. Having assumed Juliet to be nothing but a "needy traveling adventurer," they have a hard time reconciling their preconceptions of her with this new image. The revelation of Juliet's accomplishments does little, however, to assuage their distrust. Their inveterate prejudice persists: "Doubts, however, remained with all; they were varied, but not removed. The mystery that hung about her was rather thickened than cleared" (76). The effect that her playing had on them does not last. A similar scene occurs soon after they discover Juliet playing the harp. This time, the younger members of the Maple household have duped Juliet into acting in a play with them, and, when Juliet makes her appearance immediately before the play is set to begin, her fellow group of actors is astonished not by her beautiful dress or her striking beauty, but rather by the innate sense of grace she displays: "it was from the ease with which she wore her ornaments, the grace with which she set them off, the elegance of her deportment, and an air of dignified modesty, that spoke her not only accustomed to such attire, but also to the good breeding and refined manners, which announce the habits of life to have been formed in the superiour classes of society" (92). Her manners and carriage speak of her superior social status, a status that the other characters, excepting Harleigh, of course, continually refuse to support for any length of time. After seeing her act in the play, even Mrs. Maple cannot deny Juliet's superiority: "not all her pride, nor all her prejudice, could make her blind to that performer's truly elevated carriage and appearance" (97). Juliet's exquisite performance, in fact, draws the admiration of the townspeople assembled to watch the play. Afterward, they crowd around Juliet, praising her acting ability and her gentle character. Although the townspeople recognize Juliet's superior merits, however, those in Mrs. Maple's household retain their first impression of her—that of a homeless vagabond—and they treat Juliet accordingly, unwilling to modify their behavior toward her. Although struck yet once more by Juliet's refinements, the residents of Mrs. Maple's household soon fall back into their old behavior patterns, abusing Juliet and refusing to place any trust in her. Any realization of her merit that they might have held, even for the briefest of moments, is drowned out by the prejudice that, Burney takes care to show us, sits hard in their hearts.

Despite her empathy for those who doubt her intentions and character, despite her repeated emphasis on her innocence, and even despite her explanations as to why she must not disclose her identity, Juliet is thus still subject to the prejudices of her society. One of Burney's strongest criticisms in the novel is, in fact, the critique of Britons who refuse to help a fellow human being, whether foreigner or compatriot, in need. In her earliest novel, Burney had offered a different view, one that borrowed from the nationalist discourses of the time. Madame Duval in particular represented a threat to those she encountered, and, as we have seen, her dual national identity made any prejudices against her seem warranted. This time, however, we are meant to dislike those characters who mistreat Juliet merely because of her shifting identities. British society is myopic, unable, because unwilling, to look beneath the surface to discover the truth. Those characters who most seriously question Juliet and who most seriously cause her pain see her only for her surface appearance and as someone who cannot be trusted because those surface appearances have so frequently changed. The reason, of course, that Juliet so frequently becomes a blank, a nobody to be written upon, is because her lack of a name underscores what they see as her lack of a fixed and stable identity. Unable to read her or determine where she fits within society, the residents of Brighthelmstone feel threatened by Juliet's presence. A black woman from the colonies, a French emigrant, an accomplished performer, a lowly milliner, a humble paid companion: Juliet possesses all of these identities and more, and that is what makes her such a frightening prospect. Juliet is changing, shifting, and it is that which makes the other characters not know what to do with her. She has literally become Miss Polly Moore, the "daughter of a chandler's-shop woman," whom Madame Duval had held up to Evelina as an example of the myriad "opportunities" that a French education makes possible for its possessor. Whereas this fluidity threatened Evelina's world, however, it is seen as a necessary part of the Wanderer's. The reason Juliet can occupy all of these roles is because she possesses many identities within her, and Burney uses this slippery nature of identity to force her other characters to read Juliet based on her personal attributes. All of the characters who cannot look past Juliet's multiple identities or who see her as torn between conflicting affiliations are subject to Burney's overt criticism. Those other characters who look beneath the surface, however, meet not criticism, but rather a noble character who conceals but never purposely misleads. Underneath all of these names and identities, Juliet herself remains constant. In a much later scene in the novel, Lord Melbury directly makes this point when he remarks, "though we know not what Miss Ellis has been, we see what she now is;—a pattern of elegance, sweetness, and delicacy" (566). Unfamiliar with her past, they can only judge her by her present. Earlier in the novel, after Juliet finds her friend Gabriella and the two set up a sewing business together, this same point is made. In the company of her friend, Juliet experiences "the felicity of being loved because known; esteemed and valued because tried and proved" (394). Juliet's actions have revealed her to be virtuous and kind, not conniving or dishonest, and the constancy of her character has been in place throughout the novel. Juliet's multiple identities are not a cause for alarm, then, but rather a necessary condition of the modern world, where people and things are not always what they appear to be. In effect, Burney has revised her earlier view of the world as governed by surface appearances that are easily readable. It is no longer possible to know the world by appearances because those appearances are often false, and so we must instead seek some inner depth of character, a character that transcends national borders, to understand other human beings. In a world where our fellow creatures possess multiple identities, it is important to be able to look beneath the surface to discover a core inner identity.

The Changing Face of Nationalism: From Captain Mirvan to Admiral Powel

Juliet is not the only character in the novel to possess multiple identities. From Selina Joddrel's two-faced treatment of Juliet to Elinor Joddrel's own cross-dressing and disguises, everything and everyone is open to interpretation. Even relatively benign characters like Mr. Giles Arbe and Sir Jasper Herrington—male figures who should offer their protection to Juliet in a straightforward manner—exemplify this ambiguous nature of the world in that their professed aims often do not reconcile with their actual actions. Embodied in the characters of this small British town are therefore the complexities and difficulties of modern life, and the multiple identities that are a necessary part of the modern human condition as Burney now understands it. Along with a more experienced heroine, Burney has thus also given us a more experienced world. Each of these characters has a significant role in Juliet's life, and each one is infinitely more complicated than any of the characters in Burney's first novel. Unlike her predecessor, Juliet cannot accurately read the intentions of those around her; their motives remain obscure and ambiguous, as do the consequences of their actions.

Most important, Burney's new belief in the unknowability of others also carries strong nationalist overtones with it, overtones that reflect her larger overarching project of reconciliation between Britain and France. In no character is this made more evident than in Admiral Powel, who occupies a central role in the last part of the novel. Within the body of this wizened sea officer, *Evelina*'s Captain Mirvan is reincarnated, brought to life in new ways that reflect Burney's more complicated understanding of her nation and her subsequent critique of the same British nationalist discourses that she made use of in her first novel. Like his compatriots Mr. Giles and Sir Jasper, Admiral Powel possesses a personality shaded by both positive and negative attributes. Those attributes, however, are strongly linked to his nationalist prejudices; although an honest and noble man, his thoughts reflect his intolerance. Also like his predecessor Captain Mirvan, the Admiral has a pronounced dislike of the French and anything related to their country. In the opening scene of the novel, for instance, the Admiral makes his nationalist prejudices clear. While crossing the Channel on their way back to England, the small group begins to discuss their opinions of the Revolution and their reasons for having traveled to France. When he learns that Mr. Ireton, the son of Juliet's future employer, has gone over to Europe to seek a wife, the Admiral makes his thoughts on this subject clear: "a man who could go out of old England to chuse himself a wife, never deserves to set foot on it again! If I knew any worse punishment, I should name it" (16). The idea that Ireton would leave "old England" and even consider marrying a non-English woman is a severe crime for the Admiral, one that should be punished just as severely: by permanent banishment from the native land. During this same conversation in the boat, the Admiral also mistakes Juliet for a native Frenchwoman, assuming that her accent reveals her national identity. Her decision to leave France, however, greatly raises her in the Admiral's esteem. "I hope the compliment you make our country in coming to it," he tells her, "is that of preferring good people to bad; in which case every Englishman should honour and welcome you" (17). In Admiral Powel's opinion, the French are unequivocally "bad," while the British are unequivocally "good." Toward the end of the novel, the Admiral reveals his dislike of the French yet again. While standing on the coast, the Admiral watches as boatfuls of French émigrés arrive on British soil. Intrigued, he moves closer to the ocean so he can see "a small hand-ful of the enemy" disembark (853). Used to viewing the French as his enemies, the Admiral mistrusts them, and practically every sentence out of his mouth reveals his negative attitude toward this foreign land.

Admiral Powel's dislike of the French is so strong that he is even willing to disown his sister's orphaned child because the girl presumably married a Frenchman. That orphan, of course, is none other than Juliet, who, we later learn, is Admiral Powel's niece. We discover this toward the end of the novel, when the Admiral reveals his last name for the first time. When he does so, he also reveals his personal history. While stationed in the East Indies,[22] the Admiral was unable to retain contact with his sister and mother back home in Britain. Upon his return to his native land, however, he learned the true story of his sister's marriage to Lord Granville and of the existence of their daughter, Juliet, who was being raised in France. Juliet's connection to this enemy country was exceedingly disturbing to him. "I have always, in my heart," he later admits, "owed a grudge to my Lord Granville, though his lordship was my brother-in-law, for bringing up his daughter in foreign parts; whereby he risked the ruin of her morals both in body and soul" (868). He would have preferred it, he admits, if his niece had "not been brought up by the enemy" (858). Despite his disapproval of Juliet's French education, however, the Admiral determined to seek out his only living relation. "I crossed over the channel to see after her," the Admiral explains, "a great proof of my good will, I can tell you! for no little thing would have carried me to that lawless place; and from the best land upon God's earth!" (834–35). Soon after he began making inquiries about his niece, however, the Admiral learned that "Mademoiselle Juliette," as she was known, was already married to "a French monsieur" (841). His reaction is one of extreme anger: "I was told that she was married to a Frenchman, upon which I swore, God willing, never to see her face to the longest day I had to live! And I came away with that resolution" (835). Making no effort to meet his niece, the Admiral decided to return home to Britain: "He was coming away, in deep disgust, and burning wrath, when he was seized himself, and put into prison by order of Mr. Robespierre" (841). The "deep disgust" and "burning wrath" of the Admiral owe their conception to Juliet's presumed marriage to a native of the Admiral's enemy nation. Unwilling even to hear Juliet's side of the story or to meet her and her husband, the Admiral allows his nationalist prejudice to interfere with his familial connections. Hatred of the French overwhelms him to such an extent that he would rather remain alone than meet his niece—simply because she married a "French monsieur."

Like Captain Mirvan, then, the Admiral carries strong nationalist prejudices within him. Yet the differences between the two seamen do not end there, for Admiral Powel, just like his predecessor, is extremely misogynistic. Captain Mirvan's misogyny, as I argued in chapter 1, most strongly revealed itself in his desire to effectually silence not only Madame Duval, but also Evelina and Maria. Although Admiral Powel does not use similar measures, he still expresses narrow-minded views concerning the role of women within British society, in what could almost be described as a chivalrous misogyny. Late in the novel, before she learns that the Admiral is her relation, for instance, Juliet reveals to him that she is seeking passage back to the Continent. Since he has just assisted Juliet in freeing herself from the machinations of Mrs. Howel, Juliet asks for his help one more time. As soon as she makes her request, however, "Every mark of favour was now changed into disdainful displeasure; and, turning abruptly away from her, he muttered to himself, though aloud, that women's going abroad, to outlandish places, whereby they learnt more how to dizen themselves, and cut capers, than how to become good wives and mothers, was what he could not uphold; and would not lend a hand to; and then, without looking at her, he sullenly entered his own apartment" (815–16). The Admiral's muttered remarks about women "dizening themselves" and "cutting capers" resemble those that his compatriot the Captain uttered years before in response to Madame Duval's suggestion that the Captain spend some time in France. A French education, according to Captain Mirvan, would, however, only teach him to "learn to cut capers . . . and dress like a monkey . . . and palaver in French gibberish" (*Evelina*, 61). As the heir to Captain Mirvan's misogyny, the Admiral extends his forerunner's claims, incorporating women into his remarks. Women in particular should stay at home in Britain so that they can become "good wives and mothers." Travel to "outlandish places" like France, his argument runs, only makes women vain and superficial, unable to fulfill the responsibilities of British motherhood.

The Admiral's views on marriage are equally disturbing, and meant to be so. After discovering that Juliet is indeed his long-lost niece, Admiral Powel asks for her history since she left France. More particularly, the uppermost question in his mind, the first one that he asks first, is why Juliet's husband is not with her. "How came you here without your husband?" he demands, "For all I have no great goust to your marrying in that sort, God forbid I should uphold a wife in running away from her lawful spouse, even though he be a Frenchman! We should always do right, for the sake of shaming wrong. A man, being the higher vessel, may marry all over the globe, and take his wife to his home; but a woman, as she is only given him for his help-mate, must tack about after him, and come to the same anchorage" (842). Guilty as charged, Juliet has, in fact, run away from her "husband." By the time the Admiral makes this comment to Juliet, however, we have already heard the story of how Juliet's husband blackmailed her into marrying him by making her witness the guillotining of several persons. While they watched people die from a room above the square where the guillotine was placed, the commissary had promised Juliet that her friend the Bishop would be next unless she agreed to marry him. The French commissary, of course, really only married her £6,000, not her actual person, as Harleigh is so quick to point out once he learns the entire story (852). By this point, too, we have also witnessed the husband's violent attempt to force Juliet back to France with him. Her husband is more monster than human, a man described at one point as possessing "an hideous countenance" and "wearing an air of ferocious authority" (726). Never named, he is referred to instead as a "ruffian" (726), simply "the man" (726, 727), "the wretch" (852), and "this Gallic Goliath" (737). His dark presence overshadows the novel; before we even learn of his existence, he has been with us as Juliet's constant source of dread.[23] By not revealing her name or history, Juliet had been protecting both herself and her friends from the husband's merciless power. Juliet was right, we are led to think, to flee him as she did.

Shortly after the Admiral makes his views on runaway wives clear, he makes his views on gender inequality clear as well. After witnessing Juliet's joyful reaction to hearing that her husband is dead, Admiral Powel rebukes his niece. "You must have had but a sad dog of a husband," he reasons. "However, to my seeming, though he might be but a rogue, a husband's a husband; and I don't much uphold a wife's not thinking of that; for, if a woman may mutiny against her husband, there's an end of all discipline" (856). Society rests upon the foundation of marriage, according to the Admiral, with the wife inferior and subject to the husband. Without such a hierarchical structure, he firmly believes, order would not exist, for if women ever took it into their heads to "mutiny" against their husbands, there would be "an end of all discipline." Burney, however, has not only proven the Admiral's ideas to be questionable within the pages of the novel, where Juliet's flight is condoned, but also within her own life. Through her sister Susanna, Burney witnessed the consequences of marriage to a "rogue" husband firsthand. As Margaret Doody points out in her formidable biography on Burney, Susanna Burney married Molesworth Phillips in 1782 in a marriage initially based on love.[24] Although Frances was not pleased to see her sister marry at such a young age, Susanna seemed happy enough at first, until her husband forced her to move to Ireland with him. "Susanna, against her wishes and in the face of all her fears," Doody explains, "had been forced to go to the kingdom across the water, far from family and friends, in complete control of her husband. Phillips had the law on his side; a husband had the legal right to compel the companionship of his wife" (282). Susanna's life in Ireland was miserable, and her husband revealed himself to be both cruel and unfeeling. He even went so far as to carry on an open flirtation with one of Susanna's friends in front of her. Her time in Ireland eventually took a toll on her health: "Susanna's life in Ireland became increasingly lonely and more miserable, as she was subjected to Phillips's harsh temper and perhaps even to physical violence. Susanna's health declined, and it was at last clear that she was very seriously ill and not likely to improve under Molesworth Phillips's control. Charles Burney [their father] at last consented . . . to receive Susanna in his own home" (284). Because Phillips had complete control over his wife, Susanna's family had a hard time convincing him to bring her back to England. By the time Phillips finally consented to return, Susanna was very ill. The couple arrived back in England on December 30, 1799, and Susanna died within one week, on January 6, 1800.[25] Frances Burney's reaction to Susanna's death was severe, and her diaries and letters reveal that she blamed herself for not having been able to "rescue" her sister from Phillips's grasp sooner. As Doody comments, "She never got over it. She kept the sixth of January as a sorrowful anniversary for ever after, even when her father rebuked her for the practice. The grief for the lost sister endured through the rest of her life" (286). Susanna's death was obviously foremost in Burney's mind even as she was writing *The Wanderer*. In her introduction to the novel, she gives the background to its inception, explaining that although she had started the novel at the end of the eighteenth century, grief over her sister's death kept her from working on it for some time (4). Susanna's memory haunted Burney's life, haunted the pages of the novel, and Susanna's rogue husband, Burney felt, directly caused her sister's premature death. Although Admiral Powel condemns Juliet for "mutinying" against her husband, Burney had earnestly wished that her own sister Susanna had done the same.

Despite his prejudice, despite his narrow-mindedness, and even despite his misogyny, however, the Admiral still possesses a positive, benevolent side to him, a side that demonstrates Burney's changed conception of the world. While Captain Mirvan never demonstrated anything except gross and cruel behavior, Admiral Powel repeatedly demonstrates a more forgiving and gentle nature. In place of Captain Mirvan's cruel jokes and antics, in fact, Burney gives her readers the protective and generous actions of Admiral Powel. Although the Admiral dislikes the French, he is not violent or cruel toward them, and in this respect he greatly differs from Captain Mirvan. Despite his repeatedly harsh appraisals of the French, he also frequently expresses his sympathy for the French and an appreciation for national differences. Alternating between disgust and compassion, the Admiral remains a complex man. For example, when he first meets the Marchioness's servant Ambroise, the central figure who orchestrated Juliet's escape from France, the Admiral expresses a relational view of national identity. "I don't pretend to have much taste for any person who would go out of old England when once he has got footing into it," he states, "thoff if I had had the misfortune to be born in France, there's no being sure that I might not have liked it myself from knowing no better: for which reason I think nothing narrower than holding a man cheap for loving his country, be it ever so bad a one" (829–30). The reason the Admiral loves England so much is because it is natural that all men love their countries, no matter how "bad" those countries are. Hidden within his words is the key to understanding feelings that at first appear to be associated with the same kind of narrow-minded xenophobia that Captain Mirvan displayed. Whereas the Captain never questioned his belief system, the Admiral has. The Admiral recognizes that his attitudes toward the French are based on the stroke of chance that made his place of birth an English-speaking instead of a French-speaking one. If he had been born in France, he would rightfully love France just as much as he currently loves Britain, so he cannot blame others for doing the same. Besides, not all French are quite as bad as all that. "And indeed, to tell you the truth," the Admiral later sheepishly admits to Juliet, "though it is a thing I am not over fond of speaking about, I have seen some Frenchmen I could have liked mightily myself, if I had not known where they came from" (842). Once again, Burney reveals her dislike of prejudice. If the Admiral had set aside his preconceptions long enough to listen to and get to know these Frenchmen, he would have learned that they were good people, as the Admiral himself seems to recognize. National prejudice, like any other form of prejudice, has dire consequences for both personal and international understanding. After all, the Admiral was ready to leave France without meeting his only living family member merely because she had married a Frenchman. Gradually, however, the Admiral begins to realize the limited scope of his belief system; his admissions signify his willingness to look past his long-held enmity toward the French.

A recognition of the culturally constructed nature of nationalism also appears in several of the Admiral's remarks. Although he dislikes foreigners and does not always seem willing to give them a chance based on their personal merits, he also acknowledges how his sentiments are the product of his culture and environment. The Admiral's comments about a person's place of birth reveal this recognition to a certain extent, but he makes the point much clearer toward the end of the novel. A first meeting with Juliet's guardian the Bishop, for instance, gives the Admiral another opportunity to make his anti-French sentiments clear. Once he does so, however, he also reveals that these sentiments are the result of time spent in a military environment. "For it's pretty much our creed, abroad, though I don't over and above uphold it myself, except as far as may belong to the sea-service,—to look upon your nation as little better than a cluster of rogues," he reveals to the Bishop. "However, we of the upper class, knowing that we are all alike, in the main, of God's workmanship, don't account it our duty to hold you so cheap" (858). Amongst those in the military, the French are looked upon as a "cluster of rogues," and, the Admiral freely admits, when he is abroad with his peers he voices this same "creed." His situation determines his prejudices and nationalist feelings. In the main, however, he does not "over and above uphold" these sentiments, only just to the extent that he feels is "normal." In his own eyes, the Admiral is not really a prejudiced person. The anti-French sentiments that he holds are mild, he feels, in comparison with those held by some of his compatriots. Through the Admiral, then, Burney calls attention to the artificial and culturally constructed nature of nationalism, just as Charlotte Smith did in *The Young Philosopher*. The randomness of one's birthplace and peer circle, Burney points out, influences our attachments and dislikes, which ultimately influence our understanding of other nations and people.

Admiral Powel's comments about the upper class possessing a different mindset also shed light on the primary reason that he can claim to be above petty prejudices: not his status, but his *religion* separates him from those who hold the French "so cheap." "[K]nowing that we are all alike, in the main, of God's workmanship" allows the Admiral to express sympathy for the French. All humans "are all alike," he reasons, because all are the product of God's creation. National differences are brushed aside in the very fact of our humanness, and the tie of Christianity, according to the Admiral, binds everyone together. The Admiral makes this point several times in the novel, each time emphasizing how the French, despite all of their negative tendencies, are still Christians and, as such, deserve the respect of the British. When he first questions Juliet about her marriage, for instance, he concedes that her husband "may be a tolerable good Christian, mayhap, for a Papist" (842). Her husband's Catholicism alone does not necessarily make him a bad Christian. Yet during the periods both in which the novel is set and in which Burney actually published it, this view of the Admiral's was very controversial. As Doody explains in her biography on Burney, "Roman Catholicism was not only a despised persuasion in England; it was still officially proscribed, and those who practiced it were subject to special disabilities in law."[26] In her own life, Burney had witnessed the prejudice that her maternal grandmother faced as a member of the Roman Catholic church, for, as historian Linda Colley points out, Britons held "the extreme Protestant conviction that Catholic values were completely upside down."[27] Eighteenth-century Britons viewed themselves as the religious elect, subject to special treatment from God because they were members of a Protestant nation. "There existed, then," Colley reveals, "a vast superstructure of prejudice throughout eighteenth-century Britain, a way of seeing (or rather mis-seeing) Catholics and Catholic states which had grown up since the Reformation if not before, which was fostered by successive wars with France and Spain, and which encouraged many Britons, irrespective of their real income, to regard themselves as peculiarly fortunate."[28] This belief that Catholics were inferior and not actually Christians pervaded Britain, but Burney herself, by the time she penned *The Wanderer*, was not subject to it.[29] In 1793, against the wishes of her family and friends, Burney rejected nationalist prejudices by marrying Frenchman and Catholic Alexandre D'Arblay. On July 28, the two were married in a Protestant ceremony, and just two days later they recognized their marriage vows in a Catholic ceremony.[30] Later that year, in November, Burney also produced her polemical tract *Brief Reflections Relative to the Emigrant French Clergy: Earnestly Submitted to the Humane Consideration of the Ladies of Great Britain*, a 27-page pamphlet written in response to the French Revolutionary government's decision to expel refractory French priests from their nation. Without a home, many of these priests came to Britain, where they received mixed treatment from the British. Although luminaries such as Edmund Burke joined in the cause to raise funds for the priests, writing the "Case of the Suffering Clergy of France," their plight was not viewed with a very sympathetic eye.[31] After Louis XVI's execution in January of 1793, France had declared war on Britain, and the two nations had been at war for almost ten months by the time Burney's pamphlet appeared. "Still, even though the victims of revolutionary violence would seem to have ample grounds for sympathy in England," critic Claudia L. Johnson explains in her introduction to the modern-day reprint of Burney's *Reflections*, "the relief of these refugees was not a popular cause. . . . Because anti-French as well as anti-Catholic sentiments took precedence over humanitarian interests, soliciting assistance for French priests was controversial."[32] *The Wanderer*'s Admiral Powel, in his claims for the equality of all Christians, places him squarely in Burney's camp.[33]

Tolerance for others is consequently rooted in Christianity for Burney and her characters, and nowhere is this better illustrated than in the words and actions of Admiral Powel. Although the Admiral repeatedly expresses his dislike of the French, his compassion toward them makes him, in Burney's estimation, ultimately a good man. He is, after all, the one who first takes Juliet on board the small boat during her escape from France in the opening scene of the novel. Harleigh has already urged the others to allow Juliet into the boat, but it is the Admiral's decision to join his voice to Harleigh's that becomes the deciding factor in granting Juliet admission:

> "Nay, since she is but a woman, and in distress, save her, pilot, in God's name!" said an old sea officer. "A woman, a child, and a fallen enemy, are three persons that every true Briton should scorn to misuse."
> The sea officer was looked upon as first in command; the young man, therefore, no longer opposed . . . gave his hand to the suppliant. (12)

While it is true that Admiral Powel refers to his nationality as the reason why he wants to help Juliet, since "every true Briton" should help human beings in need, his reasoning depends upon his religion; it is not in Britain's name that he makes his case, but rather "in God's name." His appeal is based not in nationalism, but in religion. Juliet's uncle makes this same point toward the close of the novel. Assembled along the shore watching boatfuls of French émigrés arrive, the Admiral, Juliet, Harleigh, and Lord Melbury discuss the plight of the French. Returning to the argument he made when he first urged his own fellow boat members to take Juliet on board, the Admiral reasons, "However, though it is our duty to hold them all as our native enemies; and I shall never, God willing, see them in any other light; yet it would be but unchristian not to lend them an hand, when they are chopfallen and sorrowful; and, moreover, consumedly out of cash. So if I can help them, I see no reason to the contrary; for my enemy in distress is my friend: because why? I was only his enemy to get the upper hand of him" (854–55). The Admiral recognizes that fallen enemies deserve the help of those responsible for the fall in the first place; once an enemy is down, a true Briton will always lend a hand to help that enemy back up. One of the central concerns and criticisms that Burney develops throughout the rest of the novel is, in fact, that very few Britons help Juliet. Those characters who most recognize her worth and who most desire to help her do so by placing aside their national prejudices and by looking at Juliet's true merit. Juliet, an "enemy in distress," should be treated as a friend, but is instead shunned and turned away from social companionship.

Admiral Powel, as the first character to actively help Juliet, garners Burney's praise in several instances. Meriting the title of Juliet's "first patron" (808), the Admiral assists Juliet more than once, and reveals himself to be an able guardian. Lady Aurora, Juliet's half-sister through her father's second marriage, emphasizes this fact to Juliet, remarking that "the discovery of an uncle, a protector, in so excellent a man as the Admiral, offered a prospect of solid comfort" (846). The words of Lady Aurora carry weight in the novel, for she is one of the few characters who has always supported Juliet and believed in her innocence and value. If Lady Aurora praises the Admiral and views him as a good "protector" for Juliet, then we must feel him to be so, too. As I also argued in my discussion of *Evelina*, Burney's earlier naval officer was a man who failed in his role as protector of women. In her representation of Admiral Powel, however, Burney rewrites this character in yet another aspect, giving to the Admiral the role of guardian and protector. Knowing Burney's penchant for playing with and on names, we can also recognize the Admiral's name as a variation on Mrs. Howel's, since both names end with a single letter *l.* Mrs. Howel, however, as we shall soon see, torments and mistreats Juliet, making her name's connection to the word *howl* a strong one. She remains Juliet's worst enemy. Admiral Powel, on the other hand, protects and guards Juliet, making his name's connection to the word *power* a strong one. Whereas Mrs. Howel is the female tormentor, Admiral Powel is the male protector; what she tries to take away, he tries to restore.

What Admiral Powel ultimately restores is, ironically enough, Juliet's connection to her native land and her paternal family—her British heritage and national identity.[34] As he explains to Juliet when the two characters finally realize they are related, the Admiral possesses a copy of the codicil to Juliet's father, Lord Granville's will, a copy Juliet did not know existed. As far as she knew, the only copy of this document was lost in the fire that destroyed the Marchioness and Bishop's family chateau. Stepping back in time, the Admiral relates to Juliet the story of how, upon his first return from the East Indies, he almost forced Lord Granville to a duel, based upon the supposition that Lord Granville had not actually married his sister, Juliet's mother, who had, at that point, been dead for several years. Upon learning, however, that the marriage had legally taken place, the Admiral's anger softened. Lord Granville had only wanted to keep the marriage and the child a secret until the Admiral could properly look after Juliet in a house of his own (838–43). However, before he could make it over to France to find his mother and Juliet, both of whom were still residents of the French convent, the Admiral was called back to the East Indies, but not before, he explains, "his lordship [Lord Granville] was so honourable as to entrust to me a copy of the codicil to his will; written all in his own hand, and duly signed and sealed. . . . It's the proof and declaration of my sister's honour!" (839–40). That same codicil is, of course, also the proof and declaration of Juliet's connection to Lord Granville, and thus to her rightful inheritance. By establishing her as "the Honorable Miss Granville" (646), the codicil grants Juliet both the family name and the status that she has, until now, lacked. Juliet's entrance into British society, into the British nation, has thus been assured by her uncle's judgment and foresight. Despite his prejudices, despite his contradictory statements, Admiral Powel emerges as Juliet's ultimate protector. Through him, Juliet is restored to the two most important identities that British society sees her as lacking—through him, she can reclaim both her patronym and her *patria*.

Critiques of Nationalist Prejudice

Admiral Powel is ultimately pardoned, restored to Burney's good opinion, because he recognizes the culturally constructed nature of his anti-French sentiments and can set those feelings aside long enough, in the name of Christianity, to help Juliet, even when he believes that she is French. Other characters, however, do not get off the hook so easily. Burney's critique of nationalist prejudices carries over to a critique of many of the residents of Brighthelmstone, who not only mistreat Juliet, but also reveal their own narrow-minded views of the world. In particular, Juliet's dual national identity serves as a vehicle through which Burney can express her views on the ignorance of the British toward the French nation, an ignorance that she herself once shared. Juliet's presumed "Frenchness" provides Burney with the opportunity and excuse to comment on the people of her own nation and their prejudices toward both foreigners and foreign affairs. Burney's critique is especially apparent in two areas: in the minor characters' ignorance of French customs and in their treatment of Juliet's French friend Gabriella. Minor roles they might serve in *The Wanderer,* but these British characters reveal the insularity and ignorance of a people accustomed to viewing themselves as a chosen nation.

Whereas in *Evelina* Burney presents France as the land where bad things happen to good British subjects, in *The Wanderer* Burney presents France as a land that is misunderstood by the British. France is still dangerous, but this time it is dangerous not because of its people, but rather because of the events occurring there. Setting the novel "During the dire reign of Robespierre" (11) allows Burney to modify her earlier views on Britain's rival, while opening up her audience to a more informed understanding of political events. As mentioned, the first way Burney accomplishes this revised view of both the British and French nations is through her portrayal of some of the minor characters in the novel. Besides adding local color to the story, these characters display a surprising ignorance of the events in France, an ignorance reminiscent of the ignorance and misinformation that Charlotte Smith portrayed in her 1792 novel *Desmond.* For instance, Robespierre, the instigator of the Terror and ultimately one of its final victims, goes by many names in the novel: "Signor Robespierre" (15), "Mr. Robertspierre" (79), "Mr. Robert Speer" (93), "Mr. Robert-Spierre" (269), "Mounseer Robert Speer" (465), "Bob Spear" (466), and "Mr. Robespierre" (841). These anglicized versions of a very French name reflect not on Robespierre, but rather on the ignorance of Burney's own countrymen. They, who profess to know so much about the Revolution, do not even know the correct name of the Revolution's most important agent at that time.

Their inability to learn the notorious Frenchman's name also signals their inability to grasp the truth of the political events unfolding across the Channel, and many more examples of a misinformed British public appear throughout the novel. The play rehearsals Juliet participates in while living in Mrs. Maple's house, for instance, provide ample opportunity for the townspeople to question Juliet on what she knows about the Revolution. Assumed by the residents of Brighthelmstone to be

French, Juliet becomes their source of information about France, even though these same residents hardly ever give her a chance to respond to their inquiries. They also ultimately reveal their own ignorance during the questioning process. Mr. Scope, "a gentleman self-dubbed a deep politician," for example, explains how he has heard that in France "[a] man's wife and daughters belong to any man who has a taste for them," while the young farmer Gooch has heard that "they've got such numbers and numbers, and millions and millions of red-coats there, all made into generals, in the twinkling, as one may say, of an eye" (79). The "deep politician" Mr. Scope actually has a shortage of traits associated with his name, revealing a lack of insight instead of any depth of vision. His friend Gooch also suffers from the same degree of ignorance, confusing the color of his own nation's army uniforms with that of the French. Instances of their ignorance about the true state of affairs in France are revealed once again when Juliet meets several of Bright-helmstone's residents at church. Immediately upon seeing Juliet, the same group of men again begin to question her about France. Gooch reveals that he has learned much about the French in his political club, where "they say all the French are actors or dancers, except just them that go to the wars" (268), and Mrs. Maple's steward, Mr. Stubbs, begins to inquire yet again about the cost of rents in France. Mr. Scope also questions Juliet about "that Goddess of Reason, that, as I am credibly informed, has been set up by Mr. Robert-Spierre" (269). Without waiting for a response from Juliet, Mr. Scope offers his own opinion about "that Goddess of Reason": "And as to so many females being called Goddesses of Reason,—for I am assured there are some score of them,—one don't very well see what that means; the ladies in general,—I speak without offence, as it's out of their line,—not being particularly famous for their reason; at least not here; and I should suppose they can hardly be much more so in that light nation" (269). The women in this novel *are* reasonable beings, however, capable of using their judgment and discernment to make informed choices in their lives. Such claims, then, are meant to be ludicrous and so humorous, and Burney mocks her characters' ignorance by revealing their limited knowledge.

National differences are also not tolerated, or are looked down upon, by many of the characters. Young Gooch's father, for instance, cannot fathom how the French survive on anything other than good old British roast beef: "And as to roast beef and plum-pudding, I do hear that they do no' know the taste of such a thing. So that they be but a poor stinted race at best, for they can never come to their natural growth" (466).

Although Mr. Gooch admits that many of the tales about life in France that have made their way over to Britain are lies, he declares that he will believe the tales when they tell "somewhat that be worth a man's hearing" (466). In other words, Mr. Gooch will believe anything that is negative about the French, a land, he is firmly convinced, that is "all overrun with weeds, and frogs, and the like," and full of nothing but useless "mounseers" (467). The general British populace remains ignorant about foreign affairs and French culture, an attitude that has dire consequences for their own national identity within the novel. Complacent in their own sense of superiority, these Britons fail to discern how limited their understanding actually is. The *British*, not the French, represent the major segment of unenlightened individuals within the pages of Burney's novel.

The second way that Burney criticizes narrow-minded views is through her representation of Juliet's French friend Gabriella. The friendship between these two women has existed since they were both children in the same convent in France, and Gabriella, like Juliet, exemplifies all of the positive traits of feminine virtue as they are defined within the novel. Also like Juliet, Gabriella has been exposed to numerous hardships while trying to support her new life alone in Britain. Essentially a variation on Juliet, Gabriella functions as an alternative version of her British friend: Gabriella shares the same story of being a young foreign woman without name, family, or money who is forced to live on her own in a hostile country. Her experiences mirror Juliet's, once more allowing us a glimpse of the prejudice that is directed against foreigners, but this time from a slightly different perspective. Through her friend, Juliet witnesses the treatment that she herself has received since her arrival in Britain. This time, however, the prejudice is directed not against Juliet, but against her virtuous friend, and Juliet is allowed to see Gabriella as she herself has been seen by the other characters. Gabriella finds prejudice while residing in Brighthelmstone merely because she is French, and before we even meet Gabriella, we witness a striking example of the hostility that she must deal with on a daily basis. When Juliet first decides to give up her large apartment at the seamstress Miss Matson's in favor of a smaller, and so less expensive, room, Miss Matson, anxious to retain Juliet as a boarder, offers Juliet the use of a small chamber upstairs. Juliet's objection that the room already houses a lodger (who happens to be Gabriella) is met by Miss Matson's answer that the lodger is "known to nobody, and is very bad pay, if I can have so genteel a young lady as you" (383). These words incite Juliet to try to speak on the stranger's behalf, but the callous landlady can only say that the current boarder has little to recommend her. Miss Matson ignores Juliet's arguments, offering her own commentary on the stranger instead: "Now this person here, Ma'am, besides being poor, which, poor thing, may be she can't help; and being a foreigner, which, you know, Ma'am is no great recommendation;—besides all this, Miss Ellis [Juliet], she has some very suspicious ways with her, which I can't make out at all; she goes abroad in a morning, Ma'am, by five of the clock, without giving the least account of her haunts" (384). Gabriella's crimes, as far as Miss Matson is concerned, consist of nothing more than her being French and having "suspicious" habits. Since Gabriella does not reveal her business, she is looked at with a wary eye, just as Juliet has been. Once again, then, we have a character who is distrusted because British society refuses to look underneath surface appearances. This time, too, the critique of British society carries a nationalist tone to it, since, like Juliet, Gabriella is doubted because of her national affiliations.

Despite Miss Matson's opinion of Gabriella, the reader knows the Frenchwoman to be extremely kind and virtuous. Gabriella's dignified manner and helplessness are, in fact, what first interest Juliet on her behalf, before Juliet even realizes that this mysterious person is, in fact, her dear friend. Returning home from a visit to Elinor, Juliet first notices the stranger, whose "form and air penetrated Ellis with a feeling and an interest far beyond common curiosity" (385). Juliet immediately recognizes that the stranger possesses superior qualities, much as her own superior qualities had already been recognized and repeatedly commented upon by Harleigh and Lady Aurora. Seeking the courage to approach the foreigner to offer aid, Juliet follows her to a small hill overlooking the ocean. There the stranger stops: "she extended her arms, seeming to hail the full view of the wide spreading ocean; or rather, Ellis [Juliet] imagined, the idea of her native land, which she knew, from that spot, to be its boundary" (385). Driven by sorrow to the top of the hill, Gabriella seeks comfort by hailing, or greeting, her "native land," or at least this is what Juliet, as observer of the scene, imagines. The opening of Gabriella's arms represents her desire to welcome thoughts of her homeland, "the idea" of which seems to offer peace. Juliet's imagination is not wrong, for, when she finally speaks, the foreigner's first words are "Oh ma chère patrie!—malhereuse, coupable,—mais toujours chère patrie!" (385). Her "unhappy, guilty,—but always dear homeland" is what the stranger laments, even though, we soon learn, Gabriella has only just recently lost her infant son. The thought of her homeland, however, takes precedence in Gabriella's mind, for it encompasses all that is dear to her. The love of one's nation, as Admiral Powel himself even admitted, is natural and honorable, and Gabriella's expression of this love is meant to dignify her in our eyes.

Gabriella's homage to her homeland also unites her and Juliet, for the sound of Gabriella's words is what causes Juliet to recognize her former companion. When the two friends do finally recognize each other, their meeting also takes place entirely in French, with an extensive footnoted translation of their conversation written by Burney herself. This reunion between Gabriella and Juliet is an emotional one, and yet it, too, carries national overtones with it. In her biography of Burney, for instance, Doody refers to an 1814 review of *The Wanderer* that appeared in *The British Critic* where the critic picked out this scene in particular as worthy of his commentary. Remarking that the scene has a "French, not English pathos," the reviewer was still able to "pardon" Burney for her flagrant use of the French language: "we can therefore readily excuse our authoress from a violation of a rule of taste, in cloathing it in French garb." Gabriella herself was also declared to be "a true French character," most likely because of her excessive emotions.[35] This insertion of the French language into the text of the novel thus marked the dialogue as "French" for its contemporary readers. As Doody explains, Burney "wants a 'true French character' to impress upon the English reader that there are real French people, with their own feelings and way of putting things. She was willing to break 'a rule of taste' in giving such an extensive scene in a foreign language, because she wished to bring home to the reader the concept of another culture."[36] By importing Gabriella and Juliet's conversation into the novel, Burney gives voice to the feelings of a misunderstood people.

When he described the meeting between the two friends as one of "pathos," however, the writer from the *British Critic* chose an apt word to describe both the language in which the exchange takes place and that which is used to describe it. The emotional and excessive language is quite a change from *Evelina,* where the French expressions that litter the novel mostly consist of the oaths and complaints of Madame Duval and the pithy yet pretentious bons mots of the fop Mr. Lovel. Neither the anonymous critic nor Doody, however, recognized that the language from this scene equates *both* Gabriella *and* Juliet as French. "French pathos," they both agree, pervades the scene, yet what they fail to note is how that pathos describes not only the "true French character" of Gabriella, but also that of the British Juliet. The reaction of the two women to meeting each other is, after all, the same:

> Locked in each other's arms, pressed to each other's bosoms, they now remained many minutes in speechless agony of emotion, from nearly overpowering surprise, from gusts of ungovernable, irrepressible sorrow, and heart-piercing recollections; though blended with the tenderest sympathy of joy.
>
> This touching silent eloquence, these unutterable conflicts between transport and pain, were succeeded by a reciprocation of enquiry, so earnest, so eager, so ardent, that neither of them seemed to have any sensation left of self, from excess of solicitude for the other. . . .
>
> . . . . The fond embraces, and fast flowing tears of Ellis, evinced the keen sensibility with which she participated in the sorrows of this afflicted mother. (387–38)

Burney describes the two women's interactions by focusing not on the differences between their emotions but rather on the *similarities*. Burney does not first describe the emotions of one and then those of the other; instead, she uses the pronoun *they* to emphasize the sameness and unity of their still separate reactions. One view is presented, for each woman has the same response to meeting her friend. Essentially no difference in emotion exists between the two women: "Locked in each other's arms," both Gabriella and Juliet "remained many minutes in speechless agony of emotion . . . though blended with the tenderest sympathy of joy." Their "excess of solicitude" for the other even causes them to lose "any sensation of self," as each one loses her unique identity in her concern for her friend. In essence, Juliet's synonymous behavior marks her as indistinguishable from Gabriella, who Burney's contemporary reviewer and our own both assumed to be the only Frenchwoman present on that hill overlooking the ocean. Juliet's own "fond embraces" and "fast flowing tears" declare her to be subject to the excess of sensibility assumed to belong only to the French. If Gabriella possesses "a true French character," though, then Juliet must also since her reaction is virtually the same as her friend's.[37] Knowing, though, that Juliet is actually British causes us to question a supposed difference in national identity. If both women share the same emotional response, then how can that response be said to belong to a particular nation?

Burney provides an answer to this question when Juliet makes it clear that Gabriella possesses transnational virtues. Human beings possess, in this view, an unchanging core that remains the same, regardless of the country from which they come. So even though Gabriella was referred to as "a true French character," Juliet will later make it clear that Gabriella's virtues cut across national borders. Juliet emphasizes this while explaining Gabriella's history to Sir Jasper Herrington: "Her excellencies, her high qualities, and spotless conduct, might make the proudest Englishman exult to own her for his country-woman; though the lowest Frenchman would dispute, even at the risk of his life, the honour of her birth" (636). It is Gabriella's meritorious personal traits, and not her national ones, that give Gabriella such fluidity. Yet it is also important to note that these personal traits are linked to her gender identity as well. They make her fit not merely to be a fellow subject of the Englishman, but rather a fellow country-*woman*. The erasing of national differences thus occurs when gender identity unites its members.

GENDER IDENTITY AND FEMALE COMMUNITY

Juliet's close relationship with Gabriella and the ill treatment that both receive from Brighthelmstone society underscore one of the most sustained critiques in the novel: that British women do not help out their fellow women in times of need. Possessors of mixed national identities, Burney's novel implies, end up being wrongfully discriminated against, and gender identity, which should unite women, is often subsumed by national differences. National identity is a troubled concept for Burney in this novel, a concept that is problematic because characters like Juliet and even Burney herself can identify with more than one nation. In the modern world, where the complexities of human nature and identity have surfaced more strongly than ever before, Burney suggests, the solution is to avoid prejudice and to seek connections and community with other individuals, regardless of their nationality. Based on their actions, we can learn who other people "really" are. Women in particular need to recognize and support the claims and concerns of other women since the British nation fails to do so. In Burney's last novel, then, as in so many other texts of the period by authors such as Mary Wollstonecraft, Charlotte Smith, Hannah More, and Helen Maria Williams, gender identity is held out as the example of what should be the strongest tie between women, a form of protection in an otherwise hostile world.

One of Burney's strongest arguments in *The Wanderer* is that women need some form of protection.[38] Possessors of fragile reputations, women are subject to scandal and doubt when their actions are misunderstood by society. As several critics have pointed out, *The Wanderer* lacks powerful male figures to protect these women. Claudia Johnson, for instance, notes: "The world nightmarishly imagined in *The Wanderer* is destitute of fathers as well as of any authoritative males."[39] Women need protection to vindicate their actions, and Burney uses her novel as a way to explore what this community could look like. One striking example of what happens when women are without protection occurs when Juliet saves the young seamstress Flora from the evil machinations of Sir Lyell Sycamore. Realizing that Sir Lyell harbors plans to seduce her young friend, Juliet puts herself in his way so that he cannot be alone with Flora. Although Juliet's plan saves Flora's reputation and virtue, her own are harmed in the process, for the other women at Miss Matson's seamstress shop mistake Juliet's actions for her own interest in Sir Lyell. Juliet, the other seamstresses reason, only saved Flora from Sir Lyell so that she herself could take him as a lover. Shocked to learn their thoughts, Juliet can only reflect on the injustice of her situation: "Is there no end, then, she cried, to the evils of defenceless female youth? And, even where actual danger is escaped, must slander lie in wait, to misconstrue the most simple actions, by surmising the most culpable designs?" (470). As Juliet makes clear, young women without claims to any form of protection must submit to the "evils" of the world, and even if they escape physically unharmed, they are often forced to succumb to slander. Flora's reputation and honor remain intact, but Juliet's have suffered. Her altruistic motives, without anyone to vouch for and uphold them, leave her open to attack. Although she has protected Flora's reputation, she has no one to protect her own, and without such protection society views her as possessing "the most culpable designs." These supposed designs will even lead Sir Lyell to misconstrue her actions to such an extent that he will plan the elaborate kidnapping scheme discussed earlier.

A second example of the need for protection occurs when Juliet decides to perform in the music benefit in order to earn some desperately needed money. Harleigh pleads with her, for the sake of her family, not to take part in the concert, warning her of the severe consequences it will have on her honor and reputation. By performing in public, he cautions, Juliet would stray from the "long-beaten track of female timidity" since her female delicacy would be called into question (344). Writing in 1789, Priscilla Wakefield makes this connection between female virtue and performance clear in her educational treatise *Reflections on the Present Condition of the Female Sex; with Suggestions for its Improvement.* Wakefield explains how public life forces women into situations that undermine their purity: "The profession of an actress is indeed most unsuitable to the sex, in every point of view; whether it be considered with respect to the courage required to face an audience, or the variety of situations incident to it, which expose moral virtue to the most severe trials. . . . [acting is] a line of life, in which it is scarcely possible to preserve that purity of sentiment and conduct, which characterizes female excellence."[40] The life of a female public performer, according to Wakefield, leads women into morally dangerous terrain. Harleigh, of course, agrees with this assessment, as does Juliet herself, for she, too, does not want to perform in public. Necessity, however, compels her to perform, for, without protection, Juliet is left to herself to find a means of financial support. Extrapolating from her own story, she decries women's situation in general: "What is woman,—with the most upright designs, the most rigid circumspection,—what is woman unprotected? She is pronounced upon only from outward semblance:—and, indeed, what other criterion has the world? Can it read the heart?" (344). Returning once again to the theme of the impossibility of knowing others, Juliet reemphasizes the need to read other people through the lens of their actions. The dilemma of judging others finds its solution in looking to others' actions in order to determine their true characters. This time, however, Juliet's lament differs from those that came before it because of its gendered nature. The demands that modern society places upon women are even more severe than those placed on men. Sir Jasper may not be liked by servants and by those who know his true personality, but he is still received in Brighthelmstone society, and no mention is ever made of his terrible temper—at least not to his face. Juliet, on the other hand, as a representative of "woman unprotected," occupies a much more precarious position, one that depends upon the good will of those who decide to support her. Harleigh's argument makes that position all too apparent to her: if she performs, she becomes a fallen woman; if she does not perform, she will lose the patronage and hence protection of the Brighthelmstone women. Here the omnipotent hand of the author steps in to help out her heroine, for Burney's way out of this predicament is to have Juliet decide to perform, yet to have that performance interrupted. Elinor Joddrel's suicide attempt, which occurs at the very moment that Juliet is about to begin, absolves Juliet of any guilt, for she faints before she actually commits the sin.

Throughout the novel, Burney offers numerous examples such as these to demonstrate the necessity for female protection. Burney, through Juliet, argues that protection for women *should* be found in the domestic sphere, even though it usually is not. Late in the novel, for instance, when Juliet wanders through the Salisbury area, seeking escape from persecution, she comments upon the role that the British home should have. Tired of being repeatedly harassed by the men she meets on the road, Juliet exclaims against her vulnerability: "Alas! she cried, is it only under the domestic roof,—that roof to me denied!—that woman can know safety, respect, and honour?" (666). The British home is supposed to offer refuge to women, but throughout the novel it fails to do so when the women who seek its asylum are not British. Even when she stayed under the domestic roof, when that roof was *not* to her denied, Juliet was constantly threatened with being turned out of the houses of Mrs. Maple and Mrs. Ireton. Her national identity provokes the other characters, causing them to distrust Juliet because they see her as a foreigner without a name or certain identity. Gabriella's landlady distrusts Gabriella because she is foreign; the residents of Brighthelmstone distrust Juliet for the same reason.

The Necessity of Female Protection

The British home fails to serve as a refuge for women because it lacks a female community at its core. In Burney's assessment of British society, women are unwilling to help other women, a behavior that is strongly condemned. Through negative examples Burney demonstrates the functions that female protection should serve and the consequences of what happens to innocent women like Juliet without that protection. More specifically, female protection takes on three main forms within the novel: countenance in society, the possibility of work, and female friendship. Each of these forms confers status and validity upon women, yet, when denied, leads to "female difficulties," the term Burney chose as the subtitle for her last novel. For instance, the first shape that female protection takes—countenance within society—appears most frequently in the first volume of the novel, during that period when Juliet seeks to establish her position amongst the gentry of Brighthelmstone. After residing with Mrs. Maple and her nieces Elinor and Selina at Lewes for several weeks, Juliet, tired of Mrs. Maple's insults, decides to seek a new residence. A fortuitous visit by Miss Arbe and Miss Bydel provides Juliet with just the opportunity she seeks to venture into town, so she accepts their invitation to carry her to Brighthelmstone with them. Once in the carriage, Juliet reveals her true circumstances, that she is alone and without friends to support her. Her future, she explains to Miss Arbe and Miss Bydel, is entirely dependent upon the kindness of other women: "My situation, which seems so pleasant, is perhaps amongst the most painful that can be imagined. I feel myself, though in my native country, like a helpless foreigner; unknown, unprotected, and depending solely upon the benevolence of those by whom, accidentally, I am seen, for kindness,—or even for support!" (214). Although she is in her native country, a place where she *should* meet with compassion and protection, Juliet is instead treated like a "helpless foreigner." Because she is unknown, she is also unprotected, and the prejudice she meets with is the direct result of her being viewed by others as a nameless and friendless Frenchwoman. By openly laying her case before these two women, Juliet hopes to gain their protection. Miss Arbe and Miss Bydel are, however, extremely shocked by Juliet's revelation:

> The amazement of the two ladies, at this declaration, was equally great, though Miss Arbe, who never spoke and never acted, but through the medium of what she believed the world would most approve to hear her say, or to see her do, had no chance of manifesting her surprise as promptly as Miss Bydel. . . . Miss Arbe . . . was embarrassed how to treat her, till she could gain some information how she was likely to be treated by the world: but neither of them had entertained the most distant suspicion, that she was not settled under the roof, and the patronage, of Mrs. Maple. To hear, therefore, of her seeking a lodging, and wanting an asylum, presented her in so new, so altered, and so humiliated a point of view, that Miss Bydel herself was not immediately able to speak; and the two ladies stared at each other, as if reciprocally demanding how to behave. (214–15)

Once again, one of Burney's female characters is humiliated, brought low, although this time it is not an old, violent woman, but rather a young, modest woman who happens to be the heroine of our novel. Juliet's humiliation, like Madame Duval's, is directly brought about by another person, but Juliet's differs from her predecessor's because she did not exhibit any actions to bring the insult upon her. Her innocence, which is always exerted but never believed, has laid her open to the violence of Mrs. Maple, who has insulted Juliet so much that she is ready to take flight, alone and unaided, from Mrs. Maple's house. Juliet's humiliated state also lays her open to the pity or the ruthlessness of Miss Arbe and Miss Bydel. By revealing her actual situation to them, Juliet makes herself vulnerable, exposed. Accustomed to modifying their behavior to conform to the dictates of society, the two women do not, in fact, know how to react to Juliet's statement. They had believed that Juliet was "under the roof, and [hence] the patronage" of Mrs. Maple, but when they learn that this is not the case, they are not sure how to treat their new friend. Without knowing how "the world" will treat Juliet, they do not know how to behave. Looking to each other for guidance, Miss Arbe and Miss Bydel only draw a blank. Their uncertainty reflects their inability to offer protection to a fellow woman in need. Juliet has openly revealed her situation to them, but instead of basing their reaction to her pleas on emotion and logic, they base their reaction on what society would think.

Miss Arbe and Miss Bydel's decision to either support or reject Juliet is a crucial one, however, for without their approval, Juliet would have a hard time even finding a place to live. Without the recommendation of another woman, Juliet would be left on her own. In fact, when Miss Arbe and Miss Bydel let Juliet off in front of Miss Matson's despite her concerns, Juliet feels herself "unexpectedly abandoned" (218). Inadvertently, though, Miss Arbe has protected Juliet, for Miss Matson assumes that Juliet's presence in Miss Arbe's carriage was sanctioned by the lady herself, even though Miss Arbe was relieved to set Juliet down in order to get rid of her.[41] Although shocked by Juliet's request for a room, Miss Matson is happy to grant it, for "whatever might be the motive of her [Juliet's] return [to Miss Matson's lodgings], there could be none against her admission, since they knew her high connections, and since, even now, she was set down at the shop by Miss Arbe" (219). Juliet's association with these "high connections" thus grants her credit and guarantees her a respectable position within Brighthelmstone society. Vouched for, Juliet can procure the lodgings she needs.[42] When she receives the support of her fellow women, Juliet is given a place to live. When that support is withdrawn, however, Miss Matson becomes reserved, hostile, and familiar. Her behavior changes, and she treats Juliet "[w]ith little or no ceremony" (328).[43]

Although Miss Arbe's initial reaction to Juliet's helpless situation is one of doubt and embarrassment, she soon overcomes these feelings. In fact, Miss Arbe becomes one of Juliet's earliest protectors, yet, as her name indicates, Miss Arbe's protection remains arbitrary, subject to her own petty whims and desires. When Juliet first makes her escape from Mrs. Maple's house, she appeals to Miss Arbe in her quest to find work. Juliet hopes that Miss Arbe's position in society will grant validity to her own: "From the high influence of Miss Arbe in what is called the polite world, she hoped that to engage her favour, would almost secure prosperity to her favourite wish and plan, of exchanging her helpless dependency, for an honourable, however fatiguing, exertion of the talents and acquirements with which she had been endowed by her education; though nothing short of the courage of distress could have stimulated her to such an attempt" (212). This example brings us to the second form of female protection, that of helping another woman find suitable employment. Burney carefully emphasizes the fact that necessity alone drives Juliet to seek employment; her chances of employment, just like her chances of finding a place to live, depend, however, upon the "high influence" of Miss Arbe. Through Miss Arbe's favor alone will Juliet be able to find the means to financially support herself. Without that favor, Juliet lacks the social credit that would gain her clients for her new enterprise.

Miss Arbe ultimately agrees to aid Juliet, but only because Juliet can reciprocate the favor. Her interest in Juliet happens to coincide with her discovery that Juliet plays so well upon the harp. When Miss Arbe realizes this, she agrees to help her new protégée set up a harp lesson business, while also graciously agreeing to be Juliet's first, and most time-consuming, customer. It is then that Juliet first learns how difficult the lives of working women really are. Although she has fears about her own situation and monetary needs, Juliet soon realizes that she must grant Miss Arbe her lessons or lose the support of her powerful, because well respected, benefactress. Miss Arbe's lessons take precedence over any concerns of her own:

> And Ellis found all her painful difficulties, how to extricate herself from the distresses of penury, the horrour of creditors, and the fears of want, treated but as minor considerations, when put in competition with the importance of Miss Arbe's most trivial, and even stolen improvement.
>
> She saw, however, no redress; displeasure was unnoticed, distaste was unheeded; and she had no choice but to put aside every feeling, and give her usual instructions; or to turn a professed protectress into a dangerous and resentful enemy.
>
> She sat down, therefore, to her business. (284)

Juliet's "business" requires her to set aside any personal emotions she might have in favor of her desire to please Miss Arbe, for failure to do so would mean turning Miss Arbe into "a dangerous and resentful enemy," one who would stop at nothing to ruin Juliet's social standing. Miss Arbe essentially abuses her power as Juliet's "protectress" by manipulating Juliet into doing what Miss Arbe would like her to. This abuse is, in fact, one of the dangers of the current forms of female protection that Burney warns against. Helping other women find employment is a noble act, but the power that that help lends itself to is often abused. Because women are given so little power in other areas, they tend to abuse it in those small areas over which they do, in fact, have control. Later on, Juliet makes the connection between work, social standing, and female protection even clearer. When Miss Arbe suddenly stops showing up for her harp lessons, Juliet becomes extremely worried: "Ellis immediately experienced, that even the most superficial protection of a lady of fashion, could not, without danger, be withdrawn from the indigent and unsupported. . . . Ellis but too easily comprehended, that the ruin of her credit and consequence in private families, would follow the uselessness of her services to her patroness" (326–27). Because "a lady of fashion" countenances and supports her in society, Juliet has both "credit and consequence" with other members of Brighthelmstone society. Once that support ends, however, Juliet would lose not only her credit, but, more important, her means of making a living. Without social credit, no one would send their daughters and sisters to Juliet for harp lessons; without giving those lessons, Juliet would lose her ability to maintain herself.

This unstable balance of work and social position lies at the heart of Burney's critique of "female difficulties" in the modern British nation. A major fault of Britain is that it leads women into debt by refusing to allow them a place to work. In this respect, Burney offers a critique of the society that will not allow middle-class women the "privilege" of learning tasks that are not only pleasing, but also useful. Although the extremely accomplished Juliet can play, draw, sing, act, and sew, these talents qualify her for only a few select positions. She can become a music teacher, a paid musician, a seamstress, or even combine all of these skills by being a governess, but each of these occupations has its own drawbacks, and, without the help of a respected patroness like Miss Arbe, Juliet has little chance of doing any of them. Her limited means of employment cause Juliet to reflect once again upon the situation of women:

> How few, she cried, how circumscribed, are the attainments of women! and how much fewer and more circumscribed still, are those which may, in their consequences, be useful as well as ornamental, to the higher, or educated class! those through which, in the reverses of fortune, a FEMALE may reap benefit without abasement! those which, while preserving her from pecuniary distress, will not aggravate the hardships or sorrows of her changed condition, either by immediate humiliation, or by what, eventually, her connexions may consider as disgrace! (289)

Juliet's exploration of this problem leads her, of course, to focus almost exclusively on educated women, who do not possess the skills needed to earn a living. Lower-class women, who work all their lives, have less difficulty seeking valuable work, but middle- and upper-class women have no such skills to fall back on in times of need. When "the reverses of fortune" bring educated women low, they cannot find a way to save themselves from "pecuniary distress" since their accomplishments are so narrowly defined. Prejudice also works against educated women, for their new condition usually brings disgrace and humiliation with it. Social stigmas attach to women who, brought low, must work to support themselves, and Juliet herself experiences this stigma firsthand throughout the novel.

Juliet is not alone in her lament, however, which echoes those of other female writers from the period. Through Juliet's plea for the improved education of women, Burney joins not only prominent writers like Wollstonecraft, but also minor authors who argue that women need to find useful occupations. In her *Reflections*, for instance, Priscilla Wakefield addresses not just actresses, but also the precarious social position that women are too often left in:

> The necessity of directing the attention of females to some certain occupation is not so apparent, because custom has rendered them dependent upon their fathers and husbands for support; but as some of every class experience the loss of those relations, without inheriting an adequate resource, there would be great propriety in preparing each of them, by an education of energy and useful attainments, to meet such disasters, and to be able, under such circumstances, to produce an independence for herself. . . .
>
> . . . if it be really honourable in a man to exert the utmost of his abilities, whether mental or corporal, in the acquisition of a competent support for himself and for those who have a natural claim upon his protection, it must equally be so in a woman; nay, perhaps still more incumbent, as in so many cases there is nothing so inimical to the preservation of her virtue as a state of poverty, which leaves her dependent upon the generosity of others, to supply those accommodations which use has rendered necessary to her comfort.[44]

Like Wakefield, Burney also believes that women should be adequately educated to meet the demands of the world. When faced with disaster, women should possess the ability to lead independent lives. Dependence upon others seriously jeopardizes a woman's virtue by putting her in situations where that virtue might be compromised. Juliet's decision to perform in public serves as a good example of this. If she had actually performed, Juliet would have been stigmatized as a morally loose woman ever after.

Wakefield's comments on dependence also lead to an important element of Burney's own national critique. Besides arguing for a greater appreciation of national differences, Burney also argues for more independence for women, an independence that can only be achieved through work. Work empowers women by leading to "self-dependence," or the ability to rely upon oneself, what we nowadays refer to as "independence."[45] Gabriella accentuates this point when she remarks "self-exertion can alone mark nobility of soul; and that self-dependence can only sustain honour in adversity" (639). British society, structured as it currently is, however, leaves little opportunity for women to earn their own living, and, without self-dependence, honor and morality are compromised. As in the scene where Juliet must give Miss Arbe her harp lesson, regardless of how worried or upset Juliet is at the time, Juliet repeatedly finds that she must suffer in silence in front of those people to whom she owes money or to whom she is obliged in some way. Withstanding abuse belongs to the nature of financial dependence; debt repeatedly gives other characters emotional license over Juliet. The letter that Juliet receives from her French friends also clarifies this point in regard to gender identity. The letter lays out a course of action for Juliet to follow while she is living in Britain, and urges her to use her own talents to support herself: "That where occasion calls for female exertion, mental strength must combat bodily weakness" so that individuals, "whether female or male, [can] learn to suffice to themselves" (220). The phrasing of this passage is important, for by putting the word "female" before the word "male," Burney emphasizes her own belief in the letter's injunctions. Women, as well as men, need to be able to become self-sufficient individuals, drawing upon both their mental and physical strength to meet their goals. After reading the letter, Juliet takes the issue to heart, "declaring her firm purpose to endeavour to depend, henceforth, upon her own exertions" (220) and to seek "the self-dependence at which she so earnestly languished to arrive" (225).

Violence against Women: The Three Furies

Work, money, and independence essentially become the three components of a cycle that either propels women to safety or leaves them on morally dangerous ground. Working produces money, and money produces self-dependence, yet this cycle cannot be initiated without the protection of another woman to set it in motion. For precisely this reason, the protection of other women is crucial in the modern world.[46] In Burney's earliest novel, Evelina encountered dangerous situations while negotiating her way through British society, but France represented the truly dangerous and violent nation. British society provided Evelina with a set of challenges that she had to meet, but she always had the support and protection of her friends upon which to fall back. In Burney's last novel, in contrast, the *British* nation represents the primary site of violence against women. Captain Mirvan's brutal antics are transformed into self-inflicted acts of violence (best exemplified by Elinor's repeated suicide attempts) and into violence against helpless women (best exemplified by Juliet's "female difficulties"). The attacks that Juliet must confront, unlike those that plagued Madame Duval, come not from a vicious, bitter sea captain, who has done nothing but fight his entire life, but rather from supposedly genteel British women, who have done nothing but gossip and abuse their petty stores of power their entire lives. Instead of helping Juliet as a fellow woman, which is what Juliet wishes they would do, they make it extremely difficult for her to find a way to support herself merely because Juliet is not British, too.

Society forces women to rely on other women to make their way out of dangerous situations if they want to protect their virtue and reputations. Yet the problem is that the women who should be protectors are not willing or able to protect their fellow women: those members of society who can most appropriately offer protection are the same members of society who consistently withhold that protection. Years earlier, in 1793, Burney had made a similar argument in her *Brief Reflections Relative to the Emigrant French Clergy*. Her pamphlet, which was addressed specifically to females, urges British women to help others in need. If no one comes to the aid of this impoverished group of French priests, who were forced to leave their homeland during the Terror, then "they must soon end their hapless career, not by paying the debt of nature, but by famine."[47] The French priests, whom Burney refers to as "these destitute wanderers" (ibid.), have only one real resource open to them—and "this resource is FEMALE BENEFICENCE" (ibid., 4). Burney directs her supplication to a female audience, she explains, not because men have no sense of charity, but rather because "the ladies who patronize this plan [of financially helping the priests] are content to spread it amongst their own sex" (ibid., 7). Female community, her argument implies, assures that women will urge one another to help other humans in need. And, although the British "are too apt to consider ourselves rather as a distinct race of beings, than as merely the emulous inhabitants of rival states" (ibid., 12), they should set aside their national prejudices when charity demands it. "O let us be brethren with the good," Burney challenges, "wheresoever they may arise! and let us resist the culpable, whether abroad or at home" (ibid., 13). Although Burney's appeal refers specifically to the French priests, it could just as easily be applied to Juliet, who is, like the emigrants, also a "destitute wanderer." Female beneficence, which Burney urgently exhorts her readers to demonstrate, is what Juliet also needs. Without it, she, too, risks the danger of perishing through famine. Juliet's French husband may represent a dark, overpowering sense of danger in the novel, but the most menacing characters are actually the ones that have the power to deprive Juliet of her immediate needs and daily sustenance, and for this Burney chastises Brighthelmstone's women. Characters like Miss Arbe, Miss Bydel, and Selina Joddrel are too conscious of "what society would think" and too aware of their own concerns to provide a reliable form of protection for other women. Other female characters are even worse, taking every opportunity they can to verbally abuse Juliet and make her aware of her low and dependent status. It is also important to emphasize that Burney's critique of this practice, via her negative representations of female protection, is national in tone. The Britishness of these women is precisely what compels them to abuse Juliet, for they distrust her, as previously argued, because they perceive her as a foreigner, a nameless woman from France without a stable identity. They locate her, to state it simply, as the Other because she is not British, not easily readable. Female community fails when it refuses to overlook national difference.[48]

Female residents like Miss Arbe and Selina Joddrel pose serious challenges to Juliet's ability to support herself, but they never actively seek to harm Juliet. They are more concerned with what they can gain from Juliet, whether that be free harp lessons or transitory moments of companionship, than with intentionally causing her pain. Yet other female characters provide more serious threats to Juliet's well-being. The cruelest and most violent characters, are, in fact, other women, particularly Mrs. Maple, Mrs. Ireton, and Mrs. Howel. The "three Furies" (872), as Admiral Powel will later nickname them, do all they can to make it difficult for Juliet to sustain both her integrity and her means of financial support. Their attempts to bring Juliet low are malicious and cruel, closer in nature to the extreme pranks of *Evelina*'s Captain Mirvan than to the snubs and slights of Miss Arbe. In their hands, Juliet finds humiliation, and, through negative example, Burney uses them to illustrate what happens when women violate the sense of female community that unites them.

The first of these women, Mrs. Maple, is the least sinister of the three, yet she still has an important role in undermining Juliet's sense of safety. Mrs. Maple treats Juliet with scorn and contempt, making Juliet feel her dependent and distrusted state. It is Mrs. Maple, in fact, who devises most of the choicest appellations for Juliet, including those

of "pauper," "stroller," and "adventuress." Refusing to sit next to Juliet
during the boat ride back from France and discussing Juliet while she
is present are both damaging blows to Juliet's sense of worth, yet these
cases carry less weight than Mrs. Maple's repeated threats to kick Juliet out of her house. Admittedly, Mrs. Maple is kind to let Juliet stay
at her home in the first place, but her decision to do so is based more
on Elinor's urging and the threat that Juliet might reveal her situation
to the neighborhood than it is upon her own goodwill. Juliet's position
within Mrs. Maple's household, however, is always a precarious one,
and she is never certain as to how long Mrs. Maple's "charity" will last.
Mrs. Maple distrusts Juliet because she is without a name or country
and because Juliet has, to Mrs. Maple's way of thinking, disguised herself in the past for no good reason, even though Juliet has tried to explain her situation to Mrs. Maple on several occasions. Before Juliet's
unusual situation is publicly known, Mrs. Maple does all she can to
keep the world from knowing her guest's true state of affairs, more to
save her own reputation than to protect her house guest. Faced with
any situation that might reveal Juliet's strange situation, "All then that
occurred to her [Mrs. Maple], was her usually violent, but short measure, of sending Ellis suddenly from the house, and excusing her disappearance, by asserting that her own friends had summoned her away"
(208). Mrs. Maple's method of handling a possible embarrassing situation—a method she resorts to at regular intervals (as the word "usually"
implies)—is to dismiss Juliet from the house. Mrs. Maple does not care
where Juliet would actually go, just as long as Juliet actually leaves, an
attitude that reveals Mrs. Maple's utter lack of sympathy toward a fellow human being. Another striking instance of this occurs once Lord
Denmeath realizes who Juliet really is and what she wants. Lord Denmeath sends a letter to Mrs. Maple, requesting her to tell Juliet "to quit
the country without delay" (210). Mrs. Maple, taking pleasure in the
task assigned to her, "now, peremptorily sent word to Ellis, that she
must immediately make up her mind to leaving the kingdom" (210).
When Juliet refuses, she "was, therefore, positively ordered to seek for
charity in some other house" by Mrs. Maple herself (210). By this
point, Juliet's dismissal is a welcome one, and she decides to seek a
room at Miss Matson's in town: "It was not the design of Ellis to return
any more to Lewes. The gross treatment which she had experienced,
and the daily menace of being dismissed, were become utterly insupportable" (212). Life in Mrs. Maple's household is overshadowed by
the "daily menace" of being driven from Lewes, forced to seek a new
place to live, which is an event that could occur at only a moment's

notice, as it often has. Although Mrs. Maple has repeatedly threatened but never actually carried through with her threat, the stress, for such it is, of having this constant worry over her becomes too much for Juliet to bear, and so she finally decides to leave once and for all.

The second Fury, Mrs. Ireton, is, as her name suggests, a woman of intense wrath and anger. She becomes Juliet's employer not just once, when Juliet is her paid companion, but twice, when Juliet accompanies her from Dover to London after their boat first arrives in Britain. Both times, Mrs. Ireton takes delight in demeaning and verbally abusing Juliet.[49] Once Juliet enters Mrs. Ireton's house as a paid companion, she becomes particularly subject to Mrs. Ireton's authoritative commands. Used to dominating those around her, Mrs. Ireton will make Juliet her new object of scorn, eventually coming to view Juliet as "the creature of her power, whom she looked upon as destined for the indulgence of her will, and the play of her authority" (516). When Juliet first enters Mrs. Ireton's house, Mrs. Ireton bids her enter in a most unwelcome voice: "The authoritative tone in which this was uttered, joined to what Juliet observed of the general tyranny exercised around her, intimidated and shocked her; and she stood still, and nearly confounded" (479). After only a few days in her new position, the violence and wrath that belong to Mrs. Ireton's reign become too much for Juliet to bear, and she finds herself wondering why she ever agreed to take the position: "Juliet now stood in scarcely less dismay than she had been witnessing all around her; panic-struck to find herself in the power of a person whose character was so wantonly tyrannic and irascible" (484). Mrs. Ireton's own domestic reign of terror encompasses Juliet now, too. The tyranny that Mrs. Ireton exercises in her household also echoes that which Wollstonecraft warned about in *A Vindication of the Rights of Woman:* "women, whose minds are not enlarged by cultivation, or the natural selfishness of sensibility expanded by reflection, are very unfit to manage a family; for, by an undue stretch of power, they are always tyrannizing to support a superiority that only rests on the arbitrary distinction of fortune" (*VRW* 66). As a woman with limited education, Mrs. Ireton amuses herself by forcing others to succumb to her whims. Juliet decides to remain under Mrs. Ireton's power, however, because so few options are available to her. Without Mrs. Ireton's protection, Juliet would once more be forced back out into public life to try to make a living alone. Recognizing this, Mrs. Ireton does all she can to make Juliet's situation as miserable as possible. She uses her power over Juliet to make her young companion constantly feel her subservient state.[50]

Petty and vindictive, Mrs. Ireton thus gratifies herself by insulting others, and Juliet most often bears the brunt of her employer's attacks. We see Mrs. Ireton as spiteful and brutal, and cannot help but commiserate with Juliet for having to put up with so much cruelty. Yet underneath all of the sarcasm, underneath all of the rancor, lies an unhappy woman whose miserable fate owes its creation to the society to which it belongs. That is, Burney offers no apology for Mrs. Ireton's personality, but she does offer an explanation as to what has made Mrs. Ireton the way she is. Interestingly enough, that explanation comes from the mouth of one of the novel's most complex characters, Sir Jasper Herrington. Having known Mrs. Ireton since she was a child, Sir Jasper is intimately familiar with her personal history and her character. He reveals this knowledge to Juliet in one of their conversations, where he elucidates Mrs. Ireton's behavior: "And yet, this pale, withered, stiff, meagre hag, so odious, so tyrannical, so irascible, but a few years,—in my calculation!—but a few years since,—had all the enchantment of blithe, blooming loveliness! You, who see her only in her decline, can never believe it; but she was eminently fair, gay, and charming!" (542). Once a young, beautiful woman, Mrs. Ireton was spoiled by being indulged in every wish that she had. As she aged, however, she was "shocked and amazed to see herself supplanted by the rising bloomers; to find that she might be forgotten, or left out" (542). Her whims and fancies could no longer garner her the attention she had before been so willingly given. Thinking that her sarcasm would gain her the attention and admiration she had so recently lost, she cultivated it, gradually developing into the cruel person she now was. Sir Jasper emphasizes, however, that this pattern of maturity is common to many women:

> Such has been her maturity; such, amongst faded beauties, is the maturity of thousands. . . . in old age, without stores to amuse, or powers to instruct, though with a full persuasion that she is endowed with wit, because she cuts, wounds, and slashes from unbridled, though pent-up resentment, at her loss of adorers; and from a certain perverseness, rather than quickness of parts, that gifts her with the sublime art of ingeniously tormenting; with no consciousness of her own infirmities, or patience for those of others; she is dreaded by the gay, despised by the wise, pitied by the good, and shunned by all. (543)

Mrs. Ireton's fate is the fate of scores of "faded beauties" who wake up one morning to discover that their beauty has stolen away, taking the admiration of others with it. What Juliet had, in a passage cited earlier, referred to as "the race of the Mrs. Iretons" thus consists of a large number, a crowd of women who derive pleasure by tormenting others because they resent their own vanished glories. Sir Jasper's insightful comments also point to the role that society plays in all this. That is, his analysis of Mrs. Ireton's temperament ties in to Burney's other claims about useful employment for women. If Mrs. Ireton had been given meaningful work to do as a young woman, if she had not been petted and indulged in every whim, she would not have set such a high value on her looks. She would, in turn, have promoted her own abilities to occupy herself and to become a useful member of society. As Wollstonecraft clarifies in her second *Vindication,* "the whole tenour of female education (the education of society) tends to render the best [women] disposed romantic and inconstant; and the remainder vain and mean" (*VRW 75*). Mrs. Ireton has emerged from her adolescence as one of the remainders, as the tyrannical mistress of a household that she governs through sarcasm and cruelty. The fault, as Burney makes clear, lies not with her, however, but with British society. Her wrath is the direct result of her education and upbringing, which did not allow her to realize that she had merits besides her looks. She has become instead a woman who is dreaded, despised, pitied, and shunned by all who know her.

Mrs. Maple and Mrs. Ireton torment Juliet throughout the novel, and yet their insults and mockery remain slight when compared to that of Mrs. Howel, the last—and most terrible—of the three Furies. In Juliet's own estimation, Mrs. Howel is her worst enemy, the person whose behavior has most seriously undermined her sense of personal integrity. Whereas Mrs. Maple and Mrs. Ireton have always treated Juliet with disdain, Mrs. Howel first treated Juliet as an equal, so her departure from this behavior makes her subsequent conduct the more severe. The change in Mrs. Howel's behavior first comes about while Juliet is residing as a guest under her roof, when Mrs. Howel learns that Juliet is an 'imposter." When Mrs. Howel confronts Juliet, she enters the room, seating herself, yet without asking Juliet to do the same. Mrs. Howel, with little of ceremony or manners, then reveals that she has heard the entire narrative of how Juliet came across from France, without a name or identity. Surprise then engulfs Juliet, but such surprise mostly owes its creation to the drastic change in Mrs. Howel's attitude toward her: "[Juliet] could far better brook behaviour such as this from Mrs. Maple, from whom she had never experienced any of a superiour sort; but by Mrs. Howel she had been invited upon equal terms, and, hitherto, had been treated not only with equality but distinction: hard, therefore, she found it to endure such a change" (131). After Mrs. Howel leaves the chamber, Juliet "shut herself into her room, almost overpowered by the shock of this attack, so utterly unexpected, from a lady in whose character the leading feature seemed politeness, and who always appeared to hold that quality to be pre-eminent to all others" (133–34). Juliet's refined sensibility makes it difficult for her to reconcile Mrs. Howel's recent rudeness with her past politeness. Juliet finds the attack upon her character and intentions shocking (for her friendship with Lady Aurora and Lord Melbury has always been one based on mutual respect and integrity), but even more horrifying is the situation that Mrs. Howel knowingly leaves Juliet in, alone and without any form of protection. In sending Juliet away from the house in such a disgraceful manner, Mrs. Howel violates the trust that Juliet had reposed in her. As a house guest, Juliet could rely on the tacit agreement that Mrs. Howel would act as her temporary guardian and benefactor; when she sends Juliet away at a moment's notice, however, Mrs. Howel withdraws her protection, leaving Juliet in a precarious and even dangerous situation. In hindsight, Juliet will later refer to this scene as one in which "she had experienced the pain which she had felt *the most severely;* for there [while a guest at Mrs. Howel's] all the soothing consideration, so precious to her sorrows, had abruptly been broken off, to give place to an assault *the most shocking* upon her intentions, her probity, her character" (478, emphases added). Mrs. Howel's words and actions affect Juliet more than those of any other character in the novel, as Burney's use of the superlative shows.[51] Juliet makes it very clear that Mrs. Howel is her worst enemy and tormentor. At a later point, when Lady Aurora attempts to convince Juliet to reveal her secrets to Mrs. Howel, Juliet reacts with horror:

> I have no words to paint the terrible impression she has left upon my mind. All that I have borne from others is short of what I have suffered from that lady! The debasing accusations of Mrs. Maple, the taunting tyranny of Mrs. Ireton, though they make me blush to owe,—or rather, to earn from them the subsistence without which I know not how to exist; have yet never smote so rudely and so acutely to my inmost heart, as the attack I endured from Mrs. Howel! They rob me, indeed, of comfort, of rest, and of liberty— but they do not sever me from Lady Aurora! (556–57)

Juliet acknowledges that her "cruel situation" leaves her open to misinterpretation and doubt, and that, by choosing to guard her secrets, she cannot "repel" the attacks she receives. Yet the worst attacks of all have been those issued by Mrs. Howel: "All that I have borne from others is short of what I have suffered from that lady!" Nothing can compare to the insults that Mrs. Howel leveled at Juliet, or to the fact that Mrs.

Howel tore Lady Aurora away from her. Even comfort, rest, and liberty, as Juliet's words make clear, cannot compare to this last insult, for Lady Aurora's companionship is what has sustained Juliet in some of her most trying moments. Pursuit by her husband, the threat of having no immediate funds, the relinquishing of Gabriella's companionship—none of these episodes carries the same intensity for Juliet as her most severe pain, that of being assaulted and insulted by Mrs. Howel. Juliet's reaction seems excessive, and yet it is the very excessiveness of her reaction that underscores the extreme nature of Mrs. Howel's ability to inflict terror. One would think that Juliet's cruel French husband would inspire the most dread in her, but instead she finds that dread in the form of a fellow British woman. Mrs. Howel is a woman who delights in being the "persecutor" (805) of Juliet, a woman, who, "from her own hard conduct, [had] become the young orphan's personal enemy" (826). Mrs. Howel's personal reign of terror renders Juliet incapable of thought or action every time the two women meet.[32]

THE IMPORTANCE OF FEMALE FRIENDSHIP

Mrs. Maple, Mrs. Ireton, Mrs. Howel, and even Miss Arbe thus represent the conflicted nature of female protection in the novel. Whether it be owing to spite or adherence to the dictates of "what society would think," each one of these women possesses a reason strong enough to refuse aid to Juliet when she is most in need of female protection. Of the three versions of female protection in the novel—countenance in society, the possibility of work, and female friendship—the first two fail to offer a viable form of defense in a complex world since most of the women in the novel fail to use them to Juliet's advantage. So far, we have only looked at negative examples, none that has been positive, and yet it is through these examples that Burney most effectively argues for change since characters like the three Furies and Miss Arbe demonstrate the cruelty and solipsism that mark the behavior of women toward their fellow women in need. The female residents of Brighthelmstone resist any attempts to aid Juliet or to establish a female community that would help other women, whether British or French, or somewhere in between, when those other women need help. Discarding their national prejudices would, though, solve the problem, for then these women would seek to understand Juliet based upon her personal merits.

Burney does not rely on negative examples alone to make this point, however. Female protection also has a positive face in the novel, and that sanguine side is female friendship, which is the third form of female protection that Burney explores in *The Wanderer*. Whereas fellow writer Charlotte Smith ultimately concludes that female community is not a viable option within England, Burney still possesses hope in such community. Although Juliet repeatedly encounters hostility from some of the leaders of Brighthelmstone society, she also repeatedly encounters kindness from characters like Lady Barbara Falkland, Elinor Joddrel, and Lady Aurora, and even amongst nameless groups of women. For Burney, as for Juliet, female companionship is a necessity, a tie that links human beings together in an otherwise complex world. Juliet makes her own need for female friendship clear when she seeks intimacy from the women around her. After Gabriella returns to her husband in London, for example, Juliet continues their needlework business on her own. She desires friendship, and misses it greatly when she does not find it among her female clientele: "Now and then, however, she was surprised by sudden starts of kindness, and hasty enquiries, eagerly made, though scarcely demanding any answer, into her situation and affairs; followed by drawing her, with an air of confidence, into a dressing-room or closet:—but there, when prepared for some mark of favour or esteem, she was only asked, in a mysterious whisper, whether she could procure any cheap foreign lace, or French gloves? or whether she could get over from France, any particularly delicate paste for the hands" (406). Juliet, used to meeting with confidence and trust, here only meets with superficial concern. Expecting to receive "some mark of favour or esteem," Juliet instead finds that she is essentially being used. Her knowledge of French culture, which presumably makes her an expert on French beauty products as well as a smuggler of them, leads the women of Brighthelmstone to seek Juliet out in secret. Any concern they demonstrate, however, is merely show, exhibited so that they can gain what they really want, access to products that will increase their vanity even more. What Juliet seeks from her clients, however, is very different, for she seeks female friendship. Companionship would alleviate many of her worries for "her mind both required and merited secour as much as her circumstances" (406). Her life with Gabriella has, in fact, made this secour more necessary than ever. While working together, "No privation was hard, no toil was severe, no application was tedious, while the friend of her heart was by her side" (402). When Gabriella learns, however, that her husband is ill and that she must go to London to be with him, her absence makes Juliet more in need of companionship than ever:

> Her short but precious junction with her Gabriella, gave poignancy to every latent regret, and added disgust to her solitary toil. Thoughts uncommunicated, ideas unexchanged, fears unrevealed, and sorrows unparticipated, infused a heaviness into her existence, that not all her activity in business could conquer. . . . With an ardent love of elegant social intercourse, she was doomed to pass her lonely days in a room that no sound of kindness ever cheered. . . . she had the bitter self-experience of the weight of solitude without books, and of the gloom of retirement without a friend. (406–7)

Alone and without any form of social interaction, Juliet feels trapped. Although her circumstances require her to work unceasingly, that work becomes a burden without anyone with whom to share her thoughts. Communication, exchange, revelation, and participation—all forms of human interaction based upon friendship—would make her work less dreary and burdensome. Without them, Juliet experiences feelings of regret, disgust, bitterness, and gloom.

Although Juliet believes that female companionship would relieve all her worries, Burney shows us that this portrait remains an ideal, one tinctured by the dynamics of modern society and the role that women have within it. Juliet and Gabriella enjoy a strong bond, but that bond is based upon a mutual trust established long ago and that developed as the two women grew up together in France. With other women in the novel, women that Juliet is a stranger to, forming that bond is more difficult, usually because the other women have ulterior aims that motivate them to either seek or avoid Juliet's company. Miss Arbe's interest in Juliet, as explained earlier, fluctuates around the use-value Juliet has for Miss Arbe: if Juliet can be useful to her, then she is willing to nurture their relationship, but as Juliet's usefulness wanes, so does Miss Arbe's interest. The complex nature of female friendship within modern society is best illustrated, though, in the relationship that develops between Elinor Joddrel and Juliet.[53] Elinor is, in fact, the most likely candidate for being Juliet's companion and ally. As many critics have pointed out, Elinor is a Wollstonecraftian figure, a woman who possesses an independent fortune, and claims to laugh in the face of convention. Used to doing what pleases her, Elinor has even learned how to manipulate and control her aunt and guardian Mrs. Maple. Elinor's presence in the early part of the novel is also consistent; she is one of the earliest characters that Juliet meets, and she is the first person who offers asylum, temporary though it is, to Juliet. Their relationship, however, is problematized by two factors: Elinor's jealousy and Elinor's position within society.

Jealousy is Elinor's biggest problem. When she first realizes the man she loves does not return her affection but instead loves Juliet, Elinor turns her frustration into hatred. Juliet, of course, as the object of Harleigh's affection, becomes the target of Elinor's attacks. On one of Lady Aurora's last few days in Brighthelmstone, for instance, while Juliet is still a guest under Mrs. Howel's roof, the Lewes party is invited for dinner. Once the group begins eating, Lady Aurora is the first to notice how Elinor treats Juliet:

> Elinor, whose eyes constantly followed [Harleigh's], seemed sick during the whole repast, of which she scarcely at all partook. If Ellis offered to serve her, or enquired after her health, she darted at her an eye so piercing, that Ellis, shrinking and alarmed, determined to address her no more; though again, when any opportunity presented itself, for shewing some attention, the resolution was involuntarily set aside; but always with equal ill success, every attempt to soften, exciting looks the most terrific.
>
> Lady Aurora surprised one of these glances, and saw its chilling effect. Astonished, at once, and grieved, she felt an impulse to rise, and to protect from such another shock her new and tenderly admired favourite. She now easily conceived why kindness was so touching to her; yet how any angry sensation could find its way into the breast of Miss Joddrel, or of any human being, against such sweetness and such excellence, her gentle mind, free from every feeling of envy, jealousy, or wrath, could form no conjecture. She sighed to withdraw her from a house where her merits were so ill appreciated. (121)

Although Juliet does her best to placate Elinor by passing her plates and trying to entertain a discussion, Elinor rejects her attempts. The jealousy that makes Elinor quite literally sick envelopes her to such an extent that she can only respond to Juliet's attempts with "looks the most terrific." The unhappiness Elinor feels also prevents her from establishing a bond with Juliet, whom she views as her rival. Elinor remains unwilling to protect Juliet from others, and even initiates attacks on Juliet herself. Resentment will become the dominant emotion that Elinor has toward Juliet, especially as she comes to realize the extent of Harleigh's feelings for her rival.

Jealousy therefore impedes the formation of a lasting friendship between Juliet and Elinor, and yet equally important as a factor in their relationship is Elinor's position as a woman in modern British society. Like Mrs. Ireton, the faded beauty who has grown vindictive and sarcastic, Elinor is also a product of her society, a society that has established competing claims on her.[54] Although she desires to befriend

Juliet, she is torn between her personal inclinations and convention. Woman, Elinor's reasoning goes, is both regaled and despised by society, placed in a niche from which it is difficult for her to act with her true intentions. She explains these contradictions in one of her conversations with Juliet:

> Oh woman! poor, subdued woman! thou art as dependent, mentally, upon the arbitrary customs of man, as man is, corporally, upon the established laws of his country! . . . .
>
> This Woman, whom they estimate thus below, they elevate above themselves. They require from her, in defiance of their examples!—in defiance of their lures!—angelical perfection. She must be mistress of her passions; she must never listen to her inclinations; she must not take a step of which the purport is not visible; she must always be guided by reason, though they deny her understanding!—Frankness, the noblest of our qualities, is her disgrace;—sympathy, the most exquisite of our feelings, is her bane! (399–400)

As Elinor's comments make clear, women must adhere to the dictates of society, even when those dictates are against their natures. The "arbitrary customs of man" make as little sense, she reasons, as the laws of any nation. Both sets of injunctions require both men and women to set aside their natural preferences in favor of artificial and randomly contrived conventions. Women, of course, have a much more difficult position to occupy, since they are simultaneously both debased and elevated. They are admired for their "feminine" qualities, and yet denied the display of any qualities that might be misconstrued as nonfeminine. Self-control must become women's motto since they are forbidden to exercise their understanding and frankness, even when encouraged to be reasonable and honest. Elinor's self-loathing becomes so great that she attempts suicide not once, but twice.[55] Juliet notes this contradiction as well, remarking, "what a mixture of contrasting qualities sully, and ennoble [Elinor's] character in turn!" (401).

This contradictory set of expectations is also precisely what Elinor rejects when she rebels against all of society's rules and customs. She cannot, however, differentiate between those customs that are useful and reasonable and those customs that really do harm women. Competing claims have made her conflicted, uncertain where she should place her energies. "Throwing the baby out with the bath water" is how Elinor reacts to Juliet and her plight. Although Elinor knows what kind of modest and proper behavior is expected of her, she resists such behavior with all her energy, and even encourages Juliet to do the same.

During this same conversation, for instance, Elinor asks Juliet about her future plans and means of support:

> Juliet answered that her choice was small, and that her means were almost null: but when she lamented the severe DIFFICULTIES of a FEMALE, who, without fortune or protection, had her way to make in the world, Elinor, with strong derision, called out: "Debility and folly! Put aside your prejudices, and forget that you are a dawdling woman, to remember that you are an active human being, and your FEMALE DIFFICULTIES will vanish into the vapour of which they are formed." (397)

Hidden within Juliet's words is a plea for protection, but Elinor refuses to listen because she is so busy refusing to be what society would have her be. Although Elinor realizes that women are denied understanding, frankness, and sympathy, she still believes that they should exert their efforts to earn their own way in the world. She essentially chastises Juliet for adhering to society's dictates and for believing that her choices and means are limited. What Elinor does not realize, however, as several critics have pointed out, is that she herself occupies a privileged position in society because of her wealth and social class.[56] She does not realize how difficult it actually is for working women to earn a living, especially when they are foreign and thereby objects of prejudice before they even have a chance to demonstrate their skills. Juliet has tried to be "an active human being" so that she can achieve self-dependence, but her struggles to do so are usually thwarted because she lacks female protection. Elinor's revolt against society has thus given her a limited perspective; by refusing society's rules, she refuses even the most rationale and humane of appeals.

Once Elinor sets aside her disdain for convention, however, she reveals herself to be a generous and caring individual. Rebuking Juliet for what she sees as self-pity does not stop Elinor from sending Juliet and Gabriella a draft for £50 shortly after their conversation. Gabriella refuses the money, of course, preferring instead that Elinor exercise her influence in the community to help her and Juliet establish their sewing business. Recognizing how she can do this, "Elinor, zealous to serve, and fearless to demand, instantly attacked, by note or by message, every rich female at Brighthelmstone; urging the generous, and shaming the niggardly, till there was scarcely a woman of fortune in the place, who had not given, or promised, a commission for some fine muslin-work. The two friends, through this commanding protection, began their new plan of life under the most favourable auspices" (401). When she finally resolves the contradictions within her, Elinor becomes an excellent source of aid, providing the "commanding protection" that Juliet has been seeking all along.

Wealth and social status, the two factors that Elinor possesses in abundance, give her enough power over the women of Brighthelmstone to force them into helping Juliet. These two factors, while they are sure guarantors of power, are not, however, the only ways in which women can protect others. Even without these means of authority, Burney demonstrates how protection often lies in numbers or in names. When Juliet is alone with Sir Jasper at Arundel Castle, for instance, she is forced to comply with his wishes, forced to attend him, because there is no woman whom she can ask for help: "therefore, as there was no female in view, to whom she could apply, she was compelled to follow" (759). The mere presence of another woman would have given Juliet the ability to refuse Sir Jasper because he would be unwilling to make a scene in front of another individual. Protection in numbers also appears when Juliet's husband emerges on the scene. When he tries to force Juliet into his carriage so he can take her away with him, it is the women of the inn who come to her rescue. After collapsing while entering the coach, Juliet "now looked so sick and disordered, that all the women called upon the foreigner to let her re-enter the house, and take a little rest, before her journey. Her eyes, turned up at heaven with thankfulness, even at the proposal, encouraged them to grow clamourous in their demand" (733). Although Juliet's husband refuses to listen to the women's appeals, the very fact that they make such an uproar shows that they are concerned for a fellow creature in need. Mistreatment is something that these women will not stand for, as they make quite clear. Their efforts might fail, but they at least tried.

Besides demonstrating how numbers can protect other women, Burney also shows how names are a form of protection as well. In the version of British society that Burney presents, names offer a means of protection and also social validity. We have already seen how Juliet repeatedly encounters prejudice, for example, because she does not possess a name to guarantee her protection within society, and we have already seen the power that association with reputable members of society bestows. What Burney also demonstrates is how another person's name can also offer protection, even if that person is not present herself or is unable to offer direct support. Nowhere is this better shown than through Lady Aurora, who is one of Juliet's earliest and best allies, well before she learns that she is Juliet's half-sister.[57] Attracted to one another immediately after meeting, Lady Aurora and Juliet share a common sensibility and common tastes. Juliet's younger sister would seem to be her best form of protection, but Lady Aurora, as an underage woman, cannot welcome Juliet into her own household because she herself does not possess one. She makes this clear in one of their earliest conversations: "Oh! if I were my own mistress—with what delight I should supplicate you to live with me entirely! to let us share between us all that we possess; to read together, study our musick (*sic*) together, and never, never to part!" (136). Since she is not her "own mistress," however, and must live under the guardianship of Mrs. Howel, Lady Aurora cannot protect Juliet directly. What she can do, though, is offer Juliet her name to be used in Juliet's times of need. Lady Aurora may lack the power to protect Juliet by affording Juliet a refuge, but she allows Juliet to make use of her name as a form of protection because the two women have formed a strong friendship. In particular, Juliet often draws upon the thought of Lady Aurora for emotional strength when she feels most vulnerable. The remembrance that she retains Lady Aurora's friendship and sympathy encourages Juliet in her quest for self-dependence. When Juliet is first deciding whether or not to leave Lewes and Mrs. Maple's ill treatment of her once and for all, for example, she finds herself torn. If she stays with Mrs. Maple she can expect further persecution, but if she chooses to find a lodging in Brighthelmstone she will be utterly without protection. Her deliberations come to an end, however, when she receives an envelope with a "little coronet seal, with the cypher A. G." pressed upon it (211). After the servant gives it to her, "no sooner had she looked at the direction, than the brightest bloom glowed upon her cheeks, her eyes were suffused with tears of pleasure, and she pressed, involuntarily, to her heart, the writing of Lady Aurora Granville" (211). Her decision is made for her: the letter causes Juliet "suddenly, and most unexpectedly" to accept Miss Arbe's offer to conduct Juliet to town, where she will seek a room at Miss Matson's (211). The thought of Lady Aurora gave Juliet the emotional strength to sever her ties to Mrs. Maple and to begin her quest for self-dependence. At other points in the novel, Juliet calls upon Lady Aurora's name to help her escape the persecution of others. In one of the most memorable scenes, Juliet even uses her sister's name as protection from her own brother, who does not, of course, know yet that Juliet is his sister. When Lord Melbury approaches Juliet and offers to make her his mistress, she calls upon the name of Lady Aurora, and Lord Melbury immediately desists in his sexual advances. As the friend of his sister, Juliet should have met with his best and most polite behavior; she should have found in him succor in distress and a protector in danger. Instead, he has insulted both Juliet and his sister by assuming that Juliet's character was depraved because of the false insinuations he heard. Realizing this, Lord Melbury treats Juliet as his own sister thereafter, not knowing yet, of course, that she really is. Later on, Lord Melbury will offer Juliet financial assistance, which Juliet accepts, because "[i]t was presented in the name of his sister; a sister whom he revered as truly as he loved; such a name, therefore, sanctioned both the loan and the kindness" (573).

Throughout the novel Lady Aurora's name thus functions as a form of protection when she herself cannot protect Juliet. Although Lady Aurora does not possess the financial means to help Juliet, she offers aid in other ways. She allows Juliet to draw both emotional and physical support by freely making use of her name when she is not present, and her unwavering belief in Juliet's probity serves as a source of strength and inspiration to Juliet. Lady Aurora's behavior therefore serves as an example of what women can and should do to protect their fellow women. Even if they lack the independence needed to sustain others, they can still offer encouragement and assistance to those in need. Lady Aurora has essentially listened to the appeal Burney made years earlier in her *Brief Reflections*. Like the French émigrés, Juliet is alone and subject to prejudiced ill-treatment because of her national identity. In response to Juliet's need, Lady Aurora models the attitude that should govern a British woman's actions toward a foreigner by accepting the complexity of Juliet's identity. Doubt and distrust constitute no part of Lady Aurora's treatment of Juliet; unlike characters like Miss Arbe, Mrs. Maple, Mrs. Ireton, Mrs. Howel, and even Elinor Joddrel, Lady Aurora is consistently generous and kind. Her character, like Juliet's, remains unchanging, secure from the vagaries of modern society. Both women maintain a sympathetic bond with others and practice toleration in their relationships. They successfully integrate the principles of female community that Burney so earnestly lays out throughout the novel.

RECONCILIATION AND REVISION IN BURNEY'S WORLDVIEW

Burney's revision of *Evelina* led her to create both a world and a heroine infinitely more cryptic and obscure than those she portrayed in her first novel. By the time that *The Wanderer* appeared, Burney had witnessed the death of a beloved sister due to the mistreatment of a cruel husband; had been happily married to a Frenchman for over twenty years; and had given birth to a son of French–British heritage, upon whom she absolutely doted. She had witnessed the Napoleonic Wars firsthand during her ten years in France, and had endured the pain of being separated from her family and homeland for an extended period of time. The Frances Burney who wrote *The Wanderer* had thus experienced a great deal more than the Frances Burney who wrote *Evelina,* and those experiences are reflected in the worldview presented in *The Wanderer.* In this last novel, society is more complex, full of enigmatic personalities who often guard hidden motives or who occupy ambiguous positions. The difficulty of deciphering others is given greater emphasis, as is the flawed nature of even the kindest of characters. In this modern world, a character like Mr. Giles Arbe exists, a man who means well but who inadvertently brings pain and violence to those around him. In this modern world, a character like Admiral Powel also exists, a man who is both misogynistic and nationalistic, but who ultimately restores our heroine to her true status in society, becoming her protector in the process.

Benevolence does not necessarily wear a gentle face, then, and yet neither does malevolence necessarily wear a crooked one. The worst treatment that Juliet receives comes not at the hands of her odious and monstrous husband, but rather from the fair visages of the women of Brighthelmstone society. From them Juliet should receive protection and succor, but by them she is instead rejected and despised. Some of the most painful moments in the novel are, in fact, the scenes where Juliet must retain her dignity in the face of their open sarcasm and hostility. Juliet's ability to withstand such attacks attests to her strong personality, however, and to Burney's overt disapproval of such behavior. Through negative examples, Burney confirms her belief that women should help other women in need, regardless of where they come from or what mystery surrounds them. Female community should unite women, Burney contends, illustrating once more that women writers of this period believed that gender identity could supplant national identity in relations between women. Female community leads to female protection, which is important because without its three forms—countenance in society, aid in finding work, and friendship—women have a hard time supporting themselves both emotionally and financially. Without a friend such as Lady Aurora to support her when in company, Juliet is ridiculed and made to feel subservient. Without a friend such as Elinor to help her find gainful employment, Juliet risks starving to death or being jailed by her creditors. And without female companionship such as she receives from Gabriella, Juliet suffers from loneliness and depression. Social embarrassment is no longer the main concern of our heroine, as it was for Evelina; instead, the challenge of finding and then maintaining useful and proper work so as to eventually attain self-dependence occupies Juliet's thoughts.

Burney's desire to explore "female difficulties" ultimately initiated her into the ranks of some of the most progressive women writers of her day. Joining such liberal thinkers as Mary Wollstonecraft and Charlotte Smith, Burney emphasized women's issues and attacked the iniquities of British society. Yet Burney's association with the move toward female community also had its drawbacks, for *all* of these women were ultimately vilified for their associations with the French: Wollstonecraft for proffering radical ideas about gender roles, ideas based on her reaction to French political thought, and Smith for sympathetically portraying the Revolution and the plight of the French émigrés. Burney also did not escape the harsh pens of her critics. The central irony of her last novel is, in fact, that Burney's positive portrayal of a French–British character and her reconciliatory tone would cause her to be slandered and maligned in the press. By advocating tolerance, Burney herself was ultimately not tolerated. Vilified for her too-sympathetic treatment of the French and for her own marriage to a Frenchman, Burney became a Madame Duval of sorts, attacked by even her most admiring critics for what they saw as her adherence to French values and customs. Ideas that Burney had worked so hard to modify in her last novel were essentially used against her by the critics. They drew upon the prejudices and nationalist stereotypes of *Evelina* to attack Burney herself, using the same rhetoric and language to describe her that she herself had used years earlier to portray Evelina's grandmother. This last novel, which the reviewers unanimously agreed was her worst literary endeavor to date,[58] suffered, they claimed, from Burney's abandonment of her homeland, and they looked to national difference as an explanation for what went wrong. Her writing and her personality, they argued, suffered through exposure to French culture. One attack leveled at her was that her language use was unnatural and Latinate, contaminated by the heavy use of French-influenced words and phrases.[59] Another form of attack was that Burney was too sympathetic toward both the French and Napoleon. One particularly harsh reviewer of the novel even rebuked Burney for not being a good "Englishwoman" since she made Robespierre the archenemy of the novel, instead of Napoleon,[60] while another criticized the untimeliness of the events depicted.[61] Yet perhaps the harshest criticism that Burney received was directed not so much at the language or content of her novel as it was at herself. Most of the reviewers viewed the Burney who wrote *The Wanderer* not as a progression of her former self, but rather as a completely different person, one who left behind her homeland and her native attachments to overly sympathize with the French.[62] They blamed her for being an old woman,[63] and especially for being concerned with women's issues.[64] They criticized her, basically, for her interest in some of the most relevant and important topics of her day.

My underlying claim all along, however, has been that Burney progressed as she matured. Although *The Wanderer*'s reviewers ultimately attacked Burney for her associations with France, they missed the main points that Burney was trying to make.[65] Between the writing of her first and last novels, Burney herself underwent a revision, modifying her views and reaching a more nuanced understanding of the world. The project of reconciliation that she sets out in the introduction—that of uniting two rival nations—initially caused her to try to reconcile incongruities and contrasting character traits; she ultimately realized, however, that the world cannot always be reconciled, and that some people are meant to remain ambiguous and unknowable. Envisioning the world in this way meant that Juliet's world was more complex than Evelina's, fraught with female difficulties and dangers, but also much closer to reality. In her struggles for self-dependence, Juliet meets with prejudice and mistreatment, but the vision of female community, a community that transcends national borders, motivates her to continue to seek help from others. Heroines like Evelina might make for more amusing reading, as Burney's contemporary readers were so quick to point out, but heroines like Juliet are more representative. A heroine who is not naive, but rather wise beyond her years, also serves as a better catalyst for change. Burney's last novel is thus ultimately her richest, one replete with possibility and potential, both for Burney's world and our own.

Postscript: The Legacy of Female Community

Frances burney, mary wollstonecraft, and charlotte smith have each made significant contributions to Anglo-American feminism, numbering among a much larger group of women who used nationalist discourses in the late eighteenth and early nineteenth centuries to explore the role of women within British society and to argue for change. While modern-day critics have long recognized the significance these women writers have had in the development of feminist thought, as I suggested in the Introduction, they have largely overlooked the key role that nationalism played in their texts. This oversight reveals a greater tendency to overlook the nationalist discourses being circulated in British society on a much larger basis, for, as we have seen, it was during this period that a sense of British national identity first took shape and then solidified in the face of threats from France. By comparing themselves to the members of their rival nation, Britons strengthened their sense of purpose and meaning, leaving them complacent in the knowledge that they were "God's chosen people." For the first time, Britons began to imagine themselves as a group—a group united by its members' shared dislike of the French. Because these self-drawn comparisons were so prevalent in British society, women writers also latched onto the nationalist discourses of the period, arriving at their arguments by pulling the third term of France into their discussions of women and Britain. When women writers of this era discussed gender politics, their discussions took place within and through national politics; they took advantage of nationalist discourse to promote their various agendas regarding women's issues and concerns.

Although British women writers created imagined communities of women, the goals for doing so varied considerably. The political agendas being promoted depended on the aims of the individual author and often changed (as was the case with all three of the authors I have looked at in detail) within a single author's lifetime. As we move across the latter decades of the eighteenth century, we also see women writers progressively offering a more inclusive vision of the British nation and a more nuanced understanding of national identity. A text from the

1770s like Frances Burney's *Evelina*, I argued, is symptomatic of the earlier period in which it was written; Burney borrows from stereotypical eighteenth-century portrayals of the French, and directs her attacks against a Frenchwoman who threatens Evelina's sense of self and national identity. Yet *Evelina* also calls to the surface anxieties about such black-or-white categorizations of individuals. In her last novel, 1814's *The Wanderer*, Burney would redress her earlier mistakes, arguing for more acceptance and understanding between and within nations. Charlotte Smith also looked to France to argue for change within Britain. *Desmond*, Smith's first overtly political novel, entered into the Revolutionary debates while also addressing the current injustices within British society. Britons might be smug in their sense of superiority, but Smith demonstrated that such complacency caused Britons to overlook fundamental weaknesses in their own government and constitution, as well as their wrongful treatment of women. Toward the end of the 1790s, Smith, like Burney, would become even more interested in the vulnerable status of women within Britain, especially when they held questionable national identities. *The Young Philosopher* seeks to understand what other options are available to women (and even men) when female community fails. Like Burney and Smith, Wollstonecraft would share this desire to understand the French, and would also ground her feminist beliefs in nationalist thought. Her two *Vindications*, after all, grew out of Wollstonecraft's need to compare the current state of British society to that of the French, and her second *Vindication* was an attempt to extend the privileges that white middle- and upper-class men possessed to include women. Women (in the early days of the French Revolution) were enjoying a higher status in France than they had when they reigned over the *salons*, and Wollstonecraft wanted her own countrywomen to do the same. After attempting to understand the constructed nature of gender identity, Wollstonecraft then turned to an attempt to understand the national identity of the French so she could advocate change via revolution. All three of these women — Burney, Smith, and Wollstonecraft — thus used the idea of France relationally, as a way to explore women's roles within their own nation, and all three of them, like so many other women writers, concluded that the position of women within British society rested on a precarious foundation, one subject to both gender and national prejudices. By pointing to this weak foundation, women writers encouraged their fellow Britons to effect change.

Today a general sense of unease and dislike still exists between the British and the French, but the strong sense of acrimony and hostility that first came into being during the eighteenth century has mostly disappeared. But when, why, and how did France no longer become the third part of this triad I have been discussing? Part of the answer has to do with what happened in the early years of the nineteenth century. In recent years, of course, connections forged by the creation of the European Union have helped smooth over difficult relations, but the rivalry that once characterized their contacts disappeared much earlier. In the decades that first witnessed the transformation of the rather profligate Prince Regent into King George IV and that later ushered in the reign of Queen Victoria lies our answer to the question of how the relationship between Britain and France changed. In 1815, only one year after Burney's *The Wanderer* appeared in print, the British vanquished Napoleon, causing him to meet his final defeat at Waterloo. Reactionary and even radical Britons saw this as the end of the events that the Revolution had set in motion only twenty-six years earlier, and as the end of the empire that the French leader had tried to create. France no longer played the role of archrival that it had for so many years. With France no longer a political or military threat, Britain became the dominant world power, free to pursue the imperialist aims that it had initiated during the preceding century. As Britain solidified its trade routes and expanded its colonialist holds on other nations during the Victorian period, the idea of the Orient seized hold of the British imagination, replacing the strong hold that France once possessed.[1] Britain's imperialist longings led it to look elsewhere for the position of "Other" that France had for so long occupied. Britain's ascendancy in the arena of world affairs—as made evident in its boast that "the sun never set on the British Empire"—ensured that France would no longer occupy a central place in British thinking about nationalism and national identity.

While the idea of France slipped out of public discourse, the idea of a female community continued as the nineteenth century unfolded, and visions of female community were seen in other contexts during this period and even after. Research done into the abolitionist movement by scholars such as Moira Ferguson and Karen Sanchez-Eppler, for instance, has unveiled the ways in which the abolitionist movement inspired leagues of women to unite against the oppressive bonds of slavery.[2] These efforts became even stronger in the early 1800s, reaching a peak before slavery was finally completely abolished in Britain in 1838. To aid these efforts, women produced petitions, poems, and political tracts, imagining themselves united in their group effort to abolish the slave trade. In the latter years of the nineteenth century, women would once again unite, this time to argue for universal suffrage. The suffragists banded together as a collective entity to obtain the vote, even though their efforts met with resistance in Britain until the early twentieth century. In their willingness to unite for a common cause, women once again joined together to make claims about women's role within the nation. Even more recently, third-wave feminism has also borrowed from the notion of female community to make its claims. The early, (largely) middle-class notion of "woman" as a universal category to which each individual woman belongs echoes claims made by those writing in the late eighteenth century. Like their predecessors, those espousing this wave of feminism also overlooked differences in color, class, religion, and sexuality, essentially submerging difference in the desire to create a coherent group. Third-wave feminism thus reproduces the limits of first-wave feminism, of not recognizing individual difference among and between women. And, although third-wave feminism seeks to redress the violation of women's rights in countries such as India and China, this desire is fraught with nationalist tensions, of claiming to understand the national identity (itself, an unstable concept) of others, but then to erase it in a new emphasis on what has been called "global feminism." The twentieth-century feminist mantra that "the personal is political" also bears the imprint of our eighteenth-century forebears. The implication of this statement, after all, is that women's issues (and here, again, we see "woman" emerging as a universal category) belong to the realm of political events—of events that should be of great interest because of their influence on the welfare of the nation. Just as women writers in the late eighteenth and early nineteenth centuries urged their readers to take women's issues seriously—that women's concerns should also be the concerns of the British nation—so, too, do modern-day feminists appeal to the national significance of their claims. Modern-day women, of course, can use the political system in ways that our predecessors could not since, in the twentieth century, women were finally been granted status as citizens, however unequal that status might be. Thus it is that issues such as sexual assault, abortion, gender discrimination, and even maternity leave can today be recognized as legal (and so, nationally significant) concerns, even though not too long ago women possessed no legal standing of their own. So are there traces of nationalism and national identity still present in the idea of female community today? Perhaps national identity does not surface in global feminist issues to the extent that it once did during the late eighteenth and early nineteenth centuries, and perhaps it is more often than not subsumed under other categories, such as religious affiliation. However, contemporary feminism's move toward the global and cross-national has not completely eradicated the notion of the localized national identity. During the years leading from the eighteenth century to the twenty-first, the idea of individual national identity has still made its presence felt in feminist arenas.

Nevertheless, as I said at the outset of *Women Writing the Nation*, recognizing the connections between gender and national politics during the late eighteenth and early nineteenth centuries helps us better read and understand the texts of the period and the cultural discourses that influenced them. Gender and nation were inextricable concepts during this period, and we should no longer attempt to understand early feminism outside of the context of nationalism. But it should also be clear by now that recognizing the early formations of female community helps us also better understand our own role as feminists in modern-day society. Over two hundred years after Burney, Smith, and Wollstonecraft lived and wrote, we are still struggling to reconcile the claims of the individual woman with the claims of the larger nation. At the dawn of the twenty-first century, we stand in a position like that which these earlier writers stood in also, looking toward a new century (or, in our case, a new millennium) and hoping to effect positive change, to influence our world for the better. The legacy of female community is still very much with us today.

Notes

INTRODUCTION: BRITISH WOMEN WRITERS AND THE FRENCH CONNECTION

Epigraph: Printed for Hookham and Carpenter, London, 1793, p. 9.

1. The study of nationalism is becoming so prevalent that I here offer only a partial list of some of the seminal studies that have defined the area for future scholars. For texts that trace the genesis and development of nationalism in the eighteenth century, see Gerald Newman, *The Rise of English Nationalism: A Cultural History 1740–1830* (New York: St. Martin's Press, 1997) and Kathleen Wilson, *The Sense of the People: Politics, Culture, and Imperialism in England, 1715–1785* (Cambridge: Cambridge University Press, 1995). Key texts that follow the growth of nationalism into the Romantic period include David Simpson, *Romanticism, Nationalism, and the Revolt Against Theory* (Chicago: University of Chicago Press, 1993); Alan Richardson and Sonia Hofkosh, eds., *Romanticism, Race, and Imperial Culture, 1780–1839* (Bloomington: Indiana University Press, 1996); Katie Trumpener, *Bardic Nationalism: The Romantic Novel and the British Empire* (Princeton, NJ: Princeton University Press, 1997); and Marlon Ross, "Romancing the Nation-State: The Poetics of Romantic Nationalism," in *Macropolitics of Nineteenth-Century Literature: Nationalism, Exoticism, Imperialism,* ed. Jonathan Arac and Harriet Ritvo (Philadelphia: University of Pennsylvania Press, 1991), 56–85.

2. One of the most important of these recent studies is Anne K. Mellor's *Mothers of the Nation: Women's Political Writing in England, 1780–1830* (Bloomington: Indiana University Press, 2000). While Mellor's interests also lie in mapping out women's participation in the British nation, Mellor's analysis differs greatly from my own in that her central argument revolves around Habermas's notion of the public sphere: "In this book I argue first that Habermas's conceptual limitation of the public sphere in England between 1780 and 1830 to men of property is historically incorrect. During the Romantic era women writers participated fully in the public sphere as Habermas defined it" (2–3). Angela Keane's current work also addresses the intersections of nationalism and gender. In *Romantic Belongings: Women Writers and the English Nation in the 1790s* (Cambridge: Cambridge University Press, 2000), Keane explains, "In the Romantic national imaginary, the woman who wanders, who defines herself beyond the home and as a subject whose desires exceed or preclude maternity, divests herself of femininity and erases herself from the familial, heterosexual structure of the nation" (3). Harriet Guest's *Small Change: Women, Learning, Patriotism, 1750–1810* (Chicago: University of Chicago Press, 2000) also enters into these discussions, exploring how "a series of small changes takes place in the position of women, or the way women are perceived; and the cumulative effect of these changes is that by the early nineteenth century it had become possible or even necessary for some women to define their gen-

dered identities through the nature and degree of their approximation to the public identities of political citizens" (14). Guest's introduction chapter, in particular, usefully maps out the ways in which women writers participated in political life. Most recently, Adriana Craciun explains how "British women writers were drawn to a radicalized cosmopolitanism that had at its core a Francophilia (corresponding to an 'Anglomania' in its French Enlightenment precedent) increasingly dangerous to maintain in Francophobic Britain, thereby situating their cosmopolitanism, historically and geographically, as a deliberately oppositional strategy" (*British Women Writers and the French Revolution: Citizens of the World* [New York: Palgrave Macmillan, 2005], 6).

3. See Benedict Anderson's important and influential text *Imagined Communities: Reflections on the Origin and Spread of Nationalism,* rev. ed. (New York: Verso, 1991). Colley differs from Anderson in that Anderson believes that nations develop a sense of cohesion internally, without reference to an outside nation.

4. Linda Colley, *Britons: Forging the Nation 1707–1837* (New Haven, CT: Yale University Press, 1992), 6.

5. These threats will be discussed to a greater extent in chapter 1 in the context of Frances Burney's novel *Evelina.*

6. Colley also points to Protestantism as another bond that united the British. See chapter 1 of *Britons.*

7. Colley, *Britons,* 281.

8. Anderson, *Imagined Communities,* 6.

9. Eve Tavor Bannet has noticed a similar way in which Enlightenment women writers (whom she categorizes as either Matriarchs or Egalitarians, yet who share the same goal of delineating the role of the domestic woman) utilized the same discourses that men utilized when discussing the subject of domestic government. These writers "were joined to and separated from those of conservative and liberal men—as well as from each other—by the same language and the same domestic and political ideologies. . . . By translating hegemonic ideals in their own manner and adapting cultural values to their own ends, Enlightenment women writers both critiqued these values and ideals and moved beyond them. While carrying particular ideas, assumptions, and goals from men's texts into their own, they often analyzed them from a different place and altered, developed, and rewrote them for their own ends" (5–6). See *The Domestic Revolution: Enlightenment Feminism and the Novel* (Baltimore: Johns Hopkins University Press, 2000).

10. See Anthony D. Smith, *National Identity* (Reno: University of Nevada Press, 1991), 4ff. and Liah Greenfeld, *Nationalism: Five Roads to Modernity* (Cambridge, MA: Harvard University Press, 1992), 28–87.

11. Smith, *National Identity,* 97.

12. Colley, *Britons,* 6.

13. British men, after all, were granted more political rights than women, and were able to participate in politics to a much greater extent than women ever could. Kathleen Wilson's recent work even shows us that this involvement in politics was not just limited to white males of the upper and middle classes, but instead incorporated even those in the lower stations of life. (See Wilson, *The Sense of the People.*)

14. This creation of a universal concept of "Woman" will be addressed in the Postscript.

15. The important work of Felicity Nussbaum and Moira Ferguson also calls attention to the ways in which British women writers used the idea of the racial "Other"

to make claims about their own status. See Felicity Nussbaum, *Torrid Zones: Maternity, Sexuality, and Empire in Eighteenth-Century English Narratives* (Baltimore: Johns Hopkins University Press, 1995) and Moira Ferguson, *Subject to Others: British Women Writers and Colonial Slavery, 1670–1834* (New York: Routledge, 1992).

16. The British government's official policy, under King George III, was one of anti-Catholicism. The Whigs, who remained in opposition to William Pitt the Younger's government, did not support anti-Catholic measures, nor did Pitt himself, who resigned in 1801 over the king's refusal to grant Catholic emancipation. Chapters 1 and 5 on Frances Burney look at anti-Catholic sentiment in more detail.

17. Although her focus is on the domestic revolution that took place in the eighteenth century, Eve Tavor Bannet usefully discusses the ways in which female writers on opposite ends of the political spectrum engaged in a relationship that "was not so much one of mutual opposition as one of intertranslation and mutual articulation" (*The Domestic Revolution*, 9). Women writers exchanged ideas and arguments, often drawing upon the opposing group's arguments to express and more clearly articulate their own concerns and beliefs.

18. Although recent feminist criticism has begun to notice the subversive elements of More's work, More is usually grouped with the political conservatives. Claudia L. Johnson, for instance, notes that "More idealize[s] and defend[s] established power—power which . . . [she] do[es] not hesitate to call by its proper name: 'patriarchal'" (Claudia L. Johnson, *Jane Austen: Women, Politics, and the Novel* [Chicago: University of Chicago Press, 1988], xxi). Robert Hole, who edited several of More's texts for the Pickering Women's Classics edition, agrees: "In the late eighteenth century, there were few better exponents of the traditional, orthodox value system and view of the world than Hannah More. . . . Her thinking was traditional and conservative" (Robert Hole, Introduction to *Selected Writings of Hannah More*, Pickering Women's Classics [London: William Pickering, 1996], vii.

19. Hole, for instance, notes that "19,000 copies of her *Strictures on Female Education* were sold to the educated; the work went into seven editions before the end of 1799, and thirteen editions by 1826, in addition to being reprinted in her collected works in 1801, 1818, and 1830" (Hole, Introduction, vii).

20. *Selected Writings of Hannah More*, ed. Robert Hole, Pickering Women's Classics (London: William Pickering, 1996), 121.

21. More, *Selected Writings*, 122.

22. Colley, *Britons*, 354, 48. For Colley's extended discussion of British liberty, see especially pages 30–42.

23. Andrews, *Remarks on the French and English Ladies* (London, 1783), 184.

24. Hester Lynch Piozzi, *Observations and Reflections Made in the Course of a Journey Through France, Italy, and Germany* (London, 1789), 22–23.

25. Mary Hays, *Appeal to the Men of Great Britain on Behalf of Women*, ed. Gina Luria (New York: Garland Publishing, 1974), i.

26. Ibid., 129.

27. Ibid., n.p.

28. Ibid., 131.

29. My thanks to Nicholas Williams for pointing this out to me in his reading of an earlier draft.

30. Hays, *Appeal*, 62.

31. Matthew Bray, "Removing the Anglo-Saxon Yoke: The Francocentric Vision of Charlotte Smith's Later Works," *The Wordsworth Circle* 24.3 (1993): 155–58, 156.

32. Thomas Paine, *Rights of Man*, ed. Gregory Claeys (Indianapolis, IN: Hackett Publishing, 1992), 46. Paine devotes several paragraphs of *Rights of Man* to a critique of William the Conqueror.

33. Newman, *The Rise of English Nationalism*, 189–91.

34. Bray, "Removing the Anglo-Saxon Yoke," 156. It is also important to note that both Bray and Newman draw upon the work of Christopher Hill, who originally laid out the "Norman Yoke theory" in the third chapter of his 1958 book on Puritanism. See Christopher Hill, "The Norman Yoke," in *Puritanism and Revolution: Studies in Interpretation of the English Revolution of the Seventeenth Century*, 1958 (New York: Schocken Books, 1964), 50–122.

35. For my discussion of these dates, I used Alan Liu and Laura Mandell's extremely helpful Romantic Chronology website. See Alan Liu and Laura Mandell, eds., *Romantic Chronology*, May 23, 2006, <http://english.ucsb.edu:591/rchrono/>.

36. The irony of this fear, of course, is that the blood of William and his fellow conquerors—the blood of the *French*—had long since mixed with British blood. That the bastardization of Britishness could be overlooked in this manner testifies to the irrational level of anxiety that Britons held at this time.

37. The most recent edition of *Letters Written in France* from Broadview Press, for instance, only contains Volume 1 of her letters. The only complete edition still remains the Scholar's Facsimiles & Reprints edition, edited by Janet Todd, from 1975. I use the more contemporary Broadview edition for my discussion of Volume 1 and the Scholar's Facsimiles edition for my discussion of subsequent volumes. See Helen Maria Williams, *Letters Written in France*, ed. Neil Fraistat and Susan S. Lanser (Toronto: Broadview Press, 2002) and Helen Maria Williams, *Letters From France*, Eight Volumes in Two (1790, 1791, 1793, 1795, 1796), ed. Janet M. Todd (Delmar, NY: Scholar's Facsimiles & Reprints, 1975).

38. Gregory Claeys, ed., Introduction to *Political Writings of the 1790s*, 8 vols. (London: William Pickering, 1995), xliii.

39. Williams, *Letters Written in France*, ed. Fraistat and Lanser, 91.

40. Julie Ellison's work on emotion makes a strong case for the idea that sentiment has, since the late seventeenth century, been increasingly constructed as a man's domain, one closely aligned with his political role. If we follow this model, we can see that women like Williams began to adopt the political edge associated with sensibility. See Julie Ellison, *Cato's Tears and the Making of Anglo-American Emotion* (Chicago: University of Chicago Press, 1999).

41. Williams, *Letters Written in France*, ed. Fraistat and Lanser, 140.

42. Ibid., 109.

43. Wordsworth was so moved by the Du Fossés' tale that he based *The Prelude*'s "Vaudracour and Julia" vignette around it (as well, of course, around his own involvement with the Frenchwoman Annette Vallon). For an interesting discussion of the Du Fossés' influence on Wordsworth, see Deborah Kennedy, "Revolutionary Tales: Helen Maria Williams' *Letters from France* and William Wordsworth's 'Vaudracour and Julia,'" *The Wordsworth Circle* 21.3 (Summer 1990): 109–14.

44. Williams, *Letters Written in France*, ed. Fraistat and Lanser, 140.

45. Williams, *Letters From France*, ed. Todd, 2:4–5.

46. Ibid., 63–64.

47. Mary Wollstonecraft was also concerned with the unfortunate situations of widows. She takes great care in chapter 3 of *A Vindication of the Rights of Woman*, in fact, to

show how helpless their current state of education leaves women when their husbands die. See Mary Wollstonecraft, *A Vindication of the Rights of Woman*, 2nd ed., ed. Carol H. Poston (New York: W. W. Norton, 1988), 48–51.

48. Williams, *Letters from France*, ed. Todd, 2:80.

49. Hawkins, *Letters*, 89–90.

50. Ibid., 194–95.

51. Colley, *Britons*, 32–33.

52. Hawkins, *Letters*, 198–99.

53. As I argue in the chapter on Charlotte Smith, most prorevolutionary writers claimed that British anti-Jacobin propaganda was based on political jealousy. Britons, these writers convincingly argue, were jealous of the *French*, not the other way around, as Hawkins would have it.

54. It is interesting that Hawkins describes the path to such affection as one full of "sacrifices and absurdities" on the part of women. She seems to recognize the foolish acts that winning a husband's love requires, even though she simultaneously encourages her readers to continue to engage in these same acts.

55. I analyze these stereotypes at greater length in chapter 1 when I look at how such representations of the French play out in Frances Burney's novel *Evelina*.

56. Hawkins, *Letters*, 200.

57. Ibid., 9.

58. Hawkins herself seems to recognize this when she states, in a passage cited earlier, that English wives perform "sacrifices and absurdities" to win the affection of a man. I examine the institution of marriage in more depth in my discussions of Charlotte Smith's *Desmond*, Wollstonecraft's *A Vindication of the Rights of Woman*, and Burney's *The Wanderer*.

59. Hawkins's extreme valorization of comfort and safety might seem excessive, but, as I discuss in Smith's *The Young Philosopher* and Burney's *The Wanderer*, women without protection suffered a great deal of hardship.

60. Hawkins, *Letters*, 200–201.

61. Critic Vivien Jones points out that Hawkins was, in general, "an admirer of More" (Vivien Jones, ed., *Women in the Eighteenth Century: Constructions of Femininity* [London: Routledge, 1990], 246).

62. Anna Laetitia Barbauld, *Sins of Government, Sins of the Nation; or, A Discourse for the Fast, appointed on April 19, 1793, by a volunteer* (London: J. Johnson, 1793).

63. See Anne Francis Randell [Mary Robinson], *A Letter to the Women of England, on the Injustice of Mental Subordination*, in Jones, *Women in the Eighteenth Century*, 241.

64. For an excellent discussion of national politics in Gothic novels, see Cannon Schmitt, *Alien Nation: Nineteenth-Century Gothic Fictions and English Nationality* (Philadelphia: University of Pennsylvania Press, 1997).

65. Lord Glenthorn, or rather Christy O'Donoghue, makes this clear in the opening pages of Edgeworth's 1809 novel *Ennui*. Glenthorn/O'Donoghue attributes his laziness to the influence of French ways of life: "For this complaint there is no precise English name; but, alas! the foreign term is now naturalized in England. Among the higher classes, whether in the wealthy or the fashionable world, who is unacquainted with *ennui?*" (Maria Edgeworth, *Castle Rackrent and Ennui*, ed. Marilyn Butler [New York: Penguin Books, 1992], 144). In this respect, Edgeworth's warning about the infiltration of French *ennui* bears a striking resemblance to More's warning about the infiltration of French *persiflage*.

66. Polwhele's poem in its entirety can be found on an e-text website located at The University of Virginia. See *The Unsex'd Females*, The University of Virginia, January 3, 2006, <http://etext.lib.virginia.edu/britpo/unsex/unsex.html>, line 20.

67. Ibid., lines 195–96.

1. QUELLING THE FRENCH THREAT IN FRANCES BURNEY'S *EVELINA*

1. Frances Burney, *Diary and Letters of Madame D'Arblay*, ed. Charlotte Barrett (London, 1842–1846) 7:154–63, and *The Wanderer*, ed. Margaret Doody, Robert L. Mack, and Peter Sabor (New York: Oxford University Press, 1991), 5.

2. Macaulay, *Edinburgh Review* 76 (January 1843): 559.

3. William Hazlitt, *Edinburgh Review* 24 (February 1815): 336.

4. Ibid.

5. Martha G. Brown offers a similar analysis of Burney's characters, arguing that Burney borrows character types, as well as plots and themes, from the romance tradition. For Brown, however, Burney's borrowing of romantic tropes is a sign that Burney is not a feminist writer. See Brown, "Fanny Burney's 'Feminism': Gender or Genre?" in *Fetter'd or Free: British Women Novelists, 1670–1815*, ed. Mary Anne Schofield and Cecilia Macheski (Athens: Ohio University Press, 1986), 29–39.

6. Both Margaret Anne Doody and Julia Epstein are notable exceptions, and refer to Burney's interest in issues of nationalism and national identity. Both critics mention that interest in passing, however, without developing the idea. See Doody, *Frances Burney: A Life in the Works* (New Brunswick, NJ: Rutgers University Press, 1988), 23, 200, and Epstein, *The Iron Pen: Frances Burney and the Politics of Women's Writing* (Madison: University of Wisconsin Press, 1989), 191. Some of the other critics who overlook these nationalist tones are discussed later on in this chapter.

7. Newman, *The Rise of English Nationalism*, 124.

8. Deidre Shauna Lynch, *The Economy of Character: Novels, Market Culture, and the Business of Inner Meaning* (Chicago: University of Chicago Press, 1998), 41. Chapter 4 of Lynch's book also importantly looks at how Burney creates inner meaning in *Evelina* through images of consumption and the market: "it is in dramatizing the reification attendant on a female character's public appearances and her social exchanges that the novel of manners produces an inner consciousness that seems to operate independent of exchange relations. . . . [D]epictions of consumer society could function in the romantic era as *the* literary venue for the production of a brave new world of female interiority" (167).

9. Eve Tavor Bannet also connects Evelina's quest to learn more about the ways of the world as one indicator of the "exemplary egalitarian" nature of Burney's novel. See *The Domestic Revolution*, 75–78.

10. Fanny Burney, *Evelina, or, The History of a Young Lady's Entrance into the World*, ed. Edward A. Bloom (New York: Oxford University Press, 1991), 29. All future references are to this edition and their page numbers will appear parenthetically in the text.

11. Andrews, *Remarks*, 76.

12. Ibid., 77.

13. Piozzi, *Observations and Reflections*, 22–23.

14. Andrews, *Remarks*, 77.

15. Selections from this text are included in Vivien Jones's useful anthology of eighteenth-century writers. See Jones, *Women in the Eighteenth Century*, 50.

16. Both Margaret Anne Doody and Julia Epstein refer to Burney's interest in national identity, but both critics mention that interest in passing, without developing the idea. See Doody, *Frances Burney*, 23, 200, and Epstein, *Iron Pen*, 191.

17. As Michèle Cohen explains, the term "Grand Tour" was coined in 1670 by Lassels to refer to extended voyages made to France. The term "Il Giro" was used to refer to travel to Italy (Michèle Cohen, *Fashioning Masculinity: National Identity and Language in the Eighteenth Century* [London: Routledge, 1996], 54). Cohen also traces the demise of the Grand Tour in more detail, explaining that it fell out of favor because it created frenchified and so effeminate men who often resorted to corruption and display (69–73).

18. Writing as late as the third decade of the 1800s, Lady Morgan also noticed this tendency of the British to only consort with one another while traveling, although she viewed it as a negative trait of Englishmen abroad. In her *France in 1829–30*, Lady Morgan reports:

> The majority of Englishmen do not so much travel to acquire continental ideas, as to fortify and fix their own. They do not voyage for the sake of comparing British institutions, sentiments, and usages, with those of other countries; but for measuring all things foreign by the one infallible standard of all right and reason, "the custom of England." But the closer things can be brought into juxta position, the easier is it to form a judgment between them. It is therefore a matter of unspeakable delight to the connoisseur to be thus enabled to bring home to the senses of the Parisians, the superiority of brown stout over champagne, and of muffins and twelfth cake over *brioches* and *gâteaux de Nantes*. . . . Englishmen generally travel for the sole purpose of congregating in foreign cities, and meeting the same faces which they habitually encounter in the Rotten-row and the round room at the Opera. . . . (52–53)

Believing herself in the idea that "the closer things can be brought into juxta position, the easier is it to form a judgment between them," Morgan ridicules the extent to which the British take this idea when they only look to the false superiority of their own people. See Lady Sydney Owenson Morgan, *France in 1829–30* (London, 1829–1830).

19. Burney plays with the use of common names in her other works as well. In *The Wanderer*, for instance, Sir Jasper teasingly calls Juliet "Mrs. Betty" when she escorts him to the estate of Wilton. Sir Jasper picks this particular name for its commonality, while also choosing to tell the servants at Wilton that Juliet is a nursery-maid. See Burney, *The Wanderer*, 759.

20. Edward W. Copeland connects this snobbery to Burney's own interest in economics and money, which, he argues, was a new concern for women novelists of the period. In all of Burney's novels, he claims, the lower classes are treated with a "low, familiar comic style; the virtues of the admirable gentry (along with their estates) without fail involve her in reverent, if obscure, circumlocutions." See Copeland, "Money in the Novels of Fanny Burney," *Studies in the Novel* 8 (1976): 24–37, 26.

21. Andrews, *Remarks*, 261.

22. Mary Shelley, *History of a Six Weeks' Tour through a part of France, Switzerland, Germany, and Holland* (Oxford: Woodstock Books, 1989), 11.

23. A modern reader can see the extent to which this custom was practiced by the royal families of France in a visit to the palace of Versailles. There, a visitor can see how the French practice of receiving visitors in bed was reinforced by the arrangement of the furniture and the elaborate passages of hidden chambers where the royal family

members could prepare for receiving their morning visitors before they reentered the primary bedchamber. The bedroom's function was practical and was, in fact, designed to accommodate a morning influx of visitors.

24. During this journey, the false robbery will occur that is discussed later on in this chapter. Since *we* know that the Captain has planned the false robbery, he could also have told the drivers, who are both in his employ, to drive carelessly. Since Madame Duval does not know this, however, her statement about seeing the drivers whipped still reflects badly on her character.

25. William Ian Miller highlights the violence that underscores threats. He explains this connection in his compelling account of violence, *Humiliation:*

> Threats are words, postures, or actions intended to coerce or influence someone else's behavior by emphasizing the costs to the other of not conceding the threatener's position *and* by suggesting that the threatener will somehow be involved in bringing those costs to bear. . . . A substantial segment of the universe of threats does not involve violence at all, but the shadow of violence colors, to some extent, even the most benign threats. . . . And even though not all threats involve violence, it seems that most all violence involves threat, and this very state of affairs tends to give threat its ominous tinge. . . . The truth is that a new threat inheres in every action taken as a consequence of an original threat of violence. (87)

See William Ian Miller, *Humiliation and Other Essays on Honor, Social Discomfort, and Violence* (Ithaca, NY: Cornell University Press, 1993).

26. Quoted in Cohen, *Fashioning Masculinity*, 4.

27. Ibid., 4–9.

28. Andrews, *Remarks*, 6.

29. The *OED* lists an eighteenth-century definition of the verb *to distract* as, "To derange the mind or intellect of; to render insane, drive mad." This meaning, of course, is obsolete today.

30. Other critics read the purpose of this violence differently. The main argument of Julia Epstein's *The Iron Pen,* for instance, is that the episodes of violence that appear in Burney's novels represent Burney's "obsession with violence and hostility" (*Iron Pen*, 5). According to Epstein, Burney was not a "timid, prudish snob," as many critics have made her out to be, but rather an individual who masked her rage against society's constraints against women (4). "[S]urface propriety," Epstein writes, "was purchased at the price of internal rage" (5). Barbara Zonitch, on the other hand, reads the violence in Burney's texts as symptomatic of the declining aristocracy. In Zonitch's view, as British society moved away from being status-based and moved toward being class-based, violence broke out. Burney's fears about this new model of society emerged within her fiction as an investigation of the forms of protection that were now available for women. See Barbara Zonitch, *Familiar Violence: Gender and Social Upheaval in the Novels of Frances Burney* (Newark: University of Delaware Press, 1997).

31. Miller, *Humiliation*, 74.

32. Other critics also interpret the humorous situations differently. Margaret Anne Doody's interpretation most closely matches my own. She also connects the comedy to violence, arguing that Burney uses the jokes to point out the different power relations in society: "The practical joker for a moment seizes all the power present in the group, and shows us in extreme form the part played by aggression in social relationships" (*Frances Burney*, 57). Ronald Paulson, however, does not connect the humor with violence at all, reading the novel as pure satire. See Ronald Paulson, *Satire and the Novel in*

Eighteenth-Century England (New Haven: Yale University Press, 1967). Susan Staves only connects the comedy to Evelina's own worries: "The real tension in *Evelina* lies between the heroine's struggle to preserve her delicacy under those extraordinarily difficult conditions and the multitude of comic characters who constantly threaten it. . . . [the characters] achieve their full comic effect because they are projections of Evelina's anxieties. They actually commit all the solecisms she is afraid of committing or being thought to have committed." See Susan Staves, "*Evelina,* or Female Difficulties," *Modern Philology* 73 (1976), 376.

33. The entire Branghton household is indeed characterized by violence. Evelina accounts for one whole evening passed there as "employed in most violent quarreling between Miss Polly and her brother, on account of the discovery made by the latter, of the state of her apartment" (216). For lack of better occupation, the Branghtons pass their time in petty and yet violent displays of emotion. It is also through the Branghtons that Evelina will meet Mr. Macartney, a lodger at their house whom Evelina will later discover to be her half-brother. Evelina first notices Macartney because of his sad appearance, for he himself is overwhelmed by the "violence of his sorrows" (228). This sadness draws Evelina to him, and, in one of the most memorable scenes from the novel, Evelina rescues Mr. Macartney from becoming a potential suicide by rushing into his room and grabbing his pistols from his hands. Immediately after she saves him, Evelina reports, "I threw away the pistols, and flinging myself on the first chair, gave free vent to the feelings I had most painfully stifled, in a violent burst of tears, which, indeed proved a happy relief to me" (183). Evelina can only vent her extreme emotions and find "happy relief" through "a violent burst of tears." Because Evelina is introduced to both the Branghtons and Macartney through her grandmother, Madame Duval indirectly leads Evelina into a violent and more complex society than the one she is used to.

34. Gellner admittedly borrows his definition from the theories of sociologist Max Weber. See Ernest Gellner, *Nations and Nationalism* (Ithaca, NY: Cornell University Press, 1983), 3.

35. Miller, *Humiliation,* 74. Miller himself, however, points out: "The state's claim to a monopoly on the means of violence has an uneven application in fact and even in some ways in theory" (*Humiliation,* 80). Certain areas of society, for instance, such as the family, are allowed to exercise an unregulated violence.

36. In her otherwise insightful article "*Evelina;* or Female Difficulties," Susan Staves goes so far as to assert that Captain Mirvan is actually a positive character. Staves writes: "the Captain is a brave and essentially good-hearted man; he exposes sham and administers his corporeal punishments only to those who deserve them" (378). Julia Epstein also presents a negative portrait of Madame Duval by comparing her to the Captain. Madame Duval, according to Epstein, "is matched against Captain Mirvan as a character whose roughhewn sensibility makes it impossible for her to empathize with others" (*Iron Pen,* 113). If anything, however, Captain Mirvan is the character who possesses the "most roughhewn sensibility," not Madame Duval.

37. Walter Dorn, *Competition for Empire 1740–1763* (New York: Harper, 1940), 251.

38. It is also significant that Evelina generally refers to him as "the Captain" instead of "Captain Mirvan." Her use of the definite article emphasizes the uniqueness of his position: he is *the* captain, *the* leader of their group.

39. Miller, *Humiliation,* 130–45.

40. The *OED* defines the verb *to sob* as "to catch the breath in a convulsive manner as the result of violent emotion, esp. grief."

41. Included in Jones, *Women in the Eighteenth Century,* 47.

42. Andrews, *Remarks,* 47, 50.

43. Doody also notices this impression: "Burney uses farce and the licence farce gives to develop scenes of expressive violence. The odds are steadily raised until the laughing reader notices discomfort, protests that things have gone, as we say, beyond a joke" (*Frances Burney,* 56). Doody, however, links this unsettling nature of the violence, as mentioned in a previous note, to power relations, whereas I link it to Burney's own ambivalences about her nationalist project.

44. Miller, *Humiliation,* 137–49.

45. Julia Epstein calls Mrs. Mirvan an abused wife in passing, but never develops this point further (*Iron Pen,* 113).

46. Once again, Captain Mirvan violates Madame Duval in an episode that is both comic and yet serious. Instead of being alarmed about any permanent damage that her host may have done to her grandmother, however, Evelina is only concerned with her own feelings. Perhaps the return of Madame Duval's voice assures Evelina that her grandmother has returned to normal, but it is still surprising that Evelina's final commentary on the episode, a commentary signaled by the exclamation "Indeed," reflects only her own sense of discomfort. Burney trivializes Madame Duval's sense of pain, yet the very fact that the Captain's actions are questioned reflects upon his treatment of Madame Duval. If his behavior toward his family is subject to our disapproval, then his behavior toward Madame Duval must be also.

47. Burney's great appreciation for music is well documented. Because of her father's connections, she also had many opportunities to meet with the premier artists of her day.

48. It is also extremely disturbing to think that the primary target of the Captain's violence is an elderly woman. Age usually demands respect in Western society, but Captain Mirvan violates this custom in his treatment of Evelina's grandmother. He seems to take even greater pleasure in defiling her, in fact, because she has such pretensions to appearing youthful. His actions find their echo in the novel in another unsettling scene, the footrace between two elderly women that Lord Merton and Mr. Coverley arrange to settle a wager. One critic of the novel even goes so far as to call this cruel and discomforting scene "delightful." (See Earl A. Anderson, "Footnotes More Pedestrian Than Sublime: A Historical Background for the Foot-Races in *Evelina* and *Humphry Clinker,*" *Eighteenth-Century Studies* 14 (1980): 56–58, 56.) His comment testifies to the ways in which readers frequently mis-read the violence in Burney's novel.

49. Claudia Johnson, *Equivocal Beings: Politics, Gender, and Sentimentality in the 1790s, Wollstonecraft, Radcliffe, Burney, Austen* (Chicago: University of Chicago Press, 1995).

2. Change and Reform in Charlotte Smith's *Desmond*

1. Guest, *Small Change,* 14.

2. New archival research uncovered by Adriana Craciun suggests that Smith may even have traveled to France herself during the week of September 10–17, 1791 (*British Women Writers,* 139. If Smith really did travel to France, it could help explain why she chose to set the novel in contemporary times—as a desire to incorporate her own factual observations into her fiction.

3. Charlotte Smith, *Desmond,* ed. Antje Blank and Janet Todd, Pickering Women's

Classics (London: Pickering and Chatto, 1997), 5–6. All future references are to this edition and their page numbers will appear parenthetically in the text.

4. Although Smith positions truth and falsehood as central issues of *Desmond*, the novel—as a fictitious rendering of events—may not at first seem particularly well suited to make strong claims about truth. Yet Smith's decision to write her novel in epistolary format granted her greater authority because letters create a greater semblance of truth. Diana Bowstead concurs, noting "Smith's choice of the epistolary form has to do with the largely political and didactic form of the novel, and with advantages letters seemed to her to have over authorial narration in accommodating so weighty a burden of information and opinion" (Bowstead, "Charlotte Smith's *Desmond:* The Epistolary Novel as Ideological Argument," In *Fetter'd or Free?: British Women Novelists, 1670–1815,* ed. Mary Anne Schofield and Cecilia Macheski [Athens: Ohio University Press, 1986] 285–306, 238). Smith was hesitant to use the letter format in a novel, but her worries about writing such overtly political events outweighed her other trepidations.

5. In a similar fashion, Smith repeatedly emphasizes the arbitrary nature of the nobility's titles, which are bought and sold throughout the novel, passing from the hands of long-established, landed families to middle-class upstarts, or what Mr. Bethel at one point calls the "mushroom nobility" (24). Although the newly titled nobles claim special, "natural" rights, Smith points out that their "natural" rights have only just recently been purchased and, as such, are even more arbitrary than the special privileges that the more established nobles claim a right to. Both groups—both the newly titled and the long-titled—claim, however, arbitrary rights since both groups began as commoners, just like everyone else in Britain. See, for instance, pages 33, 36–38, 104, 107, 108, 111, 168–69, 186, 301, and 350–51.

6. Ernest Renan, "What Is a Nation?" rpt. in *Nation and Narration,* ed. Homi Bhaba (London: Routledge, 1990), 8–22, 11. Renan's central argument, one that has long since been called into question by political theorists, is that nations *will* themselves into being. His emphasis on the collective forgetting of the birth of nations, however, is an important point, one that is still widely applicable today.

7. More recently than Renan, Eric Hobsbawm has called attention to the invented nature of traditions, noting how all nations invent customs they regard as having always been in place. He explains this more fully in his introduction to the anthology *The Invention of Tradition:* "'Invented tradition' is taken to mean a set of practices, normally governed by overtly or tacitly accepted rules and of a ritual or symbolic nature, which seek to inculcate certain values and norms of behaviour by repetition, which automatically implies continuity with the past. In fact, where possible, they normally attempt to establish continuity with a suitable historical past. . . . However, insofar as there is such reference to a historic past, the peculiarity of 'invented' traditions is that the continuity with it is largely factitious. . . . The object and characteristic of 'traditions,' including invented ones, is invariance" (Eric Hobsbawm and Terence Ranger, eds., *The Invention of Tradition* [New York: Cambridge University Press, 1983], 1–2).

8. Pat Elliot makes a similar claim about Smith's ability to demystify power relations in general. Elliot notes that in *Emmeline* and *Desmond*, Smith "convey[s] strong feminist messages, clarifying and defining women's domestic and social positions, to show how the patriarchal political structure affected women's lives. Charlotte Smith demystified this structure by analyzing it on all levels; on each level, power abusers are represented as hypocritical, greedy, and weak" (111). See Pat Elliot, "Charlotte Smith's Feminism: A Study of *Emmeline* and *Desmond*," in *Living by the Pen: Early British Women Writers,* ed. Dale Spender (New York: Teachers College Press, 1992), 91–112.

9. Antje Blank and Janet Todd, eds., Introduction to *Desmond*, by Charlotte Smith, Pickering Women's Classics (London: Pickering and Chatto, 1997), xxvi.

10. Williams, *Letters From France*, ed. Todd 1:68–69. Like Smith, Williams also provides her own translations for the French phrases she uses. Here, she translates this last expression as "Become madly fond of the English" (1:69).

11. Throughout the *Letters*, Williams notes the many ways in which the French borrow from and copy the British. At one point, for example, the Revolutionaries place busts of English philosophers alongside busts of French philosophers in the Hall of Jacobins (Williams, *Letters from France*, ed. Todd, 2:114–15). Williams, like Smith, also seeks to trace to their source the causes of the misrepresentation. She finally concludes that the newspapers are to blame, for as the Revolution "advanced, it gained more of our confidence; but it proceeded so violently, and so soon outran the limits of our ideas of liberty, that it awakened a jealousy and dislike in many minds; and these prejudices were unfortunately confirmed by various other causes. One of the first and capital of these was the *misrepresentation of the newspapers*" (4:207–8). Despite their strong influence, however, "It was not the newspapers only that calumniated the French revolution. At a very early period, it was attacked with all the powers of eloquence by Mr. Burke, a writer who had long enjoyed an extensive reputation, and whose opinion, on any subject relative to politics, could not fail to excite curiosity, and to be read with attention" (4:213).

12. Smith, *Desmond*, 67.

13. I would like to thank Mary Favret for pointing this fear out to me, and also for guiding me toward an understanding of the importance of the domestic analogies and of Smith's linking of the public and the private that I discuss in the next section.

14. Anne K. Mellor, in *Mothers of the Nation*, has convincingly revised earlier notions about women's participation in the public sphere, examining the ways in which women did, in fact, participate in the public life.

15. See Mellor, *Mothers of the Nation*, 106.

16. Bowstead, "Charlotte Smith's *Desmond*," 245.

17. Montfleuri makes this statement when he informs Bethel that Geraldine's husband, Verney, has died. Although Verney died as a result of the wounds he suffered while joining a group of outlawed French nobles recently become thieves, the rumor circulating back home in Britain is that Verney was "inhumanely fallen upon by a party of the national troops, and killed" (405).

18. In an insightful analysis, Diana Bowstead links the novel's emphasis on "the consumption, distribution, and production" of food to Smith's desire to show that property is a central form of social injustice. Bowstead observes that Smith "uses table manners, gourmandizing, indulgence of sexual appetites, treatment of poachers, farming practices, estate management, and more to animate characters in ways that seem consonant with their political principles, and either attractive or repulsive to suit Smith's bias" ("Charlotte Smith's *Desmond*," 241).

19. The misplaced modifier in the last part of this sentence is worth noting. Did Smith mean to suggest that the Doctor is himself a stranger and a foreigner?

20. Smith downplays the importance of the issue of protection in *Desmond*, but, as we shall see, it becomes one of her central critiques of British society in *The Young Philosopher*.

21. One year later, in 1793, Smith would elaborate on such acts of kindness in her poem "The Emigrants." While mourning the plight of the French émigrés who had to

leave their homeland and come to Britain, Smith asserts that the French "well deserve /
To find that (every prejudice forgot, / Which pride and ignorance teaches), we for
them / Feel as our brethren" and that they should also find that "the God thou [Britons]
worshippest, delights / In acts of pure humanity!" (*The Poems of Charlotte Smith*, ed.
Stuart Curran, Women Writers in English, 1350–1850 [New York: Oxford University
Press, 1993], 148).

22. Mellor, *Mothers of the Nation*, 113.

23. Blank and Todd, Introduction to *Desmond*, xvii. Although they concentrate their
separate analyses on Smith's sonnets and letters, critics Jacqueline M. Labbe and
Sarah Zimmerman also note how Smith purposely manipulated her own self-representation to gain her readers' sympathy. See Jacqueline M. Labbe, "Selling One's Sorrow:
Charlotte Smith, Mary Robinson, and the Marketing of Poetry," *The Wordsworth Circle*
25.2 (1994): 68–71, and also Sarah Zimmerman, "Charlotte Smith's Letters and the
Practice of Self-Representation," *Princeton University Library Chronicle* 53 (1991): 50–77.

24. Keane, *Romantic Belongings*, 85.

25. Most critics who discuss Geraldine make the assertion that Geraldine is a conservative figure, even if they simultaneously believe, as do I, that Smith makes use of her
for radical ends. Antje Blank and Janet Todd, in their Introduction to *Desmond*, for
example, call Geraldine "the epitome of suffering duty so popular with eighteenth-
century sentimental writers" (xxxii). Both Chris Jones and Eleanor Ty also point this
out. Jones, for instance, refers to Geraldine as Smith's "Trojan horse" because it is her
meek demeanor that allows Geraldine to infiltrate the political sympathies of the novel's
readers (See Chris Jones, *Radical Sensibility: Literature and Ideas in the 1790s* [London:
Routledge, 1993], 163). Ty argues that Geraldine's passivity makes her a "wasted" com-
modity, but that this representation of the novel's heroine allows Smith to show how
women are abused (Eleanor Ty, *The Unsex'd Revolutionaries: Five Women Novelists of the
1790's* [Toronto: University of Toronto Press, 1993], 138). The patient woman is abused
by those who view women as objects of exchange. Ty also contrasts Smith's arguments
to those of conservative writers like Jane West and Hannah More: "Smith demonstrates, however, that this docility only prompts more exorbitant requests from the husband and causes more sorrow for Geraldine. Desmond, and even the rational Bethel,
point out the folly of adhering to her husband's commands. Unlike the novels of West
and More, Smith's *Desmond* challenges the beliefs of the conservatives, which included
suffering in silence, submission without question, and forgiveness at all costs" (Ty, *The
Unsex'd Revolutionaries*, 139).

26. Smith's female audience was a key to her success as a novel writer. As Pat Elliot
emphasizes, one of the primary differences between Charlotte Smith and Mary Wollstonecraft, for instance, is that Smith had a clear female readership in mind: "Charlotte
Smith . . . had published three novels and had an established female readership by 1792.
If her audience was not committed politically, Smith believed it could be educated
through fictional example to value rationality and to reject sentimental passivity. With
Desmond she further politicized the novel as a vehicle for social action, consciousness
raising, and change. She used the language available to women while at the same time
offering an alternative to the popular, sentimental mindless novel that both she and
Wollstonecraft deplored" (Elliot, "Charlotte Smith's Feminism," 92–93). Drawing
upon the work of Cora Kaplan and Anna Wilson, Elliot further notes that Wollstonecraft did not have such a firm base of readership: "Unlike [Thomas] Paine, who had
a clearly identifiable audience, Mary Wollstonecraft's notion of her readership shifted

throughout *The Rights* [*of Woman*]. Without the concept, and the reality, of a politically committed female audience to receive her ideas, Wollstonecraft failed to create common cause with her readers" (92).

27. Smith's connections to Mary Wollstonecraft have been noted by a number of critics. Diana Bowstead, for instance, argues that Smith is just as radical as Wollstonecraft, while Pat Elliot focuses on the connections between the two women in an entire article. Eleanor Ty also points out some of the similarities, while Elizabeth Kraft argues that *The Young Philosopher* is a prose version of Wollstonecraft's *Vindication of the Rights of Woman*. In *The Young Philosopher*, Smith herself refers to her admiration of and debt to Wollstonecraft in three separate places. Only Eleanor Wikburg claims that Smith is not as radical as Wollstonecraft. See Bowstead, "Charlotte Smith's *Desmond*"; Elliot, "Charlotte Smith's Feminism"; Ty, *The Unsex'd Revolutionaries*; Elizabeth Kraft, ed., Introduction to *The Young Philosopher*, by Charlotte Smith, in *Eighteenth-Century Novels by Women*, ed. Elizabeth Kraft (Lexington: University Press of Kentucky, 1999), ix–xxxii; and Eleonor Wikburg, "Political Discourse Versus Sentimental Romance: Ideology and Genre in Charlotte Smith's *Desmond* (1792)," *English Studies* 78.6 (1997): 522–31.

28. Smith translates this phrase herself in a footnote to the novel: "In blood and fire—or, as we say, under fire and sword" (314).

29. It is crucial to remember that Smith wrote the novel before the Terror. As Eleanor Ty, Antje Blank, and Janet Todd underscore, we cannot blame Smith for events that she could not possibly foresee. Ty, for instance, remarks that Smith's "enthusiasm for what the republican government represented should not be judged too harshly by our hindsight. Like [Helen Maria] Williams, Smith was writing as the events occurred and could not predict that the cause which promised liberty and equality to so many would become another form of oppression" (Ty, *The Unsex'd Revolutionaries*, 134). Blank and Todd mark the changing tides of reader response to *Desmond*:

> The publication of *Desmond* (1792), documenting Smith's radical enthusiasm and naive faith in the virtue of the French leadership, was particularly untimely, closely followed as it was by the reversal in French revolutionary politics that put an end to the constitutional phrase. Initially contemporary reviewers unanimously praised Smith's novel. . . . Yet only a few months later the political climate had changed dramatically and Smith found herself in a precarious dilemma. (Blank and Todd, Introduction, xx)

Although her reputation was at stake, Smith "stayed true to her progressive beliefs," like fellow writer Wollstonecraft, even though Smith did "tone down the radicalism that had characterized the authorial voice in *Desmond*" (Blank and Todd, Introduction, xxi). Although Smith continued to support the Revolution's initial ideals even after the Terror commenced, she did not support the Terror's violence and bloodshed, as we shall also see in *The Young Philosopher*.

30. See, for instance, pages 158, 164, and 302.

31. See pages 130–31 and 160.

32. Antje Blank and Janet Todd explain the power husbands had over wives during this period: "Under eighteenth-century patriarchal law a husband's power over his wife's person was absolute. . . . a wife had no legal personality in common law, was unable to enter into contracts, sue or be sued, or instigate legal actions" (Introduction, xiv). The irony, of course, is that such laws were designed to "protect" women from abuse.

33. See Bowstead, "Charlotte Smith's *Desmond*," 255, and Mary Anne Schofield,

"'The Witchery of Fiction': Charlotte Smith, Novelist," in *Living by the Pen: Early British Women Writers*, ed. Dale Spender (New York: Teachers College Press, 1992), 177–187, 177.

34. Diana Bowstead and Pat Elliot are a few of the critics who adopt this same stance. Bowstead, for instance, refers to the "radicalization" of Geraldine (Bowstead, "Charlotte Smith's *Desmond*," 261), while Elliot refers to Geraldine's process of evolution (Elliot, "Charlotte Smith's Feminism," 109). Most critics, however, take the opposite view. Eleonor Wikburg, for instance, asserts that Geraldine never really rebels, and instead simply represents "virtue-in-distress," waiting to be rescued by some man (Wikburg, "Political Discourse Versus Sentimental Romance," 528). Susan Allen Ford concedes that Geraldine rebels, but she also discredits Geraldine's act of rebellion, arguing that Geraldine only revolts to "safeguard her children" (Susan Allen Ford, "Tales of the Times: Family and Nation in Charlotte Smith and Jane West," *Family Matters in the British and American Novel*, ed. Andrea O'Reilly et al. [Bowling Green, OH: Bowling Green State University Popular Press, 1997], 15–29, 23). Alison Conway takes a more hostile stance, viewing Desmond as the "revolutionary force" of the novel, and claiming that "Geraldine produces meaning only in relation to her children, and her body takes on no specificity of its own, but rather acts as an extension of those around her" (see Alison Conway, "Nationalism, Revolution, and the Female Body: Charlotte Smith's *Desmond*," *Women's Studies* 24.5 [1995]: 395–409, 399). I disagree; Geraldine finds her voice in relation to a political event, the Revolution itself, and this is much more significant than finding her voice, or body, in relation to her children. If Geraldine only took on meaning in relation to her children, she would fulfill her role as dutiful mother and resist interpretation as a feminist agent. Because, however, Geraldine finds her voice when confronted first-hand with a political situation, it is clear that her commentary is much more significant than otherwise thought. Granted, Geraldine remains the dutiful wife, passive and willing to risk danger in a foreign country to help her husband, but the fact that she voices her thoughts makes those thoughts momentous. Even the lovely and virtuous Geraldine has a right to use argument to talk about the Revolution.

35. Smith's interest in natural landscapes would become even more important in *The Young Philosopher*. In her Introduction to this later novel, Elizabeth Kraft points to the work of Loraine Fletcher on Smith's use of landscape, noting "Like her contemporary [Ann] Radcliffe, Smith often used landscape to suggest the psychological or emotional state of her characters. . . . And, as for Radcliffe, nature is a healer and a teacher for Smith" (Kraft, Introduction, xviii). Katherine M. Rogers also comments upon Smith's use of nature, arguing that Smith even excelled over Radcliffe in her descriptions of natural surroundings, noting that "Smith's backgrounds are more authentic and more sensitively adapted to her characters' moods" (Katherine M. Rogers, "Romantic Aspirations, Restricted Possibilities: The Novels of Charlotte Smith," in *Re-Visioning Romanticism: British Women Writers, 1776–1837*, ed. Carol Shiner Wilson and Joel Haefner, [Newark: University of Delaware Press, 1990], 72–88, 73. Rogers also argues that Smith's interest in nature linked her to the great Romantic poets, although her place as a woman made it impossible for her to compete with them. Rogers explains this further: "Smith and her characters turned to Nature in the manner of the major Romantic poets, to respond to their emotional needs and help them to articulate their feelings. But there is a significant difference: they could not count on finding consolation there. . . . Smith's repeated conclusion, in her own person and through her characters, is that Nature cannot cure human misery" (Rogers, "Romantic Aspirations," 74). A more extended dis-

cussion of Smith's botanical interests can also be found in Ann B. Shteir's *Cultivating Women, Cultivating Science* (Baltimore: Johns Hopkins University Press, 1996) and Judith Pascoe's "Female Botanists and the Poetry of Charlotte Smith," in *Re-Visioning Romanticism: British Women Writers, 1776–1837,* [(Newark: University of Delaware Press, 1990), 193–209]. Shteir and Pascoe show how Smith used her knowledge of botany in her novels and how botany, as a study open to anyone, was considered to be a radical way of occupying one's time.

36. Although critics differ on the function of Josephine within the novel, I agree with Antje Blank and Janet Todd's assertion that Josephine, as Geraldine's double, exists to show that abuse of women within marriage occurs not only in France, but also in England (Blank and Todd, Introduction, xxxiv–vi).

3. NATIONAL IDENTITY AND EXPATRIATION IN CHARLOTTE SMITH'S *THE YOUNG PHILOSOPHER*

1. Smith's greater interest in the connections between women and the nation in *The Young Philosopher* is reflected in her choice of protagonists. In *Desmond,* Smith was interested in exploring the plight of women, but her desire to explore the true nature of the Revolution was equally strong. For this reason, Smith chose a male protagonist, someone who could enter more fully into the public arena and engage in overt political discussions about the Revolution. By the time she wrote the later novel, Smith's interest in female community was much stronger, so, although the novel's title refers to George Delmont, the novel really concerns itself to a much greater extent with the travails of Laura and Medora Glenmorris. The text might be named after a male character to mask its connection between women and politics, but the central action revolves around the two women characters. As Elizabeth Kraft notes on the back cover of the University of Kentucky edition, it is the Glenmorris women "who provide the emotional core of the novel."

2. For an interesting discussion of how the Revolution affected the narrative structure of Smith's 1794 novel *The Banished Man,* see Toby Ruth Benis, "'A Likely Story': Charlotte Smith's Revolutionary Narratives," *European Romantic Review* 14.3 (Sept. 2003): 291–306.

3. Dr. Winslow, his wife, and his ward Miss Goldthorp stay with Delmont, whom they have never before met, when they find themselves lost in the midst of a terrible rainstorm. Spooked by the lightning, the horses run off with Miss Goldthorp still in the carriage, until Delmont comes to her rescue. Because Miss Goldthorp's arm is injured, however, the party must remain at Delmont's until the arm heals.

4. Charlotte Smith, *The Young Philosopher,* ed. Elizabeth Kraft, Eighteenth-Century Novels by Women (Lexington: The University Press of Kentucky, 1999), 45. All future references are to this edition and their page numbers will appear parenthetically in the text.

5. Later in this same conversation we also learn that Delmont "had acquired, whether from hereditary prescription or not, a way of looking at whatever proposition was presented to him, not as Dr. Winslow had been used to do, exactly as it was shewn, but in every light it would bear. The Doctor had never thought of any object but exactly as his predecessors, his masters, had told him to think" (47). The reverend represents most of the Britons that Delmont encounters, who are unable and unwilling to think

for themselves. Whereas the reverend believes what he has been told by others, doing what has always been done, Delmont, on the other hand, has been taught to think for himself and to form his opinions through rational reflection. By thoroughly scrutinizing each issue, Delmont shows himself to merit the appellation of "young philosopher" that Smith grants him.

6. Significantly, this scene occurs immediately after Delmont "tells off" his lawyer at the end of the previous chapter. Coming back to back as these two scenes do, they provide a hard-hitting condemnation of the injustices of British society.

7. Smith's own personal entanglements with lawyers over her father-in-law's inheritance money come to mind here.

8. Spacks, *Gossip* (New York: Alfred A. Knopf, 1985), 4–6.

9. Ibid., 4.

10. Ibid., 83.

11. In this respect, Smith anticipates Frances Burney's more sustained critique of this subject in 1814's *The Wanderer*, which I discuss in the last chapter. Elizabeth Kraft also touches on the issue of gossip in her Introduction to *The Young Philosopher*, but she does not develop her arguments to any great extent. She does, however, insightfully notice in a footnote how Smith's interest in gossip had an ironic edge to it: "Smith sees gossip as an equally powerful agent of oppression. Yet her success as a writer largely depended on gossip in the sense that her career was fashioned around public interest in her private woes" (Kraft, Introduction, xxxi). Antje Blank and Janet Todd also highlight Smith's use of autobiographical elements in her texts: "Many of Smith's marginal plots are thinly veiled accounts of her own life" (Blank and Todd, Introduction, xvii). Although they concentrate their separate analyses on Smith's sonnets and letters, critics Jacqueline M. Labbe and Sarah Zimmerman also note how Smith purposely manipulated her own self-representation to gain her readers' sympathy.

12. Elizabeth Lisburne's story, which appears only in the fragments of letters, poems, and journal entries that Delmont finds, also serves as a striking example of what happens when women are alone and unprotected. See pages 182ff. for Elizabeth's story.

13. Frances Burney makes this same point earlier in the century in her 1778 novel *Evelina*, when Evelina's guardian Mr. Villars tells his ward that "nothing is so delicate as the reputation of a woman: it is, at once, the most beautiful and most brittle of all human things" (164).

14. Spacks, *Gossip*, 31–32.

15. This same situation again finds its parallel in Burney's *The Wanderer*. In this later novel, Juliet refuses to take money from Harleigh, knowing that it would compromise her in the eyes of society if it were ever found out that she had done so. Without money, however, Juliet literally risks starvation, and none of her female acquaintances are willing to help her out.

16. I would here like to thank Mary Favret for helping me realize this part of my argument. Her careful reading of an earlier version of this chapter helped me arrive at this analysis.

17. Spacks also discusses the power dynamics of gossip, but defines gossip as empowering only insofar as it creates a subtext to patriarchy's dominant tale: "gossip, 'female talk,' provides a mode of power, of undermining public rigidities and asserting private integrity, of discovering means of agency for women, those private citizens deprived of public function" (Spacks, *Gossip*, 170). What Spacks does not acknowledge is how gossip empowers women only at the expense of other women, its primary target.

18. Much later on, for instance, Armitage and Delmont first hear some of the rumors that are circulating about Laura and Medora, and "the reports which had given rise to all this, he [Armitage] traced in more than one instance to Mrs. Crewkherne" (236).

19. A high social standing itself, of course, is a form of power, but Mrs. Crewkherne does not yet (nor will she ever) possess that type of power.

20. Judith Newton, "*Evelina,* or the History of a Young Lady's Entrance into the Marriage Market," *Modern Language Studies: A Publication of the Northeast Modern Language Association* 6.1 (1976): 48–56, 48.

21. Ibid.

22. When Laura returns to Britain to claim her daughter's inheritance, Mrs. Grinsted still harbors these same feelings of jealousy and resentment: "Mrs. Glenmorris, though no longer in the bloom of youth, was so handsome that her prudent friend hated the sight of her, and was determined to believe all the ill which, the gossips of a country town having begun, had been seized with such avidity, and disseminated with such fatal success by Mrs. Crewkherne" (343). Because Laura still retains her beauty, Mrs. Grinsted remains her enemy. Alike in their desire to alter circumstances to fit their own goals, then, Mrs. Grinsted and Mrs. Crewkherne are treacherous and deceptive—ready "to alter, change, or falsify any thing, if the *existing circumstances* required it." Personal gain and personal jealousy are the motives that govern their actions. In this respect, Mrs. Crewkherne's and Mrs. Grinsted's character traits serve as a marked contrast to the honor and truth that the positive characters like Delmont, the Glenmorrises, and Armitage insist upon. Smith does not portray these old maids positively, and we are not meant to empathize with them, yet one cannot help but wonder why Smith did not portray any positive images of unmarried older women. Since Smith in both this novel and in *Desmond* viewed the family as a microcosm of the state, then perhaps she reveals here a prejudice toward the heterosexual family.

23. Medora remarks of the landlady that her "countenance towards me I thought was greatly changed" (323).

24. Admittedly, Smith falls back upon the gender stereotypes of her day in creating such roles for her characters. Yet the great intelligence and independence her female characters portray testify to Smith's belief that women *can* be strong and rational. For example, when Medora tells Delmont about her escape from the Darnells, Medora's fortitude amazes Delmont. Medora, however, views such strength of character as natural to her sex, a lesson she learned long ago from her mother. She explains this in more detail, in terms that cannot help but bring Wollstonecraft to mind: "For my mother I determined to exert that resolution, which she had often told me was a virtue as becoming in a woman, as in a man. 'It is not firmness, Medora,' she has often said, 'that gives an unpleasant and unfeminine character to a woman; on the contrary, the mind which has acquired a certain degree of reliance on itself, which has learned to look on the good and evil of life, and to appreciate each, is alone capable of true gentleness and calmness'" (306). Smith's views on how women should act in society are thus still radical ones for the period.

25. Eleanor Ty also points to what she calls, drawing upon the work of Nancy Chodorow and Carol Gilligan, the "feminine ethos" of the novel, where Mary Cardonnel "devises a 'female' solution to the case" (Ty, *The Unsex'd Revolutionaries,* 153, 154).

26. This is especially true for the Glenmorris women. As Elizabeth Kraft notices, "Both Laura and Medora exhibit extraordinary strength and courage during their trials, yet each is confronted at the moment of rescue not by praise for her strength but

by unfounded suspicions born of sexual jealousy" (Kraft, Introduction, xxv). What Kraft does not notice, and what is even more significant, is that it is the Glenmorris *women* who refuse to doubt each other. When Laura hears Mrs. Grinsted's allegations that Medora has run off with a lover, for instance, her response signals her disbelief: "Medora! Oh cruel to suppose it, Medora has no lover. Medora is incapable of leaving me. She has no lover" (209). Unlike the men in her life, Laura refuses to doubt her daughter's innocence, as her declarative sentence makes clear. Laura's own mother, Lady Mary, of course, chooses to believe the rumors that circulate about her daughter and that "Mrs. Grinsted and Mrs. Crewkherne together had persuaded her to believe" (333).

27. Newman, *The Rise of English Nationalism*, 123.

28. Angela Keane reads this issue differently, seeing not Smith's dismissal of reform, but rather Smith's portrayal of the limited resources available in her country, as "the novel's broader depiction of Britain's attenuated status as a promised land. Each corner of Britain seems to have insufficient or unevenly distributed resources" (Keane, *Romantic Belongings*, 105).

29. Adriana Craciun reads *The Young Philosopher* similarly, noting that "Smith articulates a cosmopolitan feminist alternative to British nationalism, looking toward a postcolonial future in an idealized American republic as the solution to Europe's corruption" (*British Women Writers*, 154). While Craciun focuses on the cosmopolitanism of this novel and of the novels written by other women writers of this period, I instead focus on the ways in which national identity and nationalism were articulated during this period.

30. Keane, *Romantic Belongings*, 102.

31. This is true even in the case of Desmond and Josephine's child since the boy is raised by Geraldine and Desmond along with Geraldine's children from her marriage with Verney. Smith never mentions the Anglo-French identity of the infant or any problems that might be associated with possessing such an identity since her interests lie elsewhere in this earlier novel. In *Desmond*, Smith demonstrated that the loss of British national identity was one reason the British disliked the French's imitation of them so much. Losing their national identity was a frightening prospect for most Britons since it would make them more like the French than they cared to be.

32. I differ here from critics Eleanor Ty and Elizabeth Kraft, who both argue that Smith's interest in other nations, such as the juxtaposition of Laura's story in Scotland and Medora's story in England, is meant to show that England is just as bad and "barbaric" as these other nations. Ty, for instance, contends, "Through the parallels between the stories of the mother and the daughter, which take place some twenty years apart and in different locations, Smith shows how society remains unenlightened and unprogressive, continuing a system based on violence, greed, and brutality. . . . The repetition of the wrongs the mother had suffered not only emphasizes the self-perpetuating and unprogressive nature of the social order, but also draws parallels between the cultural practices of the more 'primitive' and superstitious Scottish clans and those of the more 'civilized' and advanced society of London" (Ty, *The Unsex'd Revolutionaries*, 150). While Ty does add a nationalist slant to her interpretation, she overlooks all of the other instances of emerging national identity. Kraft follows Ty, arguing that "the novel takes us from Brighton in Sussex to northern Scotland, to London, Wales, York, and Ireland. Everywhere the characters encounter the abuses inherent in the class system, the injustices imposed by national institutions" (Kraft, Introduction,

xxvi). While this interpretation is tempting, and I agree that this was a part of Smith's aim, even more significant is how many other instances of questionable national identity emerge in the various stories that are told throughout *The Young Philosopher*. These other interpretations do not account for all of the other instances of nationalism in the novel.

33. Using a Lacanian approach to the novel, Eleanor Ty asserts that because he was raised by his mother, Delmont is outside of the Law of the Father. The novel, she claims, "celebrates female energy" (Ty, *The Unsex'd Revolutionaries*, 143). While I agree with this latter claim, I do not agree that Delmont is feminized just because he is marginalized from society. Instead, as discussed earlier, I think that Smith consciously emphasizes Delmont's "masculine" traits.

34. Frances Burney would develop this problem to an even greater extent than Smith in 1814's *The Wanderer*.

35. In her 1807 poem "Beachy Head," Smith develops the connection between the French and the British to an even greater extent, for the poem opens with the monumental splitting of France and Britain into two separate nations. Although she mentions in a note that the resemblances between France and Britain are not all that great, Smith still immortalizes the connections between the two rivals. For an interesting argument that attempts to show how Smith supported this "Norman Yoke" theory, see Matthew Bray's article "Removing the Anglo-Saxon Yoke," 155–58.

36. Delmont rebukes his brother for this last epithet, remarking, "American girl! what a way of speaking of her, brother!" (256).

37. This last question would also continue to resonate in Smith's own mind, becoming the title of the 1799 play *What Is She?* whose authorship, although slightly uncertain, is usually attributed, as Carrol L. Fry points out, to Smith. See Carrol L. Fry, *Charlotte Smith* (New York: Twayne Publishers, 1996), 92.

38. In using the term "native American," I do not wish to appropriate the designation given to those native Americans who originally possessed this nation. I use it, instead, to refer to the fact that Medora was not born in America, but elsewhere.

39. Another moment when issues of national identity surface is when Delmont travels to Ireland to straighten out Adolphus's financial affairs. Unhappy with the Irish lifestyle of drinking and gambling (a stereotype even in the eighteenth century) and with the misery of the lower classes, Delmont states that he "should [not] like" to live on this neighboring island (200). At another point in the novel, Delmont must try to get information about Laura and Medora from their Swiss servant, Susanne. When he tries to ask Susanne questions about the whereabouts of her two mistresses, Susanne "continued to lament herself, and to tell, in her motley language, which had often a ground of French, oddly embroidered with English and German, how dull and sad a life she led" (226). Smith also has this minor character relay her misunderstanding of a bilingual pun, as Elizabeth Kraft points out in her notes to the novel. When a (British) stranger tells Susanne that she is a "Franche Biche," she thinks that he is praising her for being "frank," not castigating her for being a French female (226–27). At another point, Smith herself stubbornly refuses to translate a French quotation her narrator includes from Rousseau's *Confessions*, saucily remarking in a footnote, "I give no translation, because those who are interested in such an anecdote will probably understand it as it is, and some others, who are not, may think that it [the quotation] already has taken up too great a space" (376).

40. Although at first reluctant to leave his homeland, our hero Delmont changes his mind. Medora's pleas to return to America and the injustice and harsh treatment he

witnesses in his own nation cause Delmont to desire a life abroad. At one point in the novel, while entangled in the midst of his brother's financial affairs, Delmont only wishes to depart for America: "[after] having regulated his few remaining concerns in England, to leave all his troubles behind him, and cross the Atlantic, the happy husband of the woman he adored" becomes his one desire (201).

41. Hugh F. Rankin, *The Golden Age of Piracy* (New York: Holt, Rinehart, and Winston, 1969), 5.

42. Anna Neill, "Buccaneer Ethnography: Nature, Culture, and Nation in the Journals of William Dampier," *Eighteenth-Century Studies* 33.2 (Winter 2000): 165–80, 171.

43. Ibid.

4. Mary Wollstonecraft's Nation-Building Project

1. R. M. Janes was the first to point out that, contrary to popular belief, Wollstonecraft's second *Vindication* was favorably received by her public. It was not until William Godwin published his memoirs of her that Wollstonecraft became publically vilified (R. M. Janes, "On the Reception of Mary Wollstonecraft's *A Vindication of the Rights of Woman*," *Journal of the History of Ideas* 39 [April–June 1978]: 293–302).

2. Mary Wollstonecraft, *Letter on the Present Character of the French Nation*, from *The Works of Mary Wollstonecraft*, vol. 6, ed. Janet Todd and Marilyn Butler (Washington Square, NY: New York University Press, 1989), 444. All future references are to this edition and their page numbers will appear parenthetically in the text with the abbreviation *Letter*.

3. Wollstonecraft had originally intended to expand on this text, covering events up to 1793, but she seems to have dropped the project in favor of covering other topics. No notes or manuscripts for a second volume were ever discovered among her papers.

4. A few of the more notewothy treatments of Wollstonecraft's French texts include those by Harriet Devine Jump and Steven Blakemore. Jump's main argument is that Wollstonecraft was deceived in her hope for the Revolution and subsequently had to reconcile her beliefs with the events of the Revolution. Blakemore's focus is entirely different; his interest lies in questing after the contradictions in Wollstonecraft's political thought and in tracing what he reads as the book's central thesis: that the Enlightenment led to the Revolution. See Harriet Devine Jump, " 'The cool eye of observation': Mary Wollstonecraft and the French Revolution," in *Revolution in Writing: British Literary Responses to the French Revolution*, Ed. Kelvin Everest (Milton Keynes, PA: Open University Press, 1991), 101–19, and Steven Blakemore, *Crisis in Representation: Thomas Paine, Mary Wollstonecraft, Helen Maria Williams, and the Rewriting of the French Revolution* (London: Associated University Press, 1997). Jump also points out that the *Historical and Moral View* was well received by its earliest critics. It had only one negative review (Jump, " 'The cool eye,' " 101–2).

5. Jan Wellington also notices the comparisons Wollstonecraft makes between British women and the French, but focuses her analysis on Wollstonecraft's construction of character. See Jan Wellington, "Blurring the Borders of Nation and Gender: Mary Wollstonecraft's Character (R)evolution," in *Rebellious Hearts: British Women Writers and the French Revolution*, ed. Adriana Craciun and Kari E. Lokke (New York: State University of New York Press, 2001), 33–61.

6. Wollstonecraft, *A Vindication of the Rights of Woman*, 49. All future references are

to this edition and their page numbers appear parenthetically in the text with the abbreviation *VRW.*

7. Wollstonecraft, *Historical and Moral View of the Origin and Progress of the French Revolution; and the Effect it has produced in Europe,* from *The Works of Mary Wollstonecraft,* vol. 6, ed. Janet Todd and Marilyn Butler (Washington Square, NY: New York University Press, 1989), 143, 172. All future references are to this edition and their page numbers will appear parenthetically in the text with the abbreviation *Historical.*

8. It is interesting that the Revolutionaries seek so much change among the political system in France, even while they accept their national character. As I discuss later in this paragraph, Wollstonecraft also considered the royal family to be extremely vain.

9. As Ronald Paulson points out, several writers of the period termed Burke himself a "theatrical" man, given over to a love of spectacle (Ronald Paulson, *Representations of Revolution* [New Haven, CT: Yale University Press, 1983], 81). As we shall soon see, Wollstonecraft believed that Burke shared many character traits with the French, and this seems like one more connection she could draw between the two groups.

10. Since the publication of Jean-Jacques Rousseau's *Émile, ou de l'éducation* in 1762, breastfeeding was, of course, a particularly fraught issue in France, and it became even more so during the Revolution. See, for instance, Mary Jacobus, "Incorruptible Milk: Breast-feeding and the French Revolution," in *Rebel Daughters: Women and the French Revolution,* eds. Sara Melzer and Leslie Rabine (New York: Oxford University Press, 1992), 54–75.

11. Historian Gerald Newman and literary critic Michèle Cohen both demonstrate how Great Britain eventually evolved into a nation of taciturn individuals, as compared to the volatile and loquacious French. See Newman, *The Rise of English Nationalism,* and Cohen, *Fashioning Masculinity.*

12. Wollstonecraft also criticizes Burke for his "artificial affections" throughout the first *Vindication.*

13. Cora Kaplan notes how Wollstonecraft associates female sexuality with dirt, disease, and decay throughout her second *Vindication.* See Cora Kaplan, *Sea Changes: Essays on Culture and Feminism* (London: Verso, 1986), 41.

14. Cora Kaplan, for instance, also comments on Wollstonecraft's fear of novel reading. She explains how this fear developed out of larger eighteenth-century cultural assumptions about reading practices: "Wollstonecraft's implicit theory of reading assumes the reader will identity herself with the female heroine. . . . Late eighteenth century theories of reading, as they appeared in both aesthetic and political discourses, assumed a fairly direct relationship between reading and action, especially in the naive reader, the barely literate, uneducated working-class person—and women" (Kaplan, *Sea Changes,* 122). This new connection between reader and text was based on a growing literacy rate: "An enormous expansion of literacy in general, and of the middle-class reading public in particular, swelled by literate women, made the act of reading in the last quarter of the eighteenth century an important practice through which the common sense and innate virtue of a society of autonomous subject–citizens could be reached and moulded" (160).

15. This also connects to Wollstonecraft's emphasis on the French people's penchant for extremes. Their love of emotion has made the French into a volatile group, one whose members constantly seek excess. This is a point that Wollstonecraft returns to again and again. "The enthusiasm of the French," she explains, ". . . hurries them from one extreme to another" (*Historical* 27). She makes the same point throughout the *Historical and Moral View* (see 60, 61–62, 219, 230).

16. Mary Wollstonecraft, *Collected Letters of Mary Wollstonecraft*, ed. Ralph M. Wardle (Ithaca, NY: Cornell University Press, 1979), 227.

17. Anne K. Mellor, "English Women Writers and the French Revolution," in *Rebel Daughters: Women and the French Revolution*, ed. Sara E. Melzer and Leslie W. Rabine (New York: Oxford University Press, 1992), 255–72, esp. 259.

18. See Jan Wellington's essay "Blurring the Borders" for an interesting discussion of how Wollstonecraft's previously held views on French character changed in a more positive manner during her subsequent travels north.

19. Mary Wollstonecraft, *Letters Written During a Short Residence in Sweden, Norway, and Denmark*, from *The Works of Mary Wollstonecraft*, vol. 6, ed. Janet Todd and Marilyn Butler (Washington Square, NY: New York University Press, 1989), 247.

20. Anne Mellor also concludes that Wollstonecraft blamed "the cruelties and excesses of the revolution on the French character . . . [although] she nonetheless supported the general direction of recent events in France as 'progressive'" ("English Women Writers," 259). My reading diverges from Mellor's, though, in that I am trying to locate a shift in Wollstonecraft's thought as her focus moved from women to France.

21. Incomplete as her account is, though, it still serves an important function not just as a text in which we can locate Wollstonecraft's changing belief systems, but also as an historical record of the early 1790s. Wollstonecraft's contemporary readers were able to learn more about the events occurring in France, and her modern-day readers are able to learn more about contemporary depictions of this significant time.

22. Another problem with Wollstonecraft's trying to equate women with the French is that her idea of revolution changed between the writing of her *Vindications* and her French texts. I examine this change in more detail in the closing section of this chapter.

23. Mary Wollstonecraft, *Elements of Morality*, from *The Works of Mary Wollstonecraft*, vol. 2, ed. Janet Todd and Marilyn Butler (Washington Square, NY: New York University Press, 1989), 5. All future references are to this edition and their page numbers will appear parenthetically in the text with the abbreviation *EM*.

24. Wollstonecraft's dislike of the disorderly can also be witnessed in two other areas: in her dislike of Burke and in her understanding of the French Revolution's progress. One of her main complaints against Burke in the first *Vindication*, for instance, is that Burke adopts a random, disorganized writing style that reflects his adherence to arbitrary customs and beliefs, which is her definition of prejudice. (David Simpson also links Burke's style to his politics, showing how political radicalism—anathema to Burke—was associated with symmetry and simplicity during the 1790s. See Simpson, *Romanticism, Nationalism, and Revolt.*) Throughout the *Historical and Moral View*, Wollstonecraft also portrays the Revolution as closest to failure during those moments when the events surrounding the Revolution are most disorderly and chaotic. The new political order she advocates (discussed in the conclusion to this chapter) can only be brought about if that reform takes place under the guidance of "systematic management" (*Historical* 144).

25. Whereas Wollstonecraft believed in the liberatory nature of reason, her rival Burke, as Ronald Paulson explains, viewed reason as "the false sun" (Paulson, *Representations*, 59–60).

26. Mary Wollstonecraft, *A Vindication of the Rights of Man* (Amherst, NY: Prometheus Books, 1996), 64. All future references are to this edition and will their page numbers appear parenthetically in the text with the abbreviation *VRM*.

27. Keane, *Romantic Belongings*, 113.

28. The reason, of course, that Wollstonecraft abhors the emotions produced by sensual refinement is because those emotions are artificial, unnatural, and bodily. Paris, for instance, had been one of the primary sites of decadence for quite some time, and Wollstonecraft believes that in that great city "surely the soul of Epicurus has long been at work to root out the simple emotions of the heart, which, being natural, are always moral. Rendered cold and artificial by the selfish enjoyments of the senses, which the government fostered, is it surprising that the simplicity of manners, and singleness of heart, rarely appear, to recreate me with the wild odour of nature, so passing sweet?" (*Letter* 445). As she makes clear, because the "simple emotions of the heart" are "natural," they are also "always moral." Any connection emotions might have with sensuality or pleasure taints them, making them undesirable dwellers in the human frame.

29. In this same article, Venturo also draws some interesting comparisons between Wollstonecraft's and Jonathan Swift's visions of morality, claiming they share similar moral viewpoints. Whereas Venturo believes Wollstonecraft when she says that morality is sexless, however, I do not, as I explain in the next paragraph. See David F. Venturo, "Concurring Opponents: Mary Wollstonecraft and Jonathan Swift on Women's Education and the Sexless Nature of Virtue," in *Pope, Swift, and Women Writers*, ed. Donald C. Mell (Newark: University of Delaware Press, 1996), 192–202, 193.

30. As Carolyn W. Korsmeyer remarks, one of the central paradoxes of the eighteenth-century model of female virtue was that reason was denied to women while also assumed to be necessary to raise children: "Woman's superior intuition and sensibility were supposed to grant her a moral and spiritual excellence; yet *at the same time* her deficient reason and poor cognitive ability were supposed to preclude the possibility of stable moral character!" (Carolyn W. Korsmeyer, "Reason and Morals in the Early Feminist Movement: Mary Wollstonecraft," in *Women and Philosophy: Toward a Theory of Liberation*, rpt. in *A Vindication of the Rights of Woman*, 2nd ed., ed. Carol H. Poston [New York: W. W. Norton, 1988], 285–97, 294).

31. Reason, morality, and religion thus form a foundation upon which society should be based. "What indeed," she asks in her first *Vindication*, "would become of morals, if they had no other test than prescription? The manners of men may change without end; but, wherever reason receives the least cultivation—wherever men rise above brutes, morality must rest upon the same base. And the more man discovers of the nature of his mind and body, the more clearly he is convinced, that to act according to the dictates of reason is to conform to the law of God" (*VRM* 82). Being reasonable means acting according to reasonable principles, which in turn means acting according to principles first established by God.

32. Tom Furniss reads this passage differently, connecting it to Wollstonecraft's revision of Burke's aesthetic categories (Tom Furniss, "Gender in Revolution: Edmund Burke and Mary Wollstonecraft," in *Revolution in Writing: British Literary Responses to the French Revolution*, ed. Kelvin Everest [Milton Keynes, PA: Open University Press, 1991], 65–100, 91).

33. G. J. Barker–Benfield, "Mary Wollstonecraft: Eighteenth Century Commonwealthwoman," *Journal of the History of Ideas* 50.1 (January–March 1989): 95–115.

34. Ruth H. Bloch, "The Gendered Meanings of Virtue in Revolutionary America," *Signs* 13.1 (1987): 37–58, 38, 43.

35. Barker–Benfield, "Wollstonecraft: 18th Century Commonwealthwoman," 106.

36. See esp. chapter 1 of Johnson's *Equivocal Beings*.

37. Ibid., 15–16.

38. Ibid., 24. Johnson also suggests that women could be "manly" in Wollstonecraft's formulation, although Wollstonecraft herself would ultimately become "in her own manliness an isolated and highly 'equivocal being'" (25). In the second chapter of her book, Johnson proceeds to look at the ways in which Wollstonecraft's novels do, in fact, represent the sexual difference that Wollstonecraft denies in her political treatises. It is these apparent contradictions in Wollstonecraft's thought that make her so fascinating.

39. Other critics have also noticed Wollstonecraft's dislike of the effeminate. Tom Furniss, however, links this dislike to Wollstonecraft's dislike of luxury (Furniss, "Gender in Revolution," 87ff.), while Timothy J. Reiss views this as a contradiction in Wollstonecraft's logic (Timothy J. Reiss, "Revolution in Bounds: Wollstonecraft, Women, and Reason," in *Gender and Theory: Dialogues on Feminist Criticism*, ed. Linda Kauffman [New York: Basil Blackwell, 1989], 11–50, 32).

40. Mary Poovey connects Wollstonecraft's rhetoric to her larger project of reforming the middle classes: "she refuses in *The Rights of Men* to identify herself consistently with women or even to be sympathetic to the submissiveness they have been forced to assume. . . . she rejects the female experience of helplessness and frustration for the defiant bourgeois assertion that one can, in fact, be anything one wants" (Mary Poovey, *The Proper Lady and the Woman Writer: Ideology as Style in the Works of Mary Wollstonecraft, Mary Shelley, and Jane Austen* [Chicago: The University of Chicago Press, 1984], 63). In her second *Vindication*, Poovey asserts, Wollstonecraft adopts this stance for a different reason: "It is because Wollstonecraft so thoroughly distrusts her own sexuality that she rejects a female speaking voice in *The Rights of Woman*" (79–80).

41. Wollstonecraft, *Collected Letters*, 262.

42. Ibid., 263.

43. Joan B. Landes, "Representing the Body Politic: The Paradox of Gender in the Graphic Politics of the French Revolution," in *Rebel Daughters: Women and the French Revolution*, ed. Sara E. Melzer and Leslie W. Rabine (New York: Oxford University Press, 1992), 15–37, 26, 32. Drawing upon the work of Marina Warner and Lynn Hunt, Landes also recounts how the female figures of Liberty and Marianne could, paradoxically, represent the abstract values of the Revolution, even while France's women were denied the rights that the Revolutionaries were seeking for Frenchmen.

44. Doing so would take this chapter in a different direction, but it would be worthwhile to investigate further the ways in which Wollstonecraft imagined her cross-national relationship with American Gilbert Imlay (with whom she had at one point planned on emigrating to America) and the dual national identity of her first daughter. Connections could easily be made between Wollstonecraft, Burney, and Smith on this issue. My thanks to Lisa Wood for pointing this avenue of exploration out to me.

45. Even William Godwin agreed that the second *Vindication* used a "manly" tone. Wollstonecraft had celebrated this tone during her own life; however, Godwin apologizes for it after her death, essentially siding with her critics. Several sections of his *Memoirs of Mary Wollstonecraft*, for instance, ring of contriteness:

Many of the sentiments are undoubtedly of a rather masculine description. The spirited and decisive way in which the author explodes the system of gallantry, and the species of homage with which the sex is usually treated, shocked the majority . . . . The pretty, soft creatures that are so often to be found in the female sex, and that class of men who believe they could not exist without such pretty, soft creatures to resort to, were in arms against the author of so heretical and blasphemous a doctrine. There are also, it must be confessed, occasional passages of a stern and rugged feature, incompatible with the writer's essential character. But, if they did not belong to her fixed and permanent character, they belonged to her character of the moment; and what she thought, she scorned to qualify.

Yet, along with this rigid, and somewhat amazonian temper, which characterized some parts of the book, it is impossible not to remark a luxuriance of imagination, and a trembling delicacy of sentiment. (William Godwin, *Memoirs of Mary Wollstonecraft*, ed. W. Clark Durant [New York: Haskell House Publishers, 1969], 54–55).

Godwin attributes Wollstonecraft's use of a "masculine" style as owing to the historical moment, insisting that even amidst the "stern and rugged" sections of the *Vindication of the Rights of Woman* a "trembling delicacy"—a "feminine" style—coyly peeks out. Later on in the *Memoirs*, Godwin glorifies this "womanly" tone to an even greater extent, constructing an image of Wollstonecraft as an archetypal woman in the final chapters of his text. Describing the reasons Wollstonecraft decided to write the *Letters from Sweden*, for example, Godwin praises her newly discovered "feminine" style: "The occasional harshness and ruggedness of character, that diversify her Vindication of the Rights of Woman, here totally disappear. If ever there was a book calculated to make a man fall in love with its author, this appears to me to be the book" (*Memoirs* 84).

46. Blakemore, *Crisis in Representation*, 97.

47. Wollstonecraft's comments are remarkably similar to those made by Captain Mirvan in Frances Burney's *Evelina*, where the Captain asks about the "benefits" of a French education: "What, I suppose you'd have me learn to cut capers?—and dress like a monkey?—and palaver in French gibberish? . . . And, powder, and daub, and make myself up" (Burney, *Evelina*, 61).

48. The nobility of her own country, of course, do not escape from a similar rebuke, for the British aristocracy also comes under attack in both of the *Vindications*.

49. Cora Kaplan also points this out, but only in a passing reference, remarking, "an idealized bourgeois male is the standard towards which women are groping" (Kaplan, *Sea Changes*, 46).

50. Wollstonecraft obviously disagrees with Bernard Mandeville's belief, described in his *Fable of the Bees*, that private vices create public virtues.

51. Kaplan, *Sea Changes*, 46.

52. Godwin remarks in his *Memoirs* that Wollstonecraft's own plans at the age of twenty-four involved the same goal. "Her project, five years before," Godwin writes, "had been personal independence; it was now usefulness" (25).

53. Mitzi Myers argues, for instance, that Wollstonecraft's "acceptance of natural sex roles, of rationalized marriage and motherhood as public service in the national interest . . . limits her application of egalitarian principles to women. But for Wollstonecraft, nature and reason validate the bourgeois family as a key corrective to the sins of an oppressive, class-bound establishment" (Mitzi Myers, "Reform or Ruin: 'A Revolution in Female Manners,'" rpt. in *A Vindication of the Rights of Woman*, 2nd ed., ed. Carol H. Poston [New York: W. W. Norton, 1988], 337). Joan Landes supports this position, asserting that Wollstonecraft helped define republican motherhood for her readers. Woman's major task, according to Wollstonecraft, was to instill patriotic duty into her children, making them good British citizens (Joan Landes, *Women and the Public Sphere in the Age of the French Revolution* [Ithaca, NY: Cornell University Press, 1989], 129–38). Timothy J. Reiss's analysis of Wollstonecraft's views on the principle of reason also suggests that Wollstonecraft borrowed from the major philosophical views of self-interest to form an image of women's role within Britain, one where "citizenship has

been narrowed to motherhood" (Reiss, "Revolution in Bounds," 23). As Reiss further argues, "Wollstonecraft was partly under the blinding sway of an ideology imposing marriage and motherhood as a woman's duty, and her difficulty was to put those citizenship 'duties' in terms that would not deny the equality of reason and social function. . . . Arguing her case in this manner forced Wollstonecraft to make motherhood the primary function of woman as social being, as 'citizen'. . . . Situating the statement of individuality first, Wollstonecraft found the distinguishing *human* characteristic to be the familiar one of reason, and the distinguishing *female* characteristic to be that of childbirth" (24–25). Anne Mellor also notes that Wollstonecraft, along with contemporary Helen Maria Williams and daughter Mary Wollstonecraft Shelley, believed in the power of the egalitarian family, although this family power dynamic often produced difference (Mellor, "English Women Writers," 255–72). Rajani Sudan further elucidates Mellor's arguments, showing how Wollstonecraft buys into the eighteenth century's "patriotic fervor to better the lots of British mothers for the good of the national whole" (Rajani Sudan, "Mothering and National Identity in the Works of Mary Wollstonecraft," in *Romanticism, Race and Imperial Culture, 1780–1834*, ed. Alan Richardson and Sonia Hofkosh [Bloomington: Indiana University Press, 1996], 72–89, 79.

54. Wollstonecraft also emphasizes the active role of the mother in her *Elements of Morality*. The best use for her own book of children's tales—or, for that matter, of any other—is for mothers to discuss the moral value of the stories with their children afterward. Addressing herself to her female readers, Wollstonecraft points out the serious responsibilities that belong to the role of mother: "To you does the pleasing task belong of forming their tempers, and giving them habits of virtue" (*EM* 11). (The idea of Socratic discussion is an important one for Wollstonecraft, and comes up several times in her plan for making women into better mothers. At several points in the *Vindication of the Rights of Woman*, she returns to this idea of using discussion to teach women how to think for themselves. See *VRW* 105, 168, 185.)

55. Carol Blum, *Rousseau and the Republic of Virtue* (Ithaca, NY: Cornell University Press, 1986), 208–9.

56. Lynn Hunt, *The Family Romance of the French Revolution* (Berkeley and Los Angeles: University of California Press, 1992), 42–43.

57. Encouraging each British woman to be "also an active citizen" was a radical claim for Wollstonecraft to make, one that allied her with the Revolutionaries, for the word *citizen* carried a strong Revolutionary connotation.

58. The Oath of the Tennis Court was one of the few moments when there was "an overflow of sensibility that kindled into a blaze of patriotism every social feeling. . . . in one of those instants of disinterested forgetfulness of private pursuits, all devoted themselves to the promotion of public happiness" (*Historical* 65).

59. Wollstonecraft's logic here, of course, is once again circular, revealing an underlying uncertainty about where things begin and end. Does the French people's love of their nation start in a love of the family, or does it start with a love of mankind?

60. Cora Kaplan, for instance, notes that "the debased femininity she describes is constructed through a set of social practices which by constant reinforcement become internalized parts of the self" (Kaplan, *Sea Changes*, 157). Since Wollstonecraft's belief that gender is a constructed term is so well known, I do not attempt to retread old ground here.

61. Virtue, she makes clear in her *Elements of Morality*, can also become a habit, but only if practiced consistently. "[F]or every virtue is a habit," she explains, "and habits

can only be acquired by exercise" (*EM* 14). Education, as a reified form of social conditioning, works in the same way.

62. Wollstonecraft does not leave her own nation out of this argument, either. In the *Vindication of the Rights of Men*, she repeatedly emphasizes the constructed nature of Great Britain. As she explains to Burke at one point, "private cabals and public feuds, private virtues and vices, religion and superstition, have all concurred to foment the mass and swell it to its present form" (*VRM* 55–56). Later on, she tells him how wrong he is to worship laws and customs put in place by his fellow men: "you have affixed meaning to laws that chance, or, to speak more philosophically, the interested views of men, settled, not dreaming of your ingenious calculations" (*VRM* 62). Burke's "ideal consecration of a state" makes him blind to its constructed and fallible nature (*VRM* 57).

63. Harriet Devine Jump links Wollstonecraft's goal of gradual change to her "millenialist beliefs" (Jump, "'The cool eye,'" 107). Godwin also underwent this same shift in his belief system.

64. When compared with the ideas expressed in the two *Vindications*, Wollstonecraft's opinions about the nature of revolution in her 1793 and 1794 texts show an important change in her thinking. In the earlier texts, Wollstonecraft had advocated radical, institutional change. She recognized this type of change in the Revolution's early events, and then advocated it for the women of her own nation, once more showing how a nationalist project influenced her gender politics. As the Revolution deviated from its original principles during the Reign of Terror, however, Wollstonecraft became less convinced of the benefits of sweeping change. Surprisingly, she adopted a Burkean model of gradual change.

65. Julie Ellison also realizes this, noting that "Wollstonecraft focuses on manners as the place where the subject's consciousness or inner life and social behavior coincide" (Julie Ellison, "Redoubled Feeling: Politics, Sentiment, and the Sublime in Williams and Wollstonecraft," *Studies in Eighteenth-Century Culture* 20 [1990]: 197–215, 207).

66. Mary Poovey enriches our understanding of Wollstonecraft's idea of revolution by emphasizing the meaning of the word: "When she calls for a 'revolution in female manners . . . . she is not advocating a feminist uprising to overthrow manners but rather a general acquiescence in the gradual turning that the word 'revolution' was commonly taken to mean in the eighteenth century. Women are simply to wait for this revolution to *be* effected, for their dignity to *be* restored, for their reformation to *be* made necessary. The task is primarily men's" (Poovey, *The Proper Lady*, 79). Anne Mellor links this revolution to Wollstonecraft's desire to make women into better mothers and wives (Mellor, "English Women Writers," 256–58).

67. One solution she proposes for making women useful British subjects involves making women into political agents: "I may excite laughter, by dropping an hint, which I mean to pursue, some future time, for I really think that women ought to have representatives, instead of being arbitrarily governed without having any direct share allowed them in the deliberations of government" (*VRW* 147). Government representatives would provide women with a voice against otherwise arbitrarily imposed dictates. Wollstonecraft strongly believes in the power of representative government, which she speaks more about in the *Historical and Moral View*, asserting that "[positive] consultations can take place under representative systems of government only—under systems which demand the responsibility of their ministers, and secure the publicity of their political conduct" (*Historical* 222). In this regard, it is curious that Wollstonecraft

served as a business agent for Gilbert Imlay in her travels to Scandinavia, which were undertaken to help Imlay recover gains from business transactions. See, for instance, chapters 11 and 12 of Lyndall Gordon's recent biography *Vindication: A Life of Mary Wollstonecraft* (New York: HarperCollins, 2005).

68. This passage also extends to cover Wollstonecraft's argument for why women should have more standing within Britain's legal system. To be virtuous, she reasons, women need to be able to claim the protection of Britain's laws: "But, to render her really virtuous and useful, she must not, if she discharge her civil duties, want, individually, the protection of civil laws; she must not be dependent on her husband's bounty for her subsistence during his life, or support after his death—for how can a being be generous who has nothing of its own? or, virtuous, who is not free?" (*VRW* 146). She also criticizes Britain's government for refusing to recognize women as legal entities: "is not that government then very defective, and very unmindful of the happiness of one half of its members, that does not provide for honest, independent women, by encouraging them to fill respectable stations? But in order to render their private virtue a public benefit, they must have a civil existence in the state, married or single" (*VRW* 148–49). Without a civil existence, women have a hard time being useful members of any society.

69. Rousseau, of course, was Swiss, but most eighteenth-century British associated him with the French and their Revolution since the Revolutionaries borrowed so heavily from his theories and texts.

5. Reconciliation and Revision in Frances Burney's *The Wanderer*

1. Burney recorded many of these impressions in Volume 3 of her journals and letters. See, for instance, some of the earlier diary entries in Frances Burney, *The Early Journals and Letters of Fanny Burney*, ed. Lars E. Troide and Stewart J. Cooke (Buffalo, NY: McGill–Queen's University Press, 1994), 3.

2. The April 1778 *Monthly Review* coverage of *Evelina* particularly noted the vivacity of the characters. Burney recorded the passage, with a few mistakes, in her diary: "The Characters, which are agreeably diversified, are conceived & drawn with propriety, & supported with spirit." See Burney, *The Early Journals*, 15.

3. As Margaret Anne Doody notes, "There has been a rather hazy impression that *The Wanderer* was a failure from the outset, but that is not so. The first edition sold out at once, and a second edition had to be run off at the time of publication; 3,500 copies were sold almost instantly—an extremely large issue of a novel for the time" (*Frances Burney: A Life in the Works* [New Brunswick, NJ: Rutgers University Press, 1988], 332). Contemporary reviews of the novel will be discussed in the conclusion to this chapter.

4. Some of the critics who have created a renewed interest in Burney and to whom Burney scholars owe a debt of gratitude are Margaret Anne Doody, Julia Epstein, Kristina Straub, Susan Staves, and Rose-Marie Cutting–Gray.

5. Harleigh bears the brunt of modern-day critics' barbs. Barbara Zonitch, for instance, claims that "he, like Sir Jasper, proves to be an inept protector; he can do very little to help Juliet in her frantic search for sanctuary. Lord Orville demonstrates strength. . . . But Harleigh is a mere helpless spectator" (Zonitch, *Familiar Violence*, 135). Doody agrees that Harleigh is too fussy and timid: "The sight of any woman

doing anything seems to afflict him" (Margaret Anne Doody, Introduction to *The Wanderer*, by Fanny Burney, ed. Margaret Anne Doody, Robert L. Mack, and Peter Sabor [New York: Oxford University Press, 1991], xxiii–xv, xxiv).

6. Burney, *The Wanderer*, 3. All future references are to this edition and their page numbers will appear parenthetically in the text.

7. Frances (Burney) D'Arblay, *The Journals and Letters of Fanny Burney*, ed. Joyce Hemlow, vol. 6 (Oxford: Clarendon Press, 1975), 716–17.

8. Ibid., 717.

9. As Margaret Doody states, "She hoped to serve to unite the unfortunately hostile countries, herself serving as a 'friend of humanity' by presenting both France and England in her novel" (*Frances Burney*, 317). As with many of the insightful comments about nationalism that she makes in her biography of Burney, however, Doody does not develop this idea in any detail.

10. See ftn. 6 to the Oxford University Press edition of the novel (910).

11. Burney's relationship with her husband, however, was one of continual happiness to her. As Doody points out, "Of all the women writing of her era, she seems to have made the best marriage" (*Frances Burney*, 203). Her husband continually supported her literary endeavors, and helped her pursue them as much as it was in his power to do so.

12. As Maria Jerinic points out, "Throughout her travels, the only man that Juliet can fully trust is a Roman Catholic bishop. His kindness presents him as a model of male behavior." See her "Challenging Englishness: Frances Burney's *The Wanderer*," in *Rebellious Hearts: British Women Writers and the French Revolution*, ed. Adriana Craciun and Kari Lokke (New York: State University of New York Press, 2001), 63–84, 72. Jerinic usefully focuses part of her essay on the ways in which Burney "treats" Protestant Christianity. I look at the connections between Catholicism and nationalism in more detail later on in this chapter.

13. Although she is not referring to this particular scene, Joanne Cutting–Gray talks about the double-edged sword that Evelina must bear in situations like this one. Evelina must appear innocent, with no knowledge of fleshly matters, and yet still be able to retain an awareness of the dangers around her. As Cutting–Gray puts it, "the narrated Evelina conceals her sexual and verbal power from herself and from others. Why does Evelina who writes with such acute observation and wit, who names situations so as to deflate pretension and vulgarity, seem so inept in the social world, especially in the company of young males? In a social situation where she must assume the disguise of innocence, Evelina becomes a problem to herself." I agree with Cutting–Gray's assessment, that it would not be proper for Evelina to reveal her true state of affairs, but only wish that Evelina would become angrier with Sir Clement. See Joanne Cutting–Gray, *Woman as "Nobody" and the Novels of Fanny Burney* (Gainesville: University Press of Florida, 1992), 4. Susan Staves makes a similar point when she mentions that Evelina is not supposed to know that Sir Clement might rape her (Staves, *"Evelina,"* 371).

14. Julia Epstein argues differently, claiming that Evelina's letters to Maria Mirvan are racier than her ones to her guardian, Mr. Villars. The "unstudied tone" of these letters, Epstein claims, reveals Evelina's true nature, which is that of a young woman who has learned how to "cajole, flatter, and manipulate, all with apparent innocence and real charm" to get what she wants out of men (Epstein, *Iron Pen*, 101, 111). While I agree that Evelina's letters to Maria are more candid than those she writes to Mr. Villars, I see this as a result of their friendship, not as a sign of Evelina's duplicity.

15. For the significance of Juliet's assumed identity as a black woman, see Sara Salih, "'Her Blacks, Her Whites and Her Double Face!': Altering Alterity in *The Wanderer*," *Eighteenth-Century Fiction* 11.3 (1999): 301–15. While Salih ultimately concludes that "the 'purity' of English national identity" remains intact (312), I will argue in this chapter that by the end of *The Wanderer*, Burney embraces mixed identities.

16. Most critics agree that Burney was fascinated with names. As Joanne Cutting-Gray notes, all of Burney's novels "interrogate the social practices that conceive Women as mere negation. Namelessness and identity become Burney's lifelong concern" (*Woman as "Nobody,"* 4). Most critics, however, read this lack of a name as more empowering than I think it is. Cutting–Gray, for instance, goes on to assert that because Juliet refuses to name herself, she "renames passivity and innocence, not as their opposites, but as forces complicitous with any agenda that liberates by opposition. Thus, Burney succeeds in describing a view of woman that eludes both the name imposed on her by the old social order, and the absolute freedom proposed by the new" (7). Epstein agrees, arguing that "Juliet's namelessness through most of the narrative—a namelessness far more radically isolating for Juliet than it had been for any of Burney's previous heroines—represents a daring political statement on Burney's part. A woman's name indicates not her identity *tout court*, but her social identity. . . . To lack a name is to belong to no one, that is, to belong to oneself. . . . Making her last heroine nameless was Burney's boldest stroke as a feminist novelist. Ellis's namelessness permits her to travel across classes, professions, lodgings, and appearances" (*Iron Pen*, 178). Doody makes a similar point: "The patrilinear and the patriarchal are questioned in the lack of emphasis given to Juliet's last name" (*Frances Burney*, 323). This, combined with the fact that there are no strong fathers in the novel, makes Juliet's nameless state a revisionary one for Doody. Catherine Craft–Fairchild offers an interpretation of Juliet's namelessness that is closer to my own. She claims that Juliet is a blank that the male characters appropriate as they try to incorporate her into the patriarchal culture (Catherine Craft–Fairchild, *Masquerade and Gender: Disguise and Female Identity in Eighteenth-Century Fictions by Women* [University Park, PA: Pennsylvania State University Press, 1993], 139). Unlike Craft–Fairchild, I assert that *all* of the other characters, and especially the other women, read Juliet as a blank that they can fill in with their own labels.

17. The idea of the "nobody" in Burney's writings gets taken up in greater length by Claudia L. Johnson and Joanne Cutting–Gray. Johnson traces the development of female authorship in the late seventeenth and early eighteenth centuries, showing how women writers invented similarities between being a woman and being a writer through the use of authorial personae, published books, copyrights, debts, and reputations (Johnson, *Equivocal Beings*). Cutting–Gray, on the other hand, focuses more on the use that Burney alone makes of "Nobody." She explains:

Yet Burney doesn't treat herself as the woman constructed by patriarchy; instead, she lets Nobody function as the alterity, the *unnamed* feminine that determines the structure of identity for man, the named. When Burney dismantles this opposition in her ongoing dialogue, she shows us that Woman-as-Nobody springs out of a difference that has the configuration of Somebody-as-Man. In terms of gender, this strategy enables Burney to use the conceptual vocabulary of the patriarchy without being a party to it. By using "Woman" as a conceptual name and "Nobody" as woman's place in culture, Burney imaginatively shapes herself out of the "strange medley" of an unfinished life. Her address, therefore, speaks to her heart of our concern with gender. (Cutting–Gray, *Woman as "Nobody,"* 2)

18. Doody provides an interesting analysis of this name, pointing out how it bears the sound of "Elle is," or "She is." The name also has echoes in the names of Juliet, Elinor, and Gabriella. See Doody, *Frances Burney*, 331.

19. The importance that Juliet places on the homeland is also brought to our attention in an earlier scene, one where Juliet laments her friend Gabriella's state of exile. Shortly after he discovers Juliet working in the London haberdasher's shop with Gabriella, Sir Jasper begins to express his sadness about Juliet's poverty and the "base drudgery" that she must endure (636). After listening to Sir Jasper's comments for several minutes, Juliet interrupts him, comparing her situation with that of her French friend: "Can you look, Sir, at her whom you call my partner, and think of me? She has lost her country; she wastes in exile; she sinks in obscurity; she has no communication with her friends; she knows not even whether they yet breathe the vital air!— nevertheless she works, she sustains herself by her industry and ingenuity" (636–37). Gabriella's greatest misfortune, the one that Juliet lists first, is that she "has lost her country," the tie that binds her to all those who are important in her life. Exiled in Britain, Gabriella remains alone and without any connections to her friends. Juliet has, at least, escaped from France to "this happy land" (750) that she can call home; her friend, in contrast, remains separated from the nation and people she loves.

20. Juliet has a dual national identity even while living in France. Her fellow school-children at the convent where she is educated know her "as a young English lady of fortune" (643), and refer to her as "*la sage petite Anglaise*" (644).

21. Although it might seem contradictory for Juliet to be simultaneously praised and shunned for her French "accomplishments," such behavior was common during this period. The British admired French arts and products, even though they feared being infiltrated by them.

22. In his classic study *Competition for Empire 1740–1763*, Walter Dorn traces the rise of the British and French colonial empires. As Dorn points out, both nations preferred West Indian trade routes instead of East Indian ones since these routes were thought to have more profitable resources. See Dorn, *Competition for Empire*, 260ff. Stationed as he was in the East Indies, Admiral Powel should have met with little threat from the French, which makes his strong hatred that much more unusual and pronounced.

23. In her footnotes to the novel, Doody argues that the husband represents Robespierre (881), who himself represents brutal power (878).

24. Doody, *Frances Burney*, 110.

25. Ibid., 285.

26. Ibid., 23.

27. Colley, *Britons*, 36.

28. Ibid. Not everyone, of course, felt this way. Burney's close friend Hester Lynch Thrale Piozzi, for example, made the connection between Catholics and Protestants clear in her 1789 *Observations and Reflections Made in the Course of a Journey Through France, Italy and Germany*, although she does so at the expense of non-European nations. Upon arriving in France, where she had visited once before, she notes her traveling companion's reaction to the differences between French and English culture. "But what is our difference of manners," Piozzi further reflects, "compared to that prodigious effect produced by the much shorter passage from Spain to Africa; where an hour's time, and sixteen miles only, carries you from Europe, from civilization, from Christianity" (Piozzi, *Observations and Reflections*, 5).

29. Years earlier, in 1783, Burney had pleaded with her friend Hester Lynch Thrale

not to marry the poor musician Gabriel Piozzi. In a letter dated from January of that year, Burney urged her friend to consider the effects that marriage to a Catholic Italian would have on her life: *"Children—Religion, Friends, Country, Character—*what on *Earth* can compensate the loss of all these?"* (qtd. in Doody, *Frances Burney,* 162). Although Thrale fully intended to keep her Protestant religion and English nationality, Burney assumes that marriage to a foreigner would put these areas at risk. The friendship between the two women was, of course, eventually ruptured by Burney's refusal to accept Thrale's marriage and the two women were never reconciled, even after Burney herself married a Catholic foreigner. Piozzi recognized Burney's hypocrisy, and would not forgive it.

30. Doody, *Frances Burney,* 201–2.

31. Claudia Johnson expands on this further in her Introduction to Frances Burney, *Brief Reflections Relative to the Emigrant French Clergy,* ed. Claudia L. Johnson, The Augustan Reprint Society, Publication Number 262 (Los Angeles: William Andrews Clark Memorial Library, 1990), iii.

32. Ibid., iv.

33. The Admiral's ability to get past the distinction between Catholic and Christian allies him not only with Burney, but also with our heroine Juliet. The Admiral's words about it being possible for Juliet's husband to be a "tolerable good Christian, mayhap for a Papist," echo those from an earlier scene in the novel when Lord Denmeath first pays Juliet a visit. During the meeting between Juliet and Lord Denmeath, the latter questions Juliet on the strength of her attachment to her French friends. Juliet shuns the Lord's offer to be her advisor, knowing how deceptive he really is: "I have already, my lord, a guide; and one to whose judgment I shall submit implicitly. That Bishop, whom your lordship is pleased to call officious, is my first, best, and nearly only friend; and if ever again I should be so blest as to meet with him, his opinion shall be my law,—as his benediction will be my happiness!". . . . In great emotion, yet with unappalled dignity, she was departing; but Lord Denmeath, with an air of surprize, stopping her, said, "You are then a Papist?". . . . *"No, my lord! I am firmly a Protestant! But, as such, I am a Christian; so, and most piously, yet not illiberally, is the Bishop"* (615–16). As in the several scenes discussed earlier, Juliet once again voices her attachments to French characters and the French nation. Her "first, best, and nearly only friend" is not only a Frenchman, but also a Catholic. And, while she herself is not one, she underscores the sameness of the two religions. Unlike Lord Denmeath, then, the Admiral recognizes Catholics as fellow Christians. Admiral Powel's beliefs thus mirror those of Juliet, who, in response to Lord Denmeath's inquiry, asserts that Catholics *are,* in fact, Christians.

34. As Barbara Zonitch points out, it is the maternal inheritance (since the Admiral is Juliet's *mother's* brother) that saves Juliet. This provides another instance of Burney's feminist stance. See Zonitch, *Familiar Violence,* 137.

35. Doody, *Frances Burney,* 330.

36. Ibid. Once again, Doody hints at some of the larger claims I am making, but she drops them early, before giving them full development. She writes that in this scene, "Frances Burney has recognized her own doubleness, her dual identity (as Frances Burney/Mme. D'Arblay) and the double identity which is hers by birth as the descendant of French immigrants into England" (*Frances Burney,* 331).

37. As Doody points out, this is the scene where we learn Juliet's true name, which happens to be given in both French and English (Juliet/Julie), as is Gabriella's (Gabriella/Gabrielle).

38. Zonitch makes a similar claim, but her analysis focuses on how the *aristocracy* does not effectually protect women: "we see how a long history of aristocratic rule has only served to place Juliet in grave jeopardy: it has never offered her inviolable or even adequate protection" (*Familiar Violence*, 136). Doody also mentions in her Introduction to the Oxford edition of *The Wanderer* that "Burney shows why we cannot believe that the system of mere patronage and protection actually works justly and fairly for women" (xxi).

39. Johnson, *Equivocal Beings*, 174. Johnson attributes this lack of male authority to an effect of the sentimentality of the 1790s that she is interested in tracing; I attribute it to Burney's emphasis on female community.

40. This selection was taken from Vivien Jones's anthology of eighteenth-century women writers. See Jones, *Women in the Eighteenth Century*, 126.

41. Juliet first lodged with Miss Matson under a similar recommendation, for Harleigh "had considerately named her as a young person known to Mrs. Maple" in order to obtain a room for her (67).

42. Juliet draws upon her social credit at Miss Matson's not just once, but twice. The second time, Miss Matson states once again that Juliet's connections give her validity: "you, Miss Ellis, who have been so strongly recommended; and protected by so many of our capital gentry. . . . If you really intend to take a small lodging, why should not you have my little room again up stairs?" (384).

43. A similar situation occurs when Juliet is essentially kicked out of Mrs. Howel's house. After Mrs. Howel departs and her protection of Juliet is openly withdrawn, her housekeeper treats Juliet as an equal, even going so far as to open Juliet's bedroom door without first knocking (136).

44. From Jones, *Women in the Eighteenth Century*, 123–24.

45. Rose Marie Cutting's assessment is similar to my own, as are Kristina Straub's and Julia Epstein's. Cutting's article on *The Wanderer*, one of the earliest that appeared, traces the development of Burney's feminist thought. "The preoccupation with propriety in Fanny Burney's novels," she explains, "was balanced by another sort of development—a growing rebellion against the restrictions imposed upon women. In this sense, Fanny Burney was a feminist. . . . A study of all four of her novels reveals that Fanny Burney began with a neoclassical reverence for social norms, but ended with a philosophy of self-reliance" (Rose Marie Cutting, "Defiant Women: The Growth of Feminism in Fanny Burney's Novels," *Studies in English Literature* 17 [1977]: 519–30, 519–20). Straub's analysis expands on Cutting's. She says that Burney argues for a healthy skepticism against reliance on others: "The problem with all of Juliet's lines of work is, quite simply, that none of them give her any power over others and the way in which they treat her. . . . Burney's heroines, then, illustrate the limits imposed on female labor as a means of controlling the course of one's life. Alternatively, Burney's novels suggest that women's best resources lie in an intelligent skepticism toward the romantic modes in which the plots of marriage or sexual ruin would place them" (Kristina Straub, "Fanny Burney and the Rise of the Woman Novelist," in *The Columbia History of the British Novel*, ed. John Richetti, John Bender, and Deidre David [New York: Columbia University Press, 1994], 199–219, 207–8). Epstein links her claims about the function of work within the novel to social class: "Work, despite Juliet's laments and Burney's social commentary, also energizes the heroine. . . . The economic limbo Juliet inhabits illustrates a halfway point between the degrading work available to lower- and middle-class women and the enforced leisure of upper-class women" (*Iron Pen*, 185–86).

46. Juliet's refusal to spend any of the money that Harleigh leaves with her demonstrates her understanding of how such an action could be misconstrued. By using his money, she would place herself in his debt and compromise her values.

47. Burney, *Brief Reflections*, 3.

48. It is ironic, too, that Juliet's opponents forge a sense of community out of their shared desire to not help her. Although she focuses on Burney's interest in circulating goods and forms of exchange, Deidre Shauna Lynch also points out: "What holds the book's numerous characters together and makes them a society is that each is this stranger's creditor: each lends her money, and she is what other people have in lieu of a social contract to lend to the nation and so to themselves" (*The Economy of Character*, 201).

49. During her first term in Mrs. Ireton's service, however, Juliet asserts her own claims and rights, refusing to be a victim. At this stage in their relationship, Juliet occupies a more powerful position than she will later on as Mrs. Ireton's paid companion, because Juliet is there to do Mrs. Ireton a favor. Their relationship is based upon the master–slave dichotomy, for without a female companion to attend her to London, Mrs. Ireton would be put in a questionable situation.

50. Although the threat of being denied a home is a large one for Juliet, her own sense of worth becomes increasingly important to her as Mrs. Ireton's abuse becomes increasingly extreme. A safe refuge no longer carries the same value as her own merit, and she will once again refuse to tolerate Mrs. Ireton's cruelty. During the visit to Arundel Castle, for example, the same visit where she espies Sir Jasper Herrington berating his servant, Juliet also gets taken to task by her own employer. Always ready with sarcastic comments, Mrs. Ireton delights in heaping reproaches and witticisms on Juliet. Juliet's sense of self-worth angers Mrs. Ireton, and so she constantly sets her sights on bringing Juliet down through mockery and cynicism. On this particular day, however, Juliet has heard more insults than she can stand: "Juliet could endure no more. The most urgent distress seemed light and immaterial, when balanced against submission to treatment so injurious. She walked, therefore, straight forward to the castle, for shelter, immediate shelter, from this insupportable attack. . . . Offended, indignant; escaped, yet without safety; free, yet without refuge; Juliet, hurried into the noble mansion, with no view but to find an immediate hiding-place" (550–51). In seeking shelter from the verbal attacks of this vicious woman, Juliet, without uttering a word to Mrs. Ireton, leaves and escapes toward the castle. Yet even the castle does not offer the security she needs. Although she can use it as a hiding-place, it does not provide safety or refuge, the two things of which she is most in need. Temporary as it is, her asylum cannot protect her from her most pressing need, that of finding a dignified means of supporting herself financially. For this task, she must rely upon other human beings; an empty building does not afford the same protection that another person does.

51. Juliet's use of the superlatives is echoed again when she is at a wayside inn and hears "that sound, which, of all others, *most* severely shocked her nerves, the voice of Mrs. Howel" (816, emphasis added). Burney's use of the superlative once more marks Mrs. Howel as *the most negative* character in Juliet's life.

52. Juliet's reaction to meeting Mrs. Howel is ever afterward one of absolute horror. When Lady Auora pleads with Juliet to speak with Mrs. Howel, for example, Juliet experiences violent emotions: "Juliet here, with a strong expression of horrour, interrupted her: 'Mrs. Howel? —O no! I cannot speak with Mrs. Howel! —I had nearly said I can see Mrs. Howel no more!'" (553). When she later runs into Mrs. Howel at the

inn, Juliet's reaction invokes conventions that Burney seems to borrow from Gothic novels: "[Juliet] started back involuntarily, and her countenance depicted undisguised horrour. . . . A spectre could not have made her start more affrighted, could not have appeared to her more horrible" (563). Even Juliet's reaction to seeing her "husband" is not as severe as her reaction to seeing Mrs. Howel.

53. My interest is not in whether or not the two women, or even Juliet, can be said to be opposites or partners, as it is for other critics. Judy Simons argues, for instance, that "Juliet and Elinor form two sides of the feminist coin" (*Fanny Burney* [Totowa, NJ: Barnes & Noble, 1987], 113). Craft–Fairchild (*Masquerade and Gender*, 146) and Cutting–Gray (*Woman as "Nobody,"* 85), however, take the opposite stance, arguing that Juliet and Elinor are not binary opposites. Instead, my focus is on the friendship that gradually develops between them.

54. Rose Marie Cutting briefly touches on this issue also: "Fanny Burney's female rebels may lead perverse and wasteful lives but they do so because society does not provide more constructive outlets for members of their sex" (Cutting, "Defiant Women," 522).

55. Zonitch also links Elinor's self-violence to her understanding of the world: "women's attempts to forge a new identity in a radically changing modern world provokes the community's hostile reactions and, most alarmingly, women's internalization of this violence" (*Familiar Violence*, 115).

56. Doody, for instance, notes that "Elinor is free from the basic constraints of economic life" and that her "own thinking is still too class-bound" (*Frances Burney*, 349, 360). Zonitch concurs, pointing out that the relationship between Juliet and Elinor "cannot flourish because of Elinor's selfishness, which is born of her own secure economic position . . . she does not fully reject all of the assumptions entailed in her aristocratic rank" (*Familiar Violence*, 129–30).

57. Although Juliet immediately recognizes the names of Lady Aurora and Lord Melbury, she does not let them know that they are her half-siblings. They only find out that Juliet is their sister after Sir Jasper tells them, which does not occur until late in the novel, on page 817 in the Oxford edition.

58. Even Macaulay's otherwise glowing review of Burney's published diaries and letters in his 1843 *Edinburgh Review* column claims that this is Burney's worst novel. "In 1814," he claims, "she published her last novel, The Wanderer, a book which no judicious friend to her memory will attempt to draw from the oblivion into which it has justly fallen" (Macaulay, *Edinburgh Review* 76 [January 1843]: 558).

59. Macaulay takes up this point in his review as well. Intrigued by the changes in Burney's novels, Macaulay feels compelled to "trace the progress" (564) of Burney's stylistic decline. Although her style was fresh and colloquial in her first novel, "In an evil hour the author of Evelina took the Rambler for her model" (564). After she began interacting with Dr. Johnson more, Macaulay claims, Burney's prose became more turgid and unnatural. This was nothing, however, compared to what happened when Burney went to France:

> After the publication of Camilla, Madame D'Arblay resided ten years at Paris. During those years there was scarcely any intercourse between France and England. . . . All Madame D'Arblay's companions were French. She must have written, spoken, thought, in French. Ovid expressed his fear that a shorter exile might have affected the purity of his Latin. During a shorter exile, Gibbon unlearned his native English. Madame D'Arblay had carried a bad style to France. She brought back a style which we are really at a loss to describe. It is a sort of broken

Johnsonese, a barbarous *patois*, bearing the same relation to the language of Rasselas, which the gibberish of the Negroes of Jamaica bears to the English of the House of Lords. (565–66)

Although other critics claimed that Burney was overrated to begin with, Macaulay insists, on the contrary, that "her early popularity was no more than the reward of distinguished merit, and would never have undergone an eclipse, if she had only been content to go on writing in her mother-tongue" (568). In both passages, Macaulay attaches Burney's decline in writing ability to her time spent abroad. Contact with the French language essentially contaminated her "mother-tongue," making it difficult for her to achieve the verbal artistry she had once been able to.

60. John Wilson Croker's April 1814 review of *The Wanderer* was one of the most negative published. In it he claims that "she ought not, as an Englishwoman, as a writer, to have debased herself to the little annotative flattering of the scourge of the human race" (130). Burney should have attacked Napoleon, not flattered him. See John Wilson Croker, *Quarterly Review* 11 (April 1814): 123–30.

61. An anonymous reviewer from the June 1814 edition of the *Gentlemen's Magazine* pointed this out: "Had this novel appeared when the full infatuation [of the Terror] alluded to reigned in full force, it must have made a much stronger impression upon the public mind that it will at present" (579). Despite its outdatedness, " 'The Wanderer' will have its use, and serve as an historical antidote to any lurking remnants of poisonous doctrines that still make their appearance at intervals, as our courts of justice too plainly testify" (579). Younger readers, he claims, will certainly benefit from the historical lessons the novel unfolds. See the *Gentleman's Magazine* 84 (June 1814): 570–81.

62. Macaulay's review, the review that most strongly pointed out the correlation between Burney's decline and her residence in France, makes the difference between Fanny Burney, the author, and Madame D'Arblay, the married woman, clearest. In one passage, although he had just been referring to her as "Madame D'Arblay," Macaulay suddenly switches to using "Miss Burney" to discuss her literary achievements: "Miss Burney did for the English novel what Jeremy Collier did for the English drama; and she did it in a better way. . . . She took away the reproach which lay on a most useful and delightful species of composition. She vindicated the right of her sex to an equal share in a fair and noble province of letters. . . . At present, the novels which we owe to English ladies form no small part of the literary glory of our country" (569–70). Macaulay's review, of course, is still very positive. He compares Burney's contributions to novel writing to those of a *man*, for instance, even though he also makes reference to Burney's contributions as a woman artist. Despite her affiliations with the French, Macaulay is also still quick to claim Burney as an English writer, to whom his readers owe a debt for the "literary glory" Burney has brought to their country.

63. In one of the most often cited passages from his review, for example, Croker makes the connections between the author and her novels clear:

But in the Wanderer there is no splendour, no source of delight to dazzle criticism and beguile attention from a defect which has increased in size and deformity exactly in the same degree that the beauties have vanished. The Wanderer has the identical features of Evelina—but of Evelina grown old; the vivacity, the bloom, the elegance, the purple light of love, are vanished; the eyes are there, but they are dim; the cheek, but it is furrowed; the lips, but they are withered. And when to this description we add that Madame D'Arblay endeavours to make up for the want of originality in her characters by the most absurd mysteries, the most extravagant incidents, and the most violent events, we have completed the portrait of an old coquette who endeavours, by the wild tawdriness and laborious gaiety of her attire, to compensate for the loss of the natural charms of freshness, novelty, and youth. (125–26)

Croker recognizes the similarities between the two novels, but, in Croker's analogy, Burney herself has become "Evelina grown old." The second novel, in Croker's assessment, suffers from the age of its author and her faded beauty. In addition to this cruel portrait of the author, Croker also accuses her of disloyalty to Britain. After discussing all of the improbable parts of the novel, Croker slanders Burney herself: "These, our readers will see, are proceedings as natural and well imagined as the rest; and they will conclude that her long residence in France has given Madame D'Arblay a very novel and surprising view of the state of religion, manners, and society in England" (128).

64. The most interesting example of this is William Hazlitt's review of *The Wanderer* from February 1815. Of the nineteen pages supposedly devoted to Burney's last novel, the first sixteen pages are actually given over to a history of novels in general. When Hazlitt finally gets around to discussing Burney's novel, he introduces it by stating, "It is not to be wondered, if, amidst the tumult of events crowded into this period, our literature has partaken of the disorder of the time; if our prose has run mad, and our poetry grown childish" (335). After this portentous opening, he then takes care to evaluate Burney's merits based upon her gender: "The author of the present is, however, quite of the old school, a mere common observer of manners, —and also a very woman. It is this last circumstance which forms the peculiarity of her writings, and distinguishes them from those masterpieces which we have before mentioned. She is unquestionably a quick, lively, and accurate observer of persons and things; but she always looks at them with a consciousness of her sex, and in that point of view in which it is the particular business and interest of women to observe them" (336). Overall, "There is little other power in Miss Burney's novels, than that of immediate observation. . . . The difficulties in which she involves her heroines are indeed 'Female Difficulties;'—they are difficulties created out of nothing" (337). As "a very woman," Burney's strength consists of nothing other than her ability to accurately record the events around her. Hazlitt denies her any intelligence or imagination. See William Hazlitt, *Edinburgh Review* 24 (February 1815): 320–38.

65. Or perhaps they recognized Burney's claims, which is why they attempted to criticize and demean them.

POSTSCRIPT: THE LEGACY OF FEMALE COMMUNITY

1. For some of the most important work that has been done on British imperialism during the Romantic and Victorian periods, see Kathleen Wilson, *The Sense of the People*; David Simpson, *Romanticism, Nationalism, and Revolt*; Richardson and Hofkosh, *Romanticism, Race, and Imperial Culture*; and *Macropolitics of Nineteenth-Century Literature: Nationalism, Exoticism, Imperialism*, ed. Jonathan Arac and Harriet Ritvo (Philadelphia: University of Pennsylvania Press, 1991).

2. For a compelling account of the intersections between feminism and abolitionism in Britain, see Moira Ferguson, *Subject to Others*. Karen Sanchez–Eppler explores similar connections in nineteenth-century America in *Touching Liberty: Abolition, Feminism, and the Politics of the Body* (Berkeley and Los Angeles: University of California Press, 1993).

Works Cited

Primary Texts

Andrews, John. *Remarks on the French and English Ladies, in a series of letters; interspersed with various anecdotes, and additional matter, arising from the subject.* London, 1783.

Barbauld, Anna Laetitia. *Sins of Government, Sins of the Nation; or, A Discourse for the Fast, appointed on April 19, 1793, by a volunteer.* London: J. Johnson, 1793.

Burney, Frances. *Brief Reflections Relative to the Emigrant French Clergy.* Ed. Claudia L. Johnson. The Augustan Reprint Society. Publication Number 262. Los Angeles: William Andrews Clark Memorial Library, 1990.

———. *Diary and Letters of Madame D'Arblay.* Ed. Charlotte Barrett. London, 1842–1846.

———. *The Early Journals and Letters of Fanny Burney.* Ed. Lars E. Troide and Stewart J. Cooke. Buffalo, NY: McGill–Queen's University Press, 1994.

———. *Evelina, or, The History of a Young Lady's Entrance into the World.* 1778. Ed. Edward A. Bloom. New York: Oxford University Press, 1991.

———. *The Journals and Letters of Fanny Burney.* Ed. Joyce Hemlow. Vol. 6. Oxford: Clarendon Press, 1975.

———. *The Wanderer.* 1814. Ed. Margaret Doody, Robert L. Mack, and Peter Sabor. New York: Oxford University Press, 1991.

Croker, John Wilson. *Quarterly Review* 11 (April 1814): 123–30.

Edgeworth, Maria. *Castle Rackrent and Ennui.* Ed. Marilyn Butler. New York: Penguin Books, 1992.

Gentleman's Magazine 84 (June 1814): 570–81.

Godwin, William. *Memoirs of Mary Wollstonecraft.* Ed. W. Clark Durant. New York: Haskell House Publishers, 1969.

Hawkins, Laeticia Matilda. *Letters on the Female Mind, its Powers and Pursuits. Addressed to Miss H. M. Williams, with particular reference to Her Letters from France.* London: Printed for Hookham and Carpenter, 1793.

Hays, Mary. *Appeal to the Men of Great Britain on Behalf of Women.* Ed. Gina Luria. New York: Garland Publishing, 1974.

Hazlitt, William. *Edinburgh Review* 24 (February 1815): 320–38.

Macaulay. *Edinburgh Review* 76 (January 1843): 559.

More, Hannah. *Selected Writings of Hannah More.* Ed. Robert Hole. Pickering Women's Classics. London: William Pickering, 1996.

Morgan, Lady Sydney Owenson. *France in 1829–30.* London, 1829–1830.

Paine, Thomas. *Rights of Man*. Ed. Gregory Claeys. Indianapolis, IN: Hackett Publishing, 1992.

Piozzi, Hester Lynch. *Observations and Reflections Made in the Course of a Journey Through France, Italy, and Germany*. London, 1789.

Polwhele, Richard. *The Unsex'd Females*. The University of Virginia. January 3, 2006. <http://etext.lib.virginia.edu/britpo/unsex/unsex.html>.

Randell, Anne Francis [Mary Robinson]. *A Letter to the Women of England, on the Injustice of Mental Subordination*. In *Women in the Eighteenth Century: Constructions of Femininity*. Ed. Vivien Jones, 238–43. London: Routledge, 1990.

Shelley, Mary. *History of a Six Weeks' Tour through a part of France, Switzerland, Germany, and Holland*. Oxford: Woodstock Books, 1989.

Smith, Charlotte. *Desmond*. Ed. Antje Blank and Janet Todd. Pickering Women's Classics. London: Pickering and Chatto, 1997.

———. *The Poems of Charlotte Smith*. Ed. Stuart Curran. Women Writers in English, 1350–1850. New York: Oxford University Press, 1993.

———. *The Young Philosopher*. Ed. Elizabeth Kraft. Eighteenth-Century Novels by Women. Lexington: The University Press of Kentucky, 1999.

Williams, Helen Maria. *Letters From France*. Eight Volumes in Two (1790, 1791, 1793, 1795, 1796). Ed. Janet M. Todd. Delmar, NY: Scholar's Facsimiles & Reprints, 1975.

———. *Letters Written in France*. Ed. Neil Fraistat and Susan S. Lanser. Toronto: Broadview Press, 2002.

Wollstonecraft, Mary. *Collected Letters of Mary Wollstonecraft*. Ed. Ralph M. Wardle. Ithaca, NY: Cornell University Press, 1979.

———. *Elements of Morality*. The Works of Mary Wollstonecraft. Volume 2. Ed. Janet Todd and Marilyn Butler. Washington Square, NY: New York University Press, 1989.

———. *Historical and Moral View of the Origin and Progress of the French Revolution; and the Effect it has produced in Europe*. The Works of Mary Wollstonecraft. Vol. 6. Ed. Janet Todd and Marilyn Butler. Washington Square, NY: New York University Press, 1989.

———. *Letter on the Present Character of the French Nation*. The Works of Mary Wollstonecraft. Vol. 6. Ed. Janet Todd and Marilyn Butler. Washington Square, NY: New York University Press, 1989.

———. *Letters Written During a Short Residence in Sweden, Norway, and Denmark*. The Works of Mary Wollstonecraft. Vol. 6. Ed. Janet Todd and Marilyn Butler. Washington Square, NY: New York University Press, 1989.

———. *A Vindication of the Rights of Man*. Amherst, NY: Prometheus Books, 1996.

———. *A Vindication of the Rights of Woman*. 1792. 2nd ed. Ed. Carol H. Poston. New York: W. W. Norton, 1988.

Secondary Texts

Anderson, Benedict. *Imagined Communities: Reflections on the Origin and Spread of Nationalism*. Rev. ed. New York: Verso, 1991.

Anderson, Earl A. "Footnotes More Pedestrian Than Sublime: A Historical Background for the Foot-Races in *Evelina* and *Humphry Clinker*." *Eighteenth-Century Studies* 14 (1980): 56–58.

Bannet, Eve Tavor. *The Domestic Revolution: Enlightenment Feminisms and the Novel*. Baltimore: Johns Hopkins University Press, 2000.

Barker–Benfield, G. J. "Mary Wollstonecraft: Eighteenth Century Commonwealthwoman." *Journal of the History of Ideas* 50.1 (Jan.–March 1989): 95–115.

Benis, Toby Ruth. "'A Likely Story': Charlotte Smith's Revolutionary Narratives." *European Romantic Review* 14.3 (Sept. 2003): 291–306.

Blakemore, Steven. *Crisis in Representation: Thomas Paine, Mary Wollstonecraft, Helen Maria Williams, and the Rewriting of the French Revolution*. Madison, NJ: Fairleigh Dickinson University Press, 1997.

Blank, Antje, and Janet Todd, eds. Introduction to *Desmond*. By Charlotte Smith. Pickering Women's Classics. London: Pickering and Chatto, 1997.

Bloch, Ruth H. "The Gendered Meanings of Virtue in Revolutionary America." *Signs* 13.1 (1987): 37–58.

Blum, Carol. *Rousseau and the Republic of Virtue*. Ithaca, NY: Cornell University Press, 1986.

Bowstead, Diana. "Charlotte Smith's *Desmond:* The Epistolary Novel as Ideological Argument." In *Fetter'd or Free?: British Women Novelists, 1670–1815*. Ed. Mary Anne Schofield and Cecilia Macheski, 285–306. Athens: Ohio University Press, 1986.

Bray, Matthew. "Removing the Anglo-Saxon Yoke: The Francocentric Vision of Charlotte Smith's Later Works." *The Wordsworth Circle* 24.3 (1993): 155–58.

Brown, Martha G. "Fanny Burney's 'Feminism': Gender or Genre?" In *Fetter'd or Free: British Women Novelists, 1670–1815*. Ed. Mary Anne Schofield and Cecilia Macheski, 29–39. Athens: Ohio University Press, 1986.

Claeys, Gregory, ed. Introduction to *Political Writings of the 1790s*. 8 vols. London: William Pickering, 1995.

Cohen, Michèle. *Fashioning Masculinity: National Identity and Language in the Eighteenth Century*. London: Routledge, 1996.

Colley, Linda. *Britons: Forging the Nation 1707–1837*. New Haven, CT: Yale University Press, 1992.

Conway, Alison. "Nationalism, Revolution, and the Female Body: Charlotte Smith's *Desmond*." *Women's Studies* 24.5 (1995): 395–409.

Copeland, Edward W. "Money in the Novels of Fanny Burney." *Studies in the Novel* 8 (1976): 24–37.

Craciun, Adriana. *British Women Writers and the French Revolution: Citizens of the World*. New York: Palgrave Macmillan, 2005.

Craft–Fairchild, Catherine. *Masquerade and Gender: Disguise and Female Identity in Eighteenth-Century Fictions by Women*. University Park: Pennsylvania State University Press, 1993.

Cutting, Rose Marie. "Defiant Women: The Growth of Feminism in Fanny Burney's Novels." *Studies in English Literature* 17 (1977): 519–30.

Cutting–Gray, Joanne. *Woman as "Nobody" and the Novels of Fanny Burney*. Gainesville: University Press of Florida, 1992.

Doody, Margaret Anne. *Frances Burney: A Life in the Works*. New Brunswick, NJ: Rutgers University Press, 1988.

———. Introduction to *The Wanderer*, by Fanny Burney. 1814. Ed. Margaret Anne Doody, Robert L. Mack, and Peter Sabor, xxiii–xv. New York: Oxford University Press, 1991.

Dorn, Walter. *Competition for Empire 1740–1763*. New York: Harper, 1940.

Elliot, Pat. "Charlotte Smith's Feminism: A Study of *Emmeline* and *Desmond*." In *Living by the Pen: Early British Women Writers*. Ed. Dale Spender, 91–112. New York: Teachers College Press, 1992.

Ellison, Julie. *Cato's Tears and the Making of Anglo-American Emotion*. Chicago: University of Chicago Press, 1999.

———. "Redoubled Feeling: Politics, Sentiment, and the Sublime in Williams and Wollstonecraft." *Studies in Eighteenth-Century Culture* 20 (1990): 197–215.

Epstein, Julia. *The Iron Pen: Frances Burney and the Politics of Women's Writing*. Madison: University of Wisconsin Press, 1989.

Ferguson, Moira. *Subject to Others: British Women Writers and Colonial Slavery, 1670–1834*. New York: Routledge, 1992.

Ford, Susan Allen. "Tales of the Times: Family and Nation in Charlotte Smith and Jane West." In *Family Matters in the British and American Novel*. Ed. Andrea O'Reilly et al., 15–29. Bowling Green, OH: Bowling Green State University Popular Press, 1997.

Fry, Carrol L. *Charlotte Smith*. New York: Twayne Publishers, 1996.

Furniss, Tom. "Gender in Revolution: Edmund Burke and Mary Wollstonecraft." In *Revolution in Writing: British Literary Responses to the French Revolution*. Ed. Kelvin Everest, 65–100. Milton Keynes, PA: Open University Press, 1991.

Gellner, Ernest. *Nations and Nationalism*. Ithaca: Cornell University Press, 1983.

Gordon, Lyndall. *Vindication: A Life of Mary Wollstonecraft*. New York: HarperCollins, 2005.

Greenfeld, Liah. *Nationalism: Five Roads to Modernity*. Cambridge, MA: Harvard University Press, 1992.

Guest, Harriet. *Small Change: Women, Learning, Patriotism, 1750–1810*. Chicago: University of Chicago Press, 2000.

Hill, Christopher. "The Norman Yoke." In *Puritanism and Revolution: Studies in Interpretation of the English Revolution of the Seventeenth Century*. 1958. New York: Schocken Books, 1964.

Hobsbawm, Eric, and Terence Ranger, eds. *The Invention of Tradition*. New York: Cambridge University Press, 1983.

Hole, Robert, ed. Introduction to *Selected Writings of Hannah More*, vii. Pickering Women's Classics. London: William Pickering, 1996.

Hunt, Lynn. *The Family Romance of the French Revolution*. Berkeley and Los Angeles: University of California Press, 1992.

Jacobus, Mary. "Incorruptible Milk: Breast-feeding and the French Revolution." In *Rebel Daughters: Women and the French Revolution*. Edited by Sara Melzer and Leslie Rabine, 54–75. New York: Oxford University Press, 1992.

Janes, R. M. "On the Reception of Mary Wollstonecraft's *A Vindication of the Rights of Woman*." *Journal of the History of Ideas* 39 (April–June 1978): 293–302.

Jerinic, Maria. "Challenging Englishness: Frances Burney's *The Wanderer.*" In *Rebellious Hearts: British Women Writers and the French Revolution.* Ed. Adriana Craciun and Kari E. Lokke, 63–84. New York: State University of New York Press, 2001.

Johnson, Claudia L. *Equivocal Beings: Politics, Gender, and Sentimentality in the 1790s, Wollstonecraft, Radcliffe, Burney, Austen.* Chicago: University of Chicago Press, 1995.

———. *Jane Austen: Women, Politics, and the Novel.* Chicago: University of Chicago Press, 1988.

Jones, Chris. *Radical Sensibility: Literature and Ideas in the 1790s.* London: Routledge, 1993.

Jones, Vivien, ed. *Women in the Eighteenth Century: Constructions of Femininity.* London: Routledge, 1990.

Jump, Harriet Devine. "'The cool eye of observation': Mary Wollstonecraft and the French Revolution." In *Revolution in Writing: British Literary Responses to the French Revolution.* Ed. Kelvin Everest, 101–19. Milton Keynes, PA: Open University Press, 1991.

Kaplan, Cora. *Sea Changes: Essays on Culture and Feminism.* London: Verso, 1986.

Keane, Angela. *Romantic Belongings: Women Writers and the English Nation in the 1790s.* Cambridge: Cambridge University Press, 2000.

Kennedy, Deborah. "Revolutionary Tales: Helen Maria Williams' *Letters from France* and William Wordsworth's 'Vaudracour and Julia.'" *The Wordsworth Circle* 21.3 (Summer 1990): 109–14.

Korsmeyer, Carolyn W. "Reason and Morals in the Early Feminist Movement: Mary Wollstonecraft." In *Women and Philosophy: Toward a Theory of Liberation.* Rpt. in *A Vindication of the Rights of Woman.* 2nd. ed. Ed. Carol H. Poston, 285–97. New York: W. W. Norton, 1988.

Kraft, Elizabeth, ed. Introduction to *The Young Philosopher,* by Charlotte Smith. In *Eighteenth-Century Novels by Women.* Ed. Elizabeth Kraft, ix–xxxii. Lexington: The University Press of Kentucky, 1999.

Labbe, Jacqueline M. "Selling One's Sorrow: Charlotte Smith, Mary Robinson, and the Marketing of Poetry." *The Wordsworth Circle* 25.2 (1994): 68–71.

Landes, Joan B. "Representing the Body Politic: The Paradox of Gender in the Graphic Politics of the French Revolution." In *Rebel Daughters: Women and the French Revolution.* Ed. Sara E. Melzer and Leslie W. Rabine, 15–37. New York: Oxford University Press, 1992.

———. *Women and the Public Sphere in the Age of the French Revolution.* Ithaca, NY: Cornell University Press, 1989.

Liu, Alan, and Laura Mandell, eds. *Romantic Chronology.* May 23, 2005. <http://english.ucsb.edu:591/rchrono/>.

Lynch, Deidre Shauna. *The Economy of Character: Novels, Market Culture, and the Business of Inner Meaning.* Chicago: University of Chicago Press, 1998.

Mellor, Anne K. "English Women Writers and the French Revolution." In *Rebel Daughters: Women and the French Revolution.* Ed. Sara E. Melzer and Leslie W. Rabine, 255–72. New York: Oxford University Press, 1992.

———. *Mothers of the Nation: Women's Political Writing in England, 1780–1830.* Bloomington: Indiana University Press, 2000.

Miller, William Ian. *Humiliation and Other Essays on Honor, Social Discomfort, and Violence.* Ithaca, NY: Cornell University Press, 1993.

Myers, Mitzi. "Reform or Ruin: 'A Revolution in Female Manners.'" Rpt. in *A Vindication of the Rights of Woman.* 2nd ed. Ed. Carol H. Poston. New York: W. W. Norton, 1988: 328–43.

Neill, Anna. "Buccaneer Ethnography: Nature, Culture, and Nation in the Journals of William Dampier." *Eighteenth-Century Studies* 33.2 (Winter 2000): 165–80.

Newman, Gerald. *The Rise of English Nationalism: A Cultural History 1740–1830.* New York: St. Martin's Press, 1997.

Newton, Judith. *"Evelina,* or the History of a Young Lady's Entrance into the Marriage Market." *Modern Language Studies: A Publication of the Northeast Modern Language Association* 6.1 (1976): 48–56.

Nussbaum, Felicity. *Torrid Zones: Maternity, Sexuality, and Empire in Eighteenth-Century English Narratives.* Baltimore: Johns Hopkins University Press, 1995.

Pascoe, Judith. "Female Botanists and the Poetry of Charlotte Smith." In *Re-Visioning Romanticism: British Women Writers, 1776–1837.* Ed. Carol Shiner Wilson and Joel Haefner. Newark: University of Delaware Press, 1990: 193–209.

Paulson, Ronald. *Representations of Revolution.* New Haven, CT: Yale University Press, 1983.

———. *Satire and the Novel in Eighteenth-Century England.* New Haven, CT: Yale University Press, 1967.

Poovey, Mary. *The Proper Lady and the Woman Writer: Ideology as Style in the Works of Mary Wollstonecraft, Mary Shelley, and Jane Austen.* Chicago: University of Chicago Press, 1984.

Rankin, Hugh F. *The Golden Age of Piracy.* New York: Holt, Rinehart and Winston, 1969.

Reiss, Timothy J. "Revolution in Bounds: Wollstonecraft, Women, and Reason." In *Gender and Theory: Dialogues on Feminist Criticism.* Ed. Linda Kauffman, 11–50. New York: Basil Blackwell, 1989.

Renan, Ernest. "What Is a Nation?" Rpt. in *Nation and Narration.* Ed. Homi Bhaba, 8–22. London: Routledge, 1990.

Richardson, Alan, and Sonia Hofkosh, eds. *Romanticism, Race, and Imperial Culture, 1780–1834.* Bloomington: Indiana University Press, 1996.

Rogers, Katherine M. "Romantic Aspirations, Restricted Possibilities: The Novels of Charlotte Smith." In *Re-Visioning Romanticism: British Women Writers, 1776–1837.* Ed. Carol Shiner Wilson and Joel Haefner, 72–88. Newark: University of Delaware Press, 1990.

Ross, Marlon. "Romancing the Nation-State: The Poetics of Romantic Nationalism." In *Macropolitics of Nineteenth-Century Literature: Nationalism, Exoticism, Imperialism.* Ed. Jonathan Arac and Harriet Ritvo, 56–85. Philadelphia: University of Pennsylvania Press, 1991.

Salih, Sara. "'Her Blacks, Her Whites and Her Double Face!': Altering Alterity in *The Wanderer.*" *Eighteenth-Century Fiction* 11.3 (1999): 301–15.

Sanchez-Eppler, Karen. *Touching Liberty: Abolition, Feminism, and the Politics of the Body.* Berkeley and Los Angeles: University of California Press, 1993.

Schmitt, Cannon. *Alien Nation: Nineteenth-Century Gothic Fictions and English Nationality.* Philadelphia: University of Pennsylvania Press, 1997.

Schofield, Mary Anne. "'The Witchery of Fiction': Charlotte Smith, Novelist." In *Living by the Pen: Early British Women Writers.* Ed. Dale Spender, 177–187. New York: Teachers College Press, 1992.

Shteir, Ann B. *Cultivating Women, Cultivating Science.* Baltimore: Johns Hopkins University Press, 1996.

Simons, Judy. *Fanny Burney.* Totowa, NJ: Barnes and Noble, 1987.

Simpson, David. *Romanticism, Nationalism, and the Revolt Against Theory.* Chicago: University of Chicago Press, 1993.

Smith, Anthony D. *National Identity.* Reno: University of Nevada Press, 1991.

Spacks, Patricia Meyer. *Gossip.* New York: Alfred A. Knopf, 1985.

Staves, Susan. "*Evelina,* or Female Difficulties." *Modern Philology* 73 (1976): 368–81.

Straub, Kristina. "Fanny Burney and the Rise of the Woman Novelist." In *The Columbia History of the British Novel.* Ed. John Richetti, John Bender, and Deidre David, 199–219. New York: Columbia University Press, 1994.

Sudan, Rajani. "Mothering and National Identity in the Works of Mary Wollstonecraft." In *Romanticism, Race and Imperial Culture, 1780–1834.* Ed. Alan Richardson and Sonia Hofkosh, 72–89. Bloomington: Indiana University Press, 1996.

Trumpener, Katie. *Bardic Nationalism: The Romantic Novel and the British Empire.* Princeton, NJ: Princeton University Press, 1997.

Ty, Eleanor. *The Unsex'd Revolutionaries: Five Women Novelists of the 1790's.* Toronto: University of Toronto Press, 1993.

Venturo, David F. "Concurring Opponents: Mary Wollstonecraft and Jonathan Swift on Women's Education and the Sexless Nature of Virtue." In *Pope, Swift, and Women Writers.* Ed. Donald C. Mell, 192–202. Newark: University of Delaware Press, 1996.

Wellington, Jan. "Blurring the Borders of Nation and Gender: Mary Wollstonecraft's Character (R)evolution." In *Rebellious Hearts: British Women Writers and the French Revolution.* Ed. Adriana Craciun and Kari E. Lokke, 33–61. New York: State University of New York Press, 2001.

Wikburg, Eleonor. "Political Discourse Versus Sentimental Romance: Ideology and Genre in Charlotte Smith's *Desmond* (1792)." *English Studies* 78.6 (1997): 522–31.

Wilson, Kathleen. *The Sense of the People: Politics, Culture, and Imperialism in England, 1715–1785.* Cambridge: Cambridge University Press, 1995.

Zimmerman, Sarah. "Charlotte Smith's Letters and the Practice of Self-Representation." *Princeton University Library Chronicle* 53 (1991): 50–77.

Zonitch, Barbara. *Familiar Violence: Gender and Social Upheaval in the Novels of Frances Burney.* Newark: University of Delaware Press, 1997.

Index